BAD MOON RISING

BAD MOON RISING

The Unauthorized History of Creedence Clearwater Revival

HANK BORDOWITZ

Schirmer Books
An Imprint of Simon & Schuster Macmillan
New York

Prentice Hall International
London   Mexico City   New Delhi   Singapore   Sydney   Toronto

Schirmer Books
An Imprint of Simon & Schuster Macmillan
1633 Broadway
New York, NY 10019

Library of Congress Catalog Card Number: 98-19586

Printed in the United States of America

Printing Number
1 2 3 4 5 6 7 8 9 10

Library of Congress Cataloging-in-Publication Data

Bordowitz, Hank.
    Bad moon rising : the unauthorized history of Creedence Clearwater Revival /
Hank Bordowitz.
        p. cm.
    Includes bibliographical references, discography, and index.
    ISBN 0-02-864870-6
    1. Creedence Clearwater Revival (Musical group) 2. Rock musicians—
United States—Biography. I. Title
    ML421.C75B67 1998
    782.42166'092'2—dc21
    [B]   98-19586
                                               CIP
                                               MN

This paper meets the minimum requirements of ANSI/NISO Z39.48–1992
(Permanence of Paper).

This book is dedicated to
My wife, Caren, and my boys, Michael and Larry.
It ain't easy putting up with an author around the house.
To my Mom, Dad, and Beth and Richard
And to my grandmother, Goldie Weiss,
who believed early and never stopped.

CONTENTS

Part Three ⟨ Put Us in Coach: 1972–1987

Part Four ⟨ "The Only Way We Talk to John Is Through Our Lawyers": 1988–1997

ACKNOWLEDGMENTS

The author acknowledges

The estate of Ralph J. Gleason for the use of material from the "Rolling Stone Interview With John Fogerty" from *Rolling Stone*, February 21, 1970, and "Inside the *Blue Ridge Rangers*," *Rolling Stone*, July 5, 1973, both works © The estate of Ralph J. Gleason, used by permission of Jazz Casual Productions and the Gleason Family

Straight Arrow Publishers, Inc/*Rolling Stone* magazine for the use of "The 100 Best Singles of the Last Twenty-five Years" from *Rolling Stone*, September 8, 1988; "Will Creedence Clearwater ever be revived?" by Michael Goldberg from *Rolling Stone*, September 2, 1982

DISCoveries magazine for the use of "A Revival Interview with Fortunate Son Doug Clifford," *DISCoveries*, November 1988, by Wayne Bryman, and "Creedence Clearwater Revival," *DISCoveries*, November 1988, by Jerry Orbourne (for subscription information, call 1-800-829-9132)

Steve Wynn for permission to reprint his liner notes from *John Fogerty Wrote a Song for Everyone*

John Hubner for permission to use "The Demon Fighter of Rock and Roll," *West*, 1986

Pam Bendich for the use of CCR covers and press material

Scott Isler for permission to use material from "John Fogerty's Triumph Over Evil," *Musician*, March 1995

Trish Fogerty for permission to use Tom's letters and other information

Barbara Carr and Jon Landau for permission to use Bruce Springsteen's speech at the rock and Roll Hall of Fame induction, 1993

The author wishes to thank

Richard Carlin, an editor and a gentleman

Fran Liebowitz and Jason Weinstein, from Writers' House, agents extraordinaire

Jeff Jacobson, my legal guardian

Teri Hinte, High Priestess of Publicity at Fantasy

Bob Merlis, Pope of Publicity, and his disciples at Warners Publicity

All of the critical journalists upon whose shoulders I stand

Javier Diaz, Graham Niven, Robert Aerts, Rich (Reechie) Firestone, Bengt-Ake, Lisa Taylor, Lars Petersson, Michael Bernander, Phillip Brady, Alex Aberbom (of Blue Meanie Records [are you bluish? Funny you don't look bluish]), Matt Lowen, Joe Hannigan, Dana Doaks, Dave Joens, Steve Rosen, Jeff Hickman, and Eric Schumacher-Rasmussen

Ned Garrett, my legman in the Bay Area and a man with superlative research skills

Paul Garfunkle of Blackbird Records (www.black-bird.com), a discological scholar

Gary Jackson, Stephanie Hanus, Adam Bryant, John Robinson, and the rest of the gang at the River Rising mailing list

All my cybored friends on the Velvet Rope, 'specially Julie, Joe, Lynne and Kevin Carney

Peter Koers, head of the CCR Fan Club

Lonnie Gause, Laurie Dawson and the rest of the gang at GPI

Mac Randall, Bob Doerschuck, and the rest of the gang at *Musician*

Holly George-Warren, Joe Van Plummer, and Peter Kevis at *Rolling Stone Press*

Bob Olson at Warner Publishing

Ken Levy, Steve Goldmintz, Gary Graff, Danny Lipman at *Rock Around the World*, Bob George at the Archive of Contemporary music, Dave Sprague, Ida Langsam

Malcolm Burnstein

Al Bendich

Jeff Fogerty, Bob Fogerty, Jake Rohrer, Merl Saunders, Gail Fogerty, Russ Gary, Doug & Laurie Clifford, Stu Cook

Carey Baker, of the long, industrial memory

Ron, Andre, and Ben at Renaissance for keeping the knife sharp and the hammer pounding

The research staffs at the Lincoln Center Library, the 42d Street Library, the Suffern Free Public Library, and the Ridgewood (New Jersey) Public Library and the people who run all the Internet search services

Lon Marcus and Kathy Hoy for all the empanadas

And especially to Harold Bordowitz, who has great musical taste and did even when we were kids

INTRODUCTION

"The Saddest Story in Rock and Roll"

Fame and lasting quality don't often go hand in hand during the last half of the twentieth century. When people throw away broken computers and televisions, why should entertainers, performers, and other pop stars be any less disposable? The artists that top the charts one year often never get heard of again. Those who do—by means of gifted artistry, determined craft, or even manipulation of the media that make them stars—deserve to be called "legends."

During the five years that John Fogerty, his brother Tom, and his school-mates Stu Cook and Doug Clifford made music as Creedence Clearwater Revival, they created a legacy that bands with double and triple that life span might envy. Artists as diverse as Elvis Presley, Bill Wyman, the Gun Club, Emmy Lou Harris, Def Leppard, Bill Haley, Bob Seger, and the Queen Ida Zydeco Band, to mention just a few, have covered CCR songs. By remaining true to the roots of rock, by expressing their joy in the blues and early rock and roll, the members of CCR inspired a new breed of rock, far from the trippy, psychedelic sounds that surrounded them when they played during San Francisco's "Summer of Love."

CCR created a driving, rootsy, working-class sound, a spirit artists like Bruce Springsteen (who sometimes plays the group's "Traveling Band" as an encore) and Tom Petty inherited a decade later. When Buddy Seigal accused George Thorogood of sounding like CCR in interview in the *LA Times*, Thorogood responded, "John Fogerty is an idol of mine. . . . If I ever had to say, 'This is the style I'd like to be,' it probably would be John Fogerty's. He writes the greatest songs in the world. . . . Creedence played good, fun rock 'n' roll."

Despite their short time in the spotlight, Creedence Clearwater Revival's music remains a staple on the radio. Better than a quarter century after it

1

Courtesy Laurie Clifford Archives

A European fan gets his Creedence Clearwater Revival tattoo autographed.

was first popular, long after many of their contemporaries fell into the abyss of obscurity, their songs and sound still ring in the public consciousness. They remain nearly as popular as they were when they first burst onto the music scene, even though the man who wrote, sang, and played guitar on all of the tracks refused to perform these songs live for nearly two decades.

Like Elvis or the Beatles, Creedence Clearwater Revival made such powerful music that no fewer than eight of their twenty singles had both sides hit the charts. In their time, they appealed to both hippies and rednecks. During the late '60s and throughout the '70s, their songs were as popular on truck stop jukeboxes as they were in college dorm rooms, and were played on AM top forty radio and the newly emerging FM album-oriented progressive stations. Creedence saw the world as their audience. They wanted to appeal to everyone. "Literally everyone," John Fogerty said early on. "And that's why it's hard, because I'm not trying to polarize hippies against their parents, or youth against . . . just the people who are in their twenties. . . . I think music, my concept of what music is supposed to be, shouldn't do that. It should unite, as corny as that is. You know everyone should be able to sit and tap their foot, or say, 'Wow! That's the right thing!'"

Their critical plaudits came from all sides. "Purity, not parody" declared Columbia University professor Albert Goldman, ". . . played with self-effacing skill by white boys from San Francisco."

"Creedence['s] . . . public," identified *Village Voice* critic Robert Christgau, "[is] a category that subsumes a remarkable range of high school students, truck stoppers, heads and miscellaneous. . . ."

"The finest authentic American band around," Richard Cook wrote, "was Creedence Clearwater Revival. John Fogerty's group hammered out a rural rock 'n' roll so vivid that it renders their distance from today as unimportant. His songs are lean and discreetly ingenious, often telling a cracker barrel story that bears endless repetition, and he sang them in a voice like cowhide."

"Fogerty's own homey slur," wrote Debra Rae Cohen, "lent credence to the anyone-can-do-it, dare-you democracy that was always supposed to be (but usually wasn't) at the heart of both the nation and rock & roll."

"I found myself in the midst of a song so true and so unflinching, I started to cry and would have called John Fogerty to thank him if his number was listed. I played it again and again and finally quit when I realized the song was stronger than I was," Greil Marcus wrote in *Creem*. Several years later, in the liner notes to the retrospective album *Chronicle*, Marcus added, "The tracks are deceptive: beautifully, lovingly made, they sound about as contrived as the weather. At least four tunes here—'Proud Mary,' 'Green River,' 'Fortunate Son,' and 'Up Around the Bend'—literally define rock and roll—as a musical form, as a recurring event as a version of the American spirit. Few good bands go so far, even once."

"John Fogerty's voice," wrote Pablo Guzman, ". . . can only be truly called 'country-rock' and . . . puts all the LA cowboys & girls to shame."

"Creedence Clearwater Revival defined virtually everything that's always been wonderful and timeless and true about rock and roll," wrote Allan Jones.

This appeal did not come without heartaches, treachery, and self-doubts. Before their star ascended, the group paid ten years of dues. They struggled through day jobs and road houses and the ever-rowdy crowds at California NCO clubs. During the group's heyday, they dealt with power struggles and ego trips, signed cripplingly catastrophic contracts. The members of CCR fell on themselves like hungry wolves, eventually devouring not only their success but its roots, the good time music that sounded so fresh and fun because the people playing it genuinely enjoyed what they did. After they went their separate ways, they fought over their legacy, battled about the bad business decisions. They got to a point where even the music, as powerful as it might have been, could no longer bring them together.

Like the Civil War, Creedence eventually set brother against brother. It caused a rift between friends who had been through the leanest times with nothing but each other to rely on. It sent one of the members into seclusion for years. Legal hassles and bad feelings centering around the band's breakup still linger like a stain that refuses to wash away. Their story plays like a Shakespearean tragedy. John Fogerty has all the attributes of the classic tragic hero. Like Lear and Richard III, he has it all and largely through his own machinations, it all goes wrong. As the wife of one of the members put it, "It is the saddest story in rock and roll."

Part One

BLUE VELVET GOLLIWOGS

1958–1967

1

"I WAS THE LEADER ALREADY"

In 1958 rock music had passed its infancy—it was more like a toddler—but it still was not reputable. Not many high schools had even one rock band, let alone junior highs. Especially not in a quiet, working-class suburb like El Cerrito, California. Only a twenty-mile drive from the corner of Haight and Ashbury in San Francisco, only perhaps ten miles from the University of California Berkeley, culturally those towns might have existed on another planet. During the '50s through today, El Cerrito epitomizes the quiet suburb.

Jeff Fogerty, son of Creedence rhythm guitarist Tom Fogerty, still lives a couple of towns away. He asserts, "El Cerrito is like the most un-hip place to be in the Bay Area. It's this little, small, sleepy town two towns north of Berkeley." Even so, the '50s wrought changes on the former Spanish settlement like the decade changed nearly everything in America. Classic old adobe houses gave way to more modern homes. Old sounds gave way to new.

When John Fogerty was thirteen years old, in 1958, he got the yen to form a rock band. Most parents and even a lot of kids found rock and roll distasteful. Certainly, in Eisenhower's rosy-cheeked, apple-pie America, healthy adolescents had better things to pursue—especially in El Cerrito. Fogerty, however, had entertained the idea of forming a band for close to five years. "I envisioned being exactly what I am now since I was eight," he recalled in 1986. "I remember as early as 1953, when I was about eight years old, that I was going to name my group Johnny Corvette and the Corvettes. I had already made my choice: I was thinking about making a career out of music. Of course, I was Johnny Corvette. Somehow I was the leader already."

It started when his eldest brother, Jim, turned him on to R&B, like Ray Charles. "Around 1953, I started to notice rhythm and blues songs by Bo Diddley, Chuck Berry and things like that," he told Jim Delahant in 1969.

Nearly a quarter of a century later, Fogerty commented to the *LA Times*'s Robert Hilburn, "My idols were guys who were really gritty and who were real rockers. I wanted to live up to what they did."

He recalled walking around as early as the fifth grade with a blues band playing in his head. He would sing all the parts, grunting for the drums, developing mental images of how the music would sound.

His resolve solidified when he first heard Carl Perkins. "Carl Perkins," Fogerty says, "was the first one ever to make me think about being a musician and singer. Elvis was a star, Carl was a musician. I wanted to be more like Carl."

Born on May 28, 1945, John fell smack in the middle of the five Fogerty boys. His oldest brother, Jim, was on a track that would eventually lead to work as an accountant. His immediate older sibling, Tom, had already started to make a name for himself locally as a singer when John made the momentous discovery of the power of rock and roll. Dan, about four years younger than John, eventually would own a chain of pizzerias. The youngest Fogerty sibling, Bob, took many of the photographs for his brothers' records and promotional material. He wound up in the role of John's personal manager.

Growing up in this large family could not have been easy. John's father, Gayland Robert Fogerty, worked in the print shop of the *Berkeley Gazette*. He had trouble with alcohol, and perhaps other mental disorders as well. He left home around 1953, fairly soon after Bob's birth, about the time John was eight.

Tom recalled, "We come from a strict middle class, middle income background. We got a pretty fair deal, I guess. Our parents divorced when I was eleven. Hell, everybody I knew came from a 'broken home.' "

"My grandfather and grandmother either divorced or separated because my grandfather was drinking pretty heavily at that point," Tom's son Jeff adds. "So she raised all five boys by herself. Eventually she became a full-time teacher."

The divorce left Lucile Fogerty to care for five growing boys spanning sixteen years in age. She worked as a store clerk while studying for her teaching degree. Then she taught handicapped children.

Things got pretty thin at times around the Fogerty house. Their father, Gayland, often missed child-support payments. "I come from what they are calling a dysfunctional family," John recalled. "I *did* use a lot of energy on that subject. I did hate my father. I always wished it had been better."

"Most of my struggles were mental," he said in 1970. "My old man wasn't around when I wanted an old man. My mother was a teacher who was supposedly making a good living. She really didn't get involved in my life. When she would, we finally got to the point where I said, 'Don't get involved with me. I don't want you any more. I've been doing it on my own for so long. Leave me alone.' Until a week before our first hit record, it was right there in the back of my mind, I may never get out."

John's musical life began to replace the family life he was missing: "I was always ashamed. I never brought my friends home. My room was in the basement—cement floor, cement walls. I just grabbed music and withdrew." By age fourteen, John had grabbed music hard, giving in totally to the rock and roll bug.

"John used to work relentlessly at home, in his room, for hours after school," CCR drummer Doug Clifford remembered, "maybe spending fourteen hours a day listening to the guitar parts and making sure he could play those things note for note and then listening to the vocal. That was really important. That's why John Fogerty, a white kid from El Cerrito, can sound like a black kid from the south. It was something he spent years doing and perfecting. It's a real tribute to John and a tribute to the artists that influenced his vocal style."

Tom and John came by this talent honestly. Their mother, Lucile, was musical as well. In high school, her perfect score in a "Music Memory" contest won her notice in the local *Montana Tribune*. She and twelve fellow students correctly identified several compositions, naming the composers and spelling the names correctly. By her days of parenthood in the 1950s, she gravitated toward the Bay Area's rapidly growing folk music scene:

We had this great series of music festivals in the Bay Area in the '50s and my mom took me for at least four years. You'd end up with only 100 people in an auditorium, and there's Pete Seeger talking about Leadbelly and Woody Guthrie and how music could have meaning. He spoke about songs about the unions and the depression days, but also about contemporary problems, like the House Un-American Activities Committee. It showed how music could be a force.

If Seeger reenforced the power of the message on Fogerty, another serendipitous folk festival experience solidified music's visceral power:

I'll never forget seeing Ramblin' Jack Elliot. They were testing the sound system at one of those workshops. He gave them a record to test the PA and all of a sudden, [he sings like Ray Charles] "You know the night time. . . ." All right! That was great. A lot of people didn't know what that was, but it went right through me. I saw the joining in that moment. It was all just music!

Because of their mother's interest in folk music, there was always at least a cheap guitar around the Fogerty house. John shared it with his brother Tom. He also created his own imaginary bands by copying his favorite records:

> I remember when I was eleven or twelve, Jody Reynolds' "Endless Sleep" was out. I learned to play E, A, and almost B7 on an old Stella with strings this high off the fingerboard. I was *screaming* the song, and my mom came in: "What are you doing?" It was the first time that I got that rush of playing and singing. . . . One day, I was playing the piano and this old high hat we had around the house. It was an old song by Ernie Freeman called "Lost Dreams" that had a real loud kick drum. I'm playing piano with one hand, the high-hat with the other and singing the melody. And my mom comes in again and says, "What in the heck are you doing?" It was crazy, but it all made sense to me.

"Tom and I went and rented an electric guitar for five dollars a month," he recalled. "It was a real piece of growl, but we managed to make two strings go 'bing, bing' and play the piano." They would eventually record the parts on piano, high-hat, and rhythm guitar, and John would add lead parts to this music. Once again, and not for the last time, Lucile found this "weird," but it played an important role in John's musical development.

Eventually, the "piece of growl" guitar just didn't suit John's needs. He found a Danelectro Silvertone guitar and amplifier in the Sears catalog. "I convinced my mom that I could make the time payments. The guitar cost $80. Ten months of payments, $8 interest. My mom had to co-sign and I paid for it from my paper route."

Then he cut classes and taught himself to play. "I'm really not sure how I passed eighth grade," he admits. "Some of the teachers must have been on my side."

After a few months, he felt proficient enough to look for kindred spirits. He found them in two of his schoolmates from Portola Junior High School in El Cerrito. First, he met Doug Clifford, another would-be rock-and-roller. Clifford also had lived in the East Bay area all his life. Born in Palo Alto on April 24, 1945, Clifford's father was a machinist and his mother was a cosmetic clerk. The younger (by three years) of two boys, he went to school in Livermore, Manhattan Beach, and Palo Alto, before attending Portola Junior High. Doug recalled that he tended toward hypochondria as a kid. He found polio, as it still plagued kids his age at that time, especially frightening. On the other hand, he also was a wiry, athletic kid who would put on circuses early in life. He even had a special clown suit. Later on, he'd pantomime to Elvis records.

Courtesy Laurie Clifford Archives

John on guitar and Doug on drums, both age 15.

While not bookish, Doug developed a fondness for nature well before most people showed an interest in ecology or even gave it much thought. He had a particular fondness for entomology, taking up butterfly collecting in grade school.

Around the time he started at Portola, Doug bought an old snare drum and balanced it on a flower pot stand. Then he allegedly took a couple of old pool cues into the school shop and turned them into drumsticks on the lathe. In this way, Doug took his first steps toward playing the drums.

John and Doug discovered they shared a love of the blues, the kind of blues they heard on the local R&B station in Oakland, KWBR. "For a long time," Doug recalled, "before there was any such thing as even Top 40, before that existed, the only real music . . . well, it was rock music to us. It was called rhythm and blues then. They played it on the black music station in Oakland. That was our popular music when we were young. The music . . . they call it blues, but it was such a wide variety." Fogerty recalled among his favorite songs that KWBR played were "Smokestack Lightnin'" and "Moaning in the Moonlight." With that common interest, Fogerty and Clifford started to try to bring their love of music together as musicians. "Doug wasn't the first musician I ever met," John quipped, "but he was the first sane one."

They played together and decided they sounded awful. For one thing, just guitars and drums didn't cut it. When John would start playing the licks he spent hours memorizing in his bedroom, they sounded thin over just the drums.

Doug suggested that they add another player to the band. He had been sitting in front of Stu Cook in homeroom for two years. "I was twelve or thirteen," Stu recalled. "Doug and I met in junior high. John was actually in the same junior high with us. We all met in the music room in junior high."

In addition to having alphabetically similar names, Stu and Doug discovered that they were born mere hours apart. They became fast friends, getting involved in all manner of mischief. Doug recalls one time when Stu set himself afire after finishing off some lawn work too late to bring the debris to the dump. John enjoyed reading the works of Mark Twain, but Stu and Doug had some actual Tom and Huck adventures in their time

"Doug and I met in our homeroom the first year of junior high school," Stu recalls, "and we've been blurting out ever since. A couple of fuck-offs."

Cook was born in Oakland on April 25, 1945. His father was a lawyer and his brother Gordon served as a high-ranking officer for the Australian Department of Corrections.

Clifford knew that Cook had been taking piano lessons (mostly classical) for years. Cook also played the trumpet, as had his father. Doug also knew that Stu enjoyed KWBR nearly as much as he and John did.

"I was listening to that station," Stu recalled, "the first time my mother ever told me to turn the radio off. The first time I remember, anyway. They were playing a song called 'Natural, Natural Ditty.' And if I only knew then what I know now, no wonder she wanted me to turn it off. I mean, that was the biggest boogie ever, man."

Cook and Clifford had even tried making music together at various times, but neither of them went about it with John's determination. For them it was fun; for John it was deadly serious. The three of them were able to find common ground, however, in the music itself.

"We were all on the same wavelength, really," John recalled. "I just had to decide whether I would join their band or they would join mine. I chose the latter. Once we got started we were literally the only group playing in school."

Doug decided he needed more than just his snare, and petitioned his parents for a drum set. "Both my parents worked," he recalled. "I wanted a drum set, so they gave me the opportunity to get a job. I was the gardener and the maid. I did the dishes during the week. That's how I got my bread for the set. They didn't have to do that. They could have said, 'Look, we're working, you work also.'"

Fully equipped with a small kit, a Silvertone guitar, five-watt amp, and the house piano wherever they played, John, Stu, and Doug called their group the Blue Velvets. While they all enjoyed the blues, they practiced popular instrumentals so they could play at sock hops and parties. These ranged from surf music to Duane Eddy to versions of tunes by Ray Charles. They learned the jukebox standards and hits of the day. With greased back hair and white dinner jackets, they went out and became working musicians. John remembered:

When we started, we had ducktails and the matching outfits. We were trying to be like the Viscounts and the Wailers. You know, a teen band. The first thing we played for was sock hops at Portola Jr. High School. Doug and I had been together since April, we got Stu in September, I think, of '59, and we played the school at the end of '59. And then the next summer we went around to all the county fairs representing El Cerrito Boys' Club! That kind of thing.

An early Blue Velvets show might have included tunes by Duane Eddy, Johnny and the Hurricanes, and the Ventures; "Wipe Out," "Louie, Louie," "Midnight Hour," "The Hully Gully," and "Annie Had a Baby." "We were really getting down!" Fogerty recalled fondly in 1997.

"We only knew so many songs," Doug Clifford remembered. "So what we did was play a song over again and tell the audience we had a special request for it."

In addition to the sock hops, carnivals, and fairs, another outlet for the members of the Blue Velvets was school assemblies. They played quite a few of these.

"I remember the first time I saw these guys," Jake Rohrer, a longtime friend and later general factotum for the band recalled:

> It was 1960. Word had reached me that there was a guy in school that could play the guitar and piano. They had an assembly, and out come the Blue Velvets. John was pretending that he was a heroin addict. He had a tire pump that was supposed to be his syringe. I think he held the stem of the tire pump to his arm while Doug pumped him up before they started their gig. I still remember the song they played. It was something called "Train Time." John was cranking out these great chords on his Sears and Roebuck Silvertone guitar that sounded just like a train whistle. Stu played the piano. They were really good. I was blown away because I was just the guy at school who could play piano, and here were these little punks who could play better than me!

During his first year of high school, John went from the public system to parochial St. Mary's High—where Tom had just graduated. He recalled one assembly he played there:

> St. Mary's High—the all-boys school. I got to my solo and went up on the high strings. I was jumping up and down. Everybody started freaking out. Then Brother Frederick stopped the assembly. Getting the boys excited. "The boys"—there was always this taint of homosexuality going on. Then everybody left the event in shame, as though we had done some disservice to the Christian movement.

Ever the truant, Fogerty missed a lot of his first semester at St. Mary's. They threw him out and he wound up back in El Cerrito High with his buddies in the Blue Velvets.

2

"I HAD THE MONEY TO PAY FOR THE SESSIONS"

At the same time the Blue Velvets were establishing themselves as Portola Junior High's only, and therefore preeminent, rock band, John's older brother Tom was also a working musician and singer. He played the high school dance circuit with a band called the Playboys. His vocals were so impressive that one of the top groups in the area, Spider Webb and the Insects, asked him to join. They say he did a version of Bobby Freeman's "Do You Wanna Dance" that would elicit shrieks of delight from the girls in the audience.

"Tom was singing at some assembly in High School," longtime band friend Jake Rohrer recalls. "The girls were all screaming. That was probably Tom's first inkling of rock stardom."

Born in November of 1941, Tom was three and a half years older than John. He had started playing violin, and actually took four years of lessons. When that didn't appeal to him, he switched to the accordion, then the trumpet. While he knew he wanted to do something musical, he decided that none of these instruments fit the bill.

A very athletic guy, Tom turned his interests to sports. He played halfback for the St. Mary's High football team in Berkeley until his sophomore year. By then, he had sustained enough hits and tackles that he developed calcium deposits on his femur. He had to wear a cast on his leg for a couple of months. During this time, he caught up with the blues and rented a guitar with John. He still played football when the cast came off, but he pursued music as well. He also would occasionally sit in with his brother's band, especially when the gig called for vocals.

In the meantime, the Blue Velvets were discovering that there were just so many sock hops they could play, and during the winter, county fairs are hard to come by. Still eager to perfect their craft, almost from the beginning, the Blue Velvets were hanging around the local recording studios, backing up local artists. John took pride in this early professional experience; when the band finally achieved popularity in the late '60s, he was quick to point out his long professional career: "I think it's important to know, that through high school, almost up until the time we first walked in the door at Fantasy, I had something like 5000 hours in a studio, which I'd done all through high school. Just gone in and playing with anyone." While John may have exaggerated the number of hours he logged in, by the time he left his teens he had a good deal of studio experience under his belt.

In 1960, the group made their first record with John on guitar, Doug on drums, and Stu on piano. John recalled the song:

> I was in the ninth grade. Three of us from Creedence were the backup band on a record by James Powell, a black singer from Richmond, California, on a small label, Christy Records. It was actually played on a local rhythm and blues station—I think it was KWBR—for about three weeks. It was a typical four-chord slow doo-wop song called "Beverly Angel."

In the meantime, Tom's group, Spider Webb and the Insects, was attracting some attention of their own. "We somehow landed a contract with Bob Keene, who was president of Del-Fi Records in Los Angeles," Tom said. "Del-Fi had just lost their top star, Ritchie Valens, a few weeks earlier and Keen was looking for new acts hoping to sort of pick up where Valens left off.

"By June of '59, I had my high school diploma in one hand and a signed recording contract with Del-Fi in the other. We laid down a pretty good track for them, titled 'Lyda Jane,' but for some reason, the record never came out."

Spider Webb and the Insects couldn't survive that disappointment and the band broke up in the winter of 1959. Shortly after they recorded the tune for Powell, Tom asked his brother's band to back him on a demo. While their friends and family enjoyed the recording of Tom's two tunes, they sent it around to artists like Pat Boone who quickly sent it back with rejection notices.

"The Blue Velvets backed Tom at gigs and on some recordings," Stu recalled. "Not much happened with these recordings, but they set the stage for the next sessions."

At this point, Tom was out of high school and married to Gail Skinner. "We were high school sweethearts from when we were sixteen," Gail recalls. "We got married when we were eighteen." Tom took a job with the local utility company, Pacific Gas and Electric (later to be the name for another area band). He also wanted to keep his rock and roll dreams alive, so he convinced his younger brother, Stu, and Doug that he could be an asset to them. He was, after all, considerably older and already, through his days with Spider Webb, had a following.

He also brought something the band sorely lacked: vocals. John had not yet started singing, so most of the Blue Velvets' repertoire was instrumental. Tom played some guitar and sang. In a sense, they became two bands. When they played gigs where the instrumentals would do, they were the Blue Velvets. When they needed a vocalist, they became Tommy Fogerty and the Blue Velvets. By fall of 1960, Tommy Fogerty and the Blue Velvets played all of the usual haunts, the school sock hops, fairs, and the like throughout northern California.

Tom was determined to have a new recording contract. As the elder member, lead vocalist, and the one with the largest following, he became the leader of the band. Besides, as he pointed out after he left the band in 1971, "I had the money to pay for [the] sessions. We auditioned for one record company after another, receiving one polite rejection after another. But we were determined to make records for someone, somewhere."

They also continued to record demos, working for whoever would hire them. As John recalled:

We made, I guess, five or six records before we ever went to Fantasy. We "officially" backed Powell and this other guy, this record that never came out. We did a lot of instrumentals and that sort of thing. As a group, we recorded 2000 hours in the studio. And then I would go in and be a sideman or whatever with country and western or polkas. You know, whatever you want, we'd play it, just to learn what a studio was about. I knew it would come in handy some day.

In 1961, Wayne Farlow, from a small Bay Area record company called Orchestra, decided he liked a tape of two Tom and John Fogerty compositions called "Come on Baby" and "Oh! My Love" enough to press them.

"The Blue Velvets, my backup band, were actually too young to enter into a legal contract in California," recalled Tom, "so we had a verbal agreement. I was under contract as a vocalist and I also produced the records."

"Come on Baby" enjoyed a small amount of local airplay, but didn't sell very well. Even so, a month later, another pair of Fogerty-and-Fogerty compositions, "Have You Ever Been Lonely" and "Bonita," graced the sides of a "Tommy Fogerty and the Blue Velvets" 45 on Orchestra Records.

"Casey Kasem was the program director at KEWB at that time," Tom noted. "He started playing our second record as soon as it came out. It became something of a local hit."

Courtesy Ken Levy

Tom and John in an Orchestra Records publicity photo, c. 1962.

Again, however, the records didn't sell all that well. In June 1962, Orchestra gave the band one more chance, releasing "Yes You Did," backed with "Now You're Not Mine." However, the record did even worse than the previous releases. "It died," Tom would say years later, "before it even came out."

This would be the last record Tommy Fogerty and the Blue Velvets ever released.

3

"CAST YOUR FATE TO THE WIND"

Throughout John, Stu, and Doug's years at El Cerrito High, they rehearsed constantly, played for audiences (and money) when they could, cut demos, and hung out at Sierra Recorders. As John recalled:

> There was a time, around eleventh or twelfth grade, when all three of us—Doug, Stu, and I—were going there on Sunday afternoons, just making tracks, messing with the tape recorders. The owner, Bob DiSousa, was equally interested, because *everybody's* dream is to make a hit record. Around that time, Bob started using me on little sessions that were happening. He'd need some Floyd Cramer piano or Cropper-style guitar, and he'd call me.

In June of 1963, Stu, Doug, and John graduated from high school. While they agreed to keep playing, none of them seriously saw it as a full-time job. Tom already had a job and two children. Stu and Doug enrolled at San Jose State College, about fifty miles away from home. That was close enough that they could play weekends, far enough away that they could live at school. They worked at frat parties, military bases, and, despite being considerably shy of their twenty-first birthdays, an assortment of bars in the Bay Area.

John continued to do sessions, playing guitar on everything from polkas to R&B to country and western. He also did a wide assortment of odd jobs. "Two of us worked in a gas station. . . . Doug was a janitor and we've also driven trucks. . . . When I worked in a gas station, I really took it seriously. I wanted to do it well and please everyone."

Around this time, a record by jazz pianist Vince Guaraldi started making waves on the pop music scene, both locally and nationally. As 1962 became

1963, "Cast Your Fate to the Wind" became one of the rare jazz records to make that crossover onto the pop charts. Ultimately, the record hit number 22 on the *Billboard* singles chart.

The novelty of a nominally jazz instrumental on the pop chart inspired a television documentary called *Anatomy of a Hit*. Among other choice moments from the show, it features the artist in his record company's mail room, boxing up copies of his record, commenting on how the overwhelming popularity of the recording had caught the company off guard. Guaraldi commented, "As you can see, we're not ready for success."

John, Tom, Doug, and Stu caught the show on KQED, the local National Educational Television affiliate. To their astonishment, they knew the place where all this action had happened; they lived only a few miles away. Here they were, a band that started off playing instrumentals, with a bunch of them on tape already, and there's this company with an instrumental hit right in their backyard. Within days they traveled, demo tapes of original Blue Velvets instrumentals in hand, across the San Francisco Bay Bridge to the record company's Treat Avenue office.

"We went over there," John recalled, "with the idea of 'sell the instrumentals!' And that's how it all happened, really."

Guaraldi recorded for Fantasy Records, originally an offshoot of Circle Records. Circle Records came about when an artist walked into the San Francisco-based, plastic fabrication and custom molding works run by brothers Sol and Max Weiss. The Weiss brothers pioneered plastics, having developed various processes since before the Second World War. Starting in the '40s, they produced plastic toys, utensils, and novelties.

Around the late forties, they were approached by Jack Sheedy, a trombone player and would-be music-business mogul. He asked them to press records for him, because there were no other local facilities available to him, especially not in the new long-playing format that had just been introduced.

The Weisses, recognizing an opportunity, became the only company pressing records in the Bay Area. Soon, their three presses ran twenty-four hours a day, doing a lot of custom records, hillbilly music, folk dances, and jazz. Jazz pianist Dave Brubeck's earliest records were released on Circle. In 1949 the company became Fantasy. Soon the Weiss brothers started enjoying success as record manufacturers. Brubeck sold respectably and consistently. They started to sign more artists, releasing records by sax player Gerry Mulligan, vibes player Cal Tjader, and trumpet player Chet Baker, as well as folksinger Odetta, and beat poets Lawrence Ferlinghetti and Allen Ginsberg. They put out recordings of Earl Hines and even Duke Ellington and Bill Evans. Mulligan's recording of "My Funny Valentine," with Baker on vocals and trumpet, actually made some noise in the pop market.

Through the '50s, however, Fantasy's real moneymakers were comedy records by Lenny Bruce. Despite the near-hit status of the Mulligan record and the legitimate hit status of the Guaraldi record, Fantasy had nothing in the way of real pop music. They had a jazz catalog that sold slowly and steadily, but hit records came once in a blue moon, and always by surprise.

"We recorded the kind of jazz we liked, even if it didn't sell," said Saul Zaentz, the company's longtime director of sales and promotion.

"Fantasy is primarily a jazz label," agreed Tom Fogerty. "The only reason we went to Fantasy was they were the only label there was. There was no other label in San Francisco. So we went there because we thought we want to try and do it on a national level. They have that kind of influence."

"I mean, I was eighteen years old," John added, "and I knew they were just a little jazz label. I mean, they were just sort of . . . they were . . . *strange*! I went in and I met this guy named Max Weiss." Stu described Weiss as "an eccentric, beatnik type."

"Max and Sol Weiss, they were a couple of crazy guys," recalls Merl Saunders, who also recorded for the label. "I used to bring my kids in, because I was a kind of bachelor father. Max loved kids. The kids would just follow him. He would just take them into the room and let us continue playing. We were trying to record, so we just let it go."

Off-center as he might have been, Weiss heard something in these local rockers. Maybe it was their youth, energy, and enthusiasm. Perhaps it had something to do with the pop charts. Charts that had been dominated by Steve Lawrence, the Four Seasons, and the Singing Nun in 1963 were now infested with Beatles. In these four young men, Weiss might have seen an easy way for Fantasy to venture into the hysteria that now gripped popular music.

"Max [Weiss] convinced us that instrumentals weren't the thing, which wasn't our thing anyway, but we were trying to sell them to Vince," said John, "but it got us in the door. He said 'Well, you should do vocals.' Which is what we'd been doing all along!"

One thing Fantasy did have was their own recording studio. A bit ramshackle, and certainly not state of the art, the studio was located in a lean-to-like shack behind their San Francisco offices. Here, John, Tom, Stu, and Doug put all those hours of studio expertise to work.

"We made a dumb tape, a demonstration thing . . . down in that lean-to in the back," John continued. "It was just supposed to be a demonstration. It was cut at 7 1/2 [inches per second] like a home tape recorder, and we added a few things."

Max Weiss took on the role of managing the band, and the band signed a management contract. One of the things the Weiss brothers suggested was that the band change their name. The Blue Velvets reeked of the '50s The band chose the name the Visions.

In addition to having a contract with a company with national distribution and even a couple of hits under their belts, the band was playing more. They got their first regular gig at a dive in Berkeley called the Monkey Inn, which they would later describe as "a scuzzy beer tavern." Bouncers required identification at the door, even if you looked thirty. Somehow, though, they let John, Doug, and Stu pass, despite the three younger musicians having not quite reached the legal drinking age of twenty-one. The Monkey played a formative roll in the band's development.

"The Monkey Inn was this smoke-filled, beer-filled place," Jake Rohrer recalls.

They also were booked at frat parties and dances. During the times the band wasn't active, though, John went elsewhere to keep his chops up. There was a whole scene developing in Portland, Oregon, about 600 miles north of the Bay Area. Groups like Paul Revere and the Raiders, the Kingsmen, the Sonics, and the Wailers combined the good-time R&B sound that so appealed to John with the English popcraft he was learning to love. The scene, however, was something he could live without. It didn't appeal to Fogerty to play five sets a night, six nights a week.

During the intervening nine months, though, the group hadn't heard from Fantasy. They were still waiting for news about the songs they'd submitted from the sessions in the lean-to, "Don't Tell Me No Lies" and "Little Girl (Does Your Mama Know?)." Finally, in November 1964, they got copies of their debut single for Fantasy records. Between the winter of '64 when they signed and that autumn when the record was released, more had changed than just the status of the band. The British invasion had hit the States with the force of a cultural tidal wave. If Max Weiss had not exhibited clairvoyance regarding this quartet when he signed them, the Weiss brothers certainly saw the release of this little pop confection as their opportunity to cash in on this growing wave of bands with cute names like the Beatles, the Kinks, the Mindbenders, and Herman's Hermits without even leaving the Bay Area. So when Fantasy put out the single, they redubbed the Visions the Golliwogs. As Tom later recalled:

Unfortunately, Max Weiss, the owner of Fantasy, came up with the name Golliwogs and just stuck it on the label of our first release. Weiss didn't consult us about this change. It was 1964, and the British groups were dominating the charts. I think, at least to Max anyway, "Golliwogs" sounded sort of British. We always hated the name—still do—but Max owned the label and we were new and wanted very much to make records, so we went along with things.

The Golliwogs, white fuzzy wigs and all.

"Our manager, Max Weiss, thought it fit the 'British Invasion,'" says Stu. "We figured as long as we were paying him, we'd take his advice. To Americans, it probably was no weirder than Creedence Clearwater Revival."

John was equivocal about the new name. As he recalled in his major interview for *Rolling Stone* in 1970:

> You know, I told myself, "It's okay. I like it. Yeah, it's okay, it's okay, I like it!" And I knew I didn't like it. And I couldn't face Doug and Stu! Me and Tom told 'em, "Well, it's the only way we'll ever have a record out." But we didn't like it at all. For four years after that we were laughed at. You know, we were ashamed to say the name even!

Not only that, but with the name came accouterments. There were, for example, the white fuzzy wigs the Weisses bought them and expected them to wear.

"Oh, that was so funny!" Tom and John's mother, Lucile, declared over twenty-five years later. "They were running around in wigs. They didn't want to be commonplace. They were going to be English or something. I don't know. They were very young."

"We figured if you have a manager," John said, "you take his advice. We were young and we listened to him."

With the new name and the recording contract, they tried to enlist the help of some local professionals. One person they approached was Scott Longston, a booking agent in the area.

"Agents get skatillions of submissions for booking and management every day," Longston asserts. "One of our most aggressive submissions was from some group called the Golliwogs. I wish I still had a copy of their promo picture that shows the band all dressed up in matching Sonny and Cher-type sheepskin vests and wearing white afro wigs. We laughed our asses off when their promo pack came into our offices! In a meeting with the Golliwogs soon after (with them dressed just like their promo picture), we told Mr. Fogerty and company that they were not an act we were interested in representing, and that they had a lot of maturing and rehearsing to do before anyone would ever consider them as serious artists."

"The Golliwogs and funny hats soon wore out," John recalled more sourly. "So did the dates."

The silly name and goofy wigs wouldn't be the last indignities Fantasy heaped on them.

4

"HE HAD A SOUND"

The Golliwogs started moving from dances to the next level of gigs. In addition to playing frat parties, and risking owners' liquor licenses playing underaged (except for Tom) at bars and roadhouses up and down the West Coast, they added NCO clubs on military bases to their venues.

"We were getting $50 a night," John remembered, "and all the beer we could drink. I think we were in it for the beer."

"I was mainly in it for the beer and laughs," Cook concurred.

"Those frat parties were such drunken orgies," John added, "They didn't care whether we had a mike or not. They just wanted music to sing along with."

The military bases weren't much better: "Everybody wanted either a fast or a slow number," John said, "but nobody cared if it was a blues or a polka."

The public address systems at most of these gigs were of dubious or nonexistent quality. This proved to be a bit of a strain on Tom's voice. Additionally, John's sojourns to Portland had a marked effect on him.

Up until this point, John did not consider himself a singer—or at least, wasn't brave enough to sing outside of his home. "I was very self-conscious about my voice," John remembered.

What happened was that me and some other guys went up to Portland during the summer of 1964. We found a drummer and got a two-week engagement at a club called the Town Mart. At that point, this guy named Mike Burns was the singer. Well, one day I said, "I'm going to sing." And since I was out of my hometown, away from my parents and any of my friends, I kind of told myself to go ahead and do it, don't be shy. I had taken a reel to reel tape recorder up there. I would record whole sets. Then I'd stay up until sunrise listening to myself. I heard myself improve. I'd try something like a scream. I'd hear myself try to do it on tape, and the next night I'd go back and try something else.

Somehow, the atmosphere of the smoke-filled bars gave John the confidence he needed to expand his vocal skills; at least, he could always think that not many people were listening. "There was all this beer and cigarettes and [I didn't really care] if it hurt [to scream]. I'd sing sometimes 'til I'd turn white. That was like after you'd run a mile straight up hill."

Rather magnaminously, Tom was willing to share his lead vocal duties with John, once he heard him sing. "I realized John should be singing lead," Tom recalled in 1971. "I could sing, but he had a sound." Tom started to learn to play the rhythm guitar seriously, as opposed to the kind of fooling around he and John used to do with their old rented instrument. John started taking over the vocal chores. He screamed the vocal to compensate for the poor PA systems and developed that raspy, blues-dripping holler that would be his trademark.

"I used to get sore throats," John said, "but after a while there was a power there that I didn't know I had. I began to hear a sound, so I began to try songs that would go with that. 'Hully Gully' was one of the first. I could just shriek that out."

In the meantime, the group decided that Stu should make the switch from piano to electric bass, to be more current, more rock and roll. "One day," John said, "I turned to Stu and said, 'From now on, you're the bass player. Get a bass.' And he got a cheap bass, a St. George bass, and I began to teach him."

They started working out these changes at any venue that would pay them for playing. One of these places was their regular gig at the Monkey Inn.

"We used the Monkey Inn as a coming out period, as a breakout for us as entertainers," John recalled.

We had been doing frat parties and all that, but it wasn't until just before the MI period that I began singing. I was about 18 when we first got our introduction at the Monkey. . . . We didn't know any of the people who went there. It was such a gross place—the people either made me laugh or sometimes disgusted me. I usually ended up looking at the wall while I was singing. The wall had all sorts of things written all over it, and I'd read it all. Then, about once a month the owner would paint the wall and people would write all over it again. Looking at that wall got me in the habit of singing sideways. I used to drive soundmen crazy. . . . "Sing straight into the mike!" "No, I sing sideways!"

They continued to play on their side of the Bay, almost totally ignoring San Francisco. They witnessed the birth of the whole San Francisco sound, but though they lived less than twenty miles out of the city, they may well have come from another planet.

"We never identified with it," John said. "We weren't part of that kind of music. It seemed like we were on a different road going in a different direction."

John got on the payroll at Fantasy. "Back in 1965," Saunders remembers, "he worked at Fantasy Records in the shipping department. That was back on Treat Street [*sic*] in San Francisco."

Stu and Doug continued at San Jose State College, pledging the same frat. Here Doug acquired a nickname that would follow him the rest of his life.

"When Doug and I were going to San Jose State College," Stu recalled, "one of my fraternity brothers started calling Doug 'Clifford C. Clifford.' No particular reason. Probably too many beers. At some point the question came up, 'What does the 'C' stand for?' After a few moments of deep reflection, Doug, who was very interested in nature and ecology, replied 'Cosmo.' It stuck."

The band practiced and gigged when they could. They continued the regular gig at the Monkey. John honed his chops in the studio. And the Golliwogs made records.

"This is when I started to pay attention to those guys," remarks Saunders. "They looked like a collegiate group, ties and sports jackets. They were very devoted and heavy, heavy into their own music."

In April 1965, Fantasy put out "Where You Been" b/w "You Came Walking." That summer, the company released "You Can't Be True" b/w "You Got Nothin' on Me." Neither single created much excitement.

Most of the Golliwogs' songs were written by Tom and John. They used the pseudonyms "Rann Wild" and "Toby Green." In every way they could, except for their recordings, they dissociated the band with the name. At the Monkey Inn, for example, they went unbilled. Even so, these were also formative years for John Fogerty the songwriter. He worked hard at his craft, but in retrospect, he called most of the Golliwogs' songs "very contrived. Everything I could think of in a commercial record, I'd stick in."

The latter part of 1965 marked several milestones in the lives of the young musicians. On the personal side, John married Martha Piaz, his high school steady, on September 4, 1965. From the standpoint of the band, Fantasy moved the Golliwogs onto their new Scorpio label, geared toward the rock sounds that were coming out of the Bay Area. One of the first records the Grateful Dead made, for example, also came out on Scorpio.

During October of '65 the Golliwogs recorded a song called "Brown Eyed Girl" (not the Van Morrison tune). It started to make a buzz and even sold better than 15,000 copies. It was the only single the band had ever made that actually sold a few copies. Yet in a lot of ways, John was glad that it didn't

Courtesy Graham Niven

John in the Fantasy Records warehouse, where he worked as a shipping clerk.

become a hit. He would later describe the song as "a lot of earnestness about nothing." John also believed that the song's relative failure helped the group avoid becoming just another "one-hit wonder":

If "Brown Eyed Girl" had been a hit, we would have been like every other one-hit artist. We would have never gone back and really tried to make it tight. We would have just thought, "Hey, it's simple," and that would have been it. Stu only knew three notes on the bass at the time. Tom played one string on the guitar, and then I filled in all the other instruments, organ, stuff like that. In other words, we weren't what you call an in-person group, we were a studio group.

Doug agreed. When asked why it had taken them nearly eight years of playing together to "make it," Doug laughed and said, "The reason it took us so long to make it is simple. When we started, we were terrible."

"If we had made it then," Stu adds, "we would have been the Monkees."

They followed up "Brown Eyed Girl" quickly, recording "Fight Fire" b/w "Fragile Child." Unlike "Brown Eyed Girl," though, it didn't sell. Nor did the one after that, a composition by John and Tom called "Walk on the Water," generate any excitement at all. (However, an updated version on Creedence Clearwater's debut album several years later would.) Despite these setbacks, the Golliwogs remained undaunted and kept on honing their craft and performing.

In 1965 John followed in the path of Doug and Stu and enrolled at Merritt College in Oakland. He later described the experience as his "rather unsuccessful year of college." By 1966, Doug had cut back to part-time at college, working his way through as janitor from 5 P.M. to 2 A.M. Stu's dad, a prominent Bay Area lawyer with clients like the Oakland Raiders, had a law school all picked out for his son, now into his last year at San Jose State. Tom had five years under his belt with the power company. Financially, these were really lean times.

"I was an auto dealer," Jake Rohrer recalled. "I would take care of their cars for them, give them a spare tire. Stu brought his old Chevy down and we would pull the cylinder heads out and do a valve job to keep it going." He also helped keep the band's van in working order, but they never did get around to repainting it. Wherever the band played, they were an advertisement for a local flooring company.

Toward the end of 1966, they didn't use the van much, however. Uncle Sam notified John and Doug that he wanted them. Both decided to enlist with the reserves before they were drafted. John became a reservist in the Army; Doug drew the Coast Guard. The biggest hassle for both John and Doug was the length of their hair. During their six months of active duty, the band got put on a back burner. John was particularly depressed by his enforced military service: "I was so downed by the whole affair, I didn't even touch a guitar the whole time I was in. I spent all my time and conscious efforts figuring out how I could get out. I learned how to be persistent and how to play their game. Negative examples can be great teachers."

Yet he didn't forget about music altogether. Certain ideas still burned in John's mind. They kept him going as he marched in the North Carolina heat during his tour of active duty at Fort Bragg:

I was really excited about [the song] "Porterville," which I worked on while I was in the Army. When you get into a semi-hallucinatory state, marching day after day in the heat. "Porterville" is filled with teenage angst, a kind having to deal with paying the debt his parentage had laid on him. It's about not wanting to be in the town where you live, wanting to get away. As a songwriter, "Porterville" led me to where I was going.

This direction was away from the songs of "Toby Green," John's Golliwogs nom-de-disc. The Golliwogs' songs were slight, even trite. "All through school," John said in retrospect,

I heard love songs that didn't really have much meaning. By the time I was eighteen, I made a conscious effort to steer away from that kind of songwriting. Our first Golliwogs songs, the ones that Tom and I wrote, were in that superficial vein, just rhyming words. As for love songs, you'd hear them on the radio and maybe you'd like the sound of the records or the singer's voice, but the songs were all pretty dumb. I was also self-conscious to the degree where I had trouble even saying the word "love."

John had a different vision of what a rock song could be: "I developed my style to be rhythmic and chord based with simple lead lines you could almost hum. "I think that's one of the secrets as to why some of the songs back then were memorable, and why every bar band or garage band in the world could play Creedence songs."

Stu graduated at about the same time as John and Doug finished their tour of active duty. While they still faced monthly meetings and camp, this meant nothing more inconvenient than going entire weekends without sleep every now and again. However, none of the Golliwogs were kids anymore. By the summer of 1967, the members of the band faced hard choices about what to do when they grew up. The fate of the Golliwogs was uncertain.

Still, John remained optimistic. "I'd been telling the group," John said, "all through the summer of '67—I just had this feeling—things were gonna kinda come to a head in October. And I didn't know what it was. I didn't even know if I was just giving 'em the Knute Rockne speech, you know!"

The pep talks paid off. Stu sold the car his father had given him as a graduation gift. "Stu's dad ran this high powered law firm and expected his son to go on to law school," Jake Rohrer recalls. "Stu told his dad, 'Dad, I'm sorry, I've got to do this.' He went out and sold the new car his dad had bought him for graduation to initially finance the band."

"It was a big decision for Stu," John commented, "to finally quit everything. He had to break away from his father."

Tom also sacrificed a lot, giving up his position with PG&E and his savings with a wife and young family to support. "I think I was nervous about it, but I trusted Tom and went along with it," Gail Fogerty, his ex-wife, recalls. "I didn't feel that he would let us suffer in any way. I remember that Tom quit his job. It was Tom's retirement money from PG&E and Stu sold his car that his father gave him for graduation. They pooled the money together," Gail adds. "Tom took care of the finances and paid everybody's rent and gave everybody food money. Then they started playing jobs and earning money which went back into that fund. Until they got on their feet, we did fine. None of us starved. None of us really did without. We didn't go out and buy fancy things or anything like that, but we survived fine."

"At that time," Tom noted, "I used to give everyone $20 per week to live on. That's correct: $20 per week."

John was also married with a child. Stu and Doug rented a small pink house in El Sobrante, which they called "The Shire." It became one in a line of official group "factories," places they could hang out and practice. At first, the name was an inside joke for the group, who were barely making ends meet. As Stu Cook recalls: "The original 'Factory' was a shack in Doug's backyard. We would rehearse there Monday through Friday every week. It was a joke—we were going to our jobs like other factory workers."

They paid off the creditors with the shotguns, and left the rest until they also got nasty. "I had to work pregnant to support their dreams," Laurie Clifford recalled. The group played as often as they could get jobs, and the money started to get a little better, but not much. By fall, the band was in pretty dire straits.

In 1985, recalling the sacrifices the band members made, Tom wrote to John: "In 1967, I, along with Stu, put up my life's savings to get the band started. Doug gave up everything and contributed the van so we could get to gigs and sessions." Yet, Tom really wanted to give up his day job and become a full-time performer. "I worked for the electric company for six years," he said in 1975. "Then I decided it was better that I become a musician, because that's really what I am."

"We said," Tom recalled, "'we have to devote our whole lives to music or else it won't happen.' Two or three months before our first album, we had exactly two dollars in our common checking account."

Part Two

WE'RE CREEDENCE
CLEARWATER REVIVAL
1967–1972

5

"WE KNEW SAUL MOSTLY AS A FRIEND"

Behind the scenes the summer of 1967 held all kinds of portents for the Golliwogs. While they had no way of knowing it, John must have had second sight, or perhaps he heard the rumblings coming from the Fantasy Records offices.

The Weiss brothers had been in the record business for nearly twenty years, and had run a lucrative plastics business before that. They were ready to get out of the business and take it easy. Before they could retire, however, they had to maximize the record company they'd built up over the course of the last two decades. Initially, they entered into an agreement with an East Coast company to sell Fantasy's assets.

Saul Zaentz, who had worked for Fantasy since 1955 as the director of sales and marketing, started putting out feelers for a new position. He called all of the distributors with whom he had daily contact, trying to find a safety net.

"There was some disagreement on the way the [East Coast company] contract was going to be drawn up," reports Al Bendich, attorney and VP at Fantasy. "The Weiss brothers sought to back out of the deal and [the East Coast company] sought to force the deal. There was an ongoing litigation scene there."

When this came to light, Ralph Kaffel, one of Zaentz's network of independent distributors, suggested that maybe Zaentz ought to put in a bid for Fantasy. "Saul said he didn't have the money to do that," Bendich continues. "Ralph suggested that he, as one of the distributors of the label, and others around the country, might contribute something and become partners with Saul and help him finance the purchase of the company."

Kaffel also suggested that Zaentz lease the label from the Weisses until the problems with the East Coast-based company were resolved. Zaentz put

Saul Zaentz.

together his consortium of investors from friends, family, and business associates. He formed Debut Records of California, using leased material from Fantasy as the product. He paid the Weiss brothers a fee to run Fantasy, with an option to purchase it.

Zaentz brought a colorful past with him to the Bay area. The youngest of five children, he was born in Passaic, New Jersey. He had enjoyed sports, reading, movies, and pop music as a child. He also enjoyed games of chance. "I used to gamble a lot when I was young," he recalled. "I made my living at it for a few years. They had bookies on every corner in New Jersey."

Zaentz ran away from home in his mid teens, working his way south. He hawked peanuts at the St. Louis Cardinals training camp and used that as stakes money for gambling. He hoboed his way across the country a couple of times, attending the San Francisco World's Fair in 1939. As a sergeant major enlistee in the Army during World War II, he worked on a transport, "shuttling troops to the Mediterranean, North Atlantic, South and Central Pacific. All this time, I was doing lots of reading."

The pastoral life seemed to appeal to the shipboard Zaentz. He thought about raising chickens. After the war, he studied animal husbandry at Rutgers University. However, after spending some time working on an actual chicken farm, the reality of the situation—fourteen hour days, a half day off every other week for $65 a month—changed his mind. After six weeks of that he bolted, going to St. Louis "to see the last two weeks of the baseball season."

While there, Zaentz attended business school, taking a two-year course in accounting and administration. Growing weary of St. Louis, he went back to San Francisco and put his new business skills to work with a record distributor. He went to work with jazz impresario Norman Granz, who was getting Verve Records started. Zaentz became the road manager for some of the acts Granz managed, including Duke Ellington, Stan Getz, Dave Brubeck, and Gerry Mulligan.

"Norman," Zaentz said, "was an enormous influence for me in how to work with artists. He was one of the most honest, yet the toughest men I ever knew. His word was his bond. He managed Oscar Peterson, Count Basie, and Ella Fitzgerald for years without any contracts—just a simple handshake."

The latter two artists recorded for San Francisco-based Fantasy Records, and in 1955 Zaentz took a job there as director of sales and marketing. "They didn't know anything about distribution, but they had a small plant manufacturing plastics and a bent which I shared for recording adventuresome new artists no one else would gamble on."

Zaentz hired Celia Mingus, the ex-wife of jazz great Charles Mingus, as his secretary, and eventually wound up marrying her. He must have enjoyed something about the job, because he spent a dozen years doing it before the Weiss brothers leased him the company.

As a shipping clerk, John knew Zaentz, and Zaentz knew John. They had a good relationship: "We knew Saul mostly as a friend. He worked for Fantasy. I'm not really sure what he was doing. I think it was 'sales representative,' but I never knew what those titles meant. But he was objective. He just . . . liked us, we liked him. I was working for the same company Saul was working for. It was like that, mostly just good friends."

As John predicted, things stated to break for the group in October. Zaentz formed Debut of California and sought out Fogerty and his band. John recalled, "In October, we got a phone call from Saul saying, 'I just bought Fantasy Records.' There was this phone call and we knew right away that it was momentous to us in our lives, because Saul was straight ahead. We knew what *he* was like. He said, 'I bought the company. Will you stay with it?' And we said, 'Sure.'"

Zaentz moved the company from San Francisco to the very lowest rent area of Oakland. Not far from the new space, the Black Panthers would shoot it out with the Oakland police department in 1967. The space was a one-story garage with an office.

Around this same time, the band was working on a recording of "Porter-ville," the song John wrote during his tour of active duty. Zaentz called in the band and signed them to a new contract. It didn't offer the group much.

"When Saul bought the company, basically I felt like we were in a part-nership," Fogerty asserted. "He had this little office in Oakland, there was no studio or anything. There was nothing there, just the four of us in the band and one lady to answer the phone. They didn't even have a shipping clerk at first. So, when the guy told us, 'Well, if you have a hit, we'll all share in a much bigger way in the success,' I believed him."

By 1967 standards the contract Zaentz offered the group was pretty . . . standard. Artists had not yet begun to employ lawyers to review agreements. By this time, the band had managed their own affairs for so long it was sec-ond nature to take care of it on their own. Although Stu's father practiced law as the senior partner in a Bay Area firm, they didn't even ask him to read it, though they warranted that they had gotten such advice.

While the contract ostensibly lasted seven years, the longest a personal service contract could last by California law, it took a cue from the music industry boilerplate contracts that essentially turned the artists into inden-tured musical servants at the record company's discretion. The company could drop the artist at any time, for any reason. The artist had to deliver twelve masters the first year, twelve the second year, and twenty-four masters every subsequent year of the contract. The company also had the option to demand another ten masters a year. The contract defined a "master" as a recording of under five and a half minutes. A six minute tune would count as two "masters." If the group—or the members of the group, if the group disbanded—delivered less than this, the company could "extend the then current year and/or term of this agreement until such failure to perform is so corrected." This meant that even as individual performers the group members would still be liable for any undelivered masters.

Theoretically, this meant that even if an artist could keep up with a dozen (or even twenty-two) masters over the course of the first two years, by the third year, the artist would owe a maximum of thirty-four masters. As John explained:

> You deliver ten the [third] year, because you are excited and working. The
> next year you still owe the thirty-four for that year plus twenty-four. But
> maybe you don't deliver an album so let's see. Twenty-four and thirty-four is
> fifty-eight. So all that slides into the [fifth] year. Maybe you make an album
> with ten songs on it in the [fifth] year. But in that [fifth] year you owe thirty-
> four plus fifty-eight. Then you deliver another album with maybe ten masters
> on it in that fifth year and now you only owe them eighty-two. Those eighty-

two slide into the sixth year, but maybe you don't make a record in that sixth year. Now we are looking at—how many records do we owe? You see how it gets harder and harder and harder, and as you come up with an album, you owe more and more and more every year that goes by.

Another proviso of the contract dealt with the songwriting. According to the contract, the artists assigned their publishing interests to the record company. "Fogerty, Cook, Clifford and Fogerty signed a publishing agreement with one of Fantasy's companies that gave up the rights to copyright ownership," Stu said. "It was, and still is quite common for new artists to sign such agreements. Lennon and McCartney never owned the copyrights to their compositions from the Beatles, either. When you're on the bottom, you make the best deal you can. Same when you're on the top.

"John is the only major writer from the Bay Area music scene that doesn't own his songs," Stu adds. "Steve Miller, the Dead, Jefferson Airplane, Santana, etc., all own their songs. Seems that they were astute enough to hire legal/business representation when the labels were passing out the lame contracts. I remember John referring to all those guys as drugged out, moccasin wearing hippies. I guess it's never too late to go to school," he added, ironically.

Zaentz told the band that he felt they needed to make some changes. He saw what was happening in the Bay Area music scene with the rise of "underground radio" and venues like the Fillmore presenting shows with groups like the Grateful Dead and the Jefferson Airplane. In this crowd, a band called the Golliwogs definitely wouldn't fly.

"I hated the name," Zaentz said. " 'Golliwogs,' it was ridiculous—a stupid name. They played with big white hats, ridiculous. So they said, 'What name do you want to give us?' I said no. You come up with ten names and I'll come up with ten names and the first one we like we'll use."

So with Zaentz's blessing, even encouragement, they trashed the Golliwogs sobriquet and started searching for a new name. Now that Zaentz took charge, they could use a name with more personal relevance.

Tom recalled nearly two decades later: "Many names were thrown into the hat, including: Deep Bottle Blue, Muddy Rabbit, Gossamer Wump and Credence Nuball and the Ruby . . . . I was out with a friend of mine, and he was telling me about a friend of his at work, and his name, believe it or not, his real name was Credence Nuball. He came to the Fillmore to meet us."

"Tom brought this guy's name [Credence] to the table," recalled Stu. "We tried to come up with a new name for about two weeks. We thought of nothing else."

The first name appealed to them, though they added an extra "e" to the name to create "Creedence," like a creed, something to believe in. Its connotations of believability and integrity appealed to the group. The Clearwater part also had a dual meaning. Initially, it came from an advertisement for Olympia Beer, made from cool, clear water. The notion of "Clearwater" appealed to the band's environmental sensibilities, particularly Doug's. It also called to mind a certain purity.

"Revival" meant a lot of things to the band. To the parochial-schooled Tom, there was the element of the revival show, almost a spoof on religion. More important, it represented a resurgence for the band itself.

"We'd been together for eight years at this point," Tom said, "and it looked like we were finally going to get a shot."

It also signified the revival of musical values that they had carried from the beginning, bringing back the simplicity of rock and roll in the face of the prevailing acid rock scene, especially in the Bay Area.

"Finally, John put together the three names and we surrendered to the inevitable," Stu laughs. "A name weirder than Buffalo Springfield or Jefferson Airplane."

"The most important part was Revival," John said. "I meant it as a personal resurgence within ourselves. We really needed it.

"The name was better than we were. Creedence Clearwater Revival said what we were better than what we really were in real life."

"I still have this picture in my mind of the guys walking up the stairs," says Zaentz. "They said, 'Okay, what's your first name?' I said, 'No, tell me yours.' 'Creedence Clearwater Revival.' I just tore up my list."

Zaentz asked the band what they needed. There was a lot, from a new van to replace the old '58 VW "Du-All Floor Company" van that frequently broke down. But the main thing they needed, the thing they couldn't play without for much longer, was a new guitar amp. Zaentz took a loan out against his car and bought the band that desperately needed amplifier.

"Blew 'em out at Roger Caulkins's [music shop]," John laughed, " 'cause we paid cash for it. Nobody ever did that for him."

At a gig on Christmas Eve 1967, they announced, "We're Creedence Clearwater Revival," for the first time. A month later, when "Porterville" came out, it too was under the name Creedence Clearwater Revival (though John wasn't through with pen names, listing his writing credit as "T. Spicebush Swallowtail"). While things didn't go "poof" and change in an instant, they inexorably started to go the band's way.

For one thing, the dates started getting a little better. Their main gigs were dances and NCO clubs around the Central Valley. However, they finally got over their apprehension about playing in San Francisco. "I was afraid of San Francisco," John conceded. "We'd been so bad for so long." And armed with their new name, new record company, and new attitude, they found a standing weekly gig at a club called Deno-Carlo in North Beach.

"It was a small narrow club," as Stu described it, "with an elevated stage at the opposite end from the street entrance. The stage couldn't have been more than ten feet wide. Beer and wine were the strongest drinks served. Each band had a night. I can't remember ours, but it might've been Monday."

"We were finally sure of ourselves," John said. "We had a repertoire, were able to do it well. We had whatever presence you need and we were happy with what we were doing."

So the Deno-Carlo wasn't the Fillmore, or even the Avalon, but they started building a following among people who enjoyed the band's rootsy sound as an antidote to the psychedelia all around them.

I really didn't like most of the drawn-out twenty-five-minute Ride Trans Love Airlines stuff the San Francisco groups were doing. My attention span wore out after ten minutes .... I saw precious little entertainment. I saw a lot of noodling, and I'm not made that way .... I had been weaned on James Brown ..."Yow, yow," you get in and get out.

"I remember when the ballroom scene started to happen," Stu added,

and there was a whole lot of new music going around. People wanted us to play 'Purple Haze' and things, and we were still playing 'Walking the Dog,' and all of our old favorites. Just briefly we went through this phase of going, "Are we really that far out of touch?" We really like tunes like 'Walking the Dog' and 'Green Onions'—the R&B cover stuff. We wondered if we weren't so far out of touch that we were off the planet.

Deno-Carlo let Creedence play what they wanted and build an audience, paying the band with what people would put in the beer pitcher that they passed around. "We had a lot of fun playing at Deno-Carlo and at Muir Beach and a few others," said Stu.

We weren't playing for money, per se. It was our introduction to San Francisco. I think, more than anything, the people were really ready for our music. At that time, when we needed money, we would play outside the city. That's where we would sometimes encounter the people that weren't ready for us. We got to play at Deno-Carlo one night a week and all our fans would come that night. We were always playing to people who wanted to hear us.

One occasional customer at Deno-Carlo was Zaentz. "He said," John recalled of one evening, " 'Well, I think you guys should make an album.' "

6

"WE WERE IN THE RIGHT PLACE AT THE RIGHT TIME"

"Porterville" fared no better than any Golliwogs single since "Brown Eyed Girl," but it marked a watershed. The tune symbolized the start of Creedence Clearwater Revival in more than just name. It represented a subtlely new creative direction for the band. For one thing, John wrote the tune by himself, as opposed to collaborating with Tom.

"I resolved at that point not to be mediocre," John asserts. "I resolved at that point to write real songs."

The band started woodshedding for the album. "John brought at the very least the musical structure of the song," Stu says. "He would sometimes have specific parts in the arrangement in mind and would request that we play them. Other times, we would be playing the chord changes and great parts would jump out. He'd like them and they'd stay. Sometimes he'd suggest a part and after playing it for a while, it would evolve into something else.

"Songs were introduced during the period before the recording project began," Stu added. "We usually rehearsed from Monday to Friday from about 11 A.M. to 2 P.M. We went to the Factory and worked."

"I was very careful about having the parts be true to the genre and the song," John said. "There's a certain integrity to each instrument—the rhythm lick, the bass, the drums. I was running things through that sort of filter."

The weekly gig at Deno-Carlo also played an important part in their first album. "We developed the music [by performing it there]," Stu noted. "Some of the music for the first album was fine-tuned there."

"As 1968 became a reality, we were ready," Tom wrote seventeen years later. "We had our new energy, and essentially a new record company and a whole batch of new songs. We were in the right place [San Francisco], at the right time."

42

With all that in mind, CCR went in to the studio to record their first album. In nominally producing it, Zaentz set up a paradigm that would follow him throughout his life as a producer of music and films: let the creators create.

"He was there, but not in the way," John noted. "He came around to the first couple of sessions, but he didn't say anything. He knew that I knew what to do, or at least he let me feel that he felt that way. Saul makes you feel good. If you're down, he just has a way of saying the right things."

"Early on," Stu recalled, "Saul Zaentz was like a father. John was very close to him."

Having spent so much time in the recording studio already, CCR had none of the first-album jitters. They attacked making the record like pros, cutting the bulk of the album in a week for well under $5,000. The band's attitude was all business, according to John: "Once in the studio, we'd warm up a bit, then roll the tape. We were usually really psyched up and by the second or third take, we'd just go, 'That's all.'"

Like many albums of the day, the record was essentially cut "live," although vocals were added afterward. "We tracked all of the songs together as a live band," Stu described the process. "We were prepared when we reached the studio, so three to five takes per track was common. Sometimes the track was recorded in one or two takes."

"We four track everything but the voice," John added, "putting that on last along with any filler to make the song interesting—not to make it sound like more musicians. . . . We don't use a studio to create new sounds."

John's philosophy of recording was set from the very first album, as he explained it in a lengthy 1970 interview with Ralph Gleason for *Rolling Stone:*

> I really zip through. We'll go in, we'll have maybe ten tunes, unfinished, and I'll go in and in four or five hours we'll do all the little things and finish them. I like to work that way. I've done all the thinking previously. I don't like to sit around and wait to be inspired in the studio.
>
> My basic philosophy, then and now, is that you've got to have it sounding like what you want right there in the room. That's where it all happens. Then it's up to the engineer and the producer—who was me—to get it down on tape.
>
> It was no accident that we got that sound. We all felt it had to have the muscle and the subtleties we were looking for, and we spent a lot of time looking at snare drums and going through bass strings and bass amps and all that. The idea of fixing it in the mix is totally foreign to me. Same with singing. I'd go in there and probably do two takes, and that would be it.

Yet the process of making the album marked a subtle shift in the band. John had dreamed about this since grade school. Now he had the chance to

Creedence Clearwater Revival's debut album.

make an album, to succeed in music. He recognized it as a better chance than with the Golliwogs, better than with the Blue Velvets, better than backing all the James Powells the Bay Area had to offer. This was the best chance they'd had in nearly a decade of playing together, and he wanted to make the most of it. He wrote the songs, sang the songs, and called most of the shots.

"Everybody listened to my advice," John claimed. "I don't think anybody thought too much about it."

The album featured a rerecording of the old Golliwogs tune "Walk on the Water" (which would turn out to be the last Tom Fogerty song on a CCR album), and the first CCR single, "Porterville." Other John Fogerty originals included the bluesy "Get Down Woman" and "The Working Man," the former almost a tribute to B. B. King, the latter a reflection of John's early obsession with Howlin' Wolf. "Gloomy" presaged CCR's darker side, though they also had a little fun in the studio recording it.

"My son Josh was about three years old at the time," John recalled. "Our house was full of all these wind-up toys. I recorded them at different speeds and we played some backwards and combined to make the sounds on 'Gloomy.' George Martin had a Mellotron and all that stuff, we had wind-up toys."

John had only begun to come into his own as a songwriter, but was already developing a philosophy about it. "A great record," he believed, "[has] four things, in this order: title, the sound, the words, and then the last thing, which all great rock and roll records have: a really great guitar riff."

They also cut three covers. Perhaps John's best vocal on the debut paid tribute to Wilson Pickett on "Ninety-Nine and a Half (Won't Do)." It also tipped their obsession with the Memphis sound; the coauthor of the song was MG's guitarist Steve Cropper. They also recorded Screamin' Jay Hawkins's "I Put a Spell on You," and a Bo Diddley song that didn't really come off. John stuck to his guns and rejected the cut, holding the band to the highest possible standards. "I kept telling myself," John said, " 'now if we were the Beatles, we wouldn't use that because it's no good.' We came up to the final thing, and finally I thought, 'Oh well, what the heck. If they can throw it away, we'll throw it away, too.' That's the way it worked out."

The other cover the band recorded and kept was Dale Hawkins's "Susie Q," a song that scratched the top 30 (number 27) in 1957. A favorite of the group's, they had played it since the Blue Velvets days.

"I was really hot for 'Susie Q,' John said. "I did the whole thing with it in mind of being a single eventually. That's why all the 'interesting' stuff happens at the beginning. I visualized it as two parts so we could cut it in half later."

" 'Susie Q' was a song we listened to when it came out, I guess about ten years before we did it," Doug said. "It was just classic guitar rock and roll, and we were a guitar rock and roll band."

John chose the song specifically to create a special sound for the band:

I knew I needed to work on arranging the band so that the band would sound like Creedence Clearwater Revival, would sound professional, mysterious and also have their own definition. The song I chose was "Susie Q." I decided not to write the song myself. I decided to pick something that existed because it'd just be easier. I'd be less self-conscious about doing things."

If it had been one of his own songs, John feared, he'd be too close to it to do his best as a producer/arranger:

I could worry about the sound and the musicianship on the record. I wouldn't be so involved with my own tune that I'd be all hung up on "phrasing" and all that kind of stuff. That was like a combination of everything we knew, we did it on "Susie Q." We went in and we were so ready to do it, it was one take all the way through! Just whap! And that was that.

In the context of 1968, it offered more. "Suzie Q" (as CCR spelled it) allowed the band to stretch out, and emulate a little piece of the psychedelia blooming all around them. In its way, it was a very Golliwogs-like move, more the "whatever works" ethic. Stu, who would later confess to having a personal fondness for the psychedelic scene at the time, claims, "It was my idea to record 'Suzie Q' as a psychedelic jam; I even suggested the arrangement."

John recognized the need to add a psychedelic tinge to the record in order for it to succeed commercially:

I told the other guys that the quickest way we could get on the radio, therefore get more exposure and get this thing going was to specifically go in and record an arrangement of "Suzie Q" that could be played on KMPX [the bay area's progressive radio station of the day]. It's been said that what we were doing seemed very far removed from the rest of San Francisco, but that's not quite true. "Suzie Q" was designed to fit right in. The eight-minute opus. Feedback like "East-West" [an underground hit for the Paul Butterfield Blues Band].

In selecting "Susie Q," John harked back to the band's roots-rock heritage; in arranging it with room for the band to stretch out, he recognized the need to appeal to the San Francisco sound.

John was also proud of the added vocal effect on the record. "[I] especially [liked] the little effect, the telephone box in the middle. It's a little funny sounding, but lo and behold, it worked!" Doug adds, "That was kind of a high tech thing for that period. The engineers used this new device. They said, 'We've got this pretty hip deal that makes you sound like Rudy Vallee.' We said, 'Hell, we'll use it.' John used that just for an effect. At the time, it was ahead of its time."

They also threw in some other obscure vocal effects in the background. "You know what we'd like to be asked?" Stu teased interviewer Harvey Siders. " 'What did we sing in the background of 'Suzie Q'? Nobody ever asked us about that."

"Just a whole lot of Moon-June clichés," Doug volunteered. "Nothing more."

"In the process of arranging that," Fogerty maintains, "I really came up with Creedence's—in our lifetime, in our evolution since we were thirteen-years old—I came up with our first really professional arrangement. We stepped into the next dimension with 'Suzie Q.' I kind of did the same thing with 'I Put a Spell on You.' It helped define us. It was obviously another place from where we had been for ten years."

While John was making the final touches in the studio, however, it was already clear that the band did not always share his point of view, forecasting the troubles to come. "When I mixed 'Suzie Q,' [the rest of the band was] present in the studio. This was one of those studios where the mixing console was raised, and then from down in front of it, you could look out into the recording studio. . . . I kept hearing, 'That's not going to work!' and 'Oh, that's too loud!' and 'Aw, that'll never. . . .' You know, that sort of thing for the whole two hours. . . . I never let them be in there again. Every song after that, I just refused to let them be there because it was so disruptive."

One of the reasons they targeted KMPX was that they had friends at the station. KMPX was one of the more popular free-form FM stations in the Bay Area. Slightly before the band went into the studio, the DJs at KMPX went on strike when management tried to regain control over the free-form chaos (as they saw it). The band had supported the DJ strike, playing a benefit concert for the strikers. The strike ended when most of the KMPX staff moved to KSAN. That same week, CCR finished their album. So, they brought a raw copy of the tape to KSAN.

Still, John saw no quid pro quo in the station's support of their first album. "We had supported the strike pretty strongly," John said, "but they really didn't really 'owe' us anything. What happened following us taking the tape wasn't a payoff or anything. They just played it right through for like a week and a half. It was incredible! The airplay, and the album wasn't even released yet."

The group also played out. When the music started playing on the radio, they found themselves with better gigs. They now belonged to the American Federation of Musicians Union so they now played venues that used AFM contracts. The ever-practical (and still not particularly wealthy) band members shopped carefully before selecting an AFM branch to join. "We joined Local 424, the AFM union in Richmond, California," Stu recalls, "instead of local #6 [in San Francisco] because it was cheaper and you didn't have to audition to prove to them that you were actually a musician."

Even before the debut album hit, the group had worked their way up to low billings at the Fillmore and the Avalon. Still, they were low men on the totem pole. "We were getting ready to play the Avalon Ballroom," John recalls.

Our first album was just about ready. It was 6:30 or 7:00 at night, they're getting ready to open the doors any minute, but we're on the stage sound-checking because we were the punk, opening band. The stage manager hollers, "You guys have to stop. You're wasting everybody's time. Besides, you're not going anywhere anyway!" With that remark, he'd thrown down the gauntlet. I gave him the evil eye, then looked at him and said, "Give me a year, I'll show you who's going somewhere." Then we went backstage and gathered our pride.

With all the play on KSAN, even before the record came out, it started to generate excitement on the West Coast. Yet the album still had that homegrown feel. Stu took the cover photo. "We liked the pic and the artwork," he recalls, "but Fantasy wanted a color photo, so we went back and reposed ourselves exactly as in the original photo and someone else re-shot it using color film."

The cover art was done by Laurie Clifford. She and Doug had gotten married around the same time they were making the album after going out for six years. Fantasy saw fit to include some truly curious liner notes, contributed by *San Francisco Chronicle/Rolling Stone* writer Ralph Gleason. Gleason barely mentioned the band, instead expounding on the sociology of the San Francisco rock scene. He managed to bring them into the last paragraph: "Creedence Clearwater Revival is an excellent example of the Third generation of San Francisco bands which gives every indication (as this album demonstrates forcibly) of keeping the strength of the San Francisco Sound undiminished." CCR was so new and so unknown, he apparently couldn't find anything more to say about them.

When the record hit the streets, it started to sell better than anything the band had ever put out. To keep it building, Zaentz sent them down to play a showcase at the LA club the Cheetah.

"It was a real drag," John recalled. "We drove down in the Volkswagen bus. Saul talked us into it because it was good for exposure. Sometimes that makes it, but we didn't want to pay any more dues, really. We thought, 'For ten years we've done all that junk, and now we've almost got a hit record.' We could see the importance was in the records. They could do the work for us, if we let 'em, if we were patient. But Saul really wanted us to go down there, because some record people would come. We said, 'Okay,' and we went. He showed up down there, which was far out."

Zaentz showed up for more than just the set. He came bearing news, big news. Bill Drake, one of the most powerful people in pop radio at the time, decided he really liked "Suzie Q," and recommended it to the radio stations that used his services in picking the music they programmed.

"We were convinced it was never going to happen, underground sensations and that was that," John remembered. "He told us that Bill Drake had just put it on the Chicago station and one other station and it was a cinch from there."

The single version of "Suzie Q" had come out in August. By the end of September, the record peaked at number 11 in the charts. The group's career was underway.

7

"I, FOR ONE, DIDN'T WANT TO GO BACK TO THE CARWASH"

"Our approach," John told music writer James Brewer in 1969, "was always to get a hit and that will solve everything."

Despite having a considerable hit, the band wasn't out of the woods yet. "Suzie Q" sold very well. The band took part of the fall for a brief promotional tour. They really couldn't go too far or for too long, however. John and Doug still had their duty to the Reserves, and that meant a weekend of camp every month.

"In the beginning," says Stu, "we played on weekends. When we started looking at how to get from Seattle to Miami overnight, the plan had to change."

The early reviews of the group's live shows were generally favorable. Wayne Harada reviewed a show in Honolulu on September 14, 1968, for *Billboard*. Creedence were supporting Vanilla Fudge, who were riding high on their psychedelic cover of the Supremes' "You Keep Me Hanging On." "The Revival," Harada wrote on a page that also offered a picture of the Monkees receiving a gold record and a review of a Lainie Kazan concert, "offered an equally explosive menu of rock, mainly oldies updated and dressed in now grooves. 'Suzy Q' [*sic*] and 'Good Golly Miss Molly' were durables from a decade ago, exciting in their rebirth."

The group made their New York City debut on a bill with the Beach Boys and the Turtles at the Fillmore East on October 11, 1968. Fred Kirby wrote, "Creedence Clearwater Revival, who are riding high with 'Suzie Q,' made a fine impression both nights. Fogerty has a fine blues voice and plays guitar expertly, often with mandolin effect. He also can use feedback effectively. The other three musicians in the group, drummer Doug Clifford, bass guitarist Stu Cook and rhythm guitarist Tom Fogerty were also strong performers.

"Their 'Suzie Q,'" he continued, "is an extended number with a long instrumental section, giving John Fogerty a chance to excel. Screamin' Jay Hawkins's 'I Put a Spell on You' was another top selection from the group's initial album, as John Fogerty's voice admirably put the contemporary blues numbers over.

"Other effective songs from the Fantasy album were 'Walk on the Water,' 'Porterville' and 'Ninety-Nine and a Half (Won't Do).' 'Good Golly Miss Molly' and 'Born on the Bayou' were also aces by this top new San Francisco quartet."

When 'Suzie Q' reached sales of half a million, Zaentz treated the band to a "half gold" party. But the follow-up single, "I Put a Spell on You," didn't fare as well, peaking at number 58. The album sold slowly but steadily, reaching number 52. So, despite the celebratory times, the band also had plenty on their minds. Having one hit was a fine thing. Following it up and building a career was quite another. And having to be available for Reserves camp was the biggest drag of all.

They started working out material for their new album. They'd already added "Born on the Bayou" to their show (as Kirby noted in his review). "That's my favorite Creedence tune, bar none," Doug noted some two decades later. "I just love that rhythm. That started out as a jam at the Shrine Auditorium in Los Angeles. The guys had ordered new Kustom amps. They weren't custom made, that was the brand name. They had tremendous treble, tremendous mid-range, and it made the guitar really stand out. The guys were trying out their new amps and I didn't have any toy. I started playing over that feedback thing, and John started playing that riff."

"The riff came before the words," Fogerty agrees, though he places the sound check at the Avalon. "Our first album was out, but I was already on to the next batch of songs. I had this riff for a song . . . so I screamed at Stu, 'Play these notes on the bass. Doug, play this beat. Tom, strum the back beat. Everyone stay in "E."' I was hammering this riff, screaming nonsensical vowels (I write a lot of songs that way). The feeling was great . . . The feel was definitely southern with a 'swampy' vibrato guitar."

"I can't tell you how much fun that song is to play," Clifford added. "It's almost as good as sex. I said *almost*."

The tune set the tone for the next album, and indeed for the rest of John's career, because it embodies the flavor of a mythical South. Given John's musical predilections, it made perfect sense. He credits the darkness, musically and lyrically, to Bo Diddley. "People sometimes associate me with spooky, almost voodoo imagery. If there's any one place that comes from, it's [the album] *Bo Diddley* on Checker. Bo Diddley was just the master of that

Elliot Landy/Starfile

CCR live.

primitive thing," he commented while picking his favorite records of the '50s for Rolling Stone.

With the bones of "Born on the Bayou" in his back pocket, John started writing music for the new album in earnest. He developed the insomnia that would plague him on and off, for varying reasons, throughout his life. Driven and challenged, he set out to create a great bunch of songs for the next record:

> I was writing many songs at once in 1968. I was writing these at night, and I remember that Bobby Kennedy got killed during this time. I saw that late at night. They kept showing it over and over. "Bayou" and "Proud Mary" and "Chooglin'" were all kind of cooking at that time. I'd say that was when the whole swamp bayou myth was born—right there in a little apartment in El Cerrito. It was late at night and I was probably delirious from lack of sleep. I remember that I thought it would be cool if these songs cross-referenced each other. Once I was doing that, I realized that I was kind of working on a mythical place.

Speaking to Michael Goldberg in 1993, John expounded on how he felt the record could be made more powerful through relating the material: "It is almost the Gordian knot or the key to what happened later. As I was writing it, it occurred to me that there was more power than just this one song. If there was a way to tie it all together on one album, kind of cross-fertilize, cross-relate the songs, you would have a much more interesting and maybe more powerful image."

The musical link that John discovered for the album—and for the band—was based on the entire soundscape of the South that he heard on his favorite recordings:

All the really great records or people who made them somehow came from Memphis or Louisiana or somewhere along the Mississippi River in between. I had a lifelong dream that I wanted to live there. I never even thought about the social pressures. To me, it just represented something earlier, like 1807, before computers and machinery complicated everything, when things were calm and relaxed. And singers like Howlin' Wolf and Muddy Waters gave me the feeling that they were right there, standing by the river. Carl Perkins . . . made his greatest records right by the river in Memphis. I really enjoyed the whole southern folk legend . . . Mark Twain, Tom Sawyer, Huck Finn, the River and all that went with it. The river and the South just seem to be where all the music that's kicked everything off started from or sounds like.

The genesis of a song like "Born on the Bayou" could be quite diverse, mirroring Fogerty's own widespanning interests. Speaking with Rick Clark in 1997, he described how the song was inspired by both gospel music and popular movies:

I used to listen to the religious hour on Sunday evenings. Sundays, they had a gospel show that ran for two or three hours. I would certainly remember Pops Staples's guitar and the Staples Singers. That's really why I would tune in, to hear that harmony sound and his guitar style. I'm just a kind of American sponge of all things that came before. Pops, and the gospel sound in general, is a big influence on me. So if you get any of that feel in my records, I am very proud.

I gravitated to movies that were Southern in nature. The movie *The Defiant Ones* was very southern. Another old movie that was a favorite of mine was called *Swamp Fever*, believe it or not. I think I hooked into all of that stuff because of the music first. Then I just started paying attention.

"Born on the Bayou" was . . . about a mythical childhood and a heat-filled time, the Fourth of July. I put it in the swamp where, of course, I had never lived. I was trying to be a pure writer, no guitar in hand, visualizing and looking at the bare walls of my apartment. "Chasing down a hoodoo." Hoodoo is a magical, mystical, spiritual, non-defined apparition, like a ghost or a shadow, not necessarily evil, but certainly otherworldly.

Fogerty's interest in the deep roots of southern music lent a unifying theme and sound to the group's music. Creedence Clearwater Revival's roots rock and roll sound—already an amalgam of blues, '50s blues-oriented rock, rhythm and blues, rockabilly, and even some country—mutated into something else. They found a voice in these images of a South that John had only barely touched during his active service at Fort Bragg. It turned Creedence Clearwater Revival from just the name of the band into their identity. Rather than four discrete personalities, they developed one, embodied in their name.

If "Born on the Bayou" started this metamorphosis, the joyous "Proud Mary" solidified it. "After writing 'Proud Mary,'" John says, "There wasn't a doubt in my mind. I knew it was a hit." "Proud Mary" represented the removal of two key millstones from John's back. He had toyed with the title for years. To John, the song's title made the song.

"When it came time for me to write songs," he told popular guitar player Duane Eddy in a dialogue they recorded for *Musician*, "I used that lesson I had learned from you. It was simply, if the title can mean so much without lyrics, the title must be important. If you can have a cool title like 'Ramrod,' or 'Rebel Rouser,' or 'Forty Miles of Bad Road,' 'Heartbreak Hotel,' 'Honky Tonk,' 'Bad Moon Risin',' on top of everything else, you're really setting off in the right direction."

John's compass in these matters is a notebook he maintains with ideas for lyrics, and more importantly, titles. One of the first things in the book were the words "Proud Mary." The song originally was not about a riverboat at all. John recalled, "At the time, I pictured it being about a maid in a household of rich people. She gets off the bus every morning and goes to work and holds their lives together. Then she has to go home."

He had also jotted down something Stu had said while they were watching *Maverick* on television, sitting around in a room on the road. One of the famed Mississippi River gambling boats played a part. Stu saw that and said, "Hey riverboat, blow your bell." John recalled thinking, "Yeah, that might be part of it, too."

He knew the band needed a hit. San Francisco teemed with one-hit wonders, many of them wandering around the Haight wondering whatever happened to them. To John, failure would mean going back to the gas station. Of course, he didn't feel quite like a professional musician, anyway. He still had the Reserves to deal with every month. His frustration with the situation—and its final dramatic relief—played into the creation of this best-known of all Creedence songs:

The Army Reserves had been a struggle for me at that time, the most severe thing I'd been through in my life. The Army and Creedence overlapped, so I was "that hippie with a record on the radio." I'd been trying to get out of the Army, and on the steps of my apartment house sat a diploma-sized letter from the government. It sat there for a couple of days, right next to my door. One day, I saw the envelope and bent down to look at it, noticing it said "John Fogerty." I went into the house, opened the thing up, and saw that it was my honorable discharge from the Army. I was finally out! This was 1968 and people were still dying. I was so happy, I ran out onto my little patch of lawn and turned cartwheels. Then I went into my house, picked up my guitar and started strumming. "Left a good job in the city" and then several good lines came out of me immediately. I had the chord changes, the minor chord where it says, "Big wheel keep on turnin'/Proud Mary keep on burnin' " (or "boinin'," using my funky pronunciation I got from Howlin' Wolf). By the time I hit "Rolling, rolling, rolling on the river," I knew I had written my best song. It vibrated inside me. When we rehearsed it, I felt like Cole Porter.

The song worked on many levels. Just structurally, in its simplicity, it captures classic pop song form. John would often refer to it as his "Tin Pan Alley" song. It also continued the theme of the mythical South, Mark Twain's Mississippi River brought up to the 1960s, blending paddle wheelers and pumping petrol from Memphis to New Orleans. "There's an old Will Rogers movie," Fogerty admitted, "about these old paddle wheelers, and I believe at one point they actually sing 'rolling on the river.' I know that buried deep inside me are all these little bits and pieces of Americana."

It also was a classic pop single, and Fogerty knew it in his heart. He had grown up on singles, on R&B hits. He appreciated the artistic latitude of recording an album, but ten years in the studio had honed his singles craft to a fine edge.

"A single," he believed, "means you've got to get it across in a very few minutes. You don't have twenty minutes on each side of an LP. All it really means is you've got to think a little harder about what you're doing. We learned from the singles market not to put a bunch of padding on your album. Each song's got to go someplace."

Forgerty also displayed a shrewd understanding of the commercial market. "As a songwriter," he commented in an interview with progressive radio station KSAN, "as a guy who writes a tune, I think in terms of top 40. That's where the tunes are."

Fogerty was always carefully building the group's career, carefully planning each single to maximize the band's growth and impact. He noted, "We always look ahead, always planning the next record. We always know where we're going and we're constantly evolving. In this process, we always make a conscious effort to make every side a hit."

After spending the fall supporting bands at bigger venues, rehearsing the new songs, and testing their material at Deno-Carlo, the band went down to Los Angeles, to RCA Recording Studios. "They made *Bayou Country* at RCA studios in LA," noted Russ Gary, who would engineer most of their later albums, "but there were too many distractions. Everybody was just popping into the studio. They didn't want to have anybody coming in at all."

Despite the distractions, they managed to lay down "Born on the Bayou," and the rip-roaring cover of "Good Golly Miss Molly" they'd played live at the Fillmore East. "Graveyard Train" ("That's John's tribute to Howlin' Wolf," Doug said, "one of our idols and certainly one of the major influences on John's singing voice"), and "Penthouse Pauper," mined the blues lode again. Then there were two tunes designed as concert ravers, "Bootleg," and "Keep on Chooglin'."

When it came time to lay down "Proud Mary," however, the first whiff of dissent descended on the band. The rest of the group thought the song would sound better if the group sang background on the "rolling on the river" chorus. "I knew I didn't want the band to sing that," John says. "I had it in my mind how it ought to sound, so I drew the line. Of course we had a fight about it."

But John knew how important the success of "Proud Mary" would be to the group: "We'd had a big hit with 'Suzie Q,' and then 'I Put a Spell on You' was like only top 40 or top 50. So we were balancing precariously in that position of either being on our way up or back to the car wash. We had a kind of butting of heads." Typical of John's attitude, he felt only his vocals could put the song forward and make it the hit they desperately needed.

As the group had taken on more responsibility, they hired Bruce Young, a friend of Stu's from college, as equipment manager. It fell to him to see that everything got set up properly, live and in the studio. He saw what was happening and took Tom, Doug, and Stu to Two Guys from Italy, an Italian restaurant close to the studio, to defuse the situation. John cut the vocals, double tracking his own voice. It took him about forty-five minutes. Then he went down and joined the band in the restaurant.

"I told them, 'It doesn't matter who does what,'" John says.

'What matters is that our group comes out with the best record we can possibly make. It doesn't matter who plays what part, or who's responsible, because we're competing with the rest of the world.

'We're following up a hit. We've waited all our lives for this shot. If we do something bad under the microscope, we're outta here . . .' I very clearly told the others that I, for one, didn't want to go back to the car wash again.

8

"NO SUBSTITUTE FOR PLAIN OLD TALENT"

While the debut album still credits Saul Zaentz as producer, that pretension went out the window on the *Bayou Country*. John produced it all the way, taking a tight grip of the creative reins to avoid the horror of returning to working at the car wash.

In addition to taking control creatively, John shouldered more and more of the business responsibilities (despite Stu having majored in business at San Jose). During the days when they took home what people put in the pitchers at the Deno-Carlo, money played second fiddle to music. However, now that they were a marketable commodity, they needed to consider the best way of bringing themselves to market. But they still had nightmares about their earlier experiences in the music business with managers and booking agents. Did they really want to bring these people back into their lives, even though the stakes had increased?

"We went through all that," Tom said. "Most of it was disastrous."

"Very early on in our working relationship as CCR," John says, "the four of us agreed that we would handle the group's affairs under the credo, 'all for one and one for all.' "

"We had learned more about the business itself," Tom related about their years in the studio and roadhouses, "than we did musically—what was hip and what was real."

Now, suddenly the band faced serious business. People called about shows, promotions, and other matters. But John couldn't give up even this aspect of running the group:

I wouldn't trust anybody else. I don't dig it because it's a hassle for me, answering the phones instead of somebody else or spending time thinking about things, but I've always had to do it, so it's not an extra burden at all. I'm glad I do now. It's every bit as involved as songwriting or being a musician or a singer learning a song, whatever. You've always got to be thinking about direction. I use myself as a manager sort of to oversee everything else I or the band does.

"After the first album," he added:

I realized I didn't want anybody messing with my rock and roll. Same thing with management. The first couple of decisions were what a label started saying we ought to do—"What youse guys need is a face man"—and I realized, no, that's not what we want at all. Suddenly, I found myself acting like a manager without realizing it. Finally, people started calling, and saying, "I want to talk to the manager." I would get my best gruff voice and say, "Okay, this is the manager," and kind of shut down any of the deals that were coming along. It was very effective.

"We decided to begin handling our own business affairs because we couldn't find anyone else who would give us the quality of service we wanted," John told the *LA Times*'s pop music critic, Robert Hilburn.

I was relying [on business associates] to know the right places for us to play and the right things for us to do for our career. But it didn't work. We'd ask them to make sure the sound systems were all right in the auditoriums that we were going to play and they'd tell us it had all been checked. But when we got to town the sound was a mess. The business people are after the immediate dollar. They wanted us to get involved in television commercials, movies, anything that would mean money. But we were more interested in building a career.

Fogerty's straight-shooter reputation helped the group win the respect of the rock industry. "This group," Bill Graham told Hilburn, "is the best example of honest businessmen I've met in rock. They are very straightforward."

Max Weiss had signed on as their manager and supplied them with the Golliwogs name and the attendant wigs. However, after he and his brother sold the company to Zaentz, the band had few dealings with Weiss. When he realized how well they were doing, however, Weiss initiated legal action to recover some of the money he felt the band owed him. He did, after all, have a management contract with the group. After a few months of legal wrangling and negotiation, Weiss eventually was recompensed.

Bayou Country.

Shortly after the first of the year in 1969, Fantasy released the single of "Proud Mary" with "Born on the Bayou" on the flip side. Most of the stations that played "Suzie Q" picked this one up, and once the catchy "rolling on the river" hook started blaring out of radios around the country and then around the world, others followed. Even rock's poet laureate, Bob Dylan, proclaimed it his favorite song of the year. By March, the song had topped out on the *Billboard* charts at number 2, denied the top spot by bubblegum idol Tommy Roe's tune "Dizzy." "Proud Mary," however, sold a million copies—CCR's first gold record.

Bayou Country came out in February. "A synthetic but spirited rehash of early rock is what the Creedence Clearwater Revival offers here," Peter Reilly wrote in *Stereo Review.* "I often felt that the group is a lot more sophisticated musically than it lets on, but since its members are all good performers with enormous energy and instrumental skill, *Bayou Country* is an enjoyable enough album for those who do not demand the real thing. Even those who do will, I think, find something like 'Good Golly Miss Molly' entertaining enough in its rather slick way. The best [track] here is 'Graveyard Train'; it is almost ten minutes long, but demonstrates that if the group stops looking for a gimmick and settles down to do its own thing, it has the innate ability to make a successful go of it."

"Creedence Clearwater's records," noted Professor Albert Goldman in his review in *Life*, with the oft-quoted title "Purity, Not Parody, in a Real Rock Revival," "come over the air with the dust of the '50s right in the grooves. . . . Amazing is the mastery of the black idiom which groups like the Creedence display; even more impressive is the modesty and artistic integrity with which they manipulate an alien tradition . . . holding themselves down to the hard dense core at the heart of the rock, they burn through the trash that is being spewed from the radio today. Clear water is their symbol for purity, and purity is, paradoxically, what they achieve working with the stuff that is black as perfect pitch."

"When I heard John sing 'Born on the Bayou,' " drummer Kenny Aronoff recalled, "I just couldn't get over it. It was so cool. I figured if the Incredible Hulk could sing, that's what he would sound like."

Despite hitting the stores within days of the Beatles' *Yellow Submarine*, the record took off. It reached number 7 in the *Billboard* album charts. John began to display a sixth sense about the record business. "I was so impressed with John's ability to send one of these brilliant singles up the chart," band friend Jake Rohrer remarked. "John always knew when it was time for another one."

"As soon as one single's done," John said, "I want to have another one come out." John recognized that it was time for a new single about the time "Proud Mary" peaked in March 1969. Rather than draw another song from *Bayou Country*, he took the band into the studio to cut "Bad Moon Rising" and "Lodi."

"I loved that lick on 'Bad Moon Rising' from the time I was in high school," John recalled.

I really couldn't do it exactly like Scotty Moore did it. "Bad Moon Rising" is obviously an homage to early Sun recordings. It has a little heavier beat, but the same sound and that same aural experience.

This song is definitely not about astrology. The imagery came from a 1941 movie, *The Devil and Daniel Webster*, about a senator who makes a deal with the Devil (played by Walter Huston). The idea of the film was that the Devil was protecting Daniel Webster because of the deal they had made. There's one great scene where there's a huge storm, and the neighbor's corn crop was completely knocked down. But next door, the Devil and Daniel Webster are standing side by side, looking out the barn door. You can see Daniel Webster's corn still standing tall in a straight row, six feet high. The contrast represented a very strong image to me. I took it in a biblical sense, meaning hurricanes and lightening. "Don't go round tonight/It's bound to take your life/There's a bad moon on the rise." Scary, spooky stuff.

The apocalyptic vision was somehow apropos given the times. John had gotten out of the Army just in time. The Vietnam War entered everyone's home on a nightly basis. Thousands of young men, most not too much younger than John (or even the same age), lost their lives. The threat of nuclear war hung like a sword over the head of his generation. Scary, spooky stuff.

"I remember one Sunday night when Creedence was playing a little club in North Beach," John said, "and I was the first person to inform this group of like forty-five people that Lyndon Johnson had decided not to run. Everybody whooped and hollered and thought it was great. Little did we know what we were going to get instead."

The flip side of the single was a metaphorical flip side as well. "Bad Moon Rising" set John's vision of Revelation and the end of the world to a rockabilly beat that Elvis would have loved two decades earlier (as it was, Presley had already covered "Proud Mary" live). The B-side came from John's notebook of titles. "Lodi" captured the sad desperation of the aging Golliwog who never had the opportunity to play in Creedence, doomed to work up and down roadhouses and bars of Northern California. The town of Lodi lies about ninety miles northwest of El Cerrito, nominally in wine country.

The song began for John with just the sound of the town's name:

The first time I ever heard the word "Lodi," I thought it was the coolest sounding name, so I saved it for the longest time. I finally had a vehicle to make records, so I decided to write the song, teach it to the band, and actually record it. I was determined to write a song about "Lodi." I sat down and wrote about being on the road, being a musician; not the happy, glamorous part, rather, I projected myself ahead maybe ten years, as a country musician singing that minor hit I had ten years ago. There I was. I wasn't in Los Angeles. I'm not even in Cucamonga. I'm all the way out in Lodi! The song went from "Lodi" to "Oh Lord, stuck in Lodi, again," not a happy thought.

"We made a lot of people in that town mad," Doug mused.

The younger people loved it. The older folks were very upset with that song. Lodi has grown up, and it's a fine city. It really wasn't necessarily a knock on the city. It was just a rural town—one of many we played—and those were tough ones that you played when no one cared. We used to play there a lot in the delta areas of California. I remember distinctly, we were playing in this bar and there might have been eight people in there. They were all drunk, just like the song says. We might as well not even been there.

Ironically, a few years later John nearly found himself stuck in Lodi. "I went on a fishing trip," he said, "during the energy crisis in 1973. On the way back, I came that close to running out of gas. There was one gas station open on a Sunday in Lodi, and the line was a mile and a half long."

The single marked another first for the band. Following up "Proud Mary," "Bad Moon Rising" also hit number 2 on the charts. This time, the record played second fiddle to Henry Mancini's "Love Theme from *Romeo and Juliet*." More remarkably, though, "Lodi" rose to number 52, starting a long tradition of double-sided hits for the band.

Like "Proud Mary" and any number of other Creedence songs, "Lodi" was a title John had kept in his pocket for a long time. It also was one of the few he thought he might not get a chance to use:

One night my band—part-Golliwogs/part other musicians—were playing a dance on the Cal Berkeley campus at Herbst Hall. Quicksilver Messenger Service was playing as well. This was around 1966, so they were already semi-famous. They were singing a song that, judging from the chorus, I thought was called, "Lodiiiiiii, Lodiiiiiiii!" After their set, I ran up and asked the curly headed guy, "Hey, was that song about Lodi?" He looked at me and said, "No man, codeine." I was so relieved. Talk about two concepts colliding. I was thinking Americana, and he was talking psychedelia. My secret was safe.

Part of coming from safe, square El Cerrito—despite the proximity to the den of intellectual, free thinking, free-speaking druggies at U.C. Berkeley— and having a Catholic upbringing, John disdained hard drugs. It accounted, at least partly, for his antipathy toward the San Francisco scene.

"I wasn't a prude when it came to drugs," he said, "but I never liked the idea of not being in control or not knowing where I was. And the few times I would dabble with marijuana, I would just kind of float off to some place and get a little paranoid because I wasn't in control. So, I guess in that sense Creedence tended to be separate from bands whose credo seemed to be 'tune in, turn on, drop out.'"

John's disdain for the drug culture was another facet of his personality that set him apart from the rest of the Bay Area rockers—indeed, from rock and roll stars in general. He recalled for famous music executive Joe Smith, "We may have looked like everyone else in those days, but I was anti-drug, which was a weird stance to be taking then. I did my very small share of dabbling with marijuana, but that was as far as it went. I think I was anti-drug because I was paranoid about getting caught. But I am also one of those people who do not like to be out of control. When I get stoned, I'd become paranoid and I'd stare at the wall and not be able to do anything."

"I was personally part of the psychedelic scene," Stu admitted to a chat room on Prodigy. "Professionally we tried to separate ourselves from that scene and be more universal."

But John refused to buy into the free love-hallucinogenic drug culture that was overtaking other musicians. "Good music is just that, good music," said John. "It has nothing to do with sex or drugs. Any musician who thinks he can consistently perform better stoned is really fooling himself."

CCR played out often, though haphazardly, one weekend in New York, another in Miami, another in Seattle. Within a few months, they went from bottom billing at the Fillmore to headlining, getting headliner money.

"We were sort of able to get the gravy of San Francisco right away," John recalled, adding, "It was a big change from NCO clubs and things." Indeed, an AFM contract from the spring of 1969 shows the band getting a $7,500 advance on 60 percent of the receipts of over $13,500 from a show in Sacramento.

The audience response often went way over the top. "Creedence was a good rock group a year ago," wrote Phillip Elwood of a show at the Fillmore just after "Proud Mary" peaked, "brilliant when I heard them at Fillmore East in October (opposite the Beach Boys!) and now they are the steadiest and most musically saturating ensemble going."

"Creedence Clearwater Revival is a beautifully tight hard rock group with a beat that doesn't quit," *Variety* held forth a couple of months later. "The group is very together even on their wildest feedback crescendos, swapping phrases back and forth between the drum and guitar."

"John Fogerty," Kirby wrote in *Billboard* a couple of months after that, "lead guitarist of Fantasy's Creedence Clearwater Revival, possesses one of the most distinctive voices on the pop scene. The almost incredible thing about this quartet is that they can produce the identical sound in live performance as on their string of hit recordings. And all the numbers are good! The group began with a big one in 'Born on the Bayou' and never let up. Combining old style rock, with its blues and country influences, with the longer instrumentals of today, the group was electric. Fogerty also is a bril-

Atlantic City Pop Festival

Friday • August 1
Iron Butterfly • Johnny Winter • Crosby, Stills & Nash • Chicago • Procol Harum • Joni Mitchell • Mother Earth • Santana Blues Band • Booker T & The M.G.'s

Saturday • August 2
Jefferson Airplane • Creedence Clearwater Revival • Crazy World of Arthur Brown • Tim Buckley • • B. B. King • Butterfield Blues Band • Byrds • Hugh Masekela • Lighthouse • American Dream

Sunday • August 3
Janis Joplin • Canned Heat • Mothers of Invention • Moody Blues • 3 Dog Night • Sir Douglass Quintet • Joe Cocker • Little Richard • Buddy Rich Big Band • "Dr. John" the Night Tripper

August 1-2-3
Atlantic City Race Track
Atlantic City, N.J.

Courtesy Graham Niven

Ad for the Atlantic City Pop Festival.

liant guitarist who can hold his own in these instrumentals. Drummer Doug Clifford was a tower of strength with his steady beat."

Covering the same show, the *New York Times*'s Mike Jahn noted, "Creedence Clearwater Revival . . . showed that there is no substitute for plain old talent. . . . It was really nice to have someone just get up there and wail."

The group spent a lot of time on the road. With three impressive hits, they became a draw. All this happened in 1969, the year of the rock festival. CCR played to 150,000 people at Northridge, California's, Newport Festival, to a packed house at the Denver Pop Festival at Mile High Stadium during June, and to another 140,000 on the Fourth of July in Atlanta.

These festivals all led up to one of the biggest gigs of the summer of 1969. By the middle of August, all paths led to a cow pasture about an hour and a half out of New York City (under normal driving conditions). Billed as three days of peace and music, Creedence Clearwater Revival was one of the headlining acts at the Woodstock Music and Art Fair.

"Nobody would touch the thing," Doug recalled. "The promoters were advocating this 'brotherhood' concept [i.e., working with untested organizers]. All the so-called brotherhood bands frankly, they were worried about their paycheck. Groups were waiting around to see who would go and who wouldn't."

During April, Creedence was the first band to sign on for Woodstock, agreeing to play for $10,000. In the eyes of the concert promoters, they were a supergroup. The promoters used them as a lever. Since coming up with the idea, they had experienced a lot of resistance to the idea of a three-day festival. Managers didn't want to commit their bands. Now when a manager would say, "I don't want to have the only superstar group there, the promoters could say, 'What are you talking about? We've got Creedence and plenty of dough.'"

"Once Creedence signed," Doug added, "everyone else jumped in line and all the other big acts came on."

The band headlined Saturday night at Woodstock, coming on just before the Who, but capping a day that had featured many bands from the Bay Area like Santana, Sly and the Family Stone, and Janis Joplin, the bands Fogerty hadn't even wanted to compete with a scant eighteen months before. The group flew in by helicopter, the promoters having given up on the packed roads leading to the venue early the previous day. By the time they got on, following the Grateful Dead, it was three in the morning.

"Creedence was the hottest shot on earth at the moment," John railed to *Rolling Stone* eighteen years later, reflecting his bitterness over the experience:

We were ready to rock out and we waited and waited and finally it was our turn. My reaction was, "Wow, we get to follow the band that put half a million people to sleep." I'm rocking and rocking and screaming and about three songs into the set, I look out past the floodlights and I see about five rows of bodies just intertwined—they're all asleep. Stoned and asleep. And I just looked out there and I said, "Well, we're up here having a good time. I hope some of you are, too." I was searching to see if anybody was awake, because there were a half million people asleep. These people were out. No matter what I did, they were gone. It was sort of like a painting of a Dante scene, just bodies from hell, all intertwined and asleep, covered with mud.

And this is the moment I will never forget as long as I live: a quarter mile away in the darkness, on the other edge of this bowl, there was some guy flicking his Bic, and in the night I hear, "Don't worry about it, John. We're with you." I played the rest of the show for that guy.

The Woodstock generation—Yeah, this is great. Fifty-mile-long traffic jam. No food. No water. No sleep. No shelter. Rained on, sleeping in the mud. "This is great man. What a party. Who was I watching last night? I was stoned, I forget."

When the Woodstock documentary was released in 1970, CCR wasn't in it. "Creedence was not included in the original film release or album because Fogerty thought it would be bad for our career," says Stu.

I've heard various explanations, i.e., bad performance, bad company to be associated with, feud with the promoters (CCR didn't get paid for quite a while after the concert—Fogerty, our manager, had failed to get the money up front as the Dead and Who were careful to do), etc. Fantasy Records would have loved it if we were included in the original. The film and sound-track LP sent several careers to the next level (Santana, Ten Years After, Hendrix, CSN, etc.) The set was not without technical problems, but still smoked.

"After our performance at Woodstock," Fogerty recalls, "we were asked by the producer of the *Woodstock* film to consent to the inclusion of CCR's performance of 'Bad Moon Rising' in the film. The producer sent me a reel-to-reel recording of the performances. I did not feel that the performance was our best and did not believe it would be good for it to be included in the film."

"The performances are classic CCR," says Stu sadly, "and I'm still amazed by the number of people who don't even know we were one of the headliners at Woodstock '69."

9

"FOUR INDIVIDUALS WHO MAKE UP A FIFTH PERSON"

El Cerrito, "the little hill," remained home for the CCR. As soon as "Proud Mary" hit the charts, things changed for the band, however. When they were working for the power company and the gas station, they lived in the flats.

"Highlanders and flatlanders," Laurie Clifford recalled. "No question about it. Most of us lived in the El Cerrito flatlands or foothills. Only Stu lived up and came from some wealth. The rest of us, wives included, came from middle to lower income families. We all moved up the mountain to Kensington and Berkeley with the success of CCR. But that isn't to say the families' location made the difference in the richness of our lives."

As they moved up the hill, however, they all seemed to take with them a sense of what was real. For John it was all part of his emotional baggage anyway. In many ways, he just didn't want to let go of the kid in the cinder-block basement, spending hour after hour finding solace in his guitar.

"I see things through lower-class eyes," John told *Time*. "If you sit around and think about all that money, you can never write a song about where you came from."

"They got successful after *Bayou Country*," recalls Jeff Fogerty, Tom's second oldest son, "so we moved up the hill. After my sisters were born in 1969 [Tom and Gail had twin girls, Chris and Jill], we sort of outgrew our house. Plus they made a whole bunch of money really fast, so my dad told my mom she could pick out any house she wanted. They drove all over the Bay Area, checked out everything and stumbled on the house in Berkeley that we ended up getting.

"We all lived in El Cerrito, or as it goes up the hill it becomes Kensington for about a quarter mile, then it becomes Berkeley," he added. "Doug and Stu lived on Arlington Avenue, which is the big street in the middle of the hill that ran horizontally. We lived up on the top of the hill on Woodmont, and John lived about a half a block down from Arlington on a street called Sunset. Doug and John lived about a quarter of a mile away from each other, if that. Stu lived about half a mile away from Doug and we lived about a mile up."

Laurie and Doug Clifford had a son, Brent. John and Martha now had a son and a daughter. Doug and John bought motorcycles. Jake Rohrer hooked Doug up with a new Porsche.

The band got a new Factory, a former air compressor plant in the warehouse district of Berkeley. It served as their office, rehearsal space, and clubhouse. The offices upstairs had a pool table and a Wurlitzer jukebox. Downstairs, they rehearsed on a thick, red carpet with plush blue velvet drapes hung all around to keep the room from echoing like the former industrial space it was. They hung a basketball hoop downstairs, as well. Like the people working in the plants and warehouses that surrounded them, the members of Creedence Clearwater Revival showed up for work every day to take care of the business of band membership. They rehearsed several hours a day.

"We're there nearly every weekday," the entity known as Creedence Clearwater Revival said in their fan newsletter, *Fifth St. Flash*. "It's a formal thing that happens regularly, not just if we all happen to fall by the Factory." Even though John was the leader, the rest of the group worked hard to bring to life his ideas. "The band helps with the arrangements, but John has the musical and lyrical ideas," Tom said. "We practice every day and may rehearse our songs for weeks so that everyone can play together as good on the album as they can in person."

"They would be down there all the time rehearsing," Jeff recalls, "but my dad was around pretty much every night that I remember.

"They were always around when I was a little kid," he says of his dad, his Uncle John, Doug, and Stu. "I really like them as people. We used to always go up to Uncle Dan's."

He always had a place up in the country and we would go there for Fourth of July weekend every year. I always looked forward to that, because all four uncles would be there and all their kids. We'd play baseball and talk. It was great. It's a big family. Dan has five girls, we had four kids, John had three kids, Uncle Jim had two kids. There were a lot of people up there and it was great. I used to really enjoy spending time with Uncle Dan and Uncle Bob and Uncle John. Those guys were always there. Bob was a photographer, and I was into that when I was younger, so he'd bring the camera and show me how to take pictures. It was great.

Often, the band felt as if they had two families: the ones at home and the group. Laurie Clifford, Doug's wife, gave birth to their first child without a

Courtesy Jake Rohrer

Stu, Doug, Tom, and John, four guys who make up a fifth entity.

whisper in the press. Even Stu, still the lone bachelor in the bunch, felt this way. "Creedence to me is four individuals who together make up a fifth person," he said in a way that paraphrased many a preacher at a wedding. "I like to think of that fifth individual as a perfect blend of art and science and one that voices both. All those notes have been played before so there's nothing new scientifically. Artistically, I feel we're injecting something new and with good taste."

"I wish marriage could work as loosely as our band does," he laughed. "We don't have any problems in that way. After nine years, you think it would be senseless to break up. In the early days, our music was more of a hobby and it might have happened then, but it doesn't enter our minds now."

If the band reveled in their relatively sudden change in status, Fantasy practically wallowed in it. The second quarter of 1969 was the biggest Fantasy ever had, four times as strong as any previous quarter. The company just wasn't used to selling a million records. "A jazz record that sold 50,000 copies was a hit," Zaentz marveled, "although we did have some that approached the 200,000 mark."

With all the money rolling in, Zaentz had big plans. He saw Fantasy becoming a major player in the record business, but also a purveyor of recorded art. He expanded on the spoken-word recordings and even sought to add a classical division. The label also started signing new pop talent, including Clover, a band featuring John McFee and, later, Huey Lewis.

One of the biggest signs of the company's newfound affluence was the plan to move Fantasy out of their inner-city digs and into a brand new, custom-made facility in Berkeley. Zaentz had a building designed with three state-of-the-art recording studios, and three more rehearsal halls, the better to allow his artists the leeway to create the best records they could.

"There will be no pressure in our studios," Zaentz boasted. "We won't charge studio time against an artist's royalties because we figure that as a cost of doing business. I've always felt that a record company shouldn't charge for studio time if it has its own facilities."

All of these plans hinged on their new gold mine. For his own part, John was every bit as anxious to build his career as Zaentz was to have him build it.

Late in the spring of 1969, a limousine pulled up to a black door on Hyde Street in San Francisco. The lettering on the door read "Wally Heider Recording." Bruce Young and his crew had already been there, setting up the instruments in the circle the band preferred for rehearsing and recording.

"They were one of the few bands," Russ Gary, the engineer for that and all subsequent CCR sessions recalled, "when they came to record, they were ready. They worked hard. One of the few bands that used to show up and really kick it. Really take care of business. Wally Heider used to say he never saw a band that came in and took care of business like Creedence."

"They came in," he added, "[and] wham, bam, thank you ma'am, they cut *Green River* right off the bat. It didn't take long. It was a lot of preparation."

Just as in recording *Bayou Country*, the group performed the backing tracks live, and then a vocal track was added. "We went in and did five master basic tracks," Fogerty recalled, "the ensemble, without vocals or overdubs, in one day. I think we scrapped one and redid it. Whatever was left, three songs, we did the next day. In this age of studio conceived music, I guess it seems weird, but we rehearsed first. Our first three albums each cost under $2,000 to make."

After the basic tracks were done, John would work on his own to make them richer. Band engineer Gary recalls how "John would come in and embellish things. He would play a lot of guitar, but mostly it was his own parts that he would play. He would also sing the background parts and his lead vocals and play piano and percussion instruments. I was pretty much by myself in the control room through the whole thing," Gary added, noting that the other members of the group were not too involved with this part of the process.

Within about a week, Creedence Clearwater Revival had finished their third album. "The simplicity of the project," Gary remarked, "made it unique."

Green River.

"*Green River* was the next step without changing much, format-wise," Doug said. "We did have that sort of southern thing; it was a little more focused than on the other albums. The tune 'Green River' is one of my favorites. That's just a great tune. It's fun, it's an up, happy, summer song and it can warm a heart during the middle of winter."

"I always considered *Green River* a high-water mark in my musical life," says John, "only because it felt so good. Here was the music closest to my musical center. Even though we had bigger albums, that album was my favorite. Green River was where I lived from the sound of the record, what the record's about, the riffs, the setting which spills out onto the rest of the album, the cover. It's my most comfortable place."

John had also kept this phrase in his notebook for a long time:

"Green River" was another title I'd held onto from the time I was eight years old. In my neighborhood, if you went to the soda fountain at the pharmacy, you could order different fizz drinks, like, for instance, cherry cola. One of the drinks was a Green River, a bottle of syrup that fit into the dispenser upside down. The drink was a green, lime drink on ice with fizz water, a soggy green snow cone. That's what I would order and it made me the happiest.

The content of the song also evoked joyous memories of his youth. During happier times in the Fogerty family, before his father left, they would travel about an hour north of El Cerrito to a town called Winters. Putah Creek, which had been dammed up to form Lake Berryessa, runs through the area. On the creek, just below the dam, a fellow named Cody—he claimed to be a relative of Buffalo Bill—ran a bungalow colony. The six Fogertys (this was before Bob was born) took a cabin with a kitchen and one bedroom right on the banks of the creek.

"It was exactly like the song describes it," Tom said. "There's one line, 'Up at Cody's Camp I spend my days.' Well, there was a place called Cody's Camp. That's where we used to stay. There were cabins and we'd be there for two or three weeks every summer and swim in this really great creek. John, instead of calling it 'Putah Creek,' called it 'Green River.' It's much more musical. Everything described in that song is real and actually happened."

"The day after we recorded 'Green River,'" John notes, "another young engineer in the building heard the song. He was so moved, he called me at home. 'Pick up a flat rock and skip it across the Green River.' He was a total stranger, but totally into the words, the first person to acknowledge that something special, lyrically, was happening in my music."

If *Green River* marked a watershed for John, it was in his lyrics. They reached for something beyond the abstract. If "Proud Mary" spoke universally to anyone who had left a bad job for a terrible one, but just kept rolling along, "Green River" spoke personally to nostalgia for childhood. Another *Green River* highlight, "Wrote a Song for Everyone," in addition to mining an increasing country vein in his music, spoke very personally to anyone who just couldn't find the right words at the right time.

"At one point," John recalls of the song's genesis,

my wife and I had a mild misunderstanding. I wouldn't even call it a fight. She was miffed, taking our young son out, wishing I'd be a little bit more involved. But there I was, the musician manic and possessed, holding everything up. Without me, it all collapses, so I'm feeling quite put upon. As she walks out the door, I say to myself, "I wrote a song for everyone and I couldn't even talk to you."

It was actually a true emotion that took on a larger meaning. It's still a special song in the sense that it keeps my feet on the ground. You sit and write these songs, yet you try to talk to your own son and daughter and maybe you're totally inadequate, trying to explain life to a child.

"John was better able to communicate through his music," Doug notes, "than he was speaking with people. That song was a real piece of his heart and soul."

During the sessions, they reprised the rockabilly that rocketed up the charts in the spring with "Bad Moon Rising." Not nearly as strong a song, "Crosstie Walker" was still a far more personal song, just a song about a guy with nothing in front of him but the rails. Then they dug into their old songbook and pulled out Ray Charles's "The Night Time Is the Right Time." Another tune, the B. B. King-like blues "Tombstone Shadow," grew out of another of the band's real-life adventures, a visit to a palm reader in San Bernadino.

"He told John not to take any vacations and not to fly on any airplanes," Doug laughingly told interviewer Wayne Bryman. "Those were true lyric lines from the palm reader. John, being into that sort of swampy voodoo, spooky kind of stuff, came up with that tune, I think, half tongue in cheek."

During July, Creedence also started to break overseas. "Proud Mary" hit the charts in England, reaching number 8. In August, "Bad Moon Rising" came out and topped the English charts. These singles signaled that America no longer had Creedence all to itself.

However, America would see a lot of the band that summer. In anticipation of the album and all the festivals they would be playing, CCR released a single of "Green River" backed with "Commotion" in July. Almost coincidentally with the release of the *Green River* album, the single rose to become the band's third number 2 single, shut out from the top spot on the chart by The Archies' "Sugar Sugar." "Commotion" fared even better than the previous B-side, peaking at number 30.

"Were 'Green River' on the radio today," Greil Marcus wrote in the liner notes to the 1976 *Chronicle* package, "it would jump right off it, something else entirely, just as it did in its heyday."

In his five-star review in the *Rolling Stone Record Guide*, Dave Marsh wrote, "Perhaps best of all were 'Lodi,' the story of a working rocker's depression at being stuck in another out-of-the-way gin mill, and 'Fortunate Son,' a stab at the privileged that only kids from the wrong side of the ultra-hip San Francisco area could have felt so sharply."

Don Heckman in *Stereo Review* found the album "a synthetic interpretation of black delta-style blues . . . [with] all the guts, emotion, disjunct rhythms and sometimes indecipherable black dialect . . . slicked up and packaged with a country green ribbon for all the white folks."

The band really wanted to appeal to everyone. The accusations of playing ersatz blues stung, especially John. Their massive success on pop radio and three near chart-topping singles cast them in a role that felt even more uncomfortable for the band: a "teenybopper" singles group. They wanted people to take their music as seriously as they did.

John was particularly sensitive to the charge that CCR was just a "singles" band: "Most of this is built-in uptightness. 'Singles are what I dug when I was little, therefore I have to change now. I've grown up so I don't like top 40.' That's dumb. Why not change top 40?"

With *Green River*, CCR continued that assault on the top 40. However, the group started to earn respect for their music as well.

" 'Proud Mary' should have clued us in," Bruce Miroff wrote in his review of the album in *Rolling Stone*. "It was more than simply a fine song by top-40 standards; it was a superb song by any standards. Creedence's new album, *Green River*, demonstrates convincingly that 'Proud Mary' was no fluke. Make no mistake about it; Creedence Clearwater Revival, despite some rather clear limitations, is one of the most exciting and satisfying bands around."

A big critical success, *Green River* also jumped off the shelves. Released in late August, by mid-November the album had sold close to a million copies. The group's tape sales were in the hundreds of thousands as well. While they couldn't break past number 2 on the U.S. singles chart, the English single of "Bad Moon Rising" topped the UK charts. The *Green River* album took the Eric Clapton/Steve Winwood supergroup *Blind Faith* out of the number 1 U.S. album spot, staying there for three weeks until the Beatles' *Abbey Road* knocked it out. *Green River* stayed on the charts for eighty-eight weeks.

"Our career is just starting," John opined. "There is so much untapped sound and so many songs waiting to be written."

10

"RICHARD NIXON IS A GREAT INSPIRATION"

People in the record industry saw this band on this little label becoming one of the most successful musical entities in the world. By March, the phones in the little office over the garage in Oakland started ringing—a lot. People offered to buy Creedence Clearwater Revival's contract. People offered to buy the entire label outright. Less than three years after leveraging his buy-out of the Weiss brothers, Saul Zaentz had struck his mother load. Now, everyone wanted a piece of it.

"Every couple of weeks," Zaentz said, "we get an offer—from legitimate sources—but there isn't any price. [I] wouldn't take $6 million. We have turned down much higher offers than that."

Given Fogerty's prolific nature at that time, being on an independent label did have certain advantages, as Zaentz pointed out. "We can move faster with distribution," he said. "At Columbia and Capitol, those guys are afraid to say 'boo.' All those layers and layers you have to go through to make a decision."

Finally, however, he was pretty sure Creedence wasn't going anywhere. "A contract," he asserted to John Hallowell, a magazine journalist in the midst of writing an "instant" book on the group. "That's how I hold on to them."

However, that contract became an issue between Zaentz and the band. The original contract was standard at the time. "It took us about a year after 'Suzie Q' to realize we were in big trouble," John recalled. "Zaentz promised us that he would tear up the contract as soon as we had our first hit. Well, somewhere around the time of *Green River,* I go into Saul and I'm told there'll be no tearing up of any contract."

Fantasy even contemplated going public to cash in on the group's success. Creedence was already trying to renegotiate their deal. Fantasy allegedly offered the band 10 percent of the stock, both the shares that would be offered to the public and the shares that would remain within the corporation. John wanted to tie his publishing into this offer. Zaentz refused. John turned the offer down.

"John, professing to be manager of all CCR business misconstrued this offer and refused on the other guys' behalf, without letting them know of the conversation," says a source close to the band. "That move cost the band $50 million."

For an idea of how the contract worked, Craig Modderno in the *Oakland Tribune* figured out that on a million-selling album, the band would get $40,000. Not bad, but when split four ways and covering all the overhead of the band, that left precious little. John, as the one writing the songs, got his songwriter royalties as well, both mechanical on record sales and performance from radio play.

Now that Fantasy was enjoying more money in a year than it had probably seen in all its previous years of business combined, the generators of that money wanted a taste better than the 10.5 percent of the wholesale price they were getting on LPs, with only half of that received on tapes.

In the spring of 1969, Zaentz came up with an idea. He had channeled much of Fantasy's newfound wealth into a banking scheme based in the Bahamas. He offered the same opportunity to the band, telling them, in essence it's not what you make, it's what you keep.

"Saul Zaentz introduced the band to this incredible offshore tax deal," Jake Rohrer recalls. "At the time, about two-thirds of everything Creedence earned, because of the tax situation, was going to the government. They offered this alternative of offshore trusts. It was Stu's dad's law firm that put the stamp of approval on it."

"They wanted to avoid taxes," John said, "and said that it would be like a raise. It looked great at the time."

And so, on June 5, 1969, the band actually did get a new contract. While the terms were essentially the same as the one they'd signed two years earlier, they managed to get a raise in their foreign and tape royalties. They also took on a new corporate entity, King David Distributors Limited, a Bahamian corporation, as a holding company for their newly sheltered money.

In the meantime, things were heating up at the Factory as well. John's younger brother Bob joined the entourage as group photographer. They hired longtime friend Jake Rohrer to take care of various responsibilities. They called him "press officer," but he took care of the office when they were at home and the hotels when they were on the road. His role complimented Bruce Young: Young coordinated with promoters, accountants, and venues; Rohrer took care of the band.

"When I first came to work for CCR," Rohrer says of what became a paying position in October 1969,

> I was in charge of public relations. I had no experience, but the guys didn't care. They just wanted me on board. John told me to be loose and feel my way around. We went to Europe and learned the term "press officer," so I became that. I prepared all of the press materials. As things progressed, I took on duties in other areas, helping Bruce coordinate the tours and becoming a general liaison. I traveled with the band and saw to transportation and hotels and made sure everyone got to the next stop. Personal duty was also a specialty—I carried the joints through customs. If someone got the crabs, I got them the cure or a doctor when needed. My job encompassed a lot. I just sort of flowed into areas that needed taking care of.

Rohrer had known the band for nearly ten years, almost from the start. When he came on board, he joined one of the most successful rock organizations on this side of the Atlantic. "It was an atmosphere of unity, of full support of John and his leadership. It was like magic. We were all a family. Not only was the formula working, but here were these kids who were playing in garages and sleazy bars for all these years. We were getting on top of the world. It was an incredible period of elation."

After the busy summer of touring, the band did a show in Honolulu. Then they took the band, the road crew, the support staff, and all their families for a ten-day vacation at the Hana Ranch Hotel, something that would become a fall tradition for CCR.

"We chartered two Otters," recalled Rohrer, "these little prop planes that handled ten or twelve people each and we filled them both up."

Gail Fogerty recalls these as some of the happiest times of her life:

> We used to take all of the families to Hawaii. They would play Honolulu, but it was more of a vacation. We would stay at Hana Ranch and it was absolutely fabulous. All of the children went and it was wonderful. At the height of their career, I had twins. I didn't tour a lot with them. I had babies at home. I do remember going to Hawaii. I remember taking Scott and Jeff. Right after the twins were born, we went to Hawaii and I left them with my mom. Those are the times that are very, very special to me. I did go on other trips with them, but I think that because it was the families, everyone would bring their children and we would stay there for a week or two. It was just loving and wonderful.

After the well-earned rest, the band went back to the Factory to rehearse. Not content to release two albums in the course of a year, the band went into the studio in the fall and cut *Willie and the Poor Boys*. John's idea about what the band could accomplish had grown exponentially over the course of the year, as had the band's ability to live up to those expectations. It was as if, after all the years of scuffling, the enormous public acceptance and adulation fueled John's creative engines and stoked the band's playing fire.

"Public acceptance is everything to us," Tom reflected at the time.

Paradoxically, while they were selling tons of records, people didn't know who they were. Owing to the sound and the thematic content of their music, most people assumed they were from the South.

"People thought we were a band from Louisiana," Doug recalled with a laugh. "Once, Donald 'Duck' Dunn, the great bass player from Booker T and the MGs, and the Blues Brothers—and so many others, and one of my best friends in the world said, 'I was trying to figure out what part of Louisiana you boys are from. When I found out you were from Berkeley, I burned all your records.'"

Others thought the group members were black. "When I went to get my motorcycle," John recalled, "I came back to pick it up. Some guy was telling a chick there, 'Creedence is going to come.' And the chick says, 'Oh no, he's telling you a story because Creedence are spades.' It was really far out."

"At the time, I was playing a lot of organ rooms down in the south, actually playing in the ghetto," Merl Saunders recollects. "They had that particular record on the ghetto box and everything. It was so funny, because people would play it and I'd say, 'Those are my friends back on the West Coast.' And people would say, 'Those brothers?' And I would say, 'No, they're not brothers. John is a white guy.' 'You goddam liar!' 'No, he really is, he just sings that way.' I didn't want to get into it. They got very uptight. I just laughed."

While *Willie* certainly had its swampier moments like "Feeling Blue," and its de rigueur rockabilly tune, "Don't Look Now," the overall album had a more urban edge. Even "Don't Look Now" took an attitude. The song led by example in an effort to cut the bullshit.

"There were things going on in the country that upset me," John says, "but having grown up in the 'hippie' generation, there were a lot of things about my own generation that upset me as well. The song 'Don't Look Now' was trying to address that. It wasn't that I was a fence rider, it was just that some stuff was getting out of hand."

"That's a song that'll slap you right in the face," Doug added.

It's a sobering tune, if you listen to the lyrics. It's a period of time when everyone was pointing the finger at our generation, saying "This isn't right, this isn't right." But how many people were really going to do something about it? It's real easy to point your finger and knock something, but to get in there and roll up your sleeves and change it for the better these are the real leaders in the

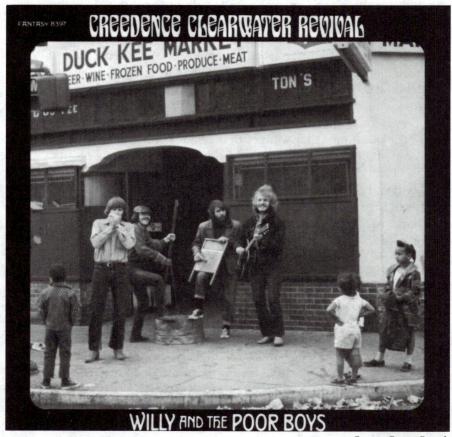

Willie and the Poor Boys.

world. That song can really ring a chord of truth about a lot of people's basic laws. That's one of my favorite songs, quite frankly. It has everything in it: Great message, nice little beat. Stu has a nice little lick in there. Stu was really an underrated bass player.

Over the course of the year, CCR had taken on this wild growth spurt. Everything they released showed rapidly maturing artistry beyond the previous release. The playing was better, the songs cut more to the quick musically and lyrically.

"When Creedence were this cohesive unit on this planned quest to see how high we could go," Rohrer recalls, "it seemed like every week we went a little higher. There was a thrill of accomplishment and mutual support and love that everybody had for everybody else. That was the most thrilling part of all of it, that we could all work together and respect one another and make it work. The accomplishment was a thrilling thing."

In 1969 the critical world in music marveled at a record from across the Atlantic, a rock opera by the Who called *Tommy*. They had played it in concert at Woodstock immediately after CCR's set. Critical opinion had it as the crest of the wave of "concept albums" that littered the pop music byways of the late '60s. While John had no pretensions of writing an opera, *Willie and the Poor Boys* certainly had the feel of a concept album, from the group starting to work out "Down on the Corner," through the "Poorboy Shuffle," played on washboard, Kalamazoo tympanic guitar, gut bass, and harmonica (the instruments outlined in the opening song).

"We were Willie and the Poor Boys," Doug mused, "another one of John's creations. The guy is brilliant—a genius in my opinion, a multitalented individual. I was the Rooster on the washboard, Stu played the gut bucket, Tom played a Kalamazoo guitar, and John played the harp; he was Willie." The inclusion of two old folk blues, "Cotton Fields" and "The Midnight Special," furthered the concept. "These were songs that we played years before we started doing our own material," Doug said.

The ever-expanding breadth of John's songs demonstrated his willingness to take a stand on the issues of the day. "It Came out of the Sky" showed John's prescience as a songwriter, taking one of the first musical swipes at Ronald Reagan, then the governor of California. "John had a vision at that point with the line, 'Ronnie the popular,'" Doug laughed. "Spiro Agnew wanted to raise the Mars tax."

Of course, the creative process couldn't go forward without a little friction. John had taken full control of material, arrangements, and production. He had an idea in his head of what he wanted the songs to sound like. Convincing the other band members to fulfill his vision could be difficult.

"The exhausting part," John recalled,

was what you'd have to go through to get everybody to want to do this. To understand that this is a good arrangement—or that it's not left field or odd. There was a lot of that. Making people do stuff they didn't want to do, and then realizing later it was okay.

With "Down on the Corner" it was just the feel. I won't say who, but we were in the studio having a rough time with it, playing it with the right feel. Then someone, in frustration, said, "This isn't rock and roll." I had to bite my lip and be the little general and wait until we got it right. Then everything would be fine. I didn't go there to fight. I went there to make a record.

Fantasy released "Down on the Corner" in November. The single was backed with another gutsy John Fogerty tune, "Fortunate Son." If "Don't Look Now" wanted to slap people in the face, "Fortunate Son" was locked and loaded for a full frontal assault.

" 'Fortunate Son' was a political statement," Doug notes, "on how unfair the nation's poor and working class had to go to war, and the people with clout were able to pull a string or two and their boys stayed at home."

"It's a confrontation between me and Richard Nixon," John says.

The haves, the people who have it all. Not a positive image of the people who live up the hill, with their big cars. People I don't respect. During the Vietnam War, these were the people who didn't have to go to war. I was thinking about David Eisenhower, the grandson of Dwight, who married Julie Nixon. I always confused her with Tricia. I guess it's easy to pick on somebody named Tricia. It sounds so silver spoon.

Anyway, I was showing the band the song. I didn't have much. I knew the chord changes and could feel the energy. I had a title, "Fortunate Son," but no song. Yet I was showing the band the structure, my normal gig as the musical director of the band.

So, I went into the bedroom, sat on the edge of my bed with a yellow legal tablet and my felt-tipped pen. Out came the song. "It ain't me, it ain't me, I ain't no fortunate son." I was screaming inside, very intense, but not saying a word. Out it came, onto three sheets of legal paper.

"It took," he added for *Rolling Stone*'s Ben Fong Torres, "about twenty minutes. It was like vrooom — it just came right out.

"I played that song at an antiwar protest. As I was walking in the hallway after our set, someone came up to me and told me what an awesome version we had played. I remember telling them, 'Richard Nixon is a great inspiration.' "

"Nixon," he recalls, "was always saying 'peace with honor' and 'my country, love it or leave it,' but we knew better 'cause the guy was obviously evil."

"The line 'When the tax man comes to the door, Lord the house looks like a rummage sale,' that's a brilliant piece of imagery," Doug marvels. "It was a brilliant observation."

Despite the inspiration for the song, John denied that it was necessarily political. "I think socially conscious is a better term," he'd say. " 'Political' always throws me, because in this country it means Democrat, Republican, or none of the above. I've been all three in my voting life. I'm one of those people who feels like, if you're going to gripe about something, you'd better vote."

Yet another stab at the political powers, Doug described "Effigy" as "a real heavy political song. It's pointing the finger at the Nixon administration when they were crumbling, the dark period, if you will. We were able to get away with it by having the rhythm section that we had. If you wanted to get heavy and get into it, you could do that. If you didn't want to do that, you could dance all night and pick up a girl or do whatever. We covered all the bases, and John would add his brilliant lyrics and took it a step forward."

Despite the emphasis on social commentary on these songs, Fogerty never forgot his primary mission: to get his audience up on their feet. "Our music," John said in 1969, "has a specific aim: to make you want to jump up and dance."

"Down on the Corner" peaked at number 3 on the charts. The B-side, "Fortunate Son," hit number 14. Christmas week 1969, *Willie and the Poor Boys* appeared in stores. The photo on the cover showed the quartet as "Willie and the Poor Boys," playing harmonica, gut bucket, washboard, and guitar in front of the Duck Kee Market in Oakland with a bunch of local kids watching.

Typically, the cover photograph was a combination of serrendipity and planning. "The Duck Kee Market on 30th Street in Oakland was on the cover of *Willie and the Poorboys*," John says.

> I had a choice of either cropping the picture or leaving the name of the market in. It was half a block from Fantasy's building. We walked out the door, half a block down the street, and took the picture. Technically, "Down on the Corner" had nothing to do with the Duck Kee Market. But the song, like the market, was vaguely urban, obviously multicultural, which is what America is and was. It worked out great. The market was Chinese, a good picture of what the song was about; semi-small-town America, certainly urban, not out in the country.
>
> An interesting sidebar occurred, when our photographer [Basul Parik], who had taken the cover of *Bayou Country*, had run out of film during "our big album cover shoot." Since they didn't have film at the Duck Kee Market, he took off in his car, leaving us duuuuuh! Playing our instruments. I remember having to give him money for the film.
>
> As for the album's title, it was vaguely inspired by Winnie the Pooh, something I saw on a kid's record. After playing around with Winnie the Pooh, I came up with Willie and the Poor Boys."

Ironically, the band were not regular patrons of the store. Fogerty could only recall actually buying something there once. "The one and only time I went into the Duck Kee Market," he recalled later, "I rode up on my motorcycle. I was on my way to some sort of meeting. In those days I smoked, and realized I didn't have any cigarettes, so I walked into the Duck Kee Market because it was the closest place. I didn't think of it as 'famous.' The people who owned it were Oriental and I assumed they had no idea their store was on an album cover. I went to pay the lady and she said, 'You're the singer!' She went to the shelf and pulled the album down."

The record earned another five-star review in the *Rolling Stone Record Guide*. In his review of the record in the magazine, Alec Dubro noted, "Fogerty's voice has ferocious power and an edge to it that can cut through the worst static on the cheapest radio. He growls and shouts and scats."

"'Don't Look Now,'" noted *Village Voice* critic Robert Christgau, "manages to encapsulate the class system in two minutes and eight seconds."

11

"A VERY HEALTHY, POSITIVE ORGANIZATION"

In retrospect, Creedence Clearwater Revival had accomplished about as much during 1969 as many bands manage during the course of a career. They had four top-10 singles, three of which reached number 2. They released three albums, all of which sold exceedingly well. Thanks to playing half a dozen or so major festivals, they played live for close to a million people. *Billboard* awarded them the Top Singles Artist of 1969 honors, as well as the Trendsetter Award. *Rolling Stone* named them Best American Band. They were incredibly prolific.

"I was a very busy guy," John reflected. "We were competing with the best people in the world—the Beatles, the Rolling Stones, Led Zeppelin, the Who. All I had was my little band with no money, no gear, no nothing. What we had were the songs."

"We were very disciplined," Doug added. "That's how we were able to do it."

Toward the end of the year, they went into the studio and cut "Travelin' Band" and "Who'll Stop the Rain." In a way, these songs represented the band's Janus-like aspect at the time. "Travelin' Band" was straight-ahead, good-time rock and roll about playing rock and roll. Not an "oh the road is hell" song, it celebrates the mind-numbing exhilaration some acts found on the road. It also found John expanding his musical horizons a little bit, adding a sax part that made the song all the more redolent of Louisiana-based rock artists like Fats Domino and Little Richard.

"I was just experimenting," John said of the sax he'd rented from a local high school band supply store. "I used to know how to play the scale on one of these.

"The sax was just my answer to Blood, Sweat and Tears," he laughed.

Portrait of a successful band: CCR with a Benz borrowed from Ray Francois, one of the band's roadies.

Conversely, "Who'll Stop the Rain," was the most personal and political song John had written to date. Very specifically about the war in Vietnam, the song would inspire both soldiers and antiwar activists. It also inspired a 1978 film starring Nick Nolte as a Vietnam vet turned drug smuggler.

"I tried to be purposefully symbolic rather than lyrically specific to things that were going on," John told *Rolling Stone.* "Certainly I was talking about Washington when I wrote the song, but I remember bringing home the master version of the song and playing it. My son Josh was four years old at the time, and after he heard it he said, '*Daddy* stop the rain.' And my wife and I looked at each other and said, 'Well, not quite.'"

That song found Creedence stretching out musically and structurally. "Stu and Tom sang background on 'Who'll Stop the Rain,'" Russ Gary points out. "There were a few little overdubs done. I believe Tom is playing acoustic guitar on that one, along with John. They both did that. They just wanted to be a little more involved."

"Travelin' Band" peaked at number 2 in March, kept from the brass ring by Simon and Garfunkel's "Bridge Over Troubled Water." "Who'll Stop the Rain" made it up to number 13, making for yet another double-sided, million-selling single.

The Factory started humming in the middle of January. Now one of the world's (and certainly one of America's) most popular recording acts, director Bob Abel brought a National General Television crew into the Factory to make a documentary about Creedence, leading up to their January 31 homecoming concert at the Oakland Coliseum.

"We're going to try and put together a special that takes music seriously," associate producer Tom Donahue told *Rolling Stone.* "We'll record the show in stereo so it can be simulcast on stereo FM when the show's broadcast."

The night before, partly for the cameras, partly for their own edification, and partly because they could, CCR invited opening act Booker T and the MGs to the Factory to jam. A longtime Creedence favorite, they had even played the MGs' hit "Green Onions" during their Blue Velvets/Golliwogs days. John would call them his favorite band for most of his career. Only drummer Al Jackson, who was not feeling well, didn't make the jam—to Doug's considerable disappointment. They started with the common tongue of rock and soul, launching into a twelve-bar blues, and winding their way through their own songs, Wilson Pickett tunes, and Otis Redding tunes before seguing into a basketball game on the Factory court at two in the morning.

"I would imagine there where about 1-2 hours of film shot at the jam," Stu figures, noting that the audio track gets bootlegged frequently (and poorly).

The next day, both bands played to a packed house at the Oakland Coliseum. Captured for the National General cameras (and recorded on tape—it would become the *The Concert* album), the crowd of 15,000 danced and screamed and packed the front of the hall.

Another phase of their popularity came into play that winter. The band had never really had a manager or a booking agent. However, the bulk of their money came from touring. The band now demanded a guarantee of $50,000 a show or more. They decided it would be in their best interests to formalize their relationship, and so formed Gort Functions.

"Gort Functions," reads the agreement, "will provide all services and equipment necessary for the public personal appearances of the CCR as singers and entertainers."

The partners included John, Tom, Doug, Stu, and their road manager, Bruce Young. "Bruce," the *Flash* introduced him, "travels everywhere with the band. He arranges booking, hotels, travel—and even this grossly understates his full situation. Bruce is a detail man, and amazes everyone by remembering even the smallest items."

The company, whimsically named after the robot in the classic science fiction film *The Day the Earth Stood Still*, mostly dealt with the in-person performances by CCR. Drawing up those papers was a timely project, as the band rehearsed for its next great on-the-road adventure, their first tour of Europe.

Creedence had made slow but sure inroads in Europe as they exploded through the States. "Bad Moon Rising" had topped the charts in England. "Green River" rose to the top 20 as did the album of the same name. *Willie and the Poor Boys* made it to the top 10. They also were doing very well in Switzerland, Norway, Germany, and Warsaw Pact countries like Poland and Czechoslovakia, not to mention places like Canada, Israel, Cambodia, and El Salvador. The time had come to take the show overseas.

Before they left for Europe, however, the group had to take care of some other business. "Travelin' Band" had peaked, and that meant Creedence Clearwater Revival had to cut a new single. With the tour looming, John needed to create. The weekend before they left, he shut himself away in his home, emerging Monday. The band rehearsed the songs one day, recorded them the next, and were off to Europe on the following Monday. By the time they got back that single—"Up Around the Bend" backed with "Run Through the Jungle"—would be well on its way to number 4. By that summer it would do better that in the UK, hitting number 3.

"That's where the gift enters in," says John. "When you're not feeling it, if you're not 'in the zone,' it's the most forlorn feeling there is. But when you've got it, and you're going into your room to write, you're almost daring the gods to send something to you."

CREEDENCE
CLEARWATER
REVIVAL
RUN THROUGH THE JUNGLE / UP AROUND THE BEND
FANTASY 641

Courtesy Graham Niven

"Run Through the Jungle"/"Up Around the Bend."

"It seems to me," says Jake Rohrer, "that within a day or two, or within a few days, he would go home and lock himself in his room and come out with 'Down on the Corner.' Then he would turn around and come out with 'Lookin' Out My Back Door' or 'Up Around the Bend.' It was just like they would roll off his mind and his tongue. He had this incredible ability to just come up with these things one after another."

The B-side, "Run Through the Jungle," resonated deeper than any of the band members knew with their less fortunate peers in Southeast Asia. This was more than a metaphor to them; it was a way of life.

"It definitely got adopted by the guys in country," John said, "but it was really my remark about American society, the metaphor being society as a jungle. When I sang 'Two hundred million guns are loaded,' I was talking about the ease with which guns are purchased in America. And it is a jungle."

"That'll put a chill up and down your back," Doug reflected. "I love it in the rhythm. It has that pounding, powerful rhythm."

"Up Around the Bend," on the other hand, was a piece of levity, a catchy rocker about getting away from it all. Replete with one of John's finest, most distinctive, and infectious guitar hooks, in many ways it typified the pop single of the early '70s.

"Even though it had all these kind of country references," Doug remarked, "it was one of the most English sounding things we did."

"I can write songs such as 'Up Around the Bend' and 'Run Through the Jungle' to challenge myself to do something different within the context of a single release," John noted at the time.

Part of getting noticed, however, meant becoming a target for the cranks. The band and Rohrer found the following letter to the editor so amusing that they included it in their press material:

As a patriotic American, I am deeply disturbed by the forces of communistic revolution at work on the minds of our young people. I particularly refer to the types of music our children are hearing and being influenced by.

Recently I listened to a recording by a group called Creedence Clearwater Revival, from California. The record in question was "Up Around the Bend," and is filled with anti-American revolutionary slogans.

The chorus to this "song" implores our youth to "come on, arise and win," the allusion being to revolution. Other words and phrases include, "fix your mind on a crystal day," a time in which the forces of the present communist oriented revolution are supposed to succeed. The song also refers to "leave the sinking ship behind." I gather from this, that American society is not good enough for youth, and should be deserted.

The final admonition is to "meet by the big red tree." This is an obvious reference to the one world, socialistic government desired by these traitors.

I think that it is time for good Americans to put an end to this sort of thing and preserve the freedoms which the Founding Fathers gave to us. We must stop this cancer of revolution before the perversions of Creedence Clearwater Revival and the other "rock groups" so poison the minds of our youth that America will go to the Russians without a shot being fired.

If only he heard the other side, he might have had apoplexy. Obscure readings of innocent songs aside—the first lyric he misquotes is "Come on the rising wind"—the single sold over two million copies.

Another crank who regularly harasssed the CCR organization was a guy they called Crazy George. "Crazy George would call," Rohrer recalls. "He'd

Photo © Robert Aerts, 1970. Used with permission

Creedence arrives at Heathrow Airport, London.

tell me raving, hands down and serious, he had a machine gun and make no fucking mistake about it, he was on his way over to the Factory to blow us all away. Then he would remit and calm down; he really liked us and wasn't going to hurt anybody. The next day he would call back, this time with a flame thrower, letting me know that now we had gone too far: Fogerty's songs were all about him; John was stealing his life, profiting at his expense. We were dead meat. Click. . . . Finally I dug this guy up in San Francisco, and sat down on his back porch with him. He was not right, but generally harmless. He had somehow gotten the Factory's phone number and had no trouble with calling us. That was our problem."

The band didn't let these generally harmless barbs distract them. They had to be ready for a whole new audience waiting to embrace them on another continent. They booked the flights, had an itinerary. Tickets sold briskly. They were off to Europe.

The *Fifth St. Flash* vividly describes the band's send-off:

As our caravan of limousines and baggage car pulled up in front of John's house, we were met by a colorful array of fluttering streamers, balloons and banners reading "Bon Voyage," "We'll Miss You," and "Hurry Back," tacked all over John's garage door. As John climbed into the back seat, he explained, "I don't know who does that—must be elves of some sort."

After a rousing reception at the London airport, we were ushered via Rolls Royce to the Britannia Hotel on Grosvenor Square. The doorman, attired in an elegant maxi-coat and top hat opened the door and stepped back, exclaiming, "Blimey! It's the bloody Revival."

The next two days were spent meeting the press, doing radio and TV shows and there were countless interviews and photo sessions. We all managed to save just half a day to ourselves before leaving for our first concert date in Holland.

In addition to appearing on the venerable BBC rock show *Top of the Pops*, they spent quite a bit of time talking to the press. One of the chief concerns involved ticket prices. The promoters were charging around seven pounds per ticket, close to $17 at that time, and an outrageous price for a ticket to a rock show in the early '70s. CCR maintained a reputation at home for the reasonable prices of their shows, despite their large guarantee. They expressed their incense at the promoters in the press.

They probably didn't get to see the stories run, however. The next morning they were on their way to Rotterdam, where they were scheduled to make their European debut.

"In Rotterdam," as the *Flash* described it, "we were again most warmly received by news media and fans alike. The concerts were held at De Doelen Hall, without a doubt the finest acoustically engineered concert hall we have ever encountered. The concerts ended with a shower of flowers from the audience. Half of them were out of their seats, filling the aisles. Some 30 or more energetic fans climbed onto the stage to dance with 'Keep On Chooglin'' and it was a minor problem keeping them out of the dressing room when it was all over."

The next day, they flew from Amsterdam to Germany. The band's hotel was in Dusseldorf, though the venue was in Essen, some fifteen minutes away. They spent the afternoon meeting with the German press, then headed out to Gruga Hall.

"It was one of the worst drives we ever had," Stu Cook recalled in *Rolling Stone*.

"As we arrived," the *Flash* recounted, "the limousine was immediately surrounded by several hundred excited fans who climbed over the bumpers and trunk, rocking the car severely. Although the boys seemed quite amused, I must admit I was a bit scared. Road manager Bruce Young somehow got out of the car and made a quick exit, to return after a 10 minute breather."

Young apparently was able to get everyone out of the car. Playing like a scene out of *Help*, the band ran for the venue door, their adoring fans in hot pursuit.

"I turned around," Tom said, "and saw thousands of people rushing toward me and at the end of this car was a big German Shepherd and a cop between us and the door."

They got in and did the show, but all was not peaceful. "Even though marked by a few minor scuffles and an all-too-big host of police (complete with dogs)," said the *Flash*, "the concert came off quite well."

The police, in an effort to keep order, pushed down or clubbed the concertgoers who had the temerity to dance. "They were supposed to be keeping order and all that crap," John told *Rolling Stone*, "but it's the police who do the scaring."

The next stop was back to London. They were booked for two nights at Royal Albert Hall. For Creedence, this was the highlight of the trip, the thing they most anticipated.

"They had always been regaled with stories about the Beatles and the Stones and the great crowd reaction at the Albert Hall," Jake Rohrer said. "When they came into the Albert Hall, they wanted to do a bang-up job and make it a special concert."

Before the shows, however, their remarks to the press about the promoters came back to haunt them. One of the promoters thought he had been libeled.

"They tried to serve papers on John, Stu, and me in London," Rohrer recalls. "These process servers were chasing us all over town. We got on the phone to Barrie [Engel, a junior partner in Herman Cook's law firm] and said, 'Hey Barrie, what should we do about this?' He said, 'Don't get served.' So we had this little comic race around London, trying to avoid these process servers."

At Albert Hall, the security was intense. Much of that had to do with the name Creedence Clearwater *Revival*. "We'd been labeled a 'rock and roll revival' band and people thought we'd bring out the rockers and mods era again," Stu told *Rolling Stone*. "They thought people would come and punch it out at Albert Hall."

"The pressure was tremendous," the *Flash* reported. "We were concerned with getting a good sound balance in the round hall. The concert was being filmed for British TV and John was having trouble getting assurance of proper lighting. On top of these technical hassles, the awesome magic of Albert Hall had caught us all. Nothing but the very best Creedence has to offer would do. I could feel the tension build over the day. I knew what was going on behind Tom's ever present smile and sensed the change in Doug and Stu as the hour drew nearer. John was, as always, cool as iced watermelon."

Rolling on the river: Creedence and friends enjoy a cruise on the Thames.

The shows, by all accounts, were extraordinary. Alan Lewis, in *Melody Maker*, wrote: "Straights, freaks, skinheads and greasers stood shoulder to shoulder. . . .

"They played with stunning precision and clarity, with John Fogerty ripping off guitar phrases which were all the more powerful for their apparent simplicity."

"Aided by a superb amplification system," the review in *Variety* ran, "Creedence really socked it to the capacity [6,200] Royal Albert Hall crowd. Creedence's sound perhaps should not be analyzed, it just works, almost at the level of brainwashing. There is something uniquely American about its character; a whiff of the backwoods, a trace of country and western, a sympathetic resonance with the black blues. In short, Creedence has come closer to the origins of rock than any contemporary British group."

In the *Flash*, the show earned the accolade of "possibly the finest night in CCR's career. There aren't words to describe the satisfaction we all felt when it was over. The audience demonstrated their approval throughout the

entire set and dancers, freaky and straight, filled the aisles. A glance at the opera boxes in the upper levels revealed elegant ladies and gents in their evening wear standing on their seats, bopping and applauding."

"There was a stomping ovation," Rohrer recalled, "that went on for fifteen minutes."

The band didn't come back for an encore, however. At some point in the previous year, the band stopped doing them. "People may think we're being a bit too cool," Doug tried to explain it at the time to *Rolling Stone*, "but in our act we build things up to a final climax. If we returned, they may have been disappointed."

The "no encores" rule was a sign of John starting to flex his leadership muscles more and more. While Doug tried to put a good face on the issue, it was an area of conflict in the band.

"One night at the Fillmore West," Stu recalled, "we played seventeen encores. The next day, Bill Graham gave us each a gold watch and told us to retire, that we'd never top it. We played most of the set over again."

Soon after that he recalled, "One night in the dressing room, with the audience going wild, Fogerty told us encores were 'phony,' and in spite of the rest of the band's objections, we never played another."

John strongly felt that encores had become an empty gesture on the part of both audiences and performers. "We hear some incredible crap get encores. When the people who deserve it get one, it means nothing."

"Encores have been part of the performing tradition since the ancient times," Stu held forth.

They are part of the presentation, for better or worse. The seed behind this tradition comes from the point of view that the audience is thanking the artist for an enjoyed performance. The artist (entertainer) may think it's phony, but what performer in his right mind wouldn't be gracious enough to respond?

CCR played from the heart every night. It had nothing to do with keeping phoniness out of the show. We weren't playing the game of "average" performance equals encore. I recall many nights when we didn't get an encore call, for whatever reason. When we earned one, we wanted to play it. Period.

John was acting more like a martyr than a person with noble intentions. Cosmo and I saw this decision as a "control" issue, as well. I suppose we could've broken up the band over it, but we chose not to.

The point of our tours was to thank the fans for their support. Forty-five minute shows with no encores may have missed the mark. By the way, Led Zeppelin was doing concerts approaching three hours in length at the time. The only negative comments I hear about Revival's concerts is that they were too short, and there was no encore.

"With Creedence Clearwater Revival," John said pointedly, "we only played for fifty-five minutes. I used to tell people that God only gets one hour a week, and that's only if you go to church on Sunday."

Creedence had developed a reputation as a pretty straight band. All the guys were married. The reports of on the road wildness that characterized many of their touring peers, like Keith Moon's legendary escapades of driving cars into swimming pools and the like, never seemed to surface about CCR.

"This was good clean living," roadie Bruce Koutz noted. "We drank a little beer, but other than that it was a very healthy, positive organization."

"We take good care of ourselves," Tom said. "It pays. When you go out on that stage for forty-five minutes, it's the moment of truth. You had better be ready. We believe in feeding our heads with rest and a little tranquillity. Then everybody's a little more ready."

While in Europe, however, they cut loose, if only a little. "Most of our evenings," reported the *Flash*, "usually lasting until daylight, were spent visiting discotheques and other points of interest. With State controlled radio in every country, the real music world was in the discotheques. All seemed to have a friendly atmosphere and each had their own live disc jockey with turntables, sometimes a glass enclosure, and superb sound systems. The mood and decor of the discotheques was extremely pleasant and exciting, as were most of the people. We all felt America had missed the boat."

After London, the band played Stockholm and Copenhagen. It was during one of these after-hour adventures in Copenhagen that John met Lucy. "Lucy was this sweet, beautiful young disc jockey," Rohrer recalls. "It was the only time I'd ever seen John get up on a dance floor and dance. He was pretty smitten with this woman."

One of the problems with playing in a traveling band, however, was that you had to move on. They went to East Berlin for a show at the Sportpalast, a building that Hitler favored for rallies. They reached the city on Lenin's Centenary and the streets were full of parades and banners. The entourage, however, found it depressing.

"They couldn't hide the despair we saw in the faces of the people," the *Flash* reported. "Amid the smiles, waving and hustle, you really didn't have to see it. You could feel it."

The last stop on the tour was Paris. After visiting the Louvre, Versailles, the Eiffel Tower, and other tourist attractions, the band played two nights at the Olympia Theater. Then it was home to another festooning of balloons, streamers, and a welcome home sign.

12

"THAT'S WHY I DO THIS"

Arriving home at the end of April didn't take the band off the road. They had dates booked in Vancouver and Seattle the first weekend of May. Two weeks later, they had a date comparable to Albert Hall in importance. They were booked into New York City's Madison Square Garden, set to play for a crowd rivaling the homecoming show they did three months earlier in Oakland.

"Creedence Clearwater Revival," Radcliffe Joe wrote in Billboard, "whipped a near capacity crowd at Madison Square Garden into a screaming frenzy of excitement with a fast paced, rhythm filled concert."

"Specializing in a distinct brand of music that strips away all pretensions and gets right to the guts of rock 'n' roll," wrote *Variety:*

> Creedence Clearwater Revival left little doubt Wednesday evening at Madison Square Garden why it is perhaps the largest draw in American rock today. Because of its phenomenal success in the radio market, Creedence is one of a handful of bands whose appeal transcends sociological and age groups. . . . Creedence Clearwater Revival make it perfectly clear that it has come to play crisp, clean and powerful rock and roll. Fogerty's raucous, yet completely coherent vocals and staccato guitar lines are reinforced by the vigorous rhythms of his brother Tom on guitar, bassist Stu Cook and drummer Doug Clifford. The resulting mix is one of the tightest and most professional concert performances in rock.

"The group was polished and obviously well rehearsed," wrote Rick Johnson in *Jazz and Pop*, "yet they projected back slapping spontaneity through their trademarks 'Born on the Bayou,' 'Proud Mary,' 'Bad Moon Rising,' 'Green River' and 'Fortunate Son.' CCR in concert is jes' fingerlicking good."

"None of the groups cashing in on our momentary nostalgia rush can match Creedence for sheer listenable energy," Richard Goldstein wrote in *Vogue*. "And that means passing for schlock rock on AM radio. It's worth noting that Creedence is a singles band, the first to do their best work in that form since the Mamas and the Papas or maybe the Animals. I guess John Fogerty has come to accept rock as something unfathomable but precious and he's worked that understanding through four albums of songs which are so thoroughly immersed in the continuing pop idiom that they imply their own tradition without seeming nostalgic."

Early in June, the band hied back to Wally Heider's studios to cut the remaining tracks for their next album. With four tunes already in the can, that left seven to do, a short week's work for the band. That's all it took, at a cost of $5,000. "We cut five complete music tracks for *Cosmo's Factory* in one eight-hour session," Fogerty asserted.

In addition to the John Fogerty originals, the band set out to cut four favorite covers. They had already recorded one of them, the Elvis (via Arthur "Big Boy" Cruddup) tune "My Baby Left Me." Talking about the song to Ralph Gleason, John said, "I think we've thrown away one song per album. . . . On the second album was an old Elvis Presley song which was much like 'Bad Moon Rising.' " In the *Flash*, however, he couched it somewhat differently. "Sometimes, after getting a song completely recorded, I'll put on my critic's hat and decide that we just weren't ready for that song, so it goes on the shelf. Two of the cuts I hope to have on this album are songs we have recorded before, but didn't use. . . . I think we are ready for them now."

Even twenty-five years later, John would question whether they got this one right. "We did our best, but we didn't have the musicality of those guys. With my guitar playing, all I could do was give an impression of Scotty Moore, who is one of my idols."

While the seven months between the release of *Willie and the Poor Boys* and going into the studio to make their next album might have seemed short to most bands, it was about right for the breakneck pace Creedence had set for themselves.

In addition to covering Elvis, they also reprised a couple of their favorites from their bar band days, Bo Diddley's "Before You Accuse Me," and Roy Orbison's "Ooby Dooby." They also cut a more recent favorite, "I Heard It Through the Grapevine." The tune had been a monster hit for Gladys Knight and the Pips in 1967, and Marvin Gaye had an enormous hit with it in 1969. For Creedence, it represented a great bass line for John to stretch out on, a tune they could jam on for ten minutes or so, and outdo the other bands from the Bay Area who were recording side-long songs.

"When I listen to the radio," John noted , "when something goes a certain way, I'll say to myself, 'That's wrong—it should have been such and such a way.' If I do that enough to a song I really like, it eventually means I'll probably do the song. 'I Heard It Through the Grapevine' came about that way."

"It was a free jam," Clifford explained, "where we got to play off of each other. What I would do is play off of John's rhythm. I don't play a lot with the bass guitar pattern. John and I would trade off little rhythms. If you listen to the record, the guitar does one thing, then I'll do something that's kind of like it."

"Our jams were never quite as totally unorganized as maybe some other groups would have done, but I really liked the way 'Grapevine' came out," John added.

We had an idea what to do. We had the first portion of the song, we knew what was going to happen. That was fairly well rehearsed. We did one take and we thought "Well, that's all right. Let's do one more." And all the pieces, for our ears, fit. It jelled. The guy in the middle turned to each face, "Did you do everything you want to do?" "Yes." "Did you do everything you want to do?" "Yes." "Okay, is there anything more to do?" "No." We were all pretty happy with that.

Stu disagreed with John's assessment of the quality of the track. "That was a tune we jammed on weeks before we recorded it," Stu says. "I had problems with 'Grapevine.' I always felt that compared to Marvin Gaye and Gladys Knight, the CCR version really blew."

Another extended jam, "Ramble Tamble," had a bridge that split the difference between savage and psychedelic. "That thing in the middle was probably too long," Fogerty noted.

"It was one of our longer songs," Doug agreed. "It's got a change of tempo in it and it's got a great guitar hook in it. And there was more political stuff: 'Mortgage on my home, mortgage on the car, mortgage on my life.' There's some pretty strong stuff there. And it's just as relevant today as it was then, maybe even more so today. There's lines like 'actors in the White House,' and 'police on the corner.' The test of time really works there."

Then there were the songs John planned for the next single. The A-side was supposed to be "Long as I Can See the Light," one of the few tunes that could even be remotely considered a love song in John's body of work.

"A real great one," Doug acknowledges, "a great love song. That's my interpretation, anyway. As a matter of fact, the word 'love' doesn't show up in any Creedence song."

One of the most controversial songs John wrote during his days with CCR he initially regarded as one of the most inconsequential. "Lookin' Out My Back Door" with it's vivid images of "all the happy creatures dancing on my lawn, a dinosaur victrola listening to Buck Owens" and "wondrous apparitions provided by magicians," was hailed by proponents and detractors of hallucinogens as John's song about tripping. Spiro Agnew, the same guy who John said would raise the Mars tax, spoke out against the song.

The band, with its antidrug stance, said this could not be more wrong. "John wrote that for his kid," Doug maintained. "The reference to a 'flying spoon'; some people thought it was about cocaine. But it's not. It's about the silver spoon you get as a little child, usually given to you by grandma, that you use to put baby food all over the room."

"This one's about coming off the road, sitting in the back where nobody can bother me," John said:

> The idea of a parade going by came from a book I read as a kid called *To Think [That] I Saw It on Mulberry Street* [by Dr. Seuss]. To a youngster, a parade is very exciting, goofy and bizarre in a kid kind of way. Elephants beating on drums, giraffes, and a monkey playing a xylophone; imagined as only a kid can. I wanted "Lookin' Out My Back Door" to be a kid's song. My son Josh was about three years old when I wrote it. I knew he would love it if he heard me on the radio singing, "doot doot doo, looking out my back door." Sure enough, when it came out, I was in the kitchen and he was on the floor scribbling on paper. The radio was playing, and the song came on. Five minutes later, he sang out, "Doot doot doo, looking out my back door." I looked down, and thought to myself, that's why I do this. The fact I still remember that incident tells you how much it meant to me at the time.

Evoking Buck Owens more than just lyrically, the song was flat out country. "During the heyday," Jake Rohrer recalls, "John and I were both closet Merle Haggard fans. Even when John came up with 'Lookin' Out My Back Door,' Tom's hackles went up, 'Hey, this is too country.' "

The resulting album, *Cosmo's Factory*, remains a favorite of the group to this day. Stu called it the apex of the group's creativity. "*Cosmo's* was the peak in a lot of ways," he enthused.

"That was our most successful album ever," Doug expanded. "Not just because it was named after me, because we were peaking at that point. It was named after me because I was the prankster, the jokester, the guy who was always saying something. John said, 'because you do that, we want to establish an image.' He was very image conscious."

Courtesy Fantasy Records

Cosmo's Factory

The cover art of *Cosmo's Factory* put Doug front and center, on his bicycle, while John hung in the background on a motorcycle behind the drums. "John Fogerty was the lead singer, the writer, the musical leader for the most part," Doug said. "I was the front man. John was uncomfortable in that role. There was a lot of pressure on him at that time, and he wanted some relief, so he said, 'We're going to do the cover of *Cosmo's Factory* to put the focus on you and take the pressure off of me.' I love it. It's our biggest selling album ever."

"It may actually be our best record," John said. "I always thought it was the culmination. By that time, Creedence had all these records and we looked back and put everything on it. It was almost redemptive, you might say. We'd done all these things and it was like 'Boom! There I said it again.'"

In July, with "Up Around the Bend," nearing the top reaches of the English charts (it would peak at number 3), Creedence released *Cosmo's Factory*. "For Creedence," Robert Christgau wrote in *The Village Voice*, "*Cosmo's Factory* is in a dozen tiny respects an elaboration. The most obvious change is in the songwriting, especially the lyrics, but there are others, e.g., John Fogerty's singing has become surer and more subtle, the four musicians are more integral, the sound of the recording is fuller, 'I Heard It Through the Grapevine' apotheosizes 'Suzie Q's' artless concept of rock improvisation."

"*Cosmo's Factory* sounds just like the previous four CCR albums," noted A. Heineman in *Down Beat*. "It's terrific: its rewards are the satisfactions of returning to a meaningful and worthwhile ritual amid the empty rituals other bands recreate out of desperation or fiscal ambition.

"That's the really fine thing about CCR's first five sessions, incidentally," he adds. "You can run through the jungle as much as you want without finding a single moment when the integrity of the material is sacrificed to melodrama, histrionics or ego. Control, logic and—above all—naturalness."

"It's an up-tempo blend of Fogerty original black-rooted Fogerty originals and Fogerty-interpreted black originals," Janice Coughlin described in *Jazz and Pop*. "All are blocked out in traditional chord progressions and delivered in a tightly controlled rhythmic frenzy with John's strident vocals working hard on top."

"It should be obvious by now," John Grissim said in *Rolling Stone*, "that Creedence Clearwater Revival is one great rock and roll band. *Cosmo's Factory* is another good reason why."

By the end of August, the album topped the American charts, with the consequently released single of "Lookin' Out My Back Door" backed with "Long as I Can See the Light," topping out at number 2, skunked by Diana Ross's "Ain't No Mountain High Enough."

When the record was out, Saul Zaentz booked a pleasure boat for a sail around the Bay. Invited were the band's entourage and families and Fantasy staffers, some sixty people all told. During the trip he presented the band with gold records for "Down on the Corner," "Travelin' Band," and "Up Around the Bend." He also had gold and platinum plaques for *Willie and the Poor Boys*.

During the cruise, they might have passed another boat, an older, smaller one called *Clearwater*. The boat made daily runs to Alcatraz Island, which had been taken over by Native American activists. It carried supplies and reinforcements for their stand. Creedence Clearwater Revival vowed to support them for as long as the they held out.

"When the American Indian Movement (AIM) was born," Stu recalls, "one of the early acts of defiance was the occupation of Alcatraz Island in

San Francisco Bay, a former federal prison. The Indians claimed it. Food and medical supplies were in short supply, as was a means to transport the same to the island. CCR, without publicity, donated a boat and supplies to the cause. The boat was eventually sunk; the Indians blame the Navy SEALS. The occupation was ended and a chapter in the struggle came to a close."

The group's fans knew about this, because it was reported in their fan letter, *The Fifth St. Flash*, but the band never really made a big deal out of it. That was part of their nature. All of them were married, but not many people knew about that. Very few people knew anything about the band. Doug's presence front and center on the cover of *Cosmo's Factory*, along with John sitting by the drums confused more than one person trying to figure out who was who. Even reasonably well-informed journalists mistook one member for another. And people still asked which one was "Creedence."

This facelessness even went so far as their biggest hit records. Already "Proud Mary" had been covered by Elvis and others. While on a business trip to Texas, Stu's father, Herman Cook, was sitting in the bar at the hotel and the pianist launched into the song. Herman, swelling bigger than life with his son's accomplishment, approached the musician.

"Where did you learn that song you just played?" he queried.

"Oh," the pianist replied, "haven't you heard that one before? That was 'Proud Mary,' a big hit by Ed Ames."

CCR might have been one of the best-selling bands in the world, but they had yet to join the cult of personality that surrounded bands like the Rolling Stones, the Beatles, and even the Jefferson Airplane. They had a love/hate relationship with the idea. On the one hand, they got upset when the journalists sent to interview them couldn't identify one member from another. On the other hand, as Doug said at the time, "I like my private life."

Events outside the band were brewing, however, things that would change the course of Creedence's destiny. Try as he might to keep a tight rein on things internally, John couldn't control outside events.

13

"JOHN AND TOM WERE AT ODDS"

Another group of four guys who made good were having problems of their own in 1970. You can draw a lot of parallels between CCR and the Beatles. Both groups started in 1959; both did their time playing grungy clubs; both groups grew up on R&B.

There were some critical differences as well. The Beatles had a manager/Svengali in Brian Epstein early in their career, whereas CCR depended on themselves for management and promotion. The Beatles also had producer George Martin in the studio, where CCR depended on John Fogerty and Russ Gary. John often joked about this, saying that they hoped Phil Spector would call, but until then, he'd have to do.

"In the beginning," John said, "we all kept waiting for someone to come along and work their magic for us, tell us what moves to make."

"There must be more than one Brian Epstein, we kept telling ourselves," Doug added.

"But he never came," John concluded, "So we had to learn to depend on ourselves."

"We told John we wanted a real manager," says Stu. "He brought us Allan Klein."

Klein was notorious as a cigar-chomping accountant and music business-man whose shrewd dealings had earned him a block of MGM stock. He had negotiated a major deal for the Rolling Stones. Ultimately Klein was one of the forces involved in polarizing the differences between John Lennon and Paul McCartney when Lennon brought him in to take the financial reins of Apple. McCartney had hoped his father-in-law, Lee Eastman, a noted entertainment lawyer, would be given the job.

John Fogerty hoped Klein could find a way out of the group's increasingly onerous deal with Fantasy. "He read our contract for us to see if there was anything he could do," John reported. "And he said, 'I'm sorry, there's nothing I can do to get you out of that.'"

In his self-appointed role as manager, John took an enormous amount on himself. By the time the group put out *Cosmo's Factory* the strain on the band was starting to show. John took the reins hard.

The band took another sabbatical in Maui after playing their annual fall date in Honolulu. They spent nine days unwinding in paradise, Doug getting to check out the flora and fauna, everyone swimming and sunning on the beach. However, despite the idyll, after ten years of struggle, the year and a half of astonishing success had started to spawn dissension in the band. The rest of the group started to question why everything had to be John's way.

Earlier, while CCR played their European tour, Paul McCartney announced a temporary break with the Beatles. He said he was leaving over "personal differences." Beyond that, he said he would no longer record with John Lennon. Over the next few months, Lennon, McCartney, and George Harrison would release solo records. The rumors swirled like whirlpools, but the upshot always pointed to the demise of the most popular group in the world. When couched like that, the next obvious question was, who would take up that mantle?

Creedence Clearwater Revival often got that nod, but that would entail their own survival. One advantage of not having a high-profile public image was that their squabbles didn't turn up on the front pages of newspapers. But internally, dissension grew. Doug already felt he was taking the front-man role in public.

Stu, a business major in college, wanted to take some of the more onerous chores of management off of John's shoulders. "I told John I wanted the band's business run like a business," he says. "I have a degree in business management. Doug backed me."

"After a couple of years," Doug stated, "Tom Fogerty, Stu Cook and I asserted more and more input into band decisions. This caused significant difference in opinions over both creative and management decisions. After much debate, Tom, Stu and I made it clear to John that each of us had an equal say in the band's decision making."

"There was a lot of push, at least on my part to have John let go of some of the things he was doing. I didn't think he was doing them as well as they could or needed to be done in terms of business management," Stu added.

I didn't think that our business was being handled well, particularly touring. We weren't making any money. When everybody was going 'We want an equal say,' it wasn't just an equal say to write and sing songs; it was that, at least for me, the whole business as a band was a shambles. John had too many things to

"I could walk away from it tomorrow," said Tom.

do. So we did change that. We did get our touring thing together, where we went out and toured for four to six weeks instead of just going out and playing weekends and flying home.

Tom wanted artistic input. He was the original lead singer, and the band had reached a level of success where it certainly would have been possible (and brotherly) for John to let Tom present material for consideration, either as a singer or a songwriter. John refused.

"There's a lot of pressure on John," Tom said, "and there's a lot of pressure on all of us because I want to live up to what John expects of me."

John, on the other hand, perhaps still afraid of the specter of the car wash, would have none of it. The tight grip he established over the group at Two Guys from Italy Restaurant continued to hold sway. Tom considered leaving.

"I could walk away from it tomorrow," he said at the time. "I almost did. No reason to pretend it's all easy, because believe me, it's not. But why should I? Why—when right now we can do so much we haven't even *thought* of yet?!

"I haven't even begun," he added, "In my own head, which is all that counts, I'm just starting. I've changed a lot in the last six months and I'm changing now."

So was the rest of the band. By the time they went in to the studio to record *Pendulum*, Tom, Stu, and Doug told John they wanted to do more than just lay down the basic tracks and hang out in the anteroom while John did all the overdubbing. "This was our first big group effort," Stu said. "I'd say it's an intentional deviation from what we usually do. Not exactly a change, but a natural evolution of our getting to be better musicians."

As the Beatles' demise became more and more of a done deal, it was generally acknowledged that CCR now held the top rung among the world's recording artists. Despite their continued inability to land a number 1 single, they were the world's number-1 singles and album band. Despite their problems with royalties, they were the number-1 band monetarily, too. However, to themselves and the people around them, little had changed.

Typically, of all the group's members, John felt the pressure of the Beatles' demise most. "I guess even if the Beatles had still been on the scene, we would have sold the same amount of records. But because they broke up, we're noticed more now. We've been put into the number 1 spot more by default than anything else." Stu, on the other hand, saw benefits to inheriting the Fab Four's mantle, effusing to rock journalist Harvey Siders, "We'd love the Beatles' bedlam!" Tom, typically, took the middle ground: "We are not setting out to 'replace' the Beatles. The Beatles didn't 'replace' Elvis. That's not the way it is."

However, Tom started to become disaffected with the whole situation. "Disaffected is a good word for it," says Jake Rohrer. "After *Cosmo's Factory*, they were approaching *Pendulum*, and all of a sudden, Tom went from considering himself just a regular guy. Things got precious for Tom. He viewed himself as a rock star. I also think he had a hard time being in the shadow of his younger brother who had this enormous talent, and he didn't. That started to come about in the late fall of 1970. *Cosmo's Factory* was such a huge, huge success. The Beatles had disbanded. Creedence was the biggest thing going. It just went to Tom's head. There may be more to it than that, but it was really depressing."

"Things were bad, a struggle," John agrees. "The trick I had been able to pull off was writing and showing everybody what to play, which held them at bay. Our success also held them at bay. Then we had a big meeting, A BAND MEETING, in capital letters, a week before the recording of *Pendulum*. This meeting didn't effect *Pendulum* too much, but the idea was that band wanted to become a democracy instead of an autocracy, or maybe a dictatorship. I was the tyrant, a dictator."

"I kinda dominated the group," he confessed five years later. "I'm saying that in the most negative way. I kind of overdid my domination, 'You do things this way, you do this that way,' because it was so clear to me how things should fit together."

Despite whatever guilt he felt at dominating the band, a more bitter John some twenty-five years later reflected on how he resented their sniping, particularly when he brought them such great success:

> For two years all I'd hear as we walked through airports were these jealous, sniping, back-biting voices behind me saying, "We should write, we should sing, we should play our own parts". . . . Here we are at Woodstock, here we are on Ed Sullivan. . . . The bigger we got, the better I did my job, the more these guys are ungrateful. Finally, right at the end of 1970, they said, "This has to be a democracy." A classic case of the inmates running the asylum.

With all this going on, the band had scheduled time at Wally Heider's, and had to get down to making their next record, with some new rules. Everyone was allowed to contribute their ideas in the studio, though the album, *Pendulum*, was totally written by John. Partly because they culled all of their previous singles from *Cosmo's Factory* and therefore had nothing in the can, rather than just go into Heider's for a week, it took them nearly a month to record *Pendulum*. "More keyboard and John's attempt at horns added up the hours," says Stu. "We were looking for a bit less of a roar and more instrumental definition."

"We were more involved on *Pendulum*," Doug reflected. "Stu played piano and I got involved in more rhythm things. We got to stretch a bit more, and that's really what we wanted to do."

"John said to me while they were making *Pendulum* that this will be the last one that he produced," Russ Gary recalls. "So the decision had been made by then that it was going to be a Creedence effort from there on out in terms of production and input. That's when I realized things had changed."

Indeed, beyond the basic Buddy Holly two-guitars-bass-and-drums that had been the hallmark of the band since the beginning, the album featured tons of organ. "We idolized Booker T and the MGs," says Doug. "We learned a lot from them. John wanted to do something that had a Hammond organ on it. John was a multitalented, multi-instrumentalist. I played it for the MGs in my living room before it came out. I had [MG bassist] Duck Dunn and [MG guitarist] Steve Cropper over. They were real quiet, and I said, 'How come you're so quiet?' They said, 'That organ sounds a lot like us.'"

Other instruments on the record included entire horn sections of John on sax. Various band members added electric and acoustic piano, harmonica, vibes, maracas, conga and tabla drums, recorder, kalimba, and even solo vox, an electronic keyboard dating back to the '30s that Stu had picked up at a garage sale. The creative floodgates had opened, but in service of what? There was some doubt internally that there would be a band after they finished the record.

The writing was on the wall, and some of John's songs on *Pendulum* reflect it. Tunes like "Chameleon" and "It's Just a Thought" chronicle the descent lyrically. "*Pendulum* starts to get into a painful period in the band's history," Stu said. "There were certainly problems between the brothers, John and Tom. Whatever disagreements they had put aside, the sibling rivalry of some sort was beginning to come to the surface again. Doug and I used to joke that we felt like we were caught in a Fogerty sandwich, the brothers were the bread and we were the bologna in the middle."

"We loved them both dearly," Doug said. "When they started fighting, Stu and I would walk, we'd go and get a cup of coffee. Being able to step back we could understand better. We could see both sides of the argument. We knew it was hopeless for us to get involved. We tried as much as we could to calm things down on either side. But to get in the middle while it was going would not have been a wise thing to do. We felt helpless in that situation."

"The band was on the verge of breaking up," Doug adds. "John was writing about the problems in the band and the problems between him and his brother. This was a very serious time. There was turmoil in the band at that point. John and Tom were at odds."

"I Wish I Could Hideaway" finds John at his most vocally vulnerable, hitting notes just at the top of his falsetto range over melancholy organ. Yet the tune bounces between that sense of naked exposure and something closer to raw rage. "John was under a lot of pressure," says Doug. "He was having problems with Fantasy, having problems internally with the band and fighting with his brother."

Even the self-deconstructing "Rude Awakening #2," which starts off with a wonderful little instrumental riff and descends into chaos points to the band's internal conflicts. "I hate that song," Doug says. "It was sort of a parody, almost a put-down on people who did long tunes." "'Rude Awakening #2' is embarrassing," says Stu. "I once told John I didn't like some of his songs, but that wouldn't stop me from giving my best to them."

The least-pointed of these songs was probably "Have You Ever Seen the Rain." "This happens in the Bay Area more often than in other places," John notes.

The sun is shining, yet you have rain falling down, rainbows and raindrops falling, as the wind blows the rain into the Bay through the Golden Gate. "Have You Ever Seen the Rain?" is about the breakup of Creedence Clearwater Revival. 'Have you ever seen the rain coming down, sunny day?' Creedence was supposed to be sunny days, the golden time, yet look at the rain falling down on us. The song was off the *Pendulum* album, which also referred to the breakup, a pendulum swinging one way toward all the wonderful times, now it was swinging back the other way, which was bad. I don't think the band realized "Have You Ever Seen the Rain" was about our breakup.

It was also one of the few songs they recorded unrehearsed. "Two songs, 'Pagan Baby' and 'Have You Ever Seen the Rain,' were written and rehearsed on the spot during the course of one of the sessions," Stu said. "To me, 'Pagan Baby' sounds just like a live cut. In fact, it only took one hour to learn and we did it in one take."

Of course, this was a Creedence album, and John had not lost his pop sense. Tunes like "Pagan Baby" were meant for the concert stage, and "Hey Tonight" had an opening lead reminiscent of Pete Townshend of the Who, but with a walking bass line that was pure CCR. "Born to Move" came out of the Memphis groove, with the overdubbed horn charts, one of John's most interesting short guitar solos, and a wailing organ break. "Molina" also sported a multi-John horn section, and "Sailor's Lament" featured some pretty group harmonies. "That was a song we spent a lot of time on," Doug remarked.

In addition to his lack of creative fulfillment, Tom had another major beef with his situation in CCR. No one knew the names of the members of the band, no one—shown a picture—could tell who was who. To Tom, the members of the most successful band in the world, the number-one singles act, the number-one money making act, should be recognizable. "People don't know us," he complained, "in spite of all the records they've bought."

The main reason CCR never got involved in the cult of personality that infected so much music from the period was probably John's natural shyness, the reticence of the kid who grew up in a bunker-like bedroom and never invited the other kids home. He just didn't like people prying into his private life.

Through a strange chain of events that started with author John Hallowell getting assigned to cover the January 1970 Oakland Coliseum homecoming concert, meeting the band, then meeting with people from Bantam Books, Hallowell was told to at least approach the band with the idea of a new kind of book Bantam was doing. Bantam called them "Extras." They covered topics ranging from the visit of Pope Paul to pornography. The book biz dubbed them "instant paperbacks," owing to the speed with which they hit the stores.

Hallowell brought the idea to the band. Under normal circumstances, the book idea probably would have died on the vine, but Tom really wanted this to happen. He suggested that a book about the band might help give the members a distinctive personality. So Hallowell spent about half of the time the band took to record *Pendulum* hanging out with the group.

Hallowell was not a great image maker, and appeared to have just the vaguest idea of what rock was about. His frame of reference seemed closer to Peggy Lee than to Jerry Lee.

"Tom was the energy behind the book," says Stu. "I never could figure out the choice of writer."

"He was around for like two weeks," recalled Bob Fogerty.

"At the time we were recording 'Have You Ever Seen the Rain,'" John recalled, "Hallowell was there. He was a sensitive guy. He knew. As we were playing it in the studio, he came up to me after with tears in his eyes. He'd figured it out."

14

"THE NIGHT OF THE GENERALS"

To the press, the band expressed nothing but positive thoughts about their forthcoming album. "This is the first time I can say I'm really proud of an album," John said at the time. "The earlier ones were nice and all that, but if I had to go to a desert island with one possession, I wouldn't have taken any of the other albums."

In an uncharacteristic move, the band hired the Hollywood PR firm of Rogers and Cowan to help launch *Pendulum*. Almost immediately, some band members were unhappy with the arrangement. "Rogers and Cowan's idea of promotion was to get you the key to the city, and have a day named after you," mused Stu. "We had no idea how to control the hype that grew out of the Rogers and Cowan PR machine."

Part of Rogers and Cowan's plan involved a huge press and VIP party to preview the album. They invited 200 journalists, deejays, and key retailers to listen to the record, watch the National General *In Concert* television show, have a couple of meals with the band, do interviews, and watch the band play on their home turf, in the Factory.

"The night of the generals," is how both Jake Rohrer and John Fogerty refer to the event. "After *Pendulum* was recorded," John recalls bitterly,

about six weeks after the BAND MEETING, we planned a big coming-out press party, just two and a half years into our career. I call it the Night of the Generals, everybody was now a general, no soldiers to do the work. We hired Rogers and Cowan to proclaim that the tyranny was over, Creedence was now a democracy. I went along with it, there wasn't much else I could do. Yet that's what they wanted, so I took a big swallow, and thought, "Ooookay." The guys all talked to *Rolling Stone* and the rest of the press about how they were going to be singing and writing, making up their own music parts instead of follow-ing John. As a surprise to me, I even had to get up and say something nice about Saul Zaentz. I swallowed hard and told the story about how Saul had loaned the band $1,200 so we could buy a new Kustom Amp.

"We had retained this high-powered, Hollywood PR firm, Rogers and Cowan," Rohrer adds.

They had heavy-duty Hollywood credentials and many big stars in their ros-ter. Bobbi Cowan was in charge of our account. I liked Bobbi, an energetic and personable gal, but the boys from Berkeley didn't really fit into the Hollywood scene. I found it all very foreign to our root beliefs. For the release of *Pendu-lum*, she wanted this big party for the press at the Factory. We'd fly in all the prestigious rock journalists from all over the country, have a big dinner party, the band would perform, and we'd show them a good time and play the new album for them. This would continue to rocket Creedence into the stratos-phere where each member would have a star of equal brilliance. Of course it was bullshit. Tom really thought it would help establish Creedence at the top of the heap, ignoring the fact that they had already arrived there just being themselves. We were all feeling the reverberations from the band's internal struggle. I worked hard to represent the band in a positive light.

"For all Creedence's immense popularity," wrote cultural critic Ellen Willis, "John Fogerty never made it as a media hero, and the group never crossed the line from best-selling rock band to cultural phenomenon . . . but then no recent pop performers have attracted anything like the Creedence audience, which during that peak year included hard-core rock-and-roll fans and hard-core freaks, high school kids and college students, AM and FM—in short, closely resembled that catholic rock audience whose loss we mourn."

As might be expected, many rock writers—fiercely independent and anti-establishment themselves—were put off by this obvious PR overkill. "John Fogerty," wrote rock journalist Al Aronowitz, "has been telling members of the Rock Press that he wants his group to have the same cultural import as the Beatles." Aronowitz quoted the itinerary for the event: "Hi! Welcome to the CREEDENCE CLEARWATER REVIVAL GALA. We've planned a wild wicked weekend (with the help of our record company—Fantasy-Galaxy Records), a once-in-a-lifetime spin through the center of American political activism."

Many members of the press questioned both why they were there and whether the trip really was necessary. After all, CCR was the most successful group in the world. *Pendulum* shipped a million copies off the bat. The group obviously didn't have anything to prove to the public—which left the press.

Pendulum.

"This would appear a somewhat redundant exercise," wrote the influential *Village Voice* critic Robert Christgau, "albeit tax deductible, but in fact it wasn't. Creedence finds itself in a quandary as perplexing as it is enviable. The band has turned off the kind of fan who exults every time he identifies a chord change, who assumes a single is a bad record and who talks about rock rather than rock and roll. Worse still, Creedence has not infused its public with the kind of ardor public idols are expected to expect. . . . Creedence is tired of being just friends.

"It was apparently John's subalterns (you remember Tom? Doug? Stu?), double bridesmaids, who felt the need for this most and pushed for the December bash in which journalists from everywhere were flown to Berkeley and housed and fed for a weekend," he added. "But it was strictly a flannel-shirt affair. Although the party was timed to coincide with the release of Creedence's sixth LP, *Pendulum*, there was none of the superliminal exposure that is the normal price of such gatherings. The sound system played classical music, unobtrusively. In return for several good meals and unlimited booze in the famous Factory, the journalists had to sit through a one-hour television film on the group, screened specially at a downtown movie house, and a twenty-five-minute set comprising two new songs and 'Grapevine' which left everyone shouting for an encore that did not materialize."

"The idea of Creedence as a new 'supergroup' or set of culture heroes is a curious one," *Rolling Stone's* John Lombardi commented. Still, the members of the group felt that they weren't getting the respect they deserved from the rock writers. "I think that the press just doesn't believe our success," John complained. "I mean, if groups like Led Zeppelin or Grand Funk Railroad or Chicago or ourselves can sell out huge stadiums, obviously some of the critics don't know what's happening."

"Everyone has the most fucking respect for the Beatles," Doug lamented to Lombardi. "Well, we're the biggest American group. We put out quality records. We go over and over our songs. We rehearse *hours* every day. *Nothing* bad gets out under our name. We have artistic control. We even carry our own sound system. We shouldn't be taken lightly. You can't sell that many records and be taken lightly."

"Sometimes, reading the reviews," John concured, "it seems like 'ho-hum, another hit for Creedence.' "

In all, the band spent about $30,000 on the junket.

There were signs of internal dissension at the junket party. Stu Cook beefed to Lombardi about lack of respect he felt the band received. "We're tired of that riff about [being] John Fogerty's backup band."

"Creedence," Jake Rohrer reflected, "was more of an entity than an individual. They always wanted to push the individual, get individual photos and names and that sort of thing out there, but it never succeeded. Creedence *was* Creedence."

Tom Fogerty, although one of the instigators of the party, ironically became reticent during the event. He's the only band member not directly quoted in the coverage. He was fighting his own personal demons.

"Tom and the other band members wanted to write songs," Gail Fogerty says. "John's songs were so good, and I think Tom was just frustrated by it all."

Everyone left the party with a copy of *Pendulum*. If the party succeeded in anything, it made the critics more thoughtful. Still, they were divided over the group's more ambitious undertaking "Grander still was the music itself," wrote Robert Christgau, "including a saxophone solo and girlie choruses and lots of John Fogerty organ and even some audible overdubbing here and there. Unfortunately, richer does not mean better. Fogerty felt he had to go somewhere from all that economical guitar-playing and hard-rocking backup, which is understandable, and that he should choose for his inspiration Booker T. Jones and a dollop of Terry Riley is typical of the fine taste in influences which his song selection has always demonstrated. In fact, the album's ambitions were so intelligent that kindness was almost mandatory. . . . Ho-hum, another brilliant Creedence album."

"There appears to be something about John Fogerty's approach that is ideally suited to the demands of a three-minute single," Jon Landau wrote in *Rolling Stone*, "and out of place in the context of a 40-minute album. His taste is too predictable, his mind too tight and his hand too heavy. Over a three minute span, tightness and orderliness can be virtues; over 40-minutes, they can be deadening.

"*Pendulum* is Creedence's attempt to prove that the album can be their medium, too," he adds. "On it, they introduce John Fogerty's piano and sax playing as regular features. . . . On 'Sailor Man' [*sic*—the song is actually called "Sailor's Lament"] some of the stylistic nuances of the album emerge. The recording is perfectly clean, with each track separate and distinct. . . . All the elements of great rock and roll are present on some of this album and yet none of it ever becomes great rock and roll."

"I confess to being awed by their professional acumen (or is it the expertise of JC Fogerty alone, who has written, arranged and produced all the tracks here that deserves such respect?)," wrote Peter Reilly in his "Super Pro"-rated performance, "Excellent"-rated recording review in *Stereo Review*. "This group is so smoothly integrated, so slick in performance, and so professionally assured that it would be like trying to take apart a wafer thin Swiss watch to analyze it."

Many commercial copies of *Pendulum* were packaged with a copy of John Hallowell's *Inside Creedence*. The book took about six weeks from the time it was conceived until it was actually published. "About a month after he was with the band," notes Bob Fogerty, "there was a book. It was so quick."

The reviews for the book were terrible. "*Inside Creedence*, written in a spastic, pseudo-Tom Wolfe style, goes from just plain silly to downright offensive," wrote Richard Cromelin.

Dripping with dropped names of Hollywood stars Hallowell has interviewed, the book is marked by a complete lack of perception into the youth culture and its music . . . One problem is the mere presence of these rock gods seemingly reduces him to a state of giddy, reeling incoherence in which he raves like a fawning and devoted press agent about every inspired blink of a Creedence eye. The potent combination of too much coffee and some loud rock sends him on mind-blown flights during which he makes such intriguing discoveries as: (1) there is a lot of sex ("S-E-X!" he sniggers more than once) in rock 'n' roll; (2) rock musicians emit much energy at a recording session, and (3) the police club kids at rock concerts.

The ever-hip *Village Voice* critic Robert Cristgau ripped the biography calling it "positively bad":

John Hallowell's *Inside Creedence*, is an authorized biography by a former *Life* staffer with a penchant for amazement and inappropriate analogies. Bantam peddled it for a dollar with merchandising keyed to *Pendulum*—both were graced with the very same dumb cover photo. It wasn't just that it looked like a fan-book, thus supporting the teen image the group is uneasily trying to shake, but that it really is a fan-book. The music, after all, simultaneously transcends and elevates its image, as rock and roll always has. John Hallowell, however, lacks John Fogerty's genius for generous deception. If John (and Tom and Doug and Stu) is less than a demigod, you won't find out from *Inside Creedence*. He is a humble leader and they his admiring but self-sufficient henchmen. Hallowell refuses to discuss drugs, and although he babbles about the group's sex appeal with all the jittery wistfulness of a man who wishes he were twenty-three again, he never explores concretely or analytically Fogerty's assertion that the group tries to "avoid the cliché uses of sex". . . . Although a silly book won't ruin Creedence, it does demonstrate how difficult the task of achieving a new level of seriousness without abandoning the old is going to be.

Despite the critics' carping, with a million copies of *Pendulum* sold out of the box, both Fantasy and the group knew that they didn't have to worry about the fans. The people who had become devoted to the group over the past two years remained devoted.

The party topped off another banner year for CCR. They received an Outstanding Contribution award from *Soul* magazine. The Music Operators of America, the organization of Juke Box Owners, named them Artists of the Year. Billboard named them Top Album Artist, as well as the top pop group in the United States, Canada, Germany, France, Switzerland, Norway, and Israel. The readers of England's *New Musical Express* voted them top international pop group, and the readers of England's *Record Mirror* named them Top Male Pop Group. The Italian critics named them the best foreign group. They received Germany's Musikmart and Golden Otto awards and Mexico's Golden Clover. The Recording Industry Association of America named them the Top Gold Record artists of the year. The National Association of Recording Merchandisers honored them as the year's top-selling artists.

They would never see the likes of such a year again.

15

"WE'RE GOING TO RETIRE TOM'S NUMBER"

Unpleasant tidings were everywhere in the CCR camp over the Christmas and New Year holidays during that winter of 1971. Reading between the lines in their official fan sheet, *The Fifth St. Flash* (admittedly with some hindsight), points to these problems. One indication that all was not well was that the members of CCR were taking separate vacations so soon after their Maui sojourn. The *Flash* reported: "Stu seems to be heading to London to spend a week or two with friends. Doug says he's heading south with his new Jeep station wagon and Tom thinks some snow and mountains would be fun. John isn't saying where he's headed, only that he would prefer not to be anywhere near a telephone for at least a month."

Another thing pointing to something afoot at the Factory came under the concert listings. That column read, "There ain't none. Not 'til March, anyway, at which time we'll have a full schedule to turn you all on to."

As it turned out, that was the height of wishful thinking.

Almost simultaneously with the release of the single "Have You Ever Seen the Rain," backed with "Hey Tonight," the subject of the A-side song let the other shoe drop. The group officially announced that Tom had left the band.

"He decided he'd had enough and he quit," Gail says.

I personally told Tom to take a vacation rather than quit. Take a six-month vacation and do something else during that time. See how he felt after that. He was very frustrated and angry at the time. I think he made a terrible mistake. It caused tension in our marriage. I didn't understand why someone could give up something they'd wanted their whole life. Just to give it up so easily. My solution was take a vacation and just be away from it for a while, then come back and see. I don't think the band would have fallen apart if they didn't do anything for six months. He didn't feel that way. I was so against that and he wouldn't listen to me.

"I was gone from my family all the time, so things were beginning to split there," Tom reflected five years later. "The communication between myself and my wife was beginning to get a little weird, and the kids were beginning to wonder who was this stranger in the house."

At the time of the announcement, the group made sure they were all away from the Factory. Stu was in London. Doug had actually headed for the mountains, enjoying the snow in the Sierras. Tom went to Acapulco. No one really knew where John went. Stu postulated he might be in Death Valley.

"I started out in this business in 1958 as a stand-up singer," Tom said later. "I got really frustrated at not being able to be everything I wanted to be when I started out. . . . I left because of a falling-out between John and I about the music itself and how much I could contribute."

Tom was frustrated because he felt his role in the development of the band was underplayed by the press—and John—who made it sound like John Forgerty *was* Creedence. "I sang lead and wrote the songs—cowrote them with John and wrote them by myself," he described the early days of the band. "The whole Creedence thing that was presented to the public was that John was the lead singer and wrote all the songs. That wasn't the whole history of the group, that was only one period. When it got into the later part of 1970, I wanted to contribute more to the group in terms of writing and singing, maybe singing backgrounds and doing two or three leads. John, at that point, was real afraid of changing anything. So I said, well, this is how it's going to be. I'm leaving. You can have it your way and do whatever you want with it. That's pretty much how it went."

The official press release, spun out of the Factory circa February 1, 1971, reads:

Tom Fogerty is leaving Creedence Clearwater Revival to remain home with his family and to record and produce on his own.

Creedence will continue as a trio and is planning to go into the studio in April.

The joint announcement was made by Tom and the other members of Creedence, John Fogerty, Doug Clifford and Stu Cook, in a statement which emphasized that the move was the beginning of new ideas and concepts for both and a natural evolution of the musical careers of all four.

"I am not retiring," says Tom. "I'm just not going to tour. My children are 8, 7, and the twins are 1, and this is the time they need a father with them and they are my first responsibility. I intend to spend as much time with them as I can.

"In addition, I hope to create on my own and come up with something individual, something unique which reflects my personal creative urge."

There will be no replacement for Tom in Creedence.

"We're going to retire Tom's number," said John Fogerty, the group's lead singer and songwriter. "Creedence will continue as a trio."

"It's a positive thing," Stu Cook said. "Not an end but a beginning of something new for all of us." Doug Clifford added, "We all understand what Tom is doing and we know why this is the thing he has to do now. The band has reached a certain point in its development and we all have, too. This is the way which we all must go for our own development as artists."

"Of course it's a change for all of us," John Fogerty says, "but change is implicit in music. We have always been a tight personal group and we will remain that way. We will miss Tom in the band but we anticipate with pleasure what we know he will bring to music on his own."

"It's really two separate things," Tom said. "If I could have given more time to my family and done what I wanted to do and still stayed in the band, I would have done it."

Creedence is officially still on vacation, though working on new material informally. They plan to get into the studio in April and Tom Fogerty is writing songs and making plans for recording about the same time.

A more personal letter accompanied the release, headed with Jake Rohrer's comment, "No doubt this will shake a few trees."

Dear Friends,

Indeed, the times the are a-changin'. Tom has left the group, yet not on a note of discord or disagreement; rather with a smile and his best wishes to all. The enclosed release says it best. . . . Creedence will remain and the music world has a new single artist. Corners must be turned and the world is still in spin. We look forward to a very fulfilling year.

And there is more. We have elected not to continue the fan club. There are many reasons for this decision but we think the most important is the fact that the band no longer has the time to give it their personal attention. And that's what the entire venture was predicated on—real involvement on the part of the band. Anyone can hire a plastics firm to send out wishy-washy hype letters and call it a fan club—that's not for us. It's been a lot of work and a lot of fun. We do hope you will understand our decision.

And so, America, 1971. We hope you'll continue, as we will, to keep on keepin' on.

God Bless you all, John Fogerty, Doug Clifford, and Stu Cook.

By February, of course, this was no surprise to the band. They had known for at least a month, probably not too long after the *Pendulum* party, possibly even before, that Tom would be leaving.

"There was all this dissension and walking on eggshells during that *Pendulum* time, which culminated in Tom leaving," Rohrer recalls. "Then there was the shock of Tom leaving. There was a couple of months there when we all kind of walked around and looked at each other and figured out what's going to happen next.

"I thought we were going to bring Duck Dunn onboard to play bass and Stu was going to move to rhythm guitar and we were going to go out and kick some ass," Rohrer continues. "I believe it was discussed, but I'm not sure. Duck was always a close friend to all the guys. I was kind of surprised when they decided to go it as a trio. I thought they were going to bring in a fourth member, and logically that would be Duck."

On announcing that he was leaving the group, Tom gave a number of interviews to the rock press. He repeated his feeling of the burden he felt under the shadow of his younger brother. "I was always under pressure," Tom said. "After a while, I found I didn't really dig success. In the group, I was frustrating my writing talents."

"John was always the most musical one," he conceded on announcing his intention to leave the group, "and therefore we considered him the leader, musically. . . . We were all talking about change and were going to contribute more. I found myself bouncing out altogether as a result of thinking that way. I couldn't even hang on to the idea of 'group' any more."

"Somehow," he added for *Melody Maker*'s Al Rudis, "it's an unnatural situation having your younger brother lead the group you're in, yet you can suppress it. Muff Winwood was in the Spencer Davis Group with Stevie. Just imagine having a younger brother like Stevie Winwood. And John is just as talented.

"Creedence had reached a point in it's evolution of twelve years together," he said, "where John was singing and playing lead and we were doing backup. My fight with John was about loosening that arrangement so that we could do more lead singing and contribute more songs.

"Creedence was together for nine years before we made it big, and sixty percent of that time, I was the lead singer," he added for *Rolling Stone*'s Michael Goldberg in an interview in the early '80s. "I wasn't a dictator, but I was more of a leader than what I ended up to be in the eyes of our fans— just the guy who stood there and played rhythm guitar. So after we were into our sixth platinum album, I though maybe I could do a little singing. But John was not going to change things, so I split."

In a letter he wrote to John in 1985, he was somewhat less sanguine about the whole thing:

In December 1970, I left Creedence for the same reason I would leave in October 1985.

Reason: your attitude.

You have never given me (or Doug or Stu) credit in public, in the press or in any media form for my contributions to Creedence. This includes my musical contributions: (Tommy Fogerty & The Blue Velvets). I was the producer, lead singer and main songwriter. Everything has to start somewhere, but in your distorted version of the band's history, you conveniently omit the Tommy Fogerty part, leading people to believe that you did it all and that I was just along for the ride. Our songwriting partnership—remember Rann Wild and Toby Green? I have *NEVER*, I repeat *NEVER* seen or heard you mention even once that you and I wrote songs together or that we shared lead vocals up until 1966. During the Golliwogs/Visions period, I wrote a song called "Walking on Water." I wrote the words and the melody, it's my song and it's also on the first Creedence LP. I shared it with you because of the Wild-Green partnership. You said I got the idea for it from some hypothetical song you wrote called "Tombstone Epitaph." I never heard that song. I got the idea for the chord changes from The Animals' "House of the Rising Sun" and the word/melody pattern from Them—"Mystic Eyes." Again, *you couldn't stand it* that somebody else in the band had talent, you wanted all the credit. Sometime next year, I'm going to negotiate with Jondora to buy *my* song back for [my publishing company] Woodmont Music.

You've never mentioned our producing partnership or my business acumen (remember I wrote the contracts, collected the money, made the phone calls, kept the books, etc.). Again, you would still lead everyone to believe that you did everything. . . . Somewhere along the line you began to believe your own press and the band went from "we" to "I" (John).

THAT'S WHY I LEFT!

In one of the many court cases that arose in the aftermath of Creedence's life, Doug described the friction between the two brothers in a formal deposition: "Tom clashed with John and said he felt restricted. He wanted to write songs and sing lead vocals, two creative areas in which John Fogerty dominated."

An "us vs. them" (or more correctly "him") mentality started to form in the group. At one point, Doug, Stu, and Tom considered collaborating on songs. "That wouldn't work," Tom admitted. "It was my fault. It was just polarizing the group. I just went one step further."

"He only left for the reasons that were bothering all of us," John conceded soon after the group broke up. "We weren't in touch with it—we didn't really know, we just felt kind of bad around each other because we, subconsciously I guess, were all responsible to the others for that feeling, whatever it was. None of us know what it was, of course."

"The fact of the matter is that Tom left because he was hip to John," Stu said bitterly many years later, reflecting the years of in-fighting and animosity that had occurred since the breakup of the band. "John never intended to 'let' any one else contribute anything."

In the midst of all this turmoil, *Pendulum* quickly peaked at number 5 on the U.S. album charts. It only hit number 23 on the English charts, just a few months after CCR topped them with *Cosmos*. "Have You Ever Seen the Rain" reached a U.S. chart peak at number 8 in March, topping out at number 36 about a month later in England. Even the B-side, "Hey Tonight," spent a hot minute on the charts in the U.S., peaking at number 90.

While they'd planned on touring through the winter, Tom's departure left them at loose ends. Instead, they decided it might be wise to take a cooling-off period. Looking for outside satisfaction, Doug had managed to produce *This House*, a record by Fantasy folk/blues musician Mark Spoelestra. "I almost went stir crazy," Doug said. "I don't ever want to do that again. I was so hungry to get back to work. The Spoelestra project came just at the right time. I knew I could learn something about recording and help him, so it was perfect for me."

Stu did the sound track for *The Museum*, a film starring Wendell Burton and shot by Stu's brother-in-law. He also agreed to produce the band Clover and spent some time in England. He was there when CCR supplanted the Beatles at the top of the *New Musical Express* popularity poll. A reporter for *NME* found Stu at a friend's apartment, perfecting his lead guitar skills on a Gibson acoustic.

"After Tom quit," Stu says, "John delivered an ultimatum to Doug and me—write and sing one third of the next album each or he would quit. We protested, saying that wasn't the goal, and it certainly wouldn't be a CCR album, but he insisted. Not being quitters, we tried to rise to the task at hand."

John continues to deny this. He asserts that the new, "democratic" CCR demanded that each member contribute equally. It all fell under the new egalitarian spirit introduced at the *Pendulum* party.

To get up to speed with the rigors of musical democracy, Stu and Doug took on the sound track and album production work. It allowed them to flex some muscles that Stu and Doug both knew they had to build. Both of them had to become more fluent musically in a big hurry if they were going to answer what they percieved as John's ultimatum. This gave John the time to take flying lessons and set up a home studio. He started a project that he'd been talking about for years.

At least since the early '70s, John had been telling the press that he wanted to make a totally solo album, on which he would play every instrument. "Really, I'd like to start making records completely on my own," he told a reporter in the spring of 1970. "I don't mean leave the group, but just to make a record where I play everything. I used to do that at home."

"I've always had a desire to do an album playing every instrument myself," he said in a another interview in the summer of 1970, "writing all the tunes, producing it, and everything . . . sort of what Paul McCartney has just done, but without my wife on it. It's still pretty far back in my mind and I don't have any immediate plans for anything like that now. . . . someday. . . ."

He had plenty of time for that, as things turned out. John's relationship with his wife, Martha, had hit the skids, to the point that by the time Tom left the band, John was living away from his family. "I wasn't real open about my feelings, even with my first wife," he concedes. "Back then, I was self-conscious about being direct or one-on-one with anybody."

So John started working on his one-man-band project. Using the same logic that fueled "Suzie Q," he decided that his best course of action would be an album of covers. He picked country music, a facet of his musical personality that he'd had to restrain in CCR.

So what was initially supposed to be a monthlong winter hiatus for the band stretched on into May, just about as long as the vacation Gail had originally recommended to Tom.

16

"BETTER AS A TRIO"

The remaining three members of CCR needed to do something so the public didn't think that the band had just evaporated and blown away in Tom's absence. The single of "Have You Ever Seen the Rain" peaked in March, and there was a danger of a singles chart appearing without a CCR record on it.

Ironically, also in March, Ike and Tina Turner put out their version of "Proud Mary." "Ike and Tina Turner opened several shows for CCR in 1970," Stu notes. "I believe this pairing gave rise to their version of 'Proud Mary.' We partied with the band, but never played the tune fast with them." John also cites a version of the song by a Phil Spector-produced band, the Checkmates. He found the versions similar. "Ike & Tina did it the fast way," he told *Rolling Stone*, "sort of like 'River Deep, Mountain High.' For me, it was almost like an Uncle Remus parody. But Ike and Tina gave it a whole new life." The cover version sold over a million copies, launching the Ike and Tina Turner Revue into the top five.

So CCR had to prepare for the studio and also had to hit the road. They had planned a three-month tour through the late winter and early spring, but canceled it when it became clear that the group would need to make some drastic changes following Tom's departure. The three original members had to get down to the business of working as a band again.

While the band regrouped, Saul Zaentz also kept busy. Fantasy's new company headquarters rose on the corner of Tenth and Parker in Berkeley. Zaentz started investing the capital he made via CCR in other ways as well. In May, he purchased Prestige records, a thirty-one-year-old jazz label formed by Bob Weinstock. The company had an archive of some of the best names in jazz, including John Coltrane, Miles Davis, Thelonious Monk, and Sonny Rollins.

Then there were three: CCR continues as a trio.

Zaentz went on a major shopping spree, picking up labels—mostly jazz-oriented ones—that solidified Fantasy's earlier position in that field. He bought Bill Grauer and Orin Keepnews's Riverside label out of bankruptcy. This added even more Monk to the library, not to mention Cannonball Adderly, Wes Montgomery, Bill Evans, and Barry Harris. He also picked up Keepnews's other label, Milestone, adding albums by Ron Carter, McCoy Tyner, and Lee Konitz. Through these acquisitions they developed a formidable library of jazz. He brought Keepnews on board to both help exploit these catalogs and to continue to record fresh sounds. "Fantasy has acquired so many other labels in the intervening years—Prestige, Riverside, Milestone, Contemporary, Specialty and Stax," notes company vice president Al Bendich, agreeing that the majority of the capital came as a result of the success of CCR.

Meanwhile, CCR was having troubles beyond just their personnel problems. With Tom no longer in the band, the National General TV special that they had rented a theater to show at the *Pendulum* unveiling suddenly became obsolete.

"The CCR special *In Concert* was surrounded by legal problems," Cook recalls. Indeed, the people who shot the special a year and a half previously couldn't find anyone to sponsor the program. The band thought the film was a dead issue. They understood that National General had to show the program within a year of production, which they took to mean after they filmed the concert in January 1970. However, they never signed any sort of contract with the company.

In a way they were glad the special wouldn't air. With Tom featured prominently, it smacked of history rather than the new trio image they needed to put forward. Even Tom didn't want it shown again. "We were promised artistic control," he told *Rolling Stone*, "but a lot of things that we said—that we wanted to get across—were cut out."

During the winter of 1971, National General sold out to Filmways, one of the bigger television distributors. Filmways finally found a sponsor and a network and set to air the show. Creedence tried to prevent them and Filmways filed suit against the band for interfering. Eventually, they reached an agreement. "A certain clause in the agreement allowed for a limited number of showings in syndication in the U.S.," says Stu. "After that, the master and all copies were supposed to be destroyed."

The special aired around the United States in June. Despite the band's trepidations, the critics in general enjoyed it. TV critic John J. O'Connor in the *New York Times* called it "first rate. The photography is excellent and the program works on its own terms, or perhaps for some, as a bit of nostalgia out to the incredibly recent past. . . . John Fogerty in plaid shirt and Prince Valiant bob, wails away at his admirers with superb professional polish. It's a nice group. It's a nice program."

"Considering all the adverse hype," wrote Don Buday in the *LA Free Press*, "the film is surprisingly good. . . . There are numerous inconsistencies, but director Bob Abel has covered a lot of ground and the editing is tight enough to keep the images flowing. The character monologues with parental references and background insights are effective. . . . The show is a vast improvement over the time that Creedence did the Ed Sullivan Show and performed 'Born on the Bayou' amidst a swamp setting with smoke pots which, I guess, was to create a foggy, vapor like effect."

With the extended break over, the original three Blue Velvets started punching the clock at the Factory again. "After Tom left and the band was a trio," Jake Rohrer recalls, "things got back to almost normal. There was this warmth among the members and support. John took off from this business of a new single up the chart every twelve weeks and we went touring, touring and partying. Things were very close and warm."

"For a band that had been playing three years without a break," Stu added at the time, "being away gave us some added perspective. It gave me a chance to look at what Creedence Clearwater Revival was all about and to see how important it was to me. I decided it was very important."

Courtesy Jake Rohrer

"I decided [Creedence] was very important," said Stu.

Late that spring, Creedence went into the studio with just two songs. One was a classic John Fogerty stomper called "Sweet Hitch-Hiker." It might have reflected his newfound freedom, or might have just been a show of bravado in the face of his recent separation from his wife. "It's about rock and roll girls in leather coats, and a lot of that stuff," Doug laughed. "I think he related that one to the mamas."

The other song they cut was "Door to Door." This one was inspired by one of Doug's many jobs held during the Golliwogs days. "I was a college student," Doug recalled, "and I was hard up to get a job. I was going to sell those pots and pans. I went through the training school—easy money in your spare time, right? But when the guy said, 'Here's the way to trick them into signing and they're hooked,' I just said, fuck you and good-bye."

The song marked a major first for the band. Although loosely based around Doug's experiences, as well as the pitfalls and pleasures of the door-to-door salesperson, it was written and sung by Stu. "It's the first Creedence song I've sung lead on," he said. "It was getting close to time to go into the studio and I brought it to rehearsal and showed it. John suggested I sing it and I was glad because in the back of my mind I really did want to sing it.

"Other parts of the inspiration were obscure," he added, citing his lyrics about the product that he's selling being effective "if you use it loosely wadded." This wording came from "the product use information on a pack of Kodak lens-cleaning tissue. The lyrics are soaked in mystical revelation and sexual innuendo."

This new order didn't thrill John, but he knew if he wanted a band, he had to give the other members some room. This had been building up since the "Proud Mary" showdown at Two Guys from Italy over two years earlier. "I realized there was no sense in trying to stop it any more," he begrudgingly said. "I had to acquire an 'arms length' agreement with myself. Just say, 'Well, go ahead and do it, but I don't have to tell myself that that's the very best that could be done at the time.' I had to convince myself that I could sit here and not have to be in charge and not have things the way I want them—good or bad."

John's discomfort was reflected in a number of interviews at the time. He felt this compromise was the only way to save the band he said to the *LA Times*'s Robert Hilburn, "It was either that, or not continue at all. We could have lasted another six months, perhaps, without the change. But that would have been worse than ever. We would really have begun to hate each other.

"I was able to accept it finally in my head that each artist has a valid contribution to make and that he is entitled to express it."

To *Melody Maker* critic Al Rudis, he admitted that compromise was the name of the game—while still equivocating over who was really compromising to make the band work. "We're all compromising," he told Rudis. "Well, really, I'm compromising because I didn't have to before. They're not compromising as much because they're gaining more. We are all producing now. We're each deciding what we want to sound like."

Stu saw the new egalitarianism in a more positive light. "We can be friends full time again. We don't have to second guess each other. We can just say what we feel. It's just the way we were in high school. It wasn't important who was the best writer or best musician. We just wanted to play in a rock 'n' roll band."

"It took us two days," Stu said about the actual recording of the single. "Well, it took us three days, but we wasted the first day just trying to get a sound on the drums. We'd been out of the studio so long we had to start all over again. But it took us two days to do the single, all the music, all the words, the mix, everything."

Once they got out of the studio, they started getting ready for their first tour as a trio, set to kick off early in July. As they were rehearsing, one of the major landmarks of their relative youth was set to disappear. Bill Graham, saying he was disillusioned with a rock scene that had bred mass commercialization, greedy performers, and drug abuse, announced he would close down his Fillmore Ballrooms on both coasts. He tried to make the closings an event, booking bands that had broken through at the Fillmore. Creedence, however, had slipped his mind. Knowing what they were going through, he actually didn't think they would play, but he called John to ask if they would at least be there for the last night of the Fourth of July weekend.

"I know you guys are switching from a quartet to a trio and don't feel like playing," he reportedly said, "but come over anyway."

"Why don't you ask us to play?" John replied.

"You wanna play?" Graham asked.

"Hell yes!" John responded. "Figure out how much you want to pay us and give it to some outfit fighting the drug battle."

Thus, Dr. Joel Fort's Fort Help got a four-figure check, and CCR debuted their trio on a bill with Santana and Tower of Power on the last night of the Fillmore West. "It was just like any other time playing the Fillmore," Stu reported, "except there was no one standing on my right."

The group leased a Lear jet for the tour, dubbing it the "Mondo Bizarro." "It was necessary," Stu says, "if we were going to party and get enough sleep."

The tour opened in Chicago, at the 8,500-seat International Amphitheater. "Although there was one less person on stage," wrote *Melody Maker* critic Al Rudis, "the sound was solidly still Creedence. . . . Hardly a word was spoken between numbers, which were all familiar except for the two on the new single. Bassist Stu Cook stepped forward for the first time to sing lead on one of these, 'Door to Door,' which he also wrote. Cook's voice is deeper than guitarist John Fogerty's, but has just as much fire. . . . The monumental stature of Creedence's hits made the audience waiver between reverence and unrestrained enthusiasm."

"I sang 'Door to Door' between 'It Came Out of the Sky' and 'Travelin' Band,'" Stu said. "It's a tough act to follow and a tougher one to precede."

By July 17, they'd made it to New York, where they played the Forest Hills Tennis Stadium. The *New York Times*'s Mike Jahn found Tom's loss noticeable, saying, "The group's dynamic hard rock and blues sound seemed flat, rather a shell of the music it presented during last year's New York appearance." Conversely, *Billboard*'s Fred Goodman noted, "The loss of Tom Fogerty did not seem to bother anyone, although there were times at which a rhythm guitar would have been nice. Creedence is one of the few groups that maintains a high artistic level as their popularity increases."

The next leg of the tour sent them for a month in Europe. Before they left, "Sweet Hitch-Hiker" peaked on the charts at number 6 in the United States, where it sold over a million copies. In England, it made it only as high as number 36.

With that news, they were off to Europe. Since John was on his way to Europe, and since he was now "at liberty" as far as his marriage was concerned, the first thing he wanted to do was get in touch with Lucy.

"On the second European tour," Rohrer recollects, "I remember we had the name of the club she worked at. We called her up and said, 'We're coming!' In the middle of this European tour, we cut out ten days and went to Copenhagen and just stayed in Copenhagen and John developed a relationship with Lucy. She wound up touring Japan and Australia with us. She was a lovely, spirited woman, but the relationship didn't last."

Stu and Doug wanted to record the tour for a possible live album. John wasn't so sure, but because the majority ruled, he went along with it. So, along with the usual entourage and equipment, Russ Gary and a slew of tape recorders traveled with the band.

The tour started in Manchester on September 5. "Creedence blew an outrageously precise set of loud, bitchy rock 'n' roll," wrote Roy Hollingsworth in *Melody Maker*. "It was too fast, too clean-cut, rather like showing you a slide show of excellent pictures and changing slides every half second. . . . Fogerty's also so well amplified and mixed that only well-trained ear specialists would be able to note any difference between studio and live work. Yes, it's as precise as all that."

The band seemed relaxed and in good spirits during this trip. The tour was marked by the trio riding bicycles into hotel lobbies for press conferences singing "There's No Business Like Show Business." John actually got up and jammed with opening act Tony Joe White after hours in a club in Berlin. At a press conference in Belgium, the hotel put out four chairs for the band. When the trio walked out and saw that, John quipped, "Well, I guess that sets us up for the first question."

The band was so upset with Hollingsworth's review of the Manchester show, they invited him to a later gig in Hamburg. Meeting the band before the show, he observed, "They're a bit clean. You'd let them marry your daughter."

He also liked the show better. "They blew a magnificent set in Hamburg that night. They were ten times better than Manchester, they went wild and Creedence wild is some good experience. Fogerty for instance, becomes raunchy to the extent of being cruel, and the last ten minutes was such a bellyful of hot things that an encore would have been physically impossible.

"Fogerty, in his white suit and dudey boots, and with sweat just drip-dripping down his face. Clifford whose gaze becomes frightening, and his action often crippling in pace and bleeding with feeling. Can't work without Cook though, he's so straight with delivery that even the mike stand looks crooked."

Once again they ended their European sojourn with two sold-out nights at Royal Albert Hall. "Other bands may have problems of musicianship ver-

Courtesy Jake Rohrer

The trio, live.

sus content, but for Creedence Clearwater Revival, such sophisticated troubles would seem laughable," wrote Robin Denselow in the *Guardian*. "In their own terms, they are probably the last rock band left on earth: They have the directness and vitality. . . . They simply stood on stage and belted out a series of their hit singles and waited for the hall to erupt around them."

The jam sessions in the hotel rooms took on a decidedly country twist during this tour. "We'd always come back to the hotel and play, just for ourselves and friends," John said.

> We'd have a party in the hotel room. At least, everyone else was having a party—I was learning to play steel guitar! A lot of people would show up—local guys and girls—expecting Creedence Clearwater, you know, loud rock and roll. I'd sit down and start playing steel, playing I guess what they'd call Okie music, hillbilly music. Pretty soon the neighbors are coming over—not to complain, but to join in. Got to admit though, the police did show up a couple of times—we called that a Stage III alert—joining in wasn't exactly what they had in mind."

"We'd have these sessions," Jake Rohrer recalls. "The show after the show was really the show. I'd sit in with them. God, Tony Joe White or Duck Dunn, who ever we were touring with would join in and we'd have these incredible hotel sessions where we would play everything and anything. We played a lot of country music and John really got interested in it."

"CCR was into country music," Stu adds.

We even had a country alter ego band, the Shit Kicker Three. I believe it started after Tom left. The 'Shit Kicker Three from Room 73' is named after a hotel room in Manchester, England, I think. John on pedal steel, Doug on a practice drum set, and me on guitar. Lot's of Merle Haggard, Buck Owens, Jimmie Rodgers, etc. We'd come back to the hotel after a show and play country music and drink all night. Some fun, huh?

On their previous European tour, there had been flack about the promoters, who the band felt were gouging the audience. On this tour, the tickets were about ten dollars less each, but that caused another worry. The tour lost money. "When I talk about losing money," longtime band road manager Bruce Young told Robert Hilburn, "I'm speaking in hundreds. The problem is you can't find good halls big enough to pay for the high cost of the show."

Like so much about Creedence, the show was deceptive in its simplicity. "You could cut costs by not bringing your own sound and lighting," Young added, "but Creedence wants to put on the same quality show in Amsterdam as it does in London or Los Angeles."

Shortly after returning from Europe, they did their annual show in Honolulu and then spent a couple of weeks vacationing in Maui. Then they finished the tour, playing the West Coast, kicking off with a show at the Forum in Los Angeles. "Creedence Clearwater Revival sounds even better as a trio," Nat Freedland reported in *Billboard*. "The sound is leaner and less cluttered with a single guitar and bass trading power blues phrases over the impressively dynamic drumming of Doug Clifford. . . . Creedence seems obviously happy to be playing at the big hall and taking home the bread."

They concluded the tour with a show in the Oakland Coliseum, before 13,000 people. "Creedence is the quintessence of rock and roll," wrote one reviewer. "They have absorbed all the roots, substance and messages of the medium, added their own personal experience, contemporized their general thrust and mastered the art of the three minute single. . . . From the moment after they finished 'Proud Mary' when the audience rushed the stage, packing the arena front (and Stu Cook admonishing 'all those people with the flashlights' to go home), the entire 13,000 seat Coliseum was a madhouse."

Now all that remained for the trio was to translate all of that into a new album.

17

"YOU DO YOURS AND I'LL DO MINE"

Tom had not been idle while his former bandmates were gallivanting around the world. After a few months of domestic tranquillity, he felt like he wanted to burst. "After I quit," he related, "I found that in just sitting around, I was frustrating my playing talents, which was as bad as the way I'd felt in the group."

So Tom embarked on his solo career, with the proviso that when "the gig is over, I can drive home." Around the time his old bandmates were in the studio cutting "Sweet Hitch-Hiker" and "Door to Door," Tom was at work on his single "Good-bye Media Man." While the record didn't chart, he did-n't particularly care. At least he was out there, and for the first time in per-haps six years, he was out there on his own terms.

"When I finished the single," Tom said, "I decided that I hadn't really clarified my own approach to music, so I went out and played some more."

"We shot a video for the song 'Good-bye Media Man,'" Merl Saunders remembers. "It was me, Bill Vitt, Tom. It was before MTV. It was that kind of shoot, in the studio with us playing, in color. It was outrageous. I don't know whatever happened to it."

Tom used this as a time to experiment and rediscover the joy and fun of playing. He also wanted to experience the process for himself again. He had done what John said for so long, even the clerical side of the studio felt good. The financial side became secondary.

"I'm not adverse to making money, but I'm happy right now," Tom added. "I'm concerned with the creative part of it, but I have to be able to take care of the business of recording—like making sure studio time is booked and that everyone fills out his W-2 form."

Robert Christgau slammed Tom's debut single, writing: " 'Good-bye Media Man,' Tom Fogerty's first single as a single, is unextraordinary musi-cally, simplistic lyrically, and also Tom doesn't sing too good. Part II is better than Part I, should you run into it on a jukebox in Lodi; it's also shorter and has less words."

In the fall, while CCR partied their way through Europe, Tom hunkered down in the studio with Merl Saunders, who had played keyboards on "Media Man." While not well known outside of the Bay Area, around San Francisco and Oakland Saunders was something of a legend. When Tom said he was going out to play some more, that's what he meant.

"Jerry Garcia and I were hanging out together and Tom came a couple of times," Saunders explained. "I said, 'Tom, you've got to come up here and play with us, you know.' Tom fell in love with what we were doing. We were called the Group in the beginning. Just called the Group." Tom played on Saunders's debut album, *Fire Up*, along with their mutual longtime buddy Jerry Garcia. Tom would work with them often during his solo career.

"I don't ever want to be a producer who sits behind the glass," Tom said. "I want to play on all the records I produce."

"I had Walter and Edward Hawkins and their sisters singing background for Jerry on my first record," Saunders says. "There was also a group called Tower of Power."

Meanwhile, the remaining members of CCR had a new bit of grief to deal with. Upon their return from Hawaii, they were served with papers notifying them that Arco Industries, which held Venice music and the copyrights to Little Richard's "Good Golly Miss Molly," had filed suit against John and one of Fantasy Records' publishing companies, Jondora. The suit alleged that "Traveling Band" plagiarized "Good Golly," which CCR had covered on *Bayou Country*.

"Probably," notes Stu, "because the song is a direct cop of Little Richard's style. They claimed it was a ripoff of 'Good Golly Miss Molly.' I always thought it sounded more like 'Long Tall Sally.' Of course, Little Richard wasn't above quoting himself, either. Fantasy settled the lawsuit by buying the song from Venice Music."

After the short tour, John ran off to Europe for two months without telling anyone, ostensibly to spend time with Lucy, although no one but John knows for certain. "He came back very bitter and very strange," Doug recalled. "He told us, 'Neither of you can sing my songs because I have a completely unique voice, and I won't sing on yours.'"

Despite all of the problems, the band was still commercially viable. By the end of 1971, they had sold more than $100 million of records and tapes.

In January, the band went into the studio for two weeks to record. *Mardi Gras* would be their seventh album in five years, but their first in over a year, their first as a trio, and their first under the new "democracy," so highly touted at the *Pendulum* party just a year earlier.

"Because their work will be compared against Fogerty's work," Robert Hilburn wrote in his review, "and because this album is Creedence's first since *Pendulum* was released in late 1970, Cook and Clifford couldn't have picked a more difficult place to begin their singing and songwriting efforts."

John denied having told Doug and Stu that they *had* to write. According to Stu, however, he did deliver such an ultimatum, and soon expanded the parameters. "John had required that Doug and I write/sing at least one third each of the *Mardi Gras* album," Stu recalls. "We protested, but it was basically the condition for his involvement. Doug and I aren't quitters. If John wanted out at that time, he could've said so. John wouldn't even play on our songs, other than rhythm guitar on the tracks. It was as though Doug and I were each doing a solo album."

"He wouldn't sing, he wouldn't play lead guitar," Stu added. "I had to teach myself to play lead guitar.

"I immediately said, 'John, that's bullshit, that won't fly. That will not even be Creedence, at least not as the fans know it. It's not something that I want to do.' He said, 'If we're going to do this album, this is the way we're going to do it.' "

However, engineer Russ Gary remembers that John was involved on some of the others' tracks. "He played leads on some of their stuff," Gary maintains. "I know Stu had made the statement that John had only played rhythm. I believe he played a solo on 'Tearing Up the Country,' Doug's song. The one on 'Door to Door' was John."

Still, John made it difficult for Stu and Doug to measure up to his level of achievement. "John made us run the hundred-yard dash before we could walk," Doug complained.

"I'm not sure what John had in mind," says Jake Rohrer.

I was flabbergasted when he held Doug and Stu to Tom's notion of "artistic democracy." I thought things had returned to normal after Tom split. I remember John putting his arms around Stu and Doug in the back of a limo, calling them his closest companions, just before he went off to Europe at the end of the tour. But I have no doubt that when they got ready to do an album, John told them: "You do yours and I'll do mine." Maybe, when something worked as well as Creedence, you shouldn't mess with it. I don't think Doug and Stu were in any hurry to come out and do several songs each. They wanted more support from John and apparently he wasn't too keen about helping. John was basically saying, "This is what you wanted. Now you can do it." Would John's support have made any difference in the relative failure of *Mardi Gras*? It might have saved the relationship. All the love in the back of that limo got sacrificed as well.

"When they were making that album," Tom recalls, "the guys were at each other's throats and there wasn't a whole lot of cooperation."

John pleaded innocence, saying that he couldn't stop the other band members from doing what they wanted to do. "I'm not even in the realm of 'is the stuff any good or not.' That's not the criterion. If someone wants to do something bad enough, you're foolish to try and stop it after a point. . . . I'm trying to be totally fair across the board about it," John told Joel Selvin at the time, commenting on Stu's tune "Door to Door." "It's not the kind of song I would write, which is the reason I didn't say anything. It's not like there's anything less there because I didn't sing it. I think Stu sang it really well. I think that side of the single sounds better, as far as recording, than 'Sweet Hitch-Hiker.' It's a better sounding record. If you want to take apart songs and all that, I don't think the song itself was all that great and if it was coming from Jim Webb I would have jumped all over it—or if it were coming from me. But it wasn't. It was Stu's first song."

"I've written a couple dozen songs, I guess, altogether," Stu said, defending the song. "Some of them I didn't finish. That just happened to be the one I thought would make the best record at the time. Not necessarily the best song I've written. At that point in the life of Creedence, I thought that would be the best one of mine."

Ironically, the one-third each formula was all they could get away with legally. Whether or not they consulted their contract before agreeing to work this way, John was legally bound to sing at least a third of the album: "In the event that the number of Artists in the Group is reduced to three (3), no less than thirty-three and one third per cent (33 1/3 %) of the masters required to be recorded by the Group . . . shall feature vocal performances by John C. Fogerty, provided that John C. Fogerty is a member of such reduced group."

The 28 minutes and 43 seconds of *Mardi Gras* often sounds like a death rattle. Though bandmembers deny it, many interpret the lyrics as little inter-band memos. In "Sail Away," Stu sings, "Spent a long time listening to the captain of the sea/Shouting orders to his crew/No one hears but me."

"Fogerty once told me he really liked 'Sail Away,' " Stu recalls ironically.

John contributed "Lookin' for a Reason" to the volley. A song that had more to do with the Hank Williams's tunes he was cutting for his semicon-cealed solo album, it was easily the most countrified song CCR ever recorded. Yet, lyrically, there was no doubt about where he aimed the song. "John was having trouble at home," Doug recalled. "Things were falling apart for the guy. It was a real terrible time for him. He was looking for a reason to stay there and looking for a reason to stay in the band."

Doug answered this with "What Are You Gonna Do?" Stu hoped that John would "Take It Like a Friend."

"Unfortunately," John commented ironically, "we had the Beatles as role models. 'I wanna be Ringo!' 'I wanna sing!' 'I wanna write songs.' Yeah, unfortunately, that wasn't our makeup. If our drummer was singing, I didn't want to play guitar in that band."

Yet, amid all the disharmony, *Mardi Gras* has two crystalline moments: one was the sprightly rockabilly version of "Hello Mary Lou"; the other was "Someday Never Comes." Sung in his most harrowing tenor, John pulled this song from his guts as a writer and a performer.

"My parents divorced when I was young," John said. "My wife and I separated around that time. We got back together for a long time and eventually did divorce, which is a very sad thing. The song was basically me talking about how it happened to me when I was young, and here I go, doing the same damn thing."

"That song was for Josh," Rohrer explains. "John and Martha were estranged and living apart when John and Lucy were happening. John was struggling."

"John had left home," Doug expanded. "He left his family and his little boy. His father left him when he was a child and had a divorce. John felt very guilty about it, and very bad. It was a deep, deep, deep song. It was the most personal song John ever did. I think it's a beautiful song. It's a song that really didn't get it's just reward, since the album was so strange."

"I've always felt 'Someday Never Comes' was John's finest song," Stu says. "It brought tears to my eyes, as well."

One of the ironies of *Mardi Gras* was that it was the first CCR album where the songwriters controlled their publishing. In the original contract they signed with Fantasy, all of the music and arrangements of works in the public domain (like "Cotton Fields") became "the subject of a copyright and [was] assigned by the Artists . . . to any publishing company or companies designated by [Fantasy]." However, when they renegotiated their contract and set up the offshore trust, one of the stipulations they changed had to do with the publishing. As of 1971, anything the band wrote could be "assigned by the Artists or their respective successors in interest to a publishing company or companies of their choice."

So the three remaining members formed publishing companies for their songs, earning all of the royalties this entailed, and not just the songwriter money. For all intents and purposes, this doubled the amount the band made as songwriters, just in time for Stu and Doug to share the wealth. And there was an initial bit of wealth to be had, as each album paid the members an equal share of the royalties. Like *Pendulum* before it, when *Mardi Gras* came out, it shipped gold.

Mardi Gras.

Mardi Gras was also the first CCR album not to have the band on the cover; instead it had a picture of a young girl in gypsy clothes shaking a tambourine. "Yeah, it's my mother's great-aunt or grandmother or something. My sister came up with that," Rohrer says. His sister, Mary Walsh, would be called the band's administrative assistant today. She took care of correspondence, including laying out *The Fifth Street Flash*. "She's quite a photographer, and she was doing some darkroom work at the time and was messing around with some old family prints. She does coloration on old black and white prints. Somehow or other, that one just got thrown onto the table one day, and they liked it."

"The girl in the photo looked like a Mardi Gras party queen," Stu notes. "It was supposed to be a subtle reference to the 'swamp rock' tag we got stuck with. New Orleans, bayous, etc. At this point CCR had become more of a country band than a rock band, anyhow."

Ellen Willis agreed in her review of *Mardi Gras* in *The New Yorker*. She also noted that "Country rock is the number one cheapo commodity in pop music; it has long since become boring and politically obnoxious besides. . . . So, on first hearing, it struck me as a lapse of taste that *Mardi Gras* should include a country-western song by Fogerty, a good-time number by Clifford, and Gene Pitney's 'Hello Mary Lou.' On the other hand, Creedence has always had good instincts in such matters and I decided that some sort of comment must have been intended. My faith was rewarded when I listened to the lyrics of . . . 'Lookin' for a Reason.' . . . The songs slide down easy, and most people will either dismiss them or batten on them."

The reviews were not all bad for this experiment. Some people understood that *Mardi Gras*, on an artistic level, marked the growing pains of a group in major flux.

"The highlight of the album is Fogerty's 'Someday Never Comes,' a song that may rank with 'Proud Mary' as the finest thing he's ever written," wrote Robert Hilburn.

Greil Marcus in *Creem* agreed:

I found myself in the midst of a song so overwhelming, so true and so unflinching I started to cry and would have called John Fogerty to thank him if his number was listed. I played it again and again and finally quit when I realized the song was stronger than I was. . . . It was a much more likable album than *Pendulum*, which is the coolest and most consistent Creedence ever made. This one had more personality and more life. Creedence had made a decision to smash the dictatorship of John Fogerty and replace genius with equality. . . . After Creedence reconstituted itself, their first assumption was that the music had to be shared; the question of whose songs were best could not be controlling. If things had not been put on this basis, the band would have broken up and this brings in the Genius vs. Equality dichotomy. I don't think Fogerty could survive as an artist outside of this little band. I think working with musicians who have known him for more than ten years, who represent, in some way, his roots and his history, keeps Fogerty in touch with himself and keeps him honest.

Bob Christgau gave the record an A-minus in his original "Consumer Guide" review (a well-regarded column that continues to run monthly in *The Village Voice*), revising it to a B when he reprinted it in his '70s *Record*

Guide. "For a while, I forgot my John Fogerty fixation and enjoyed side two of this country rock debut, which is what asking Stu Cook and Doug Clifford to sing and compose transforms the seventh Creedence album into. But facts are facts. Only 'Sweet Hitch-Hiker,' an original as unambitious as the equally effective cover of 'Hello Mary Lou,' could stand on any of Creedence's great albums. 'Lookin' for a Reason' and 'Someday Never Comes' may be major songs, but it's hard to tell from the way Fogerty sings them. And only inspired Fogerty vocals might save C&C's competent-plus to competent-minus filler from a lifetime in Lodi."

"*Mardi Gras*," wrote Arthur Levy in *Zoo World*, "is understood to be the first step in the next incarnation of Creedence Clearwater Revival, an often humorous, silly, human album that's next to impossible to ignore once listened to several times. . . . A year from now, Cook will be the most versatile singer of the three, the most stylish. . . . Bearded Doug Clifford writes with even a more sensitive, personal human regard than Cook. . . . 'Someday Never Comes' [is] in the tradition of successful CCR singles. . . . with Fogerty using his technique of hooking you into the song with a simple, mind-blowing moral built into the chorus. . . . Has it really been a year since 'Sweet Hitch-Hiker'? To those hard-core CCR followers it was like *The Day the Earth Stood Still*. But you can all relax. Gort's turned the power back on. CCR is back (changed a bit—live with it for a week before you decide)."

Of course, many heard the death rattle and weren't willing to whitewash it. "To put it simply," Michael Oldfield wrote in *Melody Maker*, "much of this album doesn't sound like Creedence Clearwater Revival. . . . 'Sweet Hitch-Hiker' is the only cut which sounds like Creedence. Fogerty, in fact, takes vocals on only four numbers and for two of these he has affected a new accent which makes him sound like a refugee from the Grand Ol' Opry. Drummer Doug Clifford and bassist Stu Cook sing three numbers each— disastrously. . . . 'Hello Mary Lou' is a straight imitation of Ricky Nelson's version. It's hard to believe that this is (almost) the same band that tore through rock 'n' roll standards such as Roy Orbison's 'Ooby Dooby' like a knife through butter."

The most scathing (and famous) summation of the album came from noted rock journalist Jon Landau in *Rolling Stone*: "In the future, *Mardi Gras* may be known as Fogerty's revenge. After all the carping about his egotism, and after the published complaints from his co-workers about his hogging the show, he has done what I never thought he would: allowed his cohorts to expose themselves in public. Ceding six of the new album's ten selections to drummer Doug Clifford and bassist Stu Cook may have been an invitation to artistic suicide for them, but it sure proves that John was right all along. Commercially, it leaves him trying to answer the new $64 Creedence Clearwater Revival question: Will the group be able to survive the catastrophe? And who will really care?. . . . *Pendulum* was a disappointment but it was honest and it was useful—just because it showed Fogerty reaching for new directions. On this album, he seems to have just given up. The result is, relative to a group's established level of performance, the worst album I have ever heard from a major rock band."

In February, between recording *Mardi Gras* and releasing it, the band went overseas again, playing in Australia and Japan. The entire Japanese leg of the tour sold out in two days, a month in advance. "The Japanese rioted at CCR's concert at the Budokan in '72," recalls Stu.

The Grammy awards offered the band yet another awkward moment. Although they were the reigning band in the world and had ridden high on the charts and critically for over two years, CCR had never won—or even been nominated for—a Grammy. However, at the March presentations for the 1971 awards, Ike and Tina Turner won the Best R&B Performance model of that year's little gramophone statuette for their version of "Proud Mary." "It's the closest I ever came to winning a Grammy," Fogerty lamented in *Rolling Stone.*

By the time the *Mardi Gras* hit the record stands, the band had hit the road again. Playing mostly through the heartland of America, they toured for close to six weeks. "Perhaps the biggest excitement generated was when the trio began the opening strains of their best-known number, 'Proud Mary,'" Lane Crockett of the *Journal* wrote of a show in Shreveport. "Deafening cheers broke out and 'peace signs' were waved in the air."

Despite the crowd's enthusiasm, John was disheartened by the tour, particularly the demands to perform the group's new material. "The review in *Rolling Stone* called *Mardi Gras* the worst album made by a major group, and they were right. The review didn't offend me; it was drivel. The only thing worse was going on tour and doing those songs live. The audiences could tell. We were so bad they started throwing money at us. I'm not kidding. I've still got a quarter I saved from Denver. Doug was singing whatever he was singing and I was getting pelted. I felt like throwing them, too."

The Denver show was the last time CCR would play together professionally.

18

"THE SUCCESS BECAME A NIGHTMARE"

If you believed Greil Marcus, *Mardi Gras* was an outstanding experiment in rock egalitarianism; if you took Jon Landau's point of view, *Mardi Gras* set CCR up to self-destruct. Either way, it became pretty evident that even in the newly democratized Creedence Clearwater Revival, Fogerty still ruled. He even seemed to have a parachute to use when the Mondo Bizarro went down in flames.

"The group hadn't officially broken up," Jake Rohrer recalls of John starting work on the *Blue Ridge Rangers* project:

It was John's project. The group was still together at the time. It was just something that he wanted to do, and he did it. There was some grumbling from Stu and Doug that John was putting his efforts into his own project, that John was putting his energies and talents into *Blue Ridge Rangers* rather than into *Mardi Gras*. He had this *Rangers* project on his mind for a couple of years before he did it. I imagine that brought some dissension. I don't recall it being open and out there, but I sensed it.

Doug and Stu don't have any doubts. "He deliberately set up the album to break up the band and blow it all apart," Doug fumed seven years later. "He obviously did a good job."

Stu is even more bitter:

Never having written or sung at the level of John's previous work, we took the heat. John set me and Doug up to take the blame for breaking up CCR, and then remained silent about it for twenty-five years. How does he think it raises him by letting us take the fall for *Mardi Gras*?

Harry Goodwin/Starfile

"He deliberately set the album up to break up the band," said Doug.

The focus of the media was John. That made it all the easier for him to run his BS on them. Doug and I never had the platform. We thought of "going public" with this information, but actually decided at the time that it would damage the memory of CCR if we ended up in a public pissing contest. The Lennon/McCartney feud was very fresh in our minds. That turns out to have been a bad decision, as the years of having to explain what happened to one person at a time have been painful, to say the least. The word will get out on this, believe me.

"I didn't want to do that album," John insists about *Mardi Gras*, reasserting that it was the band's decision to have each member contribute equally. "But it was a 'democracy,' you see. I'm sitting there saying 'This is terrible, this is worse than the Golliwogs,' and they're saying 'Sorry, two-to-one against.' Why make a record with an obvious stinko cut—just to appease one of the other musicians?"

But Stu maintains it was John who dictated that he and Doug participate equally and embarassed them by not helping them with their early songwriting efforts. "It was John's decision. I've no problem with that. He could've quit at any time, BEFORE we went down the *Mardi Gras* road. The fact that he laid down the terms for *Mardi Gras*, and then remained silent about the fallout is what takes the shine off. The world jumped to the conclusion that we forced it on him. That made us the 'bad guys.' NOTHING could be further from the truth."

"Soon enough," says John, "it all fell apart in front of my eyes. After the tyranny, fourteen months later, *Mardi Gras* came out. Ever since that album came out, the guys have spent the next twenty-seven years proclaiming, 'It wasn't our idea. John made us do that.' Baloney! All you have to do is go back and read the articles. The guys had seized the reins of power. Critics at the time called *Mardi Gras* 'Fogerty's revenge.' My only question is, revenge for what? God forbid, we had a worldclass outfit with a name that was revered and honored. Yet here we were, trashing it ourselves."

"Looking back now," John told Joe Smith in 1988, "I wish we'd had an outside manager instead of me. If we'd had a Brian Epstein, maybe we could have all been screaming at him, which would have taken the burden off of me. I know now it would have been wiser to have a fall guy."

These pressures built up, especially when the band faced the half-filled venues on the last tour. "The business pressures that John took on by trying to do everything—on and off stage—it grew to more pressure than anyone could handle, not just John," Stu observed. "Business partnerships are much more intense than a marriage, especially in a creative profession."

While the band liked to refer to him as a tyrant, John himself saw himself as "The General." "I was not popular in my own band," he reflected. "There's an old war movie where the guy says, 'When you put on the clothes of the general, you cannot be popular with your own men.'"

In the mean time, *Mardi Gras* peaked at number 12 in July having sold a million copies. "Someday Never Comes" was released as a single along with the album. It hit a chart peak of number 25 toward the end of May. However, the album didn't even chart in England.

Pursuing his declaration of freedom, Tom released his first solo album, and it hit the charts rising to number 78. It had its moments. "My Pretty Baby" actually harked back to Tom's roots, an a cappella song recalling the days of doo-wop. Several tunes took potshots at his brother, especially "The Me Song," sort of a manifesto about why he had left CCR. "This is not quite incompetent," wrote Robert Christgau acidly, "but it is exceptionally unoriginal—even a pretension or two would be welcome. Good thing identity crises weren't as fashionable in the days of David and Ricky Nelson."

That summer, the band checked their parachutes. John worked in earnest on his country music solo project. Stu and Doug had meetings with Russ

Gary about forming a production company, an idea that germinated while they were recording the concerts in Europe earlier in the year. Doug started to work on a solo album.

"Right after the band broke up, Doug Clifford made a record," Gary recalls. "Just before the end of the breakup, when everybody knew it was coming, Doug and Stu and I hired Wally Heider's truck to record his album at the Factory." So, although all the band members were busy, CCR lay in limbo.

"I think we all began to feel uncomfortable in Creedence," John said in 1973. "We began to feel trapped or restricted in ways. There were a lot of different ways we could have solved that problem, I suppose. And we didn't—well, no one ever does look at everything. At the time it was too vital, we were too interested in it, we were too close, and as a result we were all too uptight from it."

"The result was not the easier, looser, more relaxed thing we all had hoped it would be," he added. "The end result was more uptight for all of us. I would get uptight because I couldn't have my way, then I'd feel guilty for having those kinds of feelings. The tension reached a peak for me around *Mardi Gras*, but it wasn't just rough on me. It was rough on us all . . . we were all conscious things were getting more and more fragile. They were wondering what I was going to do . . . and I was wondering. I felt damned if I did, damned if I didn't."

"At that point," Doug concurred, "we should have called it a day, realizing we weren't a band anymore if we weren't going to share in the process. You've been together for fourteen years, and you love each other like brothers and you've been through as many things as we have. The last thing I ever wanted to do was to give up Creedence. Maybe it overshadowed my better judgment."

"Finally," John said, citing the fuse lit during the long-ago dinner at Two Guys from Italy, "the bomb exploded."

"John came to my house and said he didn't want to play with Doug and I any longer," Stu recalls. "At this point, the vibe was not good. By the time he decided he didn't like the 'monster' he had created, we were all ready to toss it in."

In one of the more pithy notes on the band's breakup, critic Greg Shaw observed, "Creedence Clearwater Revival called it quits. . . . If they couldn't be equal, they couldn't be John's backup band any longer either."

Interestingly, in his liner notes chronology for the *Chronicle* album, Rohrer cites the band breaking up in July. They didn't announce it, however, until October 16. "We don't regard this as breaking up," they said in a press release. "We look at it as an expansion of our activities. We will devote our time to individual rather than group projects."

"Ever since Tom split," Rohrer told *Rolling Stone*, "the rumors persisted that Creedence had split up. . . . People were wondering what the hell was going on."

At the time, label chief Saul Zaentz weighed in, saying, "They've got to do what they've got to do. Otherwise, later they'll be kicking themselves in the ass for not doing what they wanted to do. I look forward to it positively. If they are happy in their work they are going to produce better records."

In their three and a half years together, Creedence Clearwater Revival netted fifteen gold disks, seven for albums and eight for singles. They sold around twenty million albums and ten million singles all told, garnering at least $75 million in sales, putting them in a league with Elvis, the Beatles, and Bing Crosby.

"It was the biggest American thing—at least as far as groups go," Stu commented when the group announced that they were breaking up. "And one of the bigger international things."

"We always had this incredible golden rainbow, Emerald City or whatever, that dream up there," John reflected. "Once we were inside the gates, it was pretty good up until the last couple of years, until the time Tom left. That took a lot of wind out of our sails. . . . The good part was so good, I think it took me a long time to realize and admit that I was bugged by it. Doug and Stu were in touch with it longer."

"Everything that could have gone right went right," Doug mused nearly a decade later, "and everything that could have gone wrong went wrong. We grew up as kids together and before all the crap and the success, we were together for ten years. We had a dream which came true far beyond our wildest expectations."

John gave perhaps his most honest assessment of the group's brief success to record executive Joe Smith in 1988:

> The success became a nightmare, a wonderful love affair gone sour. The end of Creedence was like what Will Rogers said about real estate. They ain't making any more of it."
>
> With Creedence, we had a pretty good run of records and on every one of them I grumbled about something. I was always the grumbling leader of the band and I think I drove everyone else nuts . . . Every single we ever made was practically the top of our musical ability. Whatever got released was the absolute best take we could do. That's just the way we were. The great thing

about Creedence to me was that we had a style. That's something studio musicians don't have. They may have incredible chops, but I'll take style any day.

The tragedy with us is that we weren't ready to hang it up, and I feel like the
rug was pulled out from under us."

"After ten years of hard work climbing up the music ladder," Doug stated
in a deposition given nearly twenty-five years later, "Revival lasted as an
active band for only three and a half years. All our music, hits and albums
were created and recorded in that period of time."

However, in many ways, this is where the story really begins.

Part Three

PUT US IN COACH

1972–1987

19

"HE WANTED TO PLAY ALL THE POSITIONS"

One of the key passages in the press release announcing the group's breakup noted that the group would remain with Fantasy Records as artists, producers, and writers. While the announcement (and Zaentz's comments made to the press at the time) insinuated that they had a choice in the matter, actually they did not.

In their contract, they agreed that "in the event any one (1) or more of the Artists shall so leave the group . . . [the group] does hereby grant to [Fantasy] exclusively the services of any such individual for the purpose of making records. With respect to any such member, [the group] shall execute a form of term recording agreement substantially similar to this. . . ."

Therefore, all of the former members of CCR were bound to the contract for the term of the contract. That term ostensibly ended on December 31, 1974, a little over two years after the group broke up. However, there was another, more thorny provision in the contract. The group agreed to deliver a certain number of recordings every year. If they didn't, these got pushed into the recordings the group owed the company for the next year. At Fantasy's discretion, according to the terms of the contract, they could extend it to a "later date as suspensions or extensions of this Agreement may require."

"Fantasy's big mistake was in not treating us better," Cook says. "They could have made a deal with John for the ownership of his old songs, even at some point during the band's success if not later. They could've given the band a better recording contract. But they're the kind of folks who, when it suits them, will 'live with the deal we have.' That's called business. In the music business, as in other mixtures with the arts, there will always be this tension."

"We were always negotiating for a better contract and asking them let's try and get this thing a little bit more together than on a jazz level," Tom noted. "Here we are, supposedly the top group in the world, why don't you come through?"

For the first time in three years, there was no massive fall gathering in Maui. Instead the former members of the band were getting their solo careers underway. Within a month of the announcement, three former Creedence members put out new records.

The group's breakup coincided with several major events in Doug's life. In September, his wife, Laurie, gave birth to their second son, Grady. About that same time, Doug gave birth himself, the first of the three to hit the market with a solo recording. In addition to featuring Stu on acoustic rhythm guitar, *Cosmo* sported a fair number of impressive musicians.

Anyone looking for a Creedence Clearwater Revival record, or even a knockoff, would be sorely disappointed. *Cosmo* fell in closer to a blue-eyed, blonde-bearded, southern soul record. Duck Dunn's bass only added to this feel, as did the Hawkins Family's backing vocals, Steve Miller's organ work, and the mighty Tower of Power Horns. Adding to the countrified feel, Clover guitarist John McFee injected some pedal steel and slide work, as well as his usually tasteful licks. The album's weakest element, unfortunately, reflected badly on Doug—so soon after CCR's demise, he still composed in the shadow of John Fogerty. That shadow proved long and dark. While "Swingin' in a Hammock" had all the good time rock and roll feel any tune could muster, most of Doug's songs lacked subtlety and nuance. The record was well played, but hollow at the core.

"Some of 'Cosmo's' work on *Mardi Gras* sounded promising," wrote critic Robert Christgau, "but he must have been fibbing." Neither the album, nor the single "Latin Music" backed with "Take a Train," hit the charts.

Stu kept himself busy making demos in the studio with John McFee's band, Clover. The band, signed in the wake of CCR's popularity by Fantasy, had released two albums that just didn't fire the public's ardor like CCR (in fact, no rock of that or any other vintage the company would release ever did). The group went back to the local grind until the late '70s, when producer Nick Lowe hooked them up with a former computer programmer turned guitarist-singer-songwriter named Declan McManus. They cut his first single, then his first album. McManus's manager gave him the stage name of Elvis Costello.

Tom was preparing his second solo album as well. *Excalibur* featured most of his new friends and some of his old ones. "Tom's real happy now," John reported, "working with Doug and Stu and with Jerry [Garcia] and Merl [Saunders]."

Beyond the solo releases, Fantasy had started to exploit the sixty-five tracks that made up the body of work recorded by Creedence Clearwater Revival. Already, that past March, they started issuing twofers with a double,

Courtesy Graham Niven

John goes country.

gatefold set of *Cosmo's Factory* and *Willie and the Poor Boys*. They followed that up with the obligatory greatest hits package, just in time for the holidays. *Creedence Gold* featured most of the hits in one of the more remarkably art-directed packages on the market. The album cover had four foldaway silhouettes of all the group members. On the inside of each folded section was a picture of the silhouetted member. The album sold well, going gold. On the first album sales charts of 1973, the record peaked at number 15.

Shortly after the breakup announcement, John unleashed his first post-CCR recording. The name of the "band" was the Blue Ridge Rangers, and while he was obviously the vocalist on the project, he made no mention of who the rest of the musicians were. The Rangers' first release was "Blue Ridge Mountain Blues" backed with "Have Thine Own Way, Lord." They followed this with Hank Williams's "Jambalaya" backed with "Working on a Building." "'Jambalaya,'" recalls Rohrer, "was one of the hotel room favorites." "In our shit-kicker sessions," Fogerty concurred,

in the hotels around the country, "Jambalaya" was another one that was fun to do and when I came in with that "Well, Jambalie," and because we were using acoustic instruments and soft steel guitar, I was easily four or five times louder than the instruments, and it really hit, "wham!" I thought it was sort of a joke because the only way I can hit that one is by screeching it out. Tony Joe [White, frequent CCR opening act] used to love it—he'd say, "John, you gotta cut that one, boy!"

While the record didn't chart in England, it got to number 16 by December in the United States. Not a Creedence-like response, but respectable considering that it was a reprise of a nearly twenty-year-old country song. John played down expectations, typically, by claiming he wasn't seeking a monster hit. "I prefer now doing things that aren't so instantly commercial," John said. "I'm aware that Creedence was a commercial success beyond my wildest dreams, but I'm not ashamed of it or anything."

While working on a country record was inspired by the spirit of the "Shit-Kicker Three" hotel room sessions of CCR's last European tour, John had other reasons to make this album. Not only didn't he want the record associated with CCR, he really didn't want it necessarily to be associated with John Fogerty, per se. While subsequent releases of the record have John's name in larger type than *The Blue Ridge Rangers*, the only thing on the original recording that even connected John with the "band" was his producer's credit. "I was doing something," he said, "that was definitely not 'Creedence-y' to avoid attaching myself to that coattail."

"John Fogerty's current project is producing a seven-man band called the Blue Ridge Rangers," Christgau commented. "Strange thing is, all seven profiles on the dust jacket look just like John Fogerty. Chances are the Blue Ridge Rangers will never pursue separate careers."

"John came up with this concept," Rohrer recalls. "He saw this album cover of all Johns in silhouette, holding these different instruments."

"That's the first thing I saw," Fogerty said. "The day it all came together—I think it was in Australia or Japan. 'Blue Ridge Rangers' . . . yeah, I like that. Right away I saw the album cover, the pose, the coloring, all that stuff."

Fogerty expressed his ambivalence to personal fame—and riding his own coattails—in various interviews supporting his first solo album:

My conviction is the music is what's the most important. What's on the record. And to not capitalize on John Fogerty's name. Also vice versa. If the name was used first, you'd never know if the music's being accepted, and you might be trapped into everybody's preconceived notions of John Fogerty, which would be even worse.

I didn't want people to be playing the record just because it was John Fogerty. I didn't want to be living forever in the shadow of something I did

Courtesy Fantasy Records

The Blue Ridge Rangers.

last year, never allowed to go beyond the boundaries that had been set with Creedence. For a lot of reasons, I didn't want to get in my own way.

It also seemed like a deliberate step to avoid even the possibility of self-parody. This issue had weighed heavily on the minds of both Fogerty brothers throughout the CCR years. "We don't intend to do what Bobby Rydell or Bobby Darin did when they made it," Tom had said in 1970. "You know, those people who have two or three hits and then go legit, the nightclub trip and the TV shows. We intend to stay true to the idiom."

It also gave him the ability to make a record without composing, allow him to take a breather from the arduous rush of creativity over the last three and a half years. With this project, he could get in touch with listening and playing. "The *Blue Ridge Ranger* album," he said "was more of me just saying I think these are really outstanding songs. Not that I want to change them or do anything to them. It was the songs, not my arrangements."

Country music, while it only bubbled up occasionally, was a subtext in CCR's music almost from the start. Certainly, by the late '60s many people regarded rockabilly, once the heart of rock and roll, as country. In that light, CCR turned country around the time of "Bad Moon Rising."

"We played a lot of country music and John really got interested in it," Rohrer says.

> He'd send me up to the music library at UC Berkeley to try and figure out where some of these old songs came from, like when he did "Have Thy Own Way, Lord." He'd heard it on a Country Gentlemen album. I called up one of the members of the Country Gentlemen and asked, "Well, where did you get that song from?" He told me, "We don't know where it came from. We learned it in church." John really fell in love with Jimmie Rodgers, Hank Williams. He was really interested in all of those traditional roots. He was really interested in J. E. Mainer, the guy who did the "Blue Ridge Mountain Blues," and some of these old hillbilly families. There's just a whole list of them. I have a bunch of that music from those days. He really got involved in the roots, country, hillbilly, what have you. He really loved it. So did I.

"We've always had a warm feeling for country music and blues," John had said way back in 1969. "It's been straight ahead with that. To me, Howlin' Wolf is a country guitar player and I dig him as much as Lefty Frizzell's 'Long Black Veil' or the whole Sun record thing with Johnny Cash, Roy Orbison, Elvis, and Carl Perkins."

The *Blue Ridge Rangers* project also afforded John the opportunity to start learning again. During CCR he'd picked up the Dobro for "Lookin' Out My Back Door." Part of the reason the "Shit-Kicker Three" evolved was so John could practice his pedal steel.

"When we toured in 1971," he said,

> we found that we liked to get together and play after a concert. I finally just said, "I've been wanting to play steel guitar and I've been afraid of it all these years, but all because of those pedals and wires and everything"—it's acoustic and natural, but it's like a computer to me. Really hits me that way. Incredible variety of things you can do. But anyway, I said, "I'm going to get me a little one and play it, sitting in the hotel room and practice and make noise." I caught on really fast to it. I was amazed.

As he had done in his teens, John started teaching himself instruments so he could use them on the record. During the Japanese tour, he picked up a banjo. "I was walking by a music shop," he said, "and saw a banjo sitting there and said, 'Yeah, I think it's time.' Within an hour and a half I had a banjo, and within about a month or so we were using it in concerts.

"I did that on fiddle," he added. "Fiddle is incredibly hard. I really bit off more than I could chew. You don't just walk in and play fiddle after a month and try and sound like a champion."

Even so he acquitted himself well, playing fiddle parts on the "Blue Ridge Mountain Blues." He multitracked gospel choirs of John Fogertys and Nashville sweetening choruses of John Fogertys. "There were a multitude of reasons for doing what I did the way I did it," John said. "One of the primary ones was the idea that if I could do all the parts myself, I wouldn't have to go through that maddening process (of hearing what was missing on records)."

"We played baseball with John once after the band broke up," Stu quipped to Steve Rosen, "but he wanted to play all the positions."

What people thought of the recording seemed to depend on whether they preferred rock or roots with their country. While John sought to unearth the roots of the songs, he didn't seek to emulate them. He might be playing country, but he was still John Fogerty, still a rocker at heart.

While finding the recording "very good," Noel Coppage in *Stereo Review* called the performance "Too Much Too Soon." "The album," he wrote, "is one of the weirdest collections of old songs imaginable. . . . His reasoning becomes clear when you realize how totally befuddled he is when trying to sing 'straight' country songs. . . . 'Working on a Building,' done in a rocking gospel style that Fogerty handles very well, is an extremely strong piece. The essential flaw, I guess, is that the production involved too much hard work and not enough hard thought."

"The Rangers are . . . the finest country-rock band, even outstripping the Flying Burritos," said *Pop Music & Society*. "Fogerty's arrangements frequently improve upon the originals ('horrors' say the purists) by adding a touch of early Sun label rock. It's not rock-a-billy [*sic*] but it is not totally country. The Rangers' treatment of spirituals 'Workin' on a Building' and 'Have Thine Own Way, Lord' are hard driving and downright hand-clapping and infectious."

One important critic who was enthusiastic about the project was Jon Landau:

If he seemed immodest in Creedence Clearwater Revival, he has justified himself and proven that he can make a fine, fine record without anyone's help at all. *The Blue Ridge Rangers* may be the most successful one-man rock album yet, and if the general concept still doesn't make sense at least Fogerty had made it work. . . . The record is a crystal-clear distillation of one man's view of the rock & roll past, the source of his strength and his faith. On it, each cut seems to flow into a river of feeling in which country and city, western and blues, gospel and secular bled together in a complete body of indigenous American music.

   The center of this album is Fogerty's singing. He walks that line between concessions to the original style and maintaining his own identity as well as any white singer can. . . . He sings black material with country inflections and country tunes with black ones. And as carefully thought out as this album is, it contains not a hint of contrivance or excessive self-consciousness.

Yet, John's most compelling reason for following up his tenure leading one of the most successful rock bands of all time with a solo album of country music covers might be one he didn't even acknowledge until later. His relations with Fantasy already had become strained The same Saul Zaentz who became an idealized father figure in 1967 when he signed the band had started to grow horns and a tail in John's mind because of his refusal to modify the original CCR agreement.

   "The contract was so mind-bogglingly impossible," he said, "I came up with the one-man-band thing as a direct answer. I know this will never be really good, therefore it won't sell lots of records and they won't make any more money off me. It was as perverse as that."

   After he released the record, John was even more enraged when he discovered that it wouldn't count toward the records he owed on that contract. "I had meetings with Al Bendich during which the threat of these options were [*sic*] presented to me in response to my asking for a better contract," he said in a deposition when Fantasy sued him in 1986. "He also at this time told me that the *Blue Ridge Rangers* album would not be accepted as being included because it was country-western music, not the Creedence kind of music I had made before. Therefore I still owed whatever I had owed."

   "We had a good relationship during the *Blue Ridge Rangers* album," Fantasy president Ralph Kaffel retorted to *Rolling Stone's* Cameron Crowe. "He called all the shots and basically wrote his own ticket for everything. When he finally put out a record under his own name—'Comin' Down the Road'—it bombed. Even though we did not drop the ball, I think he held us responsible."

   "I think John's biggest disappointment with Fantasy was the *Blue Ridge Rangers* thing," Rohrer surmises.

He came out with "Jambalaya," and it was a moderate success. I think it sold several thousand copies and got a lot of airplay, both country and pop. It was a legitimate, recognized hit. He got letters from Acuff/Rose thanking him for doing Hank's tune. People like Buck Owens would write to him and congratulate him. He was pretty happy about it, that he had genuine acceptance from real people in country music. Then he released "Hearts of Stone." In John's mind, that was going to be the killer. That was the song that would put the *Blue Ridge Rangers* on the map. It didn't make it. That's a great record. He bitterly blamed Fantasy for dropping the ball on that release. That's one of the events in my mind where I saw John so bitter at Fantasy records. He felt that "Hearts of Stone," properly released and properly handled, should have been a major hit. It wasn't and his disappointment and bitterness at Fantasy over that was very apparent."

John turned "Hearts of Stone," originally a piece of southern soul as performed by The Charms and The Fontaine Sisters, into a rockabilly rager only slightly more countrified than "Bad Moon Rising." More even than "Jambalaya," it seemed like the natural song to reach old CCR fans. But the record only reached number 37. The album topped out at number 47. While faring better than his other former band mates post-CCR releases, he probably hoped for better. He was, after all, the band's leader. Because Tom's records, Doug's record, and his record didn't happen, and all of them were on Fantasy, the record company seemed as good a target for his wrath as any. He started to become obsessed with getting away from the label.

20

"A DEATH GRIP ON MY ANKLE"

The band's contract, which now applied to all the solo CCR members, required that they provide a certain number of recordings each year. Additionally, once they delivered this number of masters, the record company could ask for ten more. Basically, a master—by the terms of the contract—was a recording of a song of fewer than five and a half minutes of tape. Any more than that qualified as another master for each additional five minutes. "Heard It Through the Grapevine," at 11:05, as far as the contract was concerned, counted as three masters.

Through the end of 1969, the band had to deliver a minimum of twelve masters. Over the next year, they needed to deliver a dozen more. They met, and even exceeded these requirements. However, in the subsequent years, the contract ups the ante to twenty-four masters a year. During 1971 they delivered only ten. Under these circumstances, the contract states that the remaining fourteen masters the group owed would get tacked on to the minimum number of masters for the next year. When the group disbanded, the contract stated that they must *each* deliver twenty-four masters.

In 1972 Tom was probably the only former CCR member who released the requisite number of masters, especially if the Merl Saunders sides figured in. Doug released eleven masters for his album, Stu none at all, and John only two. In 1973, John released another ten masters, with the *Blue Ridge Rangers* album, and another two with the non-LP single "You Don't Owe Me" backed with "Back in the Hills," the last record he released under the Rangers name. That single failed to even chart, and the number of masters he owed for the year had risen into the high 30s.

To make matters worse, while the terms of the contract expired at the end of 1974, it also held a provision that the company could extend it to "such later date as any suspensions or extensions of the Agreement may require."

Further, the record company had "the absolute right in it's sole discretion to extend the current year and or term of this agreement until such failure to perform is so corrected." Therefore, if John didn't make up the ever-increasing number of masters he owed—and these masters had to get Fantasy's approval as far as commercial viability—they could hold him to the contract indefinitely.

"I owed so much product," John boiled it down for rock critic Joel Selvin, "I couldn't even brush my teeth. I couldn't focus. The pressure was there all the time. I felt like I was chained in a dungeon."

It was time, he decided to move on. He had to convince Zaentz to free him from, or at least renegotiate the terms of, his contract. He set up a meeting with Zaentz and Kaffel at the new Fantasy building at Tenth and Parker in Berkeley.

By 1973 Zaentz was becoming less and less interested in the record business. His newfound wealth allowed him to explore creative avenues he had only dared to dream of before. He produced an independent film called *Payday*, starring Rip Torn. The story must have been close to his heart, having spent so many years working with recording artists: Torn plays a fading country music star on tour. In chronicling his downfall, the film shows the underbelly of the music business. An intense piece, it was only marginally successful financially.

However, by 1973 he was engaged in coproducing a new film, with Kirk Douglas's son Michael. Ever the bohemian, he had a great fondness for the work of acid generation novelist Ken Kesey, and bought the option to make a movie out of his novel *One Flew Over the Cuckoo's Nest*. As John came to beef about his finances, Zaentz was putting together the money to actually make the film.

His film business associates point out several major characteristics in Zaentz. "He's hell to make a deal with," one Hollywood executive told Patrick Goldstein. "He's the most stubborn SOB around."

"He can spot everyone's strengths and weaknesses right away," added actor John Lithgow. "He was a killer."

"He's the most parsimonious person imaginable," *The English Patient* director Anthony Minghella said.

Obviously, Zaentz was not the kind of guy with whom to try and renegotiate a deal. Still, Fogerty went in and told Zaentz that the current contract was killing him. He told them that just the thought of having to turn out so much material paralyzed him. As John told the story, he concluded his spiel with "an unhappy John Fogerty was going to have a heck of a time producing thirty-six masters a year, or even in two years or even in five years, and it was going to be multiplied by four or five times.

"I told them, 'Look I can't make any more records this way. Not that these guys understood this. . . . I said, 'The switches are going down. I can't concentrate because I owe you so much product and it's not fair.'

"Saul looked right at me, and said, 'That's not true. The history of art shows the best stuff comes out of oppression and repression.' He was saying I didn't need to be happy or free to make good records. I said, 'That statement is pretty stupid.' I stood up real slow, went out the door and never went back there, even though my music paid for that building."

John considered returning to college. He enrolled in Contra Costa Junior College in September of 1973. Like his earlier experience at Merritt, it only confirmed that college was not the route for him. So John let another year slide away. Fantasy released "Coming Down the Road" backed with "Ricochet" (something of a collectors' item now). Although he dropped the Blue Ridge Rangers name in favor of his own, it still failed to generate any chart action. He wouldn't record anything more for Fantasy, adding another twenty-two masters to what he already owed them.

"They were stupid," he remarked.

Here they had the goose that laid the golden egg and all he wanted was to be treated fairly. . . . I wasn't hardly asking for anything. I just wanted what I thought was fair. Not only did they not want to give up anything or share anything, they wanted to hold me for the rest of my life.

My only regret is that I didn't quit sooner. I wish I had quit before I made those last two singles ["Back in the Hills" and "Coming Down the Road"]. I'm embarrassed because I stopped a little too late. Those records weren't me at all. That was my lowest personal ebb.

However, he wasn't idle. He went back into his studio and started writing songs and making another one-man-band album. He also started making it discreetly known around the music business that he might be interested in recording for anyone who could get him out of his Fantasy deal.

"He made himself available," recalls Jake Rohrer, who continued to work with John after the band split up. "[Warner Bros. president] Mo Ostin and [Elektra/Asylum chairman] David Geffen were both bidding on him."

"It was the very week all my problems with Fantasy started," John told *Rolling Stone*'s Cameron Crowe of the first call he received from Geffen. "I told him I couldn't talk and to call back in a month."

In the meantime, the rest of the band had no such angst. Fresh off the disappointment with the *Cosmo* album, Doug, Stu, and Russ Gary formed DSR Productions. The company worked out of the old Factory, which they fitted

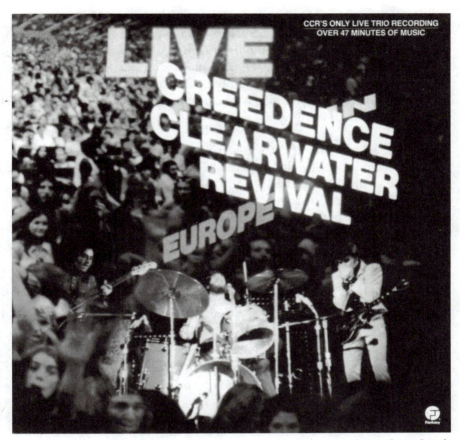

CCR'S ONLY LIVE TRIO RECORDING
OVER 47 MINUTES OF MUSIC

LIVE
CREEDENCE
CLEARWATER
REVIVAL
EUROPE

Courtesy Fantasy Records

Live in Europe.

out with a recording studio. "They had a mobile recording truck," Jeff Fogerty recalls, "which was pretty cool."

"I built a real nice echo chamber based on my favorite one up at Wally Heider's," Gary recalls.

> Bought the equipment, built the truck and away we went. I took the designs I liked over the years from Wally. Wally always had trucks. That was where he came from. That's how his business started back in '64, as a remote recording service. We worked using Doug and Stu's money, we built the truck and built up the studio a little bit. It was pretty good, because we could bring the truck

in and out through the big door of the Factory. We had something like 22,000 square feet there. We had duplicate snakes and cables made. All we had to do was back in the truck and plug everything in on the side and we were ready to go as a studio. Then we could just unplug and take off and do location. One good account was one of those live concert radio shows, "On Tour." We did a lot of location recording for that. We did a lot of hot bands, a lot of current bands at the time. It was nice.

One of their first projects was preparing the tapes of the 1971 European Trio Tour for release. The album, *Live in Europe*, came out in November of 1973. By that time, Fantasy had already compiled a companion to the *Creedence Gold* package. Called *More Creedence Gold*, it topped out on the charts at number 61 in September of 1973. However, the *Live in Europe* record didn't break the top 100, peaking at number 143.

The glut of Creedence material angered John, who was ostensibly trying to establish himself as a solo act. Commenting on the *Live in Europe* album, he asserted:

> It should never have been recorded in the first place. I got talked into the live album; outvoted as it were.
>
> I never thought Fantasy would release all that they did. Here I was with a solo career, supposedly, and they're putting out Creedence records faster than I could make my own. All the old stuff kept coming . . . *Gold, More Gold* . . . next thing to come will be *Creedence in E*. They're gonna go on forever. They released a live album, something I swore would never happen.

"They discovered," he commented ruefully, "vinyl has reproductive organs. Wow! What a discovery!"

John did play on one final Fantasy recording, however. Tom recorded his *Zephyr National* album at the Factory, now renamed DSR. Russ Gary produced it, Doug and Stu were the rhythm section. John laid down some tracks. Released in 1974, the record featured all of the former members of CCR together on a new disc for the very last time.

Fantasy's raid of the vaults to get more milk from their cash cow continued even as Fogerty worked on his new one-man-band project. In early 1975, the company struck again, releasing *Pre Creedence: The Golliwogs*. None of the band members wanted this to happen, but couldn't do much to prevent it.

"I had a solemn promise from Saul Zaentz," John said, "that *The Golliwogs* would never, ever be released. We were ashamed of it. . . . I wish I could put a disclaimer right on the record, saying 'That's not really me.'"

"I was strictly mortified, and all the other guys were, too," Tom said.

We went as far as getting copies of all the old contracts that dated back to 1964 and finding out if we could stop the company from releasing it. At the time that we went to Fantasy, in 1964, I was the only one old enough to sign a contract, so any contract we have with Fantasy before January of 1968 were all illegal in my eyes, but for some reason, the law decided that even though we had a legal right to keep the album from coming out, they were already on the market, and it wouldn't be worth it. So we decided, rather than to try and fight them legally, we could ask people to just ignore the album. It's a growing period. It isn't real Creedence material. It's like seven singles that we cut between 1964 and 1967. It was never meant to be an LP. They're all singles that we put out, they're all different types of styles.

We were just trying to grab hold of anything. We wanted to make it. That was just our thing, But I don't recommend the music at all.

Stu shares Tom and John's opinion of the material: "The Golliwogs LP was really scrapping the bottom of the barrel."

In *Rolling Stone*, Ken Barnes agreed, but added, "In scraping the bottom of their Fogerty-legacy barrel, Fantasy has unearthed a gem. These 14 single sides, recorded as the Golliwogs from 1964–68, before the band gained credence and fame, are an unabashed joy to hear . . . fascinating for their links with mature Creedence music."

Fantasy's Ralph Kaffel said they released it "because of the importance of Creedence as a contemporary rock band. *The Golliwogs* was released primarily as a historical document. There was no attempt to sweeten the sound or to pass it off as a Creedence Clearwater Revival album, and it didn't sell a damn."

Tom, in the meantime, was in the midst of a prolific, if not extraordinarily successful, period of recording. "I have four albums on my own," Tom described his post-CCR output in 1975.

Plus I produced one with Walter Hawkins and three I made with Merl Saunders and Jerry Garcia. The first solo LP was called *Tom Fogerty* in 1972. Then I did *Excalibur*, with Garcia playing lead on that particular album. It's got a whole different feel to it. That was in late '72. In 1974, I put out *Zephyr National*. That's with Doug and Stu and Russell Da Shiell and so on. And *Myopia* was last year. There wasn't any promotion at all.

I'm extremely happy with the way *Myopia* came out, sound-wise. Now that I'm writing songs again and I'm working on what will basically become my next album, I've reached another level. I'm a little let down by the lyrics on *Myopia*, but I'm happy with the sound of it.

I made this record for me. I wanted it to be the best record I ever made.

"This is Tom's calling card to the industry," Stu enthused about the album in *Billboard* in 1975 when it was released.

By this time, Tom was also becoming disenchanted with Fantasy:

I was twenty-two years old when I first signed this contract with Fantasy. For eleven years, I was with Fantasy that whole time, including the Creedence years. All that time I was with this San Francisco based jazz label. Now I'm about to enter the world of the big time, rock and roll music on a label that understands rock and roll music.

A lot of people who didn't really have to do much of anything except distribute the records, we made them millionaires. Their lack of gratitude is mind-boggling. It crushes me sometimes, to be treated so shabbily after everything we've done for them, even just on a financial level. If they don't like rock and roll, that's one thing. It's just the fact that they came into so much money as a result of it, and then to be treated so rudely is strange. I hope the next label I go to has a little more decency.

"His records weren't selling," says his son Jeff. "Fantasy never gave anyone any promotion or any push. You were lucky if you had a record out on the shelf. At the time, Tom had pretty much fulfilled his contract, so they said, 'You don't owe us any more records if you don't want.' So he moved on from there."

"I'm talking to bigger companies," Tom told *Billboard*. "Even though I want to go somewhere else, there are frightening aspects to it."

Tom also started having health problems. The former high school football star's back started acting up. In 1974, he had the first in a series of operations on his back. It prevented him from playing with Saunders and Garcia for several months.

The DSR crew had already hooked into the major label universe. In their first non-Fantasy production, Doug and Stu played and recorded on Doug Sahm's Warner Bros. Records debut, *Groover's Paradise*. Like his rhythm section, Sahm had had regional hits through high school. He moved to the Bay Area, and continued to have regional hits about the same time the Golliwogs had theirs. He hit the charts with the conjunto flavored "She's About a Mover" in 1966. In 1969, he had another hit with "Mendicino." The match of star and rhythm section seemed natural, but the resulting album only sold modestly.

"Doug Clifford and Stu Cook the rhythm section that supposedly held Creedence in thrall find a master whose core simplicity is completely unassailable," Robert Christgau wrote in his A– (abridged to B+) review of the record. "Those who consider him repetitious and derivative certainly won't enjoy these fooling songs of praise to the Lone Star State, his most unambitious music since the days of Together After Five. But they're the fools."

Ironically, Fantasy released Stu, Doug and Tom from their contract when it expired on December 31, 1974. John wasn't quite so lucky. "They tried to hang on 'til death do us part," he lamenteted. "Everybody else [in CCR] got released back in 1975, but they had a death grip on my ankle."

David Geffen called John again, exactly a month after first approaching him. This time John was ready to talk. He told Geffen why he was keeping quiet, and about how badly he felt Fantasy was treating him.

"Geffen says, 'Okay, we'll buy the company,'" John recalled for *Rolling Stone*. "I was shocked. 'I wouldn't want to own that company,' I said. 'Everything they touch turns to lead.' So he said, 'Well, we'll just buy your contract.' Which is eventually what happened."

"John went with Geffen because Geffen was there first," Rohrer elaborates, "and made the effort to come to John and open his checkbook and open his doors. Mo Ostin wanted John but wouldn't get into a bidding war. They were classy people, as were John's other suitors."

"Asylum purchased the rights to the United States and Canada for recording," says Bob Fogerty. "Zaentz got bought out. He sold the rights in the United States and Canada for Fogerty masters as part of the advance against John's royalties from Asylum. Asylum put up the money. That's why, in that period, Fantasy still owns the rights everywhere else but the U.S. and Canada. I think they proposed a number that Asylum wasn't ready to pay, so they cut it in half. That's what worked."

Geffen bought the rights to release John's records in the United States and Canada, committing to four albums. All other areas of the world, like Europe and Asia where CCR had been huge, were still controlled through Fantasy. "I went, 'Wow, that's better than twenty years. Now I can get back to work,'" John said. So John started to work in earnest, writing his first songs for publication since the three for *Mardi Gras*. "When I'm hot and my brain is working and I'm crystal clear, Jesus, I can almost do it at will," he said at the time about writing songs:

Most of the time it's just kind of busy work, like the Army: "Go over there and fold those papers for five hours." I go through all of the motions of trying to write a song. Nothing ever comes out of doing that. . . . Then, I'll be driving home on the freeway or whatever and something goes clicking! Before I know it, I've written a song before I even know I'm going to write a song. Mostly, I write a chorus. . . . I'm going home to write this song, and it might have nothing to do with anything, but I have a hook and it keeps going through my mind. . . . Half the time, I don't know what the song is going to be about. I'll have a phrase like "I like it, I like it, I like it, I like it." I didn't know what that song was going to be about for maybe a month after that, that it would become "Rockin' All Over the World." Even when it became "Rockin' All Over the World," I didn't know. Like, was I going to start in Sydney, then Melbourne? I had this idea about "Rockin' All Over the World"' Finally I decided, no, that was jive.

I think of me when I'm making the records. I think of me as the audience. What I would like, what I could live with as a listener. It comes from me. I don't know what's supposedly going to please someone else. Probably, what I play right now is different from what I liked five years ago. The change is probably more subtle to you than it is to me. To me, I might call it a big compromise. I'm playing a certain lick that I never would have dreamed of playing five years ago. It's okay now. Maybe doing a song like "You Rascal You" I might not have taken a chance doing that five years ago, but I really love that song. It was like when I started the album with "Auld Lang Syne." It was funky, crazy. How many records that you like start with "Auld Lang Syne"?

The first album in the deal was simply titled *John Fogerty*. John refers to the disc as "the Shep record" "because my dog Shep was on the cover," he said. Asylum preceded the release with a single, "Rockin' All Over the World" backed with "The Wall."

The reviews were mixed for the new album. "John Fogerty is rock-and-roll's most prominent Invisible Man," Steve Simels wrote. "After the breakup, Fogerty's reaction was a retreat to *total* anonymity—an album entitled *The Blue Ridge Rangers*. . . . He has delivered his first official solo album, but it simply isn't the masterpiece I anticipated. . . . What we've got here is a flawed record from a great talent. The flaws wouldn't have been so apparent if the wait hadn't been so long."

"In fact, some of *John Fogerty* reads like a chapter from Creedence Clearwater, Volume 57," wrote Gene Sculatti in a somewhat prophetic review:

Which shouldn't be taken as a slight either. After all, most of Fogerty's music—from garage band apprenticeship to bayou feedback and the stylistic spin-offs of the Rangers—has displayed an obsession with form, with finding some way to create within conventional structure. . . . Fogerty, above all, knows when to blow and when to quit. His reworking of Jackie Wilson's "Lonely Teardrops" gives off the unmistakable glow of a solid rocker at his strongest; in one fell swoop he brings the song down out of the hysteric pop clouds Wilson had placed it in and onto the dance floor, beer-stained and ragged, revitalized for the first time in seventeen years. . . . The point being, Fogerty can probably be counted on to retain a comparatively low profile for the rest of his natural life. . . . He'll go down rocking, which is more than can be said for all the superstars whose faces and fame surpassed his along the way.

"This is it," Michael Oldfield wrote, "a new Creedence Clearwater Revival album without the band. It finds Fogerty back in the territory he knows best—rock 'n' roll. He's a master at adapting it to the present day. . . . Nowhere can it be heard better than on his current single, which kicks off the album, 'Rocking [*sic*] All Over the World.' "

"John Fogerty single-handedly prepares records that are virtually perfect in execution as well as conception: brilliantly concise self-expression, captivating and broad based radio music," Bud Scoppa wrote. "*John Fogerty* is nearly identical in form and spirit to the best Creedence albums, *Cosmo's Factory* and *Green River*. . . . Unlike most of Creedence's albums, there's no extended rock & roll piece (such as 'Keep on Chooglin',' 'Suzie Q,' or 'Effigy'); instead, textural elements are fused into taut dramatic units. . . . I sense a yearning for some heated interaction with a packed house, a hot band and a great sound system."

John was also anxious to get together a hot band, a great sound system, and perhaps pack some houses:

> Everything inside me is saying, yeah, all systems are go. Even six months ago, I was really wondering if I want to do that. There's no question about it any more. I make records, but I grew up as a musician. You make records, you perform in person. One goes with the other. I never intended to be a hermit, and now I'm at that beginning, first step forward, where everything is possible again. I can't see any obstacles to stop the flow. It's confidence, but it may also be naiveté, too.

John wouldn't actually play another concert for over ten years.

21

"IT JUST DIDN'T RING MY BELL"

"Rockin' All Over the World" reached the top 30, topping out at number 27. The album only got to number 78. With all the muscle of Warner distribution and Elektra promotion behind him, *John Fogerty* still only barely broke the top 100 albums. The second single, "Almost Saturday Night," didn't help much either. Released in anticipation of the holidays, it rose only as high as number 78.

The relative failure of the album and singles led John to do some soul-searching. He began to doubt his own talents, suffering from the kind of self-doubts that had dogged him since childhood:

> Something was wrong. I couldn't figure it out. I was very suspicious and something was wrong. That's when I started to ask myself, "What am I working towards here?" I started having a lot of trouble sleeping and the rest of it. . . . I'd do my trip, but half my brain told me this ain't logical.
>
> I did make the . . . record on Asylum to the best of my ability, but looking back I'd have to say that a lot of the switches that had gone *click, click, click, off*, remained off. The knack to really face yourself and be brutal certainly was off. There's a couple of good tunes on there, but it's not a good record. The songwriting wasn't like before.

Looking back on the period over a decade later, John could see how his talents had slipped away:

> By the time I entered my thirties, I was slowly drying up. I kept trying and it kept coming out lousy. Suddenly, I began to feel like I could no more make a hit record than the guy down the street running a jackhammer. Creatively it

went away, and I knew it was gone and that was a terrible thing for someone who had been doing so well.

Adding to the creative switches going down, Gayland Fogerty, the father of the five Fogerty boys, passed on. "My grandfather," recalls Tom's son Jeff, "before he passed away, sort of lost it. He was also an alcoholic, so that might have led to it."

"When he died," John reflected, "we all actually felt that he was happier than being alive and so tormented. He was one of those kind of people."

Apparently, Tom's negotiations with the major record companies didn't pan out. Late in 1975, he announced that he was forming his own label, Ginseng Records. He had formed a band called Ruby, one of the names in the hat when the Golliwogs were deciding on a new moniker.

The band actually started when Tom was asked to play a benefit at Berkeley High. He needed to put together a band and found some musicians "who were kind of floating around," he related. "Randy [Oda] was one of them. He'd been working with [composer/arranger] Ed Bogas at the time. I'd remembered Anthony Davis from the Walter Hawkins album—he was the bassist on that session, and I always loved the way he played and how he was as a person." Tom wanted drummer Gaylord Birch, but he was tied up in the funk band Graham Central Station, then riding high on the R&B hit "Your Love." Birch recommended his cousin, Bobby Cochran.

"We felt we had a lot to say," Tom recalled, "because of the cultural/musical mix. Both Bobby and Anthony are black, originally from Berkeley and Oakland. Randy is from my home town, El Cerrito, but his family's from Japan and he's got a lot of Japanese/Oriental scales in his music."

They went into Wally Heider's and cut a single of "Judy/Lee," a Tom Fogerty original, backed with Jimmy Reed's "Baby, What You Want Me to Do?" "I think I'm getting more play on the Reed side," Tom noted in *Billboard* at the time, "which is all right with me."

They only pressed 5,000 copies of the first Ginseng single. The only distribution deal the company had was with Oakland-based Pacific Records and Tapes. "I realize I need a major for distribution," said Tom, "but the legal and business arrangements put me through so many changes I'd rather just go out and play. The plan is to play as much as we can and then maybe make an LP by the end of the year."

The debut album, with the Jimmy Reed track on it but not Tom's tune, came out via PBR International. Tom's first non-Fantasy record in a decade, it also was much more collaborative in nature than anything he'd recorded previously. His primary coconspirator was Oda, about a dozen years Tom's junior. The sound they made had a decidedly more contemporary pop edge to it, from the instrumental (and Oda showpiece) "Bart," to the jazzy "Running Back to Me" to the easy ballad "Life Is But a Dream." The Reed tune and a medley of Little Richard's "Slippin' and Slidin' " and the blues standard "Big Fat Woman" almost seemed like perks to the old-timer. The album, however, didn't see much play or even distribution.

"It didn't take me too long," Tom conceded, "to figure out that trying to have your own record label was not for me. Never again!"

Tom's defection was the least of the happenings at the Fantasy Building. Zaentz had mortgaged nearly everything including his chicken farm to produce the film version of *One Flew Over the Cuckoo's Nest*. Fortunately for him, it was a tremendous success. The movie grossed over $100 million and earned Zaentz his first Best Picture Oscar. The Fantasy building would be renamed the Saul Zaentz film center. If the major funding for *Cuckoo's Nest* had been earned off the sweat of CCR, Zaentz had now earned many times that investment from the film. Meanwhile, the record division of Fantasy became the domain of Ralph Kaffel.

Fantasy was not done milking the Creedence cash cow, however. In a possible attempt to cash in on the new rise in dance music, they released the full eleven-minute version of "Heard It Through The Grapevine" as a 12" single. The record actually hit number 43 on the charts. They then hit the streets with the double album *Chronicle*, an overview of the group's career that has proved to be among the most solid consistent sellers in any record company catalog.

While Tom was having trouble landing major label distribution, Stu and Doug had managed to land on Atlantic with their latest musical venture. Through their partner in DSR, they had hooked up with Don Harrison, a singer and instrumentalist from Southern California.

"I had done lots of sessions for a producer named Erik Jacobsen," Gary recalls.

The first thing I did for him was "Spirit in the Sky," by Norman Greenbaum. That turned out to be the number 1 single of 1969, by the way, even above Creedence. There was a guitar player I liked that played a lot of those sessions. He and I struck up a relationship and I did a couple of records. His name was Russell Da Shiell. That's him playing that hot stuff. He and I made two albums together with his band, Crowfoot. So, when DSR formed, Stu and Doug didn't have a guitar player, except for the occasional appearance by John on Tom's albums. I invited Russell to come over and play on the session.

Before I brought him over, I told him that CCR was history and Doug and Stu were going to get into this production company. He says, "I know this guy in Downey, California, Don Harrison. He's a good guy, a good singer, he's got

Courtesy Laurie Clifford Archives

The Don Harrison Band.

a good growl to his voice and he's a good writer." So, I went down, I made contact with him and signed him up to DSR.

"Don was signed as an artist to Factory Productions," Cook says, noting wryly, "he signed over his publishing as part of the deal. You do understand the logic. Our capital was at risk, and Don had no track record (read 'muscle') to negotiate otherwise."

Gary started grooming the company's new artist. "I rehearsed a lot of tunes with him down there. On the day I brought him up, Russell and I both went down and drove him up. All the way up, during the trip, Russell and I and Don Harrison rehearsed the tunes for the first Don Harrison Band album."

In 1976, with Russ Gary coproducing, Harrison, Stu, Doug, and Da Shiell formed the Don Harrison Band. Atlantic records signed them. It had long been rumored that Atlantic founder Ahmet Ertegun had coveted Creedence Clearwater Revival; the Don Harrison Band gave him at least a part of it. "Sixteen Tons" from their first album got some play, rising to number 47 on the single charts — a respectable figure for a song getting most of its play on album-oriented rock stations.

"When I did '16 Tons' with Don Harrison, Hugh Craig played some harmonica on that," Gary notes. "Hugh Craig, of course, became Huey Lewis. '16 Tons' had three harmonica players on it. I made one track out of it. I couldn't get what I wanted out of one guy!"

The Don Harrison Band's debut album topped out at number 159. They earned a slot on the syndicated radio show *Rock Around the World*, toured and made another record, *Red Hot*, that didn't do nearly as well. "The first DHB album is a good recording if I say so myself," Stu grins.

Meanwhile, John continued to search for direction in his solo recordings. He returned to the studio to make his next LP, *Hoodoo*, a mishmash of styles with little of the musical, vocal, or lyrical fire that vitalized his music with CCR. The album sounded fuller and deeper than *John Fogerty* from the point of view of the recording. The songs just didn't have the strength of John's previous music. New Orleans-style rock like "Telephone," with a Clarence "Frogman" Henry-style falsetto and sax break, collided with flat out rockers like the title track. "Marching to Blarney" offered up a highland fling, while "You Got the Magic," along with tunes like "Evil Thing" and "Between the Lines" were white funk just a step above KC & the Sunshine Band.

" 'You Got the Magic' was a guy living in the middle of disco," John admitted later to Scott Isler, "going, 'Well, what should I do? Oh, I'll be influenced by radio, okay.' I was like a leaf in a gale."

> The songs weren't happening, A lot of that album was just gibberish. I even ended up putting a kind of Scottish drum corps instrumental on there because I couldn't think of anything else to do.
>
> When it was done, it just didn't ring my bell. I don't know what was wrong, but there was something missing and that was confirmed by people I trusted in the business.

Even so, Fogerty delivered the album and Elektra/Asylum proceeded as if they were going to release it. They gave it a catalog number, printed up advance copies for radio and the press, designed a cover, and released a single of two of the white funk tracks, "You Got the Magic" backed with "Evil Thing."

The ill-fated *Hoodoo* album cover art.

The idea of John Fogerty doing disco made programmers and fans run for cover. These were volatile times in pop music. After a period where nearly anything went—the period that saw Creedence rise to the top—pop music entered a doldrums characterized by chart-topping albums by the Carpenters, Jim Croce, John Denver, Olivia Newton-John, and Barry Manilow. Popular music had toned down: the reign of mellow was on the charts. In this prevailing atmosphere, by May 1976 the single topped out at number 86. A week before *Hoodoo* was supposed to hit the stores, Joe Smith, the new chairman of Elektra, called Fogerty.

"After he finished *Hoodoo*," says Rohrer, "we went to Oregon where we were building John a house. We got a call that Joe Smith wanted to talk to John."

One of the people at Elektra asked if John could come down and see Joe Smith. "[Joe] said, 'John, this is not a good record,' " John recalled.

> "We'll put it out if you really want us to, but we'd rather not. Why don't you go home and work out whatever's blocking you?" He said this in a real kind and gentle way that I appreciated. I didn't feel humiliated.
>
> If it had been released, I probably . . . would have been just another used-to-be rock 'n' roller who puts out a record every year and a half or so, while everybody goes, "Ho-hum." All this time, I'd felt pressure and turmoil. I'd gone to a new label. I felt they gotta have a record. They'd paid all this money. Blah blah blah. So I'd really given myself a lot of pressure. Yet at that meeting, what he said was you don't have to do it now. Relax. I'm not demanding anything from you.

What happened then was instead of all this rushing and rushing and having an armload of half-finished tunes and just kind of a jumbled mess, I thought "Gee, I can go all the way back to the beginning and start over and build it slowly to something I can understand."

I'm really grateful. I was really dejected for just a few hours. By the time I was on the plane home, it felt more like freedom. For the first time in years, I felt I could go about building a strong foundation.

Rohrer remembers it differently. "That was a crusher," he says. "Joe Smith at Asylum was of the opinion that *Hoodoo* would do no better than his initial release, *John Fogerty*, which was disappointing, and that maybe they shouldn't release it. I know that that had quite an impact on John and myself as well."

Putting the album aside, John took stock. He knew that he had several million dollars put aside in the Castle Bank and Trust, where all of CCR's record revenues from June 5, 1969 (the day they signed the King David Contract), through that date had been deposited. He decided, since he didn't have any ready income besides his songwriter royalty checks, that he needed to explore how he could withdraw that money.

"I started working on this Bahamas tax plan," he said, "trying to separate myself. I tried to get my finances out, but the bank in the Bahamas just disappeared—gone." The bank, Castle Bank and Trust, had virtually ceased to exist. All of the bank's assets had evaporated without a trace. All that was left was the building itself. This plan that was supposed to protect CCR's assets in lieu of more royalties had suddenly rendered the members of the band paupers.

"Barrie Engel," Rohrer recalls of the CCR attorney, "went to the Bahamas to get the balance of John's money. He ended up at the Castle Bank and Trust, with the chains across the door, peered in and all that was left was a few garbage cans and the shredders."

"Practically all of Creedence's life savings were lost," John recalled. "The amount that wasn't lost—at least in my case—went to pay the taxes for the money that was lost.

"I was pretty well wiped out. People were in my bank account, taking my money without telling me."

"They stole our money!" Gail Fogerty exclaimed. "For me, it was a total shock. All our money disappeared."

"Rumors are that it's either the Mafia or the CIA that was a front for the bank," Tom intimated, "or the officers of the bank offed with it. We got left holding the bag. The *Wall Street Journal* printed a couple of stories on it, and it was on *60 Minutes* twice."

"The day I found out it was gone," John told Scott Isler,

that's when I got the earring. When it was gone for sure, nothing left, Castle Bank disappeared and I looked back over our last eight-year history—and I didn't have to look too far, only to Berkeley at all these people in their Mercedes and their big buildings and their record company—I went "You can't get away with this. You're not gonna get away with this." I need a symbol, that's what I told myself. For some reason, "earring" to me meant—maybe it's Captain Hook from childhood, I don't know—strength, integrity. I'm not going to quit. . . . I went right out to the mall here and got myself an earring.

"Miraculously, Fantasy had withdrawn all their money some months before," John added.

It may not have had the edge of malice and conspiracy John hints at, though. Fantasy was on a spending spree. Zaentz had formed his own production company and started financing films like *Three Warriors*. Their spending spree for musical properties continued as well. In 1977, they purchased the Stax catalog, ironically a label that recorded some of CCR's favorite music (Booker T and the MGs were one of its house bands).

If Fantasy was making the money work for them, all of a sudden the former members of CCR found themselves without their nest eggs. While John had his songwriter performance royalties, and Doug and Stu continued to work as producers, the situation hit Tom especially hard.

"That whole fiasco with the Castle Bank and Trust put pressure on the family," recalls Jeff Fogerty, who was fourteen at the time. "All of a sudden, we didn't have any money. That's when the trouble started, not just for our family, but for everybody's family. We went from being at the top of the world to being nowhere. Still successful on paper, but no money. That put a lot of strain on the family."

Within the year, Tom and Gail had split up. "Some of it had to do with my dad's insistence or obsession with keeping on in the music business, even though he had once become successful," says Jeff.

"I guess a nice way of saying it," Gail considers, "Tom lost perspective as to what was important. I thought the family was the most important thing. I think, at the time, he thought that music was the most important thing. I used to write him letters and talk to him and cry at him. I kept saying that all of that is superficial. It's jive. The family is most important. It was just hard for him to let go of that."

"My mom wanted to have a little home life," Jeff adds. "They had the house and the kids and some money, but my dad wanted to keep going. He had the music bug. If you do anything creative, like a painter or an architect or a writer or musician, you don't just stop after one. You keep going. It's a lifelong thing."

"He had quit the band and he was miserable because he had quit," Gail says. "He went into a depression because he was no longer with CCR. He tried different avenues, but they didn't work out for him. By that time, our marriage had really disintegrated. I just had to get out of it."

Stu also broke up with his wife, Jackie. Ironically John's marriage, which had nearly broken up with the band, was back together. However, John was in court about the same time, filing suits against Barrie Engel, the Oakland attorney who had advised the group about their investments in the trust, Edward J. Arnold, the Oakland accountant who also advised them, and Burton Kantor, the Chicago attorney who was promoting Castle Bank and Trust as an offshore tax shelter. He charged them with professional malpractice, fraud, and breach of fiduciary duty, and sought $10 million in damages. It was the first step in a long legal education for John.

22

"DEPOSITIONS IN THE CITY"

John started spending more time with lawyers than musicians, dividing his time between the courtroom and the recording studio he had built in his home. His newly diminished financial status forced him to lay off Jake Rohrer, after nearly eight years of working for the band and then for John. John's youngest brother, Bob, continued to work for him, however.

"He's been working with John the whole time, during Creedence and afterwards on his solo stuff," notes his nephew Jeff. "There was a point when I called my Uncle Bob and asked 'What's up with Uncle John?' He said, 'John's not doing anything, but I go to work every day and he pays me all the time. I feel guilty about going to work and not doing anything and getting paid.'"

"He runs my office," John explained Bob's duties. "He balances my checkbook; he handles all the mail, certainly all the incoming correspondence; talks with my lawyer when I don't understand what's going on; basically tries to keep me abreast of all the business that's involved in trying to be a working musician."

There were some bright spots. Status Quo did what John couldn't do, at least in England: they took "Rockin' All Over the World" to number 3 on the English charts. If nothing else, this brought some much needed songwriter's revenue into John's coffers.

Tom's career continued its downward slide. His second album with Ruby, *Rock and Roll Madness*, failed to light up request boards and cash registers. "It didn't get much distribution," Tom admits, "and by then I was getting disillusioned with the whole business." They called it a day. Randy Oda eventually tasted the success that evaded him with Ruby. He wrote a gold record, "Think I'm in Love," for Eddie Money in 1982.

With his marriage, his deal with Fantasy, and his new band over, Tom tried to bring CCR back together. "He got on the phone and he called Doug and Stu and John and said he wanted to talk to them, so they all came over," Jeff recalls.

> They had a big, many hour discussion, with lots of yelling and screaming and all kinds of stuff at the kitchen table at the house, about putting the band back together and the problems with it and the pros and cons of it. My dad really wanted to put the band back together, and Doug and Stu did as well, but John was on the fence. He didn't want to do it. They were yelling and screaming. My dad sent me to the back room and told me to put on records and keep playing them as loud as I could. Stay out of the kitchen. They were getting into it. This started about four in the afternoon, and they stayed until two or three in the morning. I think John left first and I think Doug left last. Doug and my dad were really good pals. They were really, really close.

Ironically, all but the Fogertys had music on their plate. Doug was hard at work putting together a band called California Gold with former Derek and the Dominoes vocalist and keyboard player Bobby Whitlock. Stu was working behind the glass, producing various projects. Both would have dropped them in a minute to play again as CCR.

When it was settled that the band would not be getting back together, Tom finally decided to take Gail's advice. He escaped. "For a six-month period I had moved to Hawaii," he said.

"I moved there with him," says Jeff. "I stayed there for a few months. We were on the smallest Island, Kauai, and there was nothing really going on for me."

Zaentz was having some minor troubles of his own. While *One Flew Over the Cuckoo's Nest* had been a major success, his next production was an epic animation of J. R. R. Tolkien's *Lord of the Rings*, directed by the enfant terrible of cartoons, Ralph Bakshi. The film was made on a paltry $8 million, and eventually did recoup its costs, but disappointed audiences were booing the end of the film, which only took Tolkien's trilogy about halfway to it's finish.

"We knew from the beginning that there would be two films," Zaentz told the *New York Times.* "It simply wasn't possible without doing violence to Tolkien's wonderful story or making a four-hour movie to get it all in one film." The second part was never made, at least not by Zaentz and Bakshi.

By 1978 change was rampant in popular music. That year, following the demise of the Don Harrison band, Stu and Doug recorded with DHB guitarist Russell Da Shiell. Epic released the album *Elevator* but it disappeared without a trace. Meanwhile, out of the pop-music doldrums, groups like the Clash were stripping rock down to its rawest core again. CCR was a touchstone for many of these groups. "When Fogerty's name came up in an interview with Joe Strummer," Robert Hilburn reported about a piece on the former Clash guitarist, "it took nearly ten minutes to get Strummer to talk about his own music again."

People still had a tremendous amount of affection for CCR. Before Hilburn was able to get Strummer back on track and talking about his own music, "Strummer asked the same thing that so many other Creedence fans were asking: 'Whatever happened to him?'"

In 1979 a band from Finland called Eppu Normaali (Abby Normal) wrote a song called "John Fogerty." A loose translation of the tongue-in-cheek lyrics reads, "If all the girls of the world died, or Chinese came and ate them, my only consolation, would be the music of John Fogerty."

Dave Marsh wondered where he had disappeared to for two pages in *Musician*: "It's hard to decide what case to use with Fogerty. . . . At a time when Tom Petty screams about the possible retail price of his records, and Rotten makes harassing record companies his favorite sport, it's typical that Fogerty never spoke a word of public complaint. I wouldn't be surprised if he never made another record again—or if a new one showed up tomorrow. That's fatalism for you, and Fogerty's fatalism is about as great as any American artist since Mark Twain."

Privately, there was a tremendous amount of infighting among the members of CCR, however, about how to use their catalog. The contract gave Fantasy carte blanche to exploit the masters any way they saw fit, and Fantasy continued to think of creative ways to repackage CCR's music. In 1978, for example, they repackaged the first six albums as double record gatefolds under the titles of *1968/1969*, *1969*, and *1970*. However, the band members retained the rights to determine what outside use was made of their old hits. They were in large demand. People wanted them for compilations, film sound tracks, even commercials. For the most part, Stu, Doug, and Tom were game for any use of the masters, as it always put a few thousand dollars in their pockets. John however was dead set against it. This set off enormous amounts of friction among the band's former members.

"We had been informed by a Fantasy executive," Doug related, "that Fantasy and John had entered into a separate written agreement wherein Fantasy agreed to obtain John's express approval before exploiting any of our recordings."

Tom found this extremely frustrating. He wrote to Fantasy attorney Malcolm Burnstein:

> I felt it was time you were informed of what was really going on.
> First of all, you have catered to & let John dictate all the decisions on this matter and all of the Creedence recordings. Stu & Doug & I have

always felt it should be a majority rules vote & the three of us have usually said "YES!" but have been outvoted by one "NO!" I guess legally
John has this right, but all four of us made the recordings and it's
absurd that we don't have any rights in *this so-called democracy.*

I guess your logic is that since John is still under contract to you out
of the USA & Canada that you must look to his needs as an artist in
order to maintain a relationship of sorts.

If I were to take John's point-of-view, I would probably not wish to
help the cause of a record company (Fantasy-Saul) that was constantly
behind in it's royalty payments (six to seven years, not months) & yet
has the money to invest in movies & new office buildings. I mean, don't
you think it's a show of a complete lack of priorities?

Fantasy can make 10% or better in simple Time-Deposits & only have
to pay Creedence 7% on back royalties due. Fantasy as a company loses
approx. 400,000 dollars in the Castle Bank, Burton Kanter fiasco while
the personal money of Creedence members, approx. 6 (SIX) million dollars, our rainy day money is stolen. Fantasy Records (Saul Zaentz) intro-
duces Creedence to Burton Kanter & the whole nightmare & then punts
it's responsibility into the "I KNOW NOTHING" end zone.

On the other hand, John felt that he was protecting the work they had
done when he still had "the gift": "Tom wanted to earn as much revenue
from exploiting our recordings right away and in any way possible, whereas
I believed (and continue to believe) that our music would be more valuable
for a longer period of time if our recordings did not appear in compilation
recordings, advertisements and film and television sound tracks."

So when he received a carbon copy of Tom's letter, he responded as to
why he hated compilation records so much. He felt that they were bad for
the band's image. Albums featuring a hodgepodge of artists ranging from
Donna Summer to ZZ Top to Hall and Oates to Sister Sledge demeaned the
band's output. The Beatles never did it. Why? "Because the Beatles were special," he said.

He claimed consumers couldn't find consumer albums with Elvis, the
Rolling Stones, Rick Nelson, and Bob Dylan that paired them with the pop
phenomenons and one-hit wonders. Those artists were special, he declared,
and one way they maintained their specialness was not to use their music
this way. "No amount of wishing can make you special again," he write. "The
thing is not a virgin anymore. It's been spoiled beyond recognition."

He then pointed out that even financially he didn't think reissues were
worth the band's while. He pointed out that if a company paid $100,000 to
license a song, after splitting it four ways, paying taxes and lawyers and oth-

ers, they came home with perhaps $10,000 each. "Do you sell specialness for a few thousand bucks?" he wondered. "Why am I cast in the role of someone who would do injury? For chrissake! My only motive, 'lo these many years, has been to protect the specialness of Creedence against the winds of bull-shit that blow, unthinking, in all directions."

In the end, though, he allowed the band to use the material as they all saw fit. "Just don't ask me to endorse it."

While it might not read that way, John claims that he did this out of com-passion, "worn down by Tom's complaints and understanding that he was under great financial constraints at the time."

Tom's son Jeff sees it differently, however:

John was really against anything that had to do with Creedence. Whenever there was a movie that came up they wanted to use a song for, or a compila-tion album, anything, John would vote it down. He didn't want Fantasy to make another dime off Creedence stuff. My dad, Doug, and Stu would always say yes, here's another $10,000 for something we did in 1970. They would always vote yes and John would always call Tom up and give him this big rou-tine, "How can you do that? You're my brother! It all goes to Fantasy! Fuck Fantasy!" and on and on. My dad, at one point, just got sick of it. Every time, every single time something would come up, John would call up and give this big tirade. Finally my dad called Fantasy and said, "Listen, I rescind my vote. I give it to you. It's always 'Yes.' You can do whatever you want with it. I don't want to be called. Just send me the check." He didn't want to get the phone calls from John, but John kept calling anyway. John would write nasty letters and be really bitter and angry. He threatened to sue my dad.

It got really unfriendly, and it was ugly because dad couldn't just be John's brother any more. There was always some sort of tension.

Because of this tension, John started to reconsider his relationship with Fantasy again. While "the Shep record" had come out on Asylum in the United States and Canada, Fantasy still owned him everywhere else:

The inner conflict was just mind-boggling. "Waitaminute! You just lost your entire life savings! And you've been working already . . . years on this record. You're gonna hand it over to Fantasy Records?" The two things just would sit in my stomach; it was like swallowing jalapenos and straight brandy. About '78, '79, I finally got an ulcer; that was one of the contributing factors.

I was going to an alpha-wave clinic to learn how to relax so I could go to sleep. But I didn't do much of the training because I'd sit there at the beginning of each session and I'd start complaining about how I owed them three albums!

Courtesy Jake Rohrer

Doug was playing live
with Doug Sahm's bands.

I decided I had to get away. So, I got a lawyer and said, "I just cannot record
for Fantasy anymore."

They owed me some foreign royalties, so I said, "All right, I'll trade you
that, the foreign royalties, and I'll trade you my artist royalties from now on. I
don't get paid as an artist on Creedence records any more, forever."

I was getting such a low rate that giving up artist royalties was not that big
a deal to me. It was like cutting off your leg to save the rest of your body.

I traded my past for my future.

This acrimony didn't keep the band from getting back together, however.
By the early '80s, the group members' various lawsuits against the Castle
Bank advisers had been consolidated for hearing. Their former attorney, Barrie Engel, who worked at the law firm in which Stu's father had been a partner, settled out of court. So did Burton Kantor, the Chicago attorney who had

promoted the deal. However, the accountants, Edward J. Arnold and Company, did not. So the former members of CCR got ready to go to trial.

"I was hung up in depositions in the city," Tom remarked one day in 1981. "The deposition I was at, I was with the other three members of Creedence."

When they weren't in court, they were working. Doug was spending a lot of time drumming for Doug Sahm's various Sir Douglas bands. Stu found himself in the studio with another psychedelic survivor, former 13th Floor Elevator member Roky Erikson and his band, the Aliens. They also spent some time working with Tom.

> With Doug and Stu, we're doing an album that we started. I don't know how long that's going to take. We can't get together very often to do it, but we have some songs that we've written together. We're trying to get that going on the side. It will take some time until it really gels into something. For the first time in all the time we've known each other, we're going to really try to help each other on each other's songs. And try to make something together.

A couple of the tunes came out on Tom's next solo album, *Deal It Out*, which found him, once again, recording for Fantasy. Tom was also playing out nearly every weekend. He sounded like he was having the time of his life. "I wanted to concentrate on communicating with the audience," he said, "and needed to get over my shyness and always being thought of as someone from Creedence."

Deal It Out featured former members of Van Morrison's band, who brought with them two previously unreleased Morrison tunes. It also featured members of the local group Tom was working with live, a band called Festival that featured future jazz stalwarts Marc Russo and Tom Lilienthal. "Their own music is a cross between Stuff and the Crusaders," Tom said, "R&B jazz. But when they back me up, they do a really good country rock feel. One of the tunes we do is 'Mustang Sally,' with horns. All together, with me singing, it's six pieces."

People around Tom at the time, however, hint that he was having problems with drugs and alcohol. As one musician who worked with him intimated (on condition of anonymity), "We all did. Tom saw going into the studio as an opportunity to party. We didn't get much work done. The times were wild, and so was Tom."

As Tom saw it, though, he was still in a much more enviable position than John. "He still wants to do his one-man-band trip," Tom said.

> Nobody's heard anything musically from him. He hasn't played live in about eight years. He's been working on a solo LP. I guess it's into it's sixth year now.

Nobody gets to hear it. He gets about halfway through it, then he scraps the whole thing and starts over. Sorry to say, I think he's into sort of a bad place right now. He's not able to really function as a musician. A lot of it has to do with all of this litigation.

Doug's view was a lot less charitable: "He's become like Brian Wilson without drugs," he reflected in 1979. "He's just locked himself into a closet bent on making perfect records, which I think is really destroying him. . . . He's been at work on the same album for four years. . . . He's doing another self-destruct number, but this time he's only doing it to his own career."

23

"THAT MAKES ME CHOKE"

John was, as his brother observed, not functioning well as a musician. But he was working. As he did in CCR, John says he went to work every day. He bought a house in Albany, California, about four miles from his house, and converted it into an office and demo studio. The period after the rejection of *Hoodoo* became a time of intense woodshedding:

> It was a real job. I'd start work usually about 9:30 and knock off about 6:30 or 7:00. Then I'd come home, go running for about forty minutes and have dinner. Then I'd rehearse until about 11:30, another three and a half hours of chops, on bass and guitar and drums especially. And no weekends off!
>
> [I] always had it in my head that I wanted to become a good guitar player, not just sort of a rock guitar player, but really play. Use all my fingers. I really started practicing then—scales, alternate picking, using my little finger.
>
> Once you stop, the next step is backward and you're going to end up in a bar some place in Albuquerque.

While he didn't take weekends off, he had a growing family. On weekends, *Time* magazine's Jay Cocks reported, he would play in the TV room "where my family could see I was actually alive. I just had to get better and better."

What he didn't do was write anything. At least anything that he was willing to share. His bad experiences from the past continued to weigh heavily on him.

> When things aren't right especially when you've been ripped off or your so-called friends turn out to be your worst enemies, you're walking on thin ice.

You just don't step very solidly, or with a lot of authority. Then you tend to retire and start being real timid about things. You get confused, which is what happened to me. You don't write very good songs, you don't play very good music. The thing that really leaves you is you lose the vision of what is correct.

The pain of knowing that Fantasy was profitting off his best material continued to gnaw away at him.

I went to the studio everyday, but how is a guy who is so tormented and unhappy going to write? I didn't want to write about myself and my problems. I mean, what a bummer! I wanted to write about the little world I'd created, but I couldn't. I'd hear my old stuff on the radio and think about how it was keeping the big bucks flowing in their door and *they hadn't done anything*. This whole thing came out of *this brain*, not theirs. My work didn't give me pride, it caused me pain.

Rather than even think about writing, he continued to hone his chops and take care of things at home. Initially, he found it hard to work up any enthusiasm for nearly anything. His professional woes had worn away John's most important asset, the one that kept the band playing in 1967 when they were living on $20 a week His depression deepened:

I had no confidence. I was scared to go into a department store. It was such a hassle just to buy a pair of socks.

I could see people looking at me like I was a loser. I hated that, but all I could do was keep working. I understood why they felt that. If I had been someone else looking at me alone in that studio every day, I would have thought, "Hey, this man is crazy."

Even with the intense schedule he maintained, John found time for the family that he nearly walked out on as CCR disintegrated. "I tried to hit all the high spots with my kids," he says, "but some of it I missed." He claims to have attended every little league game his sons, Josh and Sean, played in. He took family vacations in a van, and personal vacations to hunt and fish, hobbies he began to indulge when CCR broke up. "I took my kids to McDonalds," he said. "We did a lot of fishing and camping. We went to ball games and watched *Saturday Night Live.*

"I bought socks at Penney's and pizza at Shakey's. I paid the light bill, mowed the lawn, all that normal sort of stuff. Elvis never figured out how you do that. If you build your own prison, you're going to be your own jailer. You'll destroy yourself because that ain't living."

He also took Josh to shows. At a Def Leppard concert, he recalled, "They came back out [for an encore] and the drummer started, 'Boom de de de,' the whole thing. Then they said, 'We'd like to do a song by a bloke that lives around here . . . his name is . . . *JOHN FOGERTY*!!' " With that, the English hard rock band launched into "Travelin' Band." "It was a great moment for a father and a son."

Fortunately, John could afford to do this. Although he bartered his royalties for his freedom from Fantasy, he still collected songwriter royalties. Despite his long absence from recording and performing, CCR songs were still a staple on the radio in any number of formats. Every quarter, he would get a nice check from BMI. "BMI won't pay royalties to an entity, to an 'it,' " he noted to Scott Isler. "They want to pay it to a person, bless their heart."

As far as the public—from old CCR fans to Hilburn to Joe Strummer— was concerned, Fogerty had disappeared. If you were around the East Bay, you might have seen him at Shakey's when you went to grab a slice. But by 1980, it had already been nearly five years since his last record. He also refused to talk to the media, despite frequent requests.

I told Joe Smith "I don't wanna be the Howard Hughes of rock!" I didn't want to be bleeding in front of everybody. You don't have a record to talk about, so what are you gonna talk about? So I stopped doing anything.

The picture I always have is of a dog who goes away. He doesn't sit there and lick his wounds in front of you. Animals are pretty smart that way. Nothing is worse than a has been rock 'n' roll singer telling you his problems.

But most of all, it was his bitterness over the continuing problems with Fantasy that kept him from speaking out:

A few years ago, Russ Gary . . . called and said I must be proud that all the old records were still being played on the radio. But I said, "No. It wasn't worth it. The way I am living . . . not getting any sleep, worrying over what is going to happen to my music and how I'm going to provide security for my wife and family."

But what good would it have done to say all that publicly? It wouldn't have made me feel any better.

The strain was telling on his family. John's temper would erupt upon hearing from the lawyers and accountants preparing the Castle Bank case. His daughter, Laurie, said, "Dad was always mad." "I came home and kicked the door on that one," he reported to Scott Isler. He peppers his recollections of that time with phrases like "banging at the door," and "kicking things."

John, Stu, and Tom play at Tom's wedding.

As John festered along, Doug became the first former member of the boys from El Cerrito to uproot his family permanently from the East Bay. He took his wife, Laurie, and the kids and moved to Lake Tahoe, where taxes were low, the living was easy, and he could play golf to his heart's content when not on the road with Sir Douglas.

In 1980 Tom met Trish Clapper at the telephone company office in Walnut Creek, about twenty-five miles inland from the East Bay. They got married on October 19, 1980. While he had not achieved his goal of getting the band together for a professional reunion a year earlier, all of the former members of Creedence were at his wedding.

The last CCR photo? The quartet together again at Tom's wedding. "A couple of days went by and John was gone again."

Festival, with whom Tom was still working, began playing the music at the wedding reception. By the end of the evening, Tom, John, Doug, and Stu were up on stage. They played for nearly an hour, doing tunes from the Blue Velvets days. They did "In the Midnight Hour," "Down Home Girl," and even "Suzie Q." "I was hoping there would be a lot of discussion," Tom said about his aspirations for reforming the band after the event. "Doug and Stu would put the band back together in a second. But a couple of days went by and John was gone again."

By this time, however, Stu began to have his doubts. "Obviously, John doesn't want to bring Creedence back together," he said.

> Even if he did, I would have my misgivings about such a venture. We just have never been able to recapture the camaraderie that existed when we started out. Why should we get together unless it's just to make a lot of money?
>
> There's a bitter emotional problem that's evolved, and there's these differences that I would have thought in time would have disappeared. It's like you have fights with people and then you have a hurt and then time heals. I would think it would have just dissolved by now, but it hasn't.

Many of these differences related to Fantasy. With Tom once again signed to the label, John felt like he'd thrown in with the enemy. In a vituperative 1980 letter to Doug, John continued to vent his frustration with his ex-bandmates, alluding to letters that Tom and Doug sent, "using the word 'honest' and *that* makes me choke. Even though no single thing broke Creedence up, I would say lack of honesty sure helped."

John then went on to enumerate the ways he saw the band lacking honesty. He traced it back to that dinner all those years ago at Two Guys restaurant when they agreed to make the records right, that is, John's way. Despite this, he pointed out that they spent the rest of the band's time together trying to get him to allow them to do things like singing backup in the studio, playing on more than the basic tracks, and even having a larger role in the band's business. John felt that none of them was competent to take on these tasks.

He alluded to members of the band attacking songs like "Bad Moon Rising," "Lodi," and "Down on the Corner" as not rock and roll. In John's opinion they were griping because they couldn't play the songs. He characterized their behavior as jealous and backbiting. He called *Mardi Gras* a direct offshoot of the highly touted democracy, declared within the band at the *Pendulum* meeting and to the world at the subsequent press conference. "You still haven't accepted *Mardi Gras*," he wrote, "but all it was was me saying O.K., you told the whole world so go do it. Then you wanted me to arrange your stuff—honest?"

He outlined all the business differences he had with the band. John felt they shouldn't have even recorded the *Live in Europe* record, but if they had to, they should have bought the remotes, not rented them. He again laced into them on the issue of compilations, touching once more on how it cut into the band's "specialness." He insinuated that they were lazy, that they wouldn't practice by themselves because they found it too boring. Finally, he brought up his management skills: "I got us to number one in the world," he asserted. "There ain't no spots higher."

In a later letter he continued, "You got your shots—you could not handle it."

The Castle Bank lawsuit had some unexpected results. While the band members became more and more personally estranged, they once again banded together to protect CCR. "During the course of the lawsuit that Tom, Cook, Clifford and I had brought against our former accountants and attorneys," John stated, "it came to our attention that no trademark registration had ever been filed for the CCR name. As a result, Tom located a trademark attorney who took care of the necessary paperwork to register the group's service mark on behalf of the four members of CCR." So, for the first time in the fourteen years that the name existed, the band owned it legally.

Interest in John's music continued. English roots rocker Dave Edmunds released a version of "Almost Saturday Night" as a single in March 1981. The record got a good deal of rock airplay but topped out at number 58 on the UK charts and number 54 in the United States. One of John's musical heroes, Ricky Nelson (it was his version of "Hello Mary Lou" that CCR had covered, not Gene Pitney's) also recorded a version of the tune.

Meanwhile, Fantasy continued to exploit the CCR catalog. In 1981 they unearthed a tape box from the archives, and on playing it heard an excellent live concert by CCR as a quartet. They thought they had found the master recordings of the 1970 Albert Hall concerts. However, these tapes were actually from the "In Concert" TV special. Stu noted wryly:

> Fantasy has made it a policy to release product without talking to anyone from the band. Example: *The Royal Albert Hall Concert*. It was Coz [aka Doug "Cosmo" Clifford] that called them and broke the news that it was actually the Oakland, California concert. They said, "Why didn't you listen to the test pressing we sent you?" He replied to the effect that they hadn't chosen to consult us at the beginning of the project, why should we get involved at the end?

John explained Fantasy's haphazard approach to CCR reissues in more amusing terms to Don Everly of the Everly Brothers: "They put 'em in a closet, turn on a light, play a little soft music, somehow vitalize the reproductive organs."

Despite the misleading title, the new "live" CCR album helped renew interest in the band. In the absence of anything new by John, the critical community greeted the record with enthusiasm. It was like someone had brought back a long-lost brother. It also allowed many to reassess just how great a *band* Creedence actually was. During their heyday, many critics couldn't get past CCR as a hit-making machine. With the benefit of ten years without the band, they could look at them in a new light.

CREEDENCE CLEARWATER REVIVAL
-THE CONCERT-

Courtesy Fantasy Records

The Concert.

"A feel for the bedrock mysteries of the American experience is usually associated with sacrosanct heavyweights like, say, The Band rather than with a Berkeley (California) aberration with a knack for chart-topping singles," wrote Milo Miles in his *Boston Phoenix* review, in which he *still* managed to mix up the instruments Stu and Doug played. "But Fogerty neatly proves he has it all — the common touch with uncommon perceptions. . . . *Albert Hall* is an unexpected reward from the past."

In her four-and-a-half-star review in *Rolling Stone*, Debra Rae Cohen wrote, "Thank goodness . . . for *The Concert*, newly mined from the vaults of Fantasy, a live album that captures the group circa 1970—all raw edges, roar and spunk. If the populist gusto of John Fogerty's tunes hasn't dated a bit, neither has the band's bluesy drive."

In *The Village Voice*, Pablo Guzman called the record a "serious piece of entertainment. Fourteen tracks of prime four part Creedence, which is primo

American rock. Creedence sounds damn contemporary and fresh here; they sound *necessary* against so much of the current pollution. It stands up and blows most of what's heard today on [the radio] out of the water."

"Ultimately, he who lives by the simple singles, dies by them, as *The Royal Albert Hall* concert proves," wrote one of the few critical voices of dissent on the album, *Melody Maker*'s Michael Oldfield. "The band perform carbon copies of their greatest hits with so little deviation that it makes the album a bad buy for anyone with *Creedence Gold*."

The generally positive reaction reflected something John maintained from the beginning. He always claimed that he was writing music that would sound as good ten years down the road as it did when it was new. Ten years later, while he might have hated the source, *The Concert* proved him correct. The record rose to number 62 on the album charts. In addition to spurring a critical reevaluation of the band, it spawned a consumer resurgence. "Their records never stopped selling," Fantasy's head of sales, Kirk Roberts, said in 1982, "but after the release of *The Concert* two years ago, sales of Creedence records started to pick up. They sell like the Beatles for us."

If nothing else, Fantasy was resourceful in how they prepared the reissues. For the holiday season of 1982, they put out a set of CCR extended jams called *Chooglin'*. "We felt that since reissue product had concentrated on the single versions," Kaffel said, "it might be a good idea to put together an album of original longer cuts where the band gets to stretch out." Fantasy remastered the recordings using a relatively recent development, digital audio, and pressed it on heavier virgin vinyl. "We did special packaging and used rice paper sleeves, and we came up with what is not strictly speaking an audiophile record, but one which is certainly superior to a regular record," Kaffel explained.

However, John felt that this decision to do a "quasi-audiophile" reissue was yet another example of Fantasy's penny-pinching attitude toward the Creedence catalog: "It's like, how can you rape something that much? But to them, if they can sell one more copy and make one more dollar—the consequences as far as artistically being distasteful and being odorous—it doesn't bother them at all. If you can make one more dollar, then do it."

After pursuing the matter for nearly seven years, John was starting to wonder if the Castle Bank case would ever go to trial by the winter of 1983. When he wasn't consulting with his attorney, he worked away in his home studio, refining his playing. He still wasn't able to write. This didn't stop people from calling. It had been close to a six years since John had dealt with anyone at Elektra. Early in February Mo Ostin got something he had wanted ten years ago, when he and David Geffen had been bidding against each other for John's services as a solo artist: Elektra agreed to transfer Fogerty's contract to their sister company within the Warner Communications empire, Warner Bros. Records, which Ostin chaired.

"I was informed that Mo Ostin and Lenny Waronker would like to meet with me at Warner Bros." John said. "Basically they informed me that if I so desired, I was now on Warner Brothers and not on Elektra/Asylum. . . . They asked, 'How is it coming musically?' And I said, 'I'm woodshedding; I don't have anything right now.'"

Lenny Waronker, Warner's president and an important producer in the pop music business, was particularly interested in getting John back to work. John recalled: "Lenny Waronker said, 'So how about it, Fogerty, have you been writing songs?' 'No I haven't.' 'Don't you have any songs backed up?' 'Well, no.' 'What have you been doing?' 'I've been trying to get my chops up.' 'No songs, huh?' He and Mo Ostin looked at each other and said, 'God, I wonder if he's ever going to make a record.'"

Toward the end of February 1983, a jury in San Francisco County Superior Court started hearing the case of CCR versus Edward Arnold's CPA firm regarding the Castle bank affair. It took seven weeks of testimony, and another eight days for the jury to find that the CPA firm was responsible for the loss of the money. They also decided that Fantasy bore no responsibility in the case, although the record company made the payments to the accounting firm. However, the jury maintained that Fantasy just forwarded the money to the accountants, but the firm failed to supervise the investment closely enough. "They just let Castle Bank do what they wished with the money," John Herron, who represented Stu, Doug and Tom, told *Variety*. "It has disappeared."

The jury awarded Stu $1,525, 491; Doug $1,441,352; Tom $1,540,505, and John $4,142,545—a total of $8,649,893. Of course, no one got any cash. Arnold's firm appealed the verdict. Even so, John felt he had won a moral victory. "I think," John said later, "I felt really more the fact that we had won a fight, or at least won at a certain stage."

Despite this victory, though, the case dragged on. "It still goes on, up and up the ladder of justice," Fogerty complained to Scott Isler a couple of years later. "The whole thing may take another ten years."

At a press conference sometime after the jury's decision, however, John told reporters, "I feel more relieved than anything." He also confessed that he hadn't been able to do much in the way of songwriting. "I haven't been able to focus on what I want to say because of the lawsuit, but I feel the next album is finally on the way."

24

"A NICE METAPHOR FOR MY COMEBACK ALBUM"

John was out fishing when the creative switches started to turn on again. It was in May 1983, not long after the jury had found for the band and they at least had legal right to their money, if not the actual dollars in hand.

"I went to the San Pablo reservoir out there by El Sobrante," he says—El Sobrante being where Stu and Doug had rented their Pink House, the Shire, nearly twenty years earlier. "I rented this little boat, taking my fishing pole and my little tackle box as an excuse, my note pad and my pen stashed inside. I motored around the lake, thought about the words, going around in circles, trolling."

He had been nurturing an idea for a song for several years at that point, a remembrance of things past for the TV generation. He tried to recall the images that television had cathode rayed into his impressionable mind:

Then the first line came to me: "They sent us home/to watch the show/comin' on the little screen/a man named Ike was in the White House/Big Black Limousine." That actually happened to me. Most of us barely had a TV in the fifties. I remember coming home from school first or second grade seeing this line of big black limousines on the screen. That was the first image that came to me.

It was one of the toughest things I'd ever done . . . trying to go back to when I was twelve years old and remember what it was really like. I'd already written an outline for the song, which is how I do most of my stuff. I know I'm getting serious when I do the outline. Just like English lit. . . . Anyway, I kept trolling up and down that lake. I'm good on water. I don't know why. Maybe it's got something to do with negative ions or something. . . . I spent the day on it, up and down the lake. I didn't get one bite, which is probably a

Courtesy Laurie Clifford Archives

From flyer commemorating twentieth reunion of the El Cerrito high school class of '63.

good thing. . . . By 6 o'clock I had a verse and a half and I knew where the rest of it was going. When I finally got out of the boat, I said to myself, "I got it. I can do this now." It was the first time that switch had gone on in maybe nine years. . . . I was waiting for that feeling down in my solar plexus and that's what happened with "TV."

It hit me like a ton of bricks. In that instant, twelve to fourteen years melted away. It meant "Here we go! It's back. You can work."

Apart from children being born or getting married, that was one of the bigger moments of my life.

That fall, John, Doug and Stu met at the twentieth reunion of the El Cerrito High class of 1963. "Doug and I didn't think John would come," Stu said, "because he's not a real socializer. But he and his wife showed up and we talked for a couple of hours and had dinner. Then afterward, John came up to us and asked if we wanted to play."

"I was shocked that he even showed up—and even more shocked when he asked me if I wanted to play," Doug recalled. "John said, 'We'll do three tunes and the last one will be "Proud Mary" and by the time we get up there I'll figure out what the other two will be.'"

"It was very sincere and honest," John said.

For one thing, we had all just been in this trial which we won. And also we were seeing our class after twenty years. The first three people in line ahead of us that saw me said, "You're going to play, aren't you?" It wasn't my idea to play. And finally, the girl running the thing—you know, all those people that you haven't seen except that you knew as kids—I mean, I realized, "My god, we came out of their high school, they were proud of us." So I thought to myself, "What kind of asshole goes to his twenty year reunion and *won't play?*"

We opened up with "Hully Gully," and everybody understood. That was what the Blue Velvets always played.

"We played a mixture of old Creedence tunes and some blues covers that we used to do before we were called Creedence," Stu concurred. "It all seemed so natural."

"An hour and ten minutes later," Doug continued, "we did 'Proud Mary.' We would have liked to play longer, but we ran out of tunes. We did 'Hully Gully' and 'Annie Had a Baby' and a lot of tunes that we did when we were the Blue Velvets.

"From the moment they announced the Blue Velvets were gonna play," he added, "everyone went nuts."

The only sign that things had even been bad, or that anything had changed between them musically, was John's voice. "We dropped 'Good Golly Miss Molly' a half step," mused Stu.

Nineteen-eighty-four was another big year for Saul Zaentz. He spent a good portion of the year producing Milos Forman's film version of Peter Shaffer's hit Broadway play *Amadeus*. He mortgaged the Fantasy building to finance it, once again drawing on his CCR legacy. The film opened to some of the best reviews since *Cuckoo's Nest.*

John was hard at work in his home studio. After getting the parts right, he started approaching music more holistically again. He ran through all the contemporary pop styles—but kept returning to his original sound. "I tried a little disco," he told Scott Isler. "I tried a little mellow, I tried a little Holiday Inn lounge, a little punk, English synthesized art-rock—I did all that stuff, and I didn't like it! It didn't ring true. I felt comfortable when I got something raw and swampy. Not only was it fun to play, it sounded good to me!"

He wrote twelve songs, making elaborate demos, playing all the instruments himself.

He started sometimes with something as small as a guitar riff or chord progression, and perhaps a phrase that stuck in his mind. One of the first songs he wrote in this way was "The Old Man Down the Road." He described the process this way:

I do most of my writing on the guitar, and every time I come up with a good thing, I put it on tape with the other instruments. . . . Eventually, I'll have cassette after cassette with these little riffs on them. Then I'll listen to them when I'm driving around and eventually some of them are strong enough that I want to write a song. That's exactly what "Old Man" was. To me, that's the most obvious way to make a rock and roll record.

I have a little notebook full of song titles. I'll look over and see if any of these look like they might go with this music I'm making. In this case it was "Somewhere Down the Road." So I wrote out the whole musical structure, then I started working on the words. Not at the same time—I was on vacation on a houseboat and wrote out all the words, and they didn't seem as strong as what the music was doing. "Somewhere Down the Road" is kind of abstract, not a very powerful title. It was a hook cliché, but not very strong. The song was about leaving home and all the crud you meet. One of the images was this guy with a suitcase covered with rattlesnake hide, and he stands right in the road. Gee, I like that. Okay, scrap the song and keep that part. And I just did it all over again, into "The Old Man Down the Road," which is a much more powerful image and fit the music. It's a swampy thing and seemed much cooler to me, anyway.

A second song, "Rock and Roll Girls," had a similar gestation. "[It's] just those three great chords," he said about this song inspired by his fourteen-year-old daughter, Laurie. "I mean, it's just a simple, straight ahead song. But to me, there's a lot of meaning. That certain age that girls all go through. For them, it's that wonderful time between being a child and being a woman. Right in between, but still the age of innocence. I have a daughter and you look in her face . . . 'Secrets on the telephone' . . . you know, it's true."

"A title will help me get a handle on what I'm trying to say," he related. "A really obscure example would be 'Searchlight.' I had the phrase, 'Oh, the midnight, need a searchlight' for three months, but had no idea what the song was about. I had the music to it, got the groove goin', and knew what I wanted it to sound like, but . . . it made no sense to me. Later, when I made it literal and you could see the rocky beach, I thought, 'That works.'"

Perhaps most important among these songs was "Centerfield," which became the title track of the album. It drew an analogy between John's two favorite obsessions, music—and his musical career specifically—and baseball. "I was never good enough to play ball," he confessed to Scott Isler, "like twenty million frustrated centerfielders.

I packed several images into "Centerfield." The only thing I didn't include was that quote "Son, it's a game of inches." All the baseball stuff I could remember is in there. I really do love baseball, so I didn't have to research it. Baseball is something I've researched practically my whole life. When I sing, "And you can tell that one good-bye," I'm quoting former Giants and A's announcer Lon Simmons.

I decided that the concept of playing in center field in the manner that a twelve-year-old or younger boy might feel about playing center field in Yankee Stadium would be symbolically a nice metaphor for my first comeback album.

Shortly after attending the baseball All-Star Game at Candlestick Park in 1984, he started recording, once again playing all the instruments by himself. "You can get every bit as much spontaneity doing it by yourself as you can with having a group of people sitting there," John believed. "Whatever instrument I choose to be playing at the time, you can make it spontaneous. Within five minutes of having an idea, you can be playing that if you're doing it yourself."

By August he had six songs done. He set up an appointment with his new label, and on September 10, 1984, he went to Burbank armed with a tape of "I Can't Help Myself," "The Old Man Down the Road," "Rock and Roll Girls," "Searchlight," "Zanz Can't Danz," and "I Saw It on TV":

I came down to LA to let Warner Bros. hear it. I kept thinking, "Is this worth it, or am I nuts?" Remember the guy in *The Shining* who's been working on his novel for six months and his wife comes down and sees it and it's all one line, over and over again. I wanted to know if that's what I'd been doing.

I didn't know if this was even in the ballpark, as far as what they wanted, if it would be acceptable on a commercial level. So I went to play the tapes for Lenny.

"Well Lenny, [John said] how does a thirty-nine-year-old has-been rock singer get you to listen to his records?"

"I guess we'll just listen," was Waronker's reply.

He was thinking, "What if it's bad? How can I tell him?" John added. About five seconds into the first song, he *overreacted*—he was so happy. He told me later he was so relieved.

John got home late that night. His wife and three children were already asleep. He found a piece of paper and wrote, "The monkey is off my back." Below it he drew a dancing chimpanzee. He posted the note for his family on the refrigerator and went to bed.

25

"ALL I DID WAS WRITE A SONG ABOUT A PIG"

John finished the album in another couple of weeks. The entire recording reportedly cost $35,000, in an era when bands like Fleetwood Mac and Foreigner were spending in excess of a million dollars and a year in the studio. In a final touch of irony, on the inner sleeve of the album, he paid homage to his old band: "This album is dedicated to Gossamer Wump and dreams that survive."

Lenny Waronker and Mo Ostin were excited. John Fogerty breaks his silence after nearly ten years! They wanted to get the hype machine jump-started in a big way. "They had a large listening party," John related. "They flew in . . . the entire field staff of Warner Bros. records to be at this listening."

Suddenly, in the fall of 1984, the musical grapevine started buzzing with rumors of a new record by legendary rock recluse John Fogerty, the first music he'd made that anyone had heard in nearly a decade. When *Centerfield* came out in January 1985, it was like D. B. Cooper had emerged from the north woods with hundred dollar bills for everyone. It was a "cause to celebrate the return of one of rock's favorite sons," wrote David Hiltbrand in *People.*

"From the opening strains of 'The Old Man Down the Road,' it's apparent that the one-time driving force of Creedence Clearwater Revival has lost nothing in his 10-year layoff," wrote Bill Milkowski. "Apart from anything Bruce Springsteen or NRBQ has done recently, this album is the most honest, sincere, and American-sounding collection of rock & roll music to come along in some time. And it's come along just in time."

In John Swenson's five star review in the *Saturday Review*, he asserted, "Fogerty has returned with a vengeance. He balances personal and moral concerns deftly in some of his strongest songwriting ever."

"Hush children: we are in the presence of greatness," Allan Jones wrote in *Melody Maker*. "Since 1975's *John Fogerty*, he has been silent, a brooding enigma. It was as if Fogerty, having reached definitive peaks with Creedence, simply couldn't contemplate the potential embarrassment of releasing anything that failed to match his previous achievements. Listening to [*Centerfield*] is like finding new lips for a familiar passion."

"While Fogerty hews close to the Creedence outline," J. D. Considine wrote in *Musician*, "the texture of the music—clean, crisp, lean and uncluttered—is far more 80s than 70s. . . . But Fogerty's greatest talent is an ability to construct songs that are such perfect metaphors he never has to state his case. . . . Here's hoping it won't be another ten years for our next chance to get this excited."

In assessing his reason for including it in the *Top 100 Albums of the 80s*, Parke Putterbaugh said, "Look a little deeper and one finds an intensely autobiographical album: a survivor's tale that celebrates the durability of rock & roll and the power inherent in remaining true to one's own belief."

"After a ten year absence," Kurt Loder wrote in his four-star *Rolling Stone* review, "Fogerty has returned with *Centerfield*, a near-seamless extension of the Creedence sound and a record that's likely to convert a whole new generation of true believers."

Even other musicians weighed in on the record. Eddie Van Halen told Steve Rosen it was one of his favorites. "It's so simple," he said.

One of the musicians the album failed to move, however was Stu. "I am not impressed," he told a critic at the time. "Don't get me wrong. I wish him well. But if he was going to copy an old Creedence tune, he should have picked 'Proud Mary' instead of 'Run Through the Jungle.' If we weren't good enough to play in his band, and this is what he's come up with by playing all the instruments himself, I am glad I didn't play on this album."

Even John felt somewhat humble about his playing, telling *Time* magazine's Jay Cocks, "I'm a pretty good bar band."

Almost universally, the first question people asked when they interviewed John was "What have you been doing for the last ten years?" Invariably John would tear into Fantasy Records and Saul Zaentz, as he did with Scott Isler, saying things like "My problems were more legal than musical. It's basically a fight between an artist and a greedy record company."

The second question was how he felt about making a comeback. To this he replied, "This is more than a comeback! This is a triumph over evil. . . . I was legally bound to Fantasy Records. It was not one of the greatest places. They're cruel. That word was *cruel*. They realized they could make a lot of money off me. Without saying the word 'greedy,' I guess I'll just say [they were] greedy."

Every time a Fogerty-composed Creedence song got played on the radio, Fantasy (or more correctly Jondora, one of Fantasy's music-publishing arms) made money. Every time anyone played a Fogerty-composed Creedence song in public, Jondora made money. Consider that Fantasy was ostensibly ready to offer CCR 10 percent of the company at one juncture, but never offered John the opportunity to reclaim his publishing. If the money from the CCR records continued to swell their coffers, the publishing royalties from the CCR hits, many achieving BMI "Millionaire" status (i.e., a song that had over a million airplays), was also very important to the label.

Fogerty was against anything that would make Fantasy another dollar off of his creative vision. Therefore, he vowed to Scott Isler:

> I'm not gonna do the old Creedence songs ever again. It'd be almost pandering for me to sing "rollin' on the river" at this point. I had to divorce myself from all that. There was all this ill will between the guys in the group and me, and between me and Fantasy. I had to make a mental divorce. Up to that point, I'd been defending and trying to protect the, quote, good name of Creedence the best I could—not wallow in all the things they do as a record company, like 147 reissues of Golliwogs material. That's enough, that's not me anymore. Go ahead: You guys can use it all you want. You can ride on the coattails, you can squeeze it, milk it, do whatever you want. It has nothing to do with me. I ain't defending or protecting it anymore.

The bitterness over the long battle to control his publishing would continue for years to come. As he stated in one of the many court cases involving his publishing rights, "When I hear 'Proud Mary' on the radio, it reminds me more of all the seventeen years of baloney than it does of any personal pride I may feel about the song."

In the interim between 1980—when John renounced his rights to royalties from his Fantasy recordings—and when *Centerfield* came out, much had changed in the record business. A new medium, the compact disc (CD), rapidly began replacing the LP as the standard means for the commercial dissemination of sound recordings. This offered every record company the opportunity to resell its back catalog, as people replaced their scratchy, skippy vinyl recordings with the laser-read, immaculate sounding digital discs. A catalog like CCR's gave forth another rain of gold into the Fantasy coffers. John, having signed over his royalties, saw none of it.

"I think the reason for all the vitriol," Fantasy attorney Norman Rudman commented in 1986, "is that [Fogerty] thinks he made a bad deal in 1980 and he won't accept responsibility for it. He's very conscious of money and I think he wants his due. Most of John's complaints come down to the fact that he doesn't like to see other people making money when he's not."

"John didn't *have* to 'give up' his royalties," comments Stu. "It was his idea, and in my opinion, a very poor business decision. Of course, the label jumped at it."

While this decision cost him a fortune, it freed him up to say anything he wanted about his old band and his old record company. He really felt he had nothing to lose. Tom, however felt differently. In a letter to John, he complained bitterly about the many interviews John gave over the years in which—Tom claimed—John destroyed Tom's ability to make a living:

The best example in the past of your whitewashing the facts is *Rolling Stone* magazine, February 1970. Every time I read it, I wonder why I put up with your ego. Oh well, I left nine months later.

The best example in the present of completely misleading the public is *Musician* magazine, Jan./Feb. 1985. You don't know the difference between hearsay and fact.

Most people, when they reach forty, mellow out. They reflect on the past and count their blessings. Not John Fogerty. Fifteen years later, his attitude is even worse. In fact, "I" is the dominant word in every interview.

You have sabotaged and severely damaged my career and my source of income. Because you gave up your Fantasy royalties, you felt you had nothing to lose by blasting Saul, Fantasy, and Creedence in the press and on the radio—not only in San Francisco but in Los Angeles, New York, all over the U.S. and in other countries.

The problem is, Doug, Stu, and I haven't given up our share of the royalties and by hurting Fantasy's image you have severely damaged the royalty income that Doug, Stu and I are entitled to. You had no right to say those things, *it's not your group!* We own it, *we* own the name and the rights to the royalty income.

You speak of the "triumph of good over evil"; it's more like the "triumph of madness over reason."

To make matters even worse, your diatribes totally sabotaged my chances of success. When my LP and video came out in May 1985 on Fantasy Records, the radio and TV people who read and heard your interviews immediately got the wrong image of the label and all my efforts were in vain. In order to have any kind of career in the future, I'm going to have to change labels. This is not by choice but by necessity.

You have convinced the family and you're working on convincing the whole world that Saul is a bad person and that Fantasy ripped you off. I find it all very amusing!

Thanks to Tricia's love, Saul and I "buried the hatchet" in 1980 and we've been closer than ever. I couldn't ask for a better friend.

As for money, Fantasy has paid me approximately $150,000 per year in royalties since 1980. I settled my last Fantasy audit in 1980 without accountants and lawyers. I work everything out on the same basis I used before we hired Ed Arnold and Barrie Engel: common sense. I conduct my business within an atmosphere of trust and friendship.

I have informed my kids and will inform my grandkids of your "suppression of truth" concerning the history of Creedence. I will not go to the media about your mendacious exaggerations regarding Fantasy Records as I think the public deserves better. I say, leave the whining to Richard Penniman and Albert Goldman.

Perhaps as a way of getting back at John, Fantasy sank a little more money into Tom's musical legacy. They took the two independently released albums Tom made with the group Ruby, and picked the strongest tracks for a best-of release, titled *Precious Gems*. "I thought we never really had a decent shot at it when this music was first recorded," Tom said. "Actually, I feel we were somewhat ahead of our time."

No one except Tom expected it to do any better than the initial releases, but that didn't seem to matter to Fantasy. They even gave the group money to make a video, bringing them back together on a soundstage. "The video consists pretty much of straightahead studio shots," Tom remarked, "I had a blast doing it and learning as I went along. I think the video explosion has been really good for rock and roll, and music in general, for that matter."

To further help Tom (and perhaps to tweak John), Fantasy executives started touting the Ruby record as "The recording by the founding member and original vocalist of Creedence Clearwater Revival . . . Tom Fogerty." It was, of course, a stretch of the truth. Tom hadn't sung lead since the Golliwogs—that was one of the reasons he left CCR in the first place.

By this time, Tom and Trish had moved away from the Bay Area. They settled in Arizona. They had a daughter, and Trish enrolled in Northern Arizona University while Tom stayed home with the baby. Tom needed all the royalties he could get. By 1985, his bad back had largely sidelined his career. He was getting treatment and surgery that would last for another year or two. The money from the Castle Bank affair was still tied up in the courts, and Tom was not doing much work.

Zaentz, on the other hand, was very busy. *Amadeus* won eight Academy Awards at the 1985 Oscar presentations. He came home with the Best Picture Oscar statuette. By the end of the year, the film nearly cleared $100 million at the box office worldwide. He was able to pay off the mortgage he'd taken on the Fantasy building to fund the film. With the added income, Fantasy strengthened their record division, buying the catalog of Contemporary and Good Time Jazz records, and Pablo records from Zaentz's former employer Norman Granz.

Despite having minimal involvement in the running of Fantasy Records at this point, the ghost of the artist that had created the initial funds for these activities continued to haunt him. To John, Fantasy was Zaentz, the father figure who had abandoned him, just like his real father had. He referred to the company and the company's owner almost interchangeably. Beyond that, two of the songs on *Centerfield* were aimed like spears directly at Zaentz. Every critic even remotely familiar with John's situation knew whom John was describing in "Mr. Greed." Even more obvious was the final song on the album. The most unusual song musically, with a jazzy, almost reggae feel, "Zanz Can't Danz" told the story of a break-dancer who would assemble crowds for his pocket-picking pet pig to rob.

Zaentz didn't like "Zanz." He took exception to "Mr. Greed." Nor did he like all the things John was saying about him in the press. By the time he took home his Oscar, he'd already threatened John with a lawsuit about "Zanz." Warner Bros. urged John to alter the song to render it somewhat less provocative. "Lenny Waronker called me and asked me to make a change," John testified. "I remember I had to do the remix the night of my daughter's father-daughter dance. So it took me from midnight until 8:00 in the morning to do it." Suddenly, pressings of the record replaced the original song with a new one called "Vanz Can't Danz." Many assumed that John had already recorded the altered track anticipating, perhaps even relishing, Zaentz's reaction.

"Saul was hurt, injured, outraged, and he felt himself to have been very badly abused," Fantasy lawyer Norman Rudman fumed. "Was he surprised at the song? Sure. I don't think it comes as a surprise that John Fogerty harbors a certain feeling of resentment, maybe even, as some people have characterized, vengeance against him. Certainly we were surprised to see it expressed in that way."

The altered version didn't appease Zaentz. The record had sold nearly three quarters of a million copies before John made the change. Zaentz wanted the cut removed altogether. Fantasy decided to go forward with the threatened suit.

"It's defamatory," Rudman added. "It's slanderous or libelous, depending only on the medium that's used to perpetrate it. When you call someone a thief, or say that somebody stole your money or acted like a slave driver, you've gone beyond the bounds of saying merely unfavorable things about people and gone into the kinds of statement that are just plain, irreducible defamations."

In the suit, Zaentz sought $144 million in damages. The suit claimed that John's lyrics portrayed Zaentz as "a thief, robber, adulterer and murderer." These allegations, according to the suit, undermined Zaentz's image and the image of Fantasy records. Artists under contract and in negotiations lost faith in the company. The public was turned off to the label because of these remarks.

"All I did," John would claim somewhat disingenuously time and time again, "was write a song about a pig."

Tom wrote a letter to the *Chronicle* saying that he trusted Zaentz "to the max." Clifford called *Centerfield* a "mediocre copy of something that was once and still is great."

When Fantasy finally took its case to court, on July 26, 1985, it also got the ball rolling on one of the most unusual lawsuits of the decade. They sued John for copyright infringement, claiming that the song "The Old Man Down the Road" infringed on the copyright, controlled by Jondora Music, of "Run Through the Jungle." It didn't matter that John wrote both songs. Jondora owned the copyright to "Run Through the Jungle." If they could convince a jury that the it was essentially the same song as "The Old Man Down the Road," Jondora would be entitled to the publishing royalties from John's new top-10 hit.

John initially assumed that Doug had brought the song to Zaentz. Doug, however, swore under oath that he didn't. While Stu had mentioned it in passing to the *Los Angeles Times*, as recently as June 1997, John told the *Toronto Star*, "And you should know, it was Stu Cook who took 'Old Man' and played it for Saul, who then couldn't decide whether it sounded like 'Green River' or 'Run Through the Jungle."

"This is a total load of crap," asserts Stu. "Whether or not he stole from himself is not the point. The publisher of the songs felt he had and pursued it in the courts. . . . Neither Doug nor I pointed out the obvious similarities of the songs in question to Zaentz. Doug signed a sworn court document on behalf of Fogerty that it didn't happen."

Centerfield blew away the charts. In March, the album spent a week at the top of the charts (sandwiched by Wham! and Phil Collins). "Old Man Down the Road" got heavily played on album-oriented rock stations, and cracked the top 10 on the pop charts as well. The single "Rock and Roll Girls" hit the top 20. Both songs had videos in rotation on MTV. The "Old Man" video cleverly used a continuous tracking shot to establish its atmosphere, while "Rock and Roll Girls" had a more conventional "band-in-concert" video. *People* magazine mused, "It would have been a lot more fun, not to mention more honest, to have Fogerty racing from instrument to instrument, or at least appearing in various disguises. What America needs is a truth in video law."

In true Creedence fashion, the B-side of "Rock and Roll Girls" got nearly as much attention. It was the title track from the album, "Centerfield." Ultimately, it may be one of the most valuable songs John owns, because it gets used during nearly every major league baseball broadcast, and at every ballpark with a sound system. John recalled:

I was up in Oregon at my little place. It was 1985, with all these hunters and loggers, it felt like the end of the earth, watching the World Series off a satellite dish at this little cafe that served burgers and beer. The network started to play "Centerfield." One of my friends was working as a waitress during the busy season, she looked over at me and I looked at her. She could tell I was bursting with fatherly pride at my little child, my little song being played during the World Series. Nobody else in the room knew I had written the song.

I'm very tough about people using my songs in films and things. That other guy [i.e., Zaentz] who controls the Creedence stuff, he hardly ever says "No," but I almost always say "No" to anybody using the songs I control. But when Little League teams call up and say they're making a video, and they ask for rights, usually that could mean thousands of dollars. But I say, hell yes, go ahead and use it, that's what the song is for; it's about baseball and America. No charge.

I'm proud of it just because of the way it's been endorsed and adopted by baseball. I mean, I love baseball, and I never dreamed anything like this would happen to me.

John's next single was almost as notable at the time. For the requisite video for "Vanz Can't Danz," rather than use the standard formula, he brought in Will Vinton, the creator of Claymation, to do the clip. MTV played the animation, but the single never got released to the public. It only came out as a Warner promotional.

That summer, Bob Geldof used John's song "Rockin' All Over the World" as the theme music to kick off the *Live Aid* concerts at London's Wembly Arena and Philadelphia's JFK Stadium on July 13, 1985. The shows raised over $100 million for the relief of famine-stricken areas of eastern Africa.

John was itching to play live again, but because he refused to play his old CCR songs, and the tunes from the Shep album were nearly ten years old and—he had now concluded—not very strong, he didn't have enough songs to perform. He decided to wait until he put out one more album and had enough material to tour. He got the opportunity to get his feet wet in front of an audience when Showtime asked him to play a special. Rather than make that special a tribute to *Centerfield* or to CCR or even a celebration of himself, John used the show to do two things. One thing was to gather some of his favorite musicians. Booker T Jones and Duck Dunn were obvious choices. Sax player Steve Douglas, a Phil Spector staple, made the date, as did drummer Prairie Prince and guitarist Albert Lee. With this stellar band, Fogerty played music that he loved, tunes by Hank Ballard, the Swan Silvertones, Bo Diddley, and Ray Charles. "Centerfield" was used as the show's theme song.

Ironically, the use of footage from the Oakland Coliseum show (which had supposedly been destroyed) during the special required that Bob contact the other former CCR members. "In John's recent Showtime special," he wrote, "a little over one minute of film footage from CCR's 'In Concert' 1970 film was included. . . . Irregardless [sic] of how you might have voted on this usage, I'm assuming you would have and do want to get paid." He sent each member $1,283.

One of the running vignettes in the special showed John and George Thorogood at a spring training game. A longer aside showed him at a crawdad fiesta in New Orleans playing a song called "My Toot Toot," with the song's composer, veteran zydeco performer Rocking Sidney. During the course of the year the song had generated something of a mania. No fewer than a half dozen different versions were in the stores. Fogerty heard it via Warner's head of publicity, Bob Merlis, and decided that it would be the perfect addition to the Showtime special.

The only *Centerfield* song the band performed was the current single "Rock and Roll Girls." Performed in front of an audience comprised mostly of Warner employees, it was still the first time John had performed live professionally and the first time he had recorded with a band in any medium since 1972.

26

"DEVIOUS PERFIDY"

Just as John was making his comeback, Stu had fallen back in with an old friend. Former Clover guitarist John McFee had been around in the years since Stu and he had worked together. He had played guitar on Elvis Costello's debut, *My Aim Is True;* he had been a Doobie Brother; and in 1985 he hooked up with singer/songwriter Tim Goodman and Doobie percussionist Keith Knudson and put together a country-rock band—called Southern Pacific—with a definite emphasis on the country. When the original bassist didn't work out, McFee asked if Cook would audition. Cook did, and got the job.

In an article about the band for the 10,000 readers of the South Holland, Illinois, *Lansing Economist Pointer* concentrating on the former CCR member, writer Lawrence Arendt stated that "Cook remains on friendly terms with Zaentz." John's name cropped up in the piece. Southern Pacific was also a Warner act. John subscribed to Burrell's, a service that searches newspapers nationwide for clippings that mention the people that hire them. Somehow, via one of these means, a copy of the article got into John's hands.

When John saw the statement about Zaentz, he dashed off a letter to Stu calling the interview a "load of self-serving shit." Not even deigning to comment on the music, John expressed incredility at the idea that Stu and Saul could be friends. Zaentz was the man who had cheated them, promised a better contract, and gave them a tax dodge in the Bahamas. "Never forget the promise, devious perfidy!" he wrote.

The promise referred to the promise circa 1967 of a new contract. This was not the kind of news Stu wanted to find in his mailbox. Over the years, John had become increasingly estranged from the former members of CCR. He communicated with them mostly through his attorneys and via short

209

Chuck Pulin/Star File

Southern Pacific.

letters like this one. Frankly Stu was getting tired of these little *billet doux* arriving in his mailbox, and even more tired of John bemoaning his status as a victim to anyone who would let him moan.

"The same contract has my signature on it," Stu says. "I guess I've done better at getting over it. At least I recognize that no one made me sign it."

Stu and John were both now Warner Bros. recording artists, because Southern Pacific recorded for the Nashville division of the company. They both lived in LA by 1986. Stu had moved to be where his band was based. John and Martha had finally split, and John spent most of his time in LA to be closer to his business, taking an office in the basement of Warner Bros. records. Even by his own admission, as a single man in LA, the notorious puritan of rock started living that stereotypical musician's lifestyle he had so long disdained.

"I was living the life of a bachelor rock 'n' roll party animal," he said. "No responsibilities, sleep whenever I want, get up whenever I want, get drunk, etc., whenever I want.

"I was carousing. I spent a lot of time going to bars and looking for cocktail waitresses. I did everything I thought I should to feel like a rock star."

Los Angeles County is a big place, but the music business is a small world. A few weeks later, John and Stu encountered each other in a hallway at Warner's Burbank offices. "Hey Stuey," John allegedly said. "I hear you're working in a [heh, heh] country band."

"I stopped him in the hall to ask him to stop writing me rude letters," Stu recalls, adding wryly, "I believe the conversation was slightly heated."

For Stu, Southern Pacific was his first experience in a band since the Don Harrison band fell apart nearly a decade earlier. It was the first time he'd played country since the Shit-Kicker Three hotel jams. He didn't find anything in Southern Pacific that strange, though.

"Creedence was pretty much a root-fifth band [i.e., it used simple chord progressions, like I-V]," he said.

> A lot of stuff that Creedence recorded would not get played on rock radio if it were released today; it would be on country radio. So it's not a large change in approach for me. I just try to look at each song and see what would complement the arrangement when I'm trying to decide on a bass part. And if I err, it's usually on the more straightforward side, the simpler side, rather than over-arrange or overplay. I would rather err on the side of simplicity and cleanness because all of the parts have to fit together to help support the song.

What he did find unusual was the situation. In CCR, John had been the front man. In the Sir Douglas bands, Doug Sahm was the leader. Even the Don Harrison band had a "face." However, Southern Pacific was a true group effort. "I find it interesting to be working in a band where there is no one person as the sole focal point," he commented. "I think it makes it more interesting for the listener, in that we can—because there's a lot of talent in this band—pass around the spotlight a bit and really show off more than just one guy or one aspect or one sound or one lead vocal."

As he hadn't been in a band, he hadn't needed to tour. Belonging to a country band it meant spending a lot of time on the road. This was a new experience for Stu:

> We drove rental cars across America for two or three years. Then we got a bus. Some of them were so bad you could find them in the parking lot with your nose.

Southern Pacific was opening some shows for Neil Young when he was in his "country" faze. He had a pretty good band, Johnny Gimble was playing fiddle, I recall. After our first show with him he came to our dressing room and asked us to "tone it down." We all smiled and nodded. After he left we all said, F . . . you, Neil." We never got any more shows, but the nerve of the guy pissed us off. Guess he didn't like following our act.

Stu had spent a good part of his time since CCR producing other artists. Now he found himself in the studio with a country music legend, Jim Ed Norman, who was producing the group's album. Over several decades, Norman had worked with musicians ranging from the Bay Area rockers The New Riders of the Purple Sage to the Osmond Brothers. His work with Mickey Gilley had solidified his reputation in Nashville and beyond. Still, Stu had some problems working with this representative of the old Nashville:

Jim Ed Norman is quite a guy. The classic son of a southern preacher, he's got a wild streak completely dominated by an anal drive to turn everything he produces into Ann Murray. He was the exec who got Southern Pacific signed as Jimmy Bowen was leaving Warner Bros., Nashville. The band had a killer deal, about $250,000 per album budget, etc., but WB never figured out how to promote the project. Jim Ed always wanted us to record lame Nashville written tunes. There are a few on *Kilbilly Hill*. The band gradually took more control of the writing and producing, but Jim Ed was always around to get on a soapbox about what country music really needed. I must say he really believed that between us all there could be big success. I enjoyed getting to know and work with him.

Mostly, though, Stu enjoyed being with a band. "It's totally democratic," he commented, "and I like that. That's what people think bands are about. Creedence started out that way, but somewhere along the line it actually did turn into John's band—although he couldn't have done it without us."

"In Southern Pacific," he quipped about the nature of working among equals, "whenever I played a 'wrong' note the other guys would accuse me of playing jazz."

Perhaps spurred by the two-pronged success of Stu in country and the triumphant return of John to the rock wars, CCR records were selling at unprecedented rates. During a generally lackluster February 1986, *Chronicle* went platinum and *The Concert* went gold.

After the long layoff, spun into a big hit, John's CCR reflexes sprung into play. He knew he had to do two things: the first was make a new album; the other was get a band together so that he could hit the road. He decided to take care of both at the same time. When the songs for his next album were ready, he brought in a band to play them:

> I had to let go of the idea that I was going to do the whole album by myself, like *Centerfield*. I was writing a lot in a little room down in the basement of Warner Bros, and that was taking up all my time. It would have taken so much effort just to get my chops back up. . . . I hadn't played drums or sax in over a year. Then it dawned on me, being in LA and so close to all these prime players, that it would be great to put together the very best talent available and make great records . . . using other musicians is a way to keep the work interesting and fresh.

He also got daring. After disappearing from the public eye for a decade, *Centerfield* had to be close to home. Now that he had a number 1, certified platinum record under his belt, he felt he could take musical chances, perhaps as much an effort to update his sound as to shuck off the CCR association just a little:

> While it was nice that I was received well on *Centerfield*, I kept hearing roots and roots rock 'n' roll and I don't wanna be typecast in that role. I love old records and all that sort of thing, but I'm not stuck there.
> I've always used whatever the latest studio technology happens to be, going back to Creedence days. "Suzie Q" has as much studio technique going for it as "Eye of the Zombie." It's just twenty years later. I get real uncomfortable when people call me the keeper of the roots rock flame. I don't like to carry that mantle around. I'd much rather be thought of as aware and making use of whatever's out there to create the best possible songs. Microchips, computers, synthesizers and digital samplers are just ways to make sounds people are going to remember, that they're going to want to hear again. When I use technology it's filtered through my own musical approach. I'm not bowing at the fount of electronics, but by the same token, I'm not stubbornly holding on to fifties rock and roll as the last good thing that happened in pop music.

While digital drums and some synthesizers showed up on *Centerfield*, his next album was going to be positively high tech. "I decided I needed to know all the options myself before I could make the right choice," he said. "It meant tracking from noon to seven at night and coming back to my little cubbyhole in the basement and working with digital sampling synths, a Macintosh computer and a pile of manuals six feet high . . . until the next morning. I know all three shifts of the maintenance people at Warner Bros. on a first-name basis."

If the music was more modern, so were the album's concerns. " 'Eye of the Zombie,' " he said, "is about terrorism. I have another song on the album called 'Violence Is Golden' which is pretty self-explanatory. The setup is the guy in the middle of any struggle, be it a street struggle or a nation by nation struggle. The guy in the middle selling weapons to both sides is the one making out, and that's what the tune is about.

"I'd been playing with 'Violence Is Golden' for nearly twenty years," he noted. "I had written it in this little notebook I keep. Finally it all came together. It didn't belong on a happy album; it belonged here."

Clearly, John was in a dark frame of mind. He had to deal with renewed hostilities with Zaentz, defending himself against copying his own song in the plagiarism case. His marriage was crumbling. Now that he began to enjoy another moment in the sun, he lived 300 miles away from his hometown, an hour or so even by plane.

Yet, there were also good things that came from his newfound successs. In 1986 the Rock and Roll Hall of Fame had its first induction of members. Among the original inductees was Buddy Holly, and the Hall's committee asked John to enroll him. So John gave a short speech and joined in the jam session afterward.

On March 28, 1986, the federal appeals court ruled in the band's favor in the Castle Bank case. The decision noted that the Castle Bank "consisted primarily of an empty room with a small table on one side." They further pointed out that Burton Kantor had been indicted as early as 1976 (and later acquitted) on charges that he used the bank, his favorite offshore tax shelter, as a means of fostering tax evasion.

With this news recently in hand, John flew back to El Cerrito. In about a month, Warner Bros. would release "Eye of the Zombie," the first single from the new album of the same name. However, he had not come to play, but rather to be recognized as the town declared July 15, 1986, John Fogerty Day. The mayor gave John the following proclamation:

> WHEREAS, John Fogerty, the creative genius force within Creedence Clearwater Revival, one of the best rock and roll bands ever, was raised in El Cerrito, and
>
> WHEREAS, in 1959 John Fogerty started playing with friends Doug Clifford and Stu Cook from Portola Junior High School and continuing through El Cerrito High School representing the El Cerrito Boys Club on a tour of county fairs under the name of the Blue Velvets, and
>
> WHEREAS, Creedence Clearwater Revival, consisting of John playing on guitar and harmonica and singing the vocals; Doug on drums,

Photo © 1986 by Dana Doak. Used with permission.
John accepts a proclamation from El Cerrito mayor Charles R. Lewis IV.

Stu on electric bass; and Tom Fogerty on guitar; burst onto the rock scene in 1968 with a remake of the 1950s hit "Suzie Q," and

WHEREAS, the band established itself as a major attraction by recording an unprecedented list of hits, written, arranged and produced by John, including "Proud Mary," "Bad Moon Rising," "Green River," "Lodi," "Fortunate Son," and "Down on the Corner," in 1969; and continued with hits like "Travelin' Band," "Who'll Stop the Rain," "Up Around the Bend," "Run Through the Jungle," "Long as I Can See the Light," and "Lookin' Out My Back Door" in 1970 and added "Hey Tonight" and "Sweet Hitch-Hiker" in 1971, and

WHEREAS, although John Fogerty never lived in the South, he displayed a talent for writing songs showing a deep understanding of rhythm and blues without betraying the fact that he grew up in El Cerrito, and

WHEREAS, after the fission of Creedence in 1972, John formed the Blue Ridge Rangers and added a couple of more hits to his credit with "Hearts of Stone" and the revival of Hank Williams' tune "Jambalaya," retaining the rock group sound he had made famous with Creedence while, actually, the Rangers was not a group at all, but John himself playing all the instruments and singing all the vocals, and

WHEREAS, more recently, John recorded a new album, *Centerfield*, including the hits "The Old Man Down the Road" and "Rock and Roll Girls," and becoming the number one album in the country, and

WHEREAS, this year John received a Grammy nomination as vocalist on *Centerfield* and he received the Bammy (Bay Area Music Award) for Outstanding Album for 1985.

NOW, THEREFORE, in recognition of his musical talent, his achievements and his contributions to rock music, to his fans around the world and to the citizens of El Cerrito, the El Cerrito City Council does hereby proclaim the Fifteenth Day of July, 1986, as John Fogerty Day.

Signed
Charles R. Lewis, IV
Mayor, of the City of El Cerrito

"I'm truly, deeply honored about this," John said. "I feel strongly about growing up in El Cerrito and living in El Cerrito. It's the small-town values. That's why I'm still here. That's why I raised my kids here. This is neat. This is really neat! This kind of thing reaffirms what this country is all about."

Then he flew back to LA to continue getting his band ready for his first tour in fifteen years.

27

"THERE THEY ARE, SCREWING ME AGAIN"

A few days after Warner Bros.' release date for *Eye of the Zombie*'s first single, the title track, backed with the recording of "I Confess," a non-LP tune, John did something he hadn't done in fourteen years: he went on tour. "That's the energy that's got nothing to do with the brainy guy who sits around and writes songs in the middle of the night," he said about the road.

The "Rockin' All Over the World" tour kicked off with a show at the Mud Island Amphitheater in Memphis on August 28. "I wanted to start here," he told Robert Palmer, "because this city is sort of the center of my musical roots and orientation." Palmer found one flaw with the show, that the band of studio musicians—the same ones who played on the forthcoming album—"provided only intermittently the sort of cohesive group chemistry that Mr. Fogerty's tough, soulful brand of music demands."

But John was exhilirated by performing again before an audience. "I forgot totally what live is," John said at the time. "When the frenzy of emotion first swept over me in Memphis, it made me want to cry. It was like 'Oh yeah! Madison Square Garden, 1970.'"

Throughout the tour, John relied on material from the new album, a couple of songs from the Shep album, and material from *Centerfield*. He played "Centerfield" on a guitar shaped like a Louisville Slugger baseball bat made specially by Kubicki Guitars. He also did some of the old soul and gospel tunes from the Showtime program. However, as he had told anyone who would listen, he did not play any CCR songs during the show. In Memphis, no one called for them. Nor did anyone at a show in Cincinnati. A couple of nights after Memphis, though, at the tour's second stop in Pittsburgh, every song was punctuated by the crowd chanting "Creedence . . . Creedence . . . Creedence. . . ." The same thing occured at a show at Poplar Creek in Chicago.

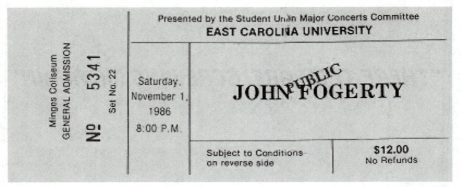

Ticket to John's first tour in over a decade.

Fogerty, however, did not blame the fans, but continued to make his point about Fantasy:

> I know they're doing it because they love those songs.. But it wasn't their fight. There are certain principles at stake that I simply won't subvert. And it won't change. . . . I have no interest in being an oldies act, singing "rolling on the river" until I die. . . . I do think I'm going to have to get to the point where I can at least respond to the audience when they're chanting for Creedence. I mean, I *am* the same guy. I was in Creedence. I still wear flannel shirts. So, it's not like I had a lobotomy. I'm just not doing those particular songs.
>
> I'm still proud of those songs, but I don't own them. They're all owned by Fantasy, and I've been fighting with them since 1970. We're going to court yet again after the first month of the tour. When I hear "Proud Mary" on the radio, I just think of a lawsuit, and I don't want to keep reminding myself of all that.

But some of the fan disaffection came from more than unfamiliarity with the material. John had taken his new spirit of modernism on tour with him. Many fans who hoped for some of the old CCR magic got the voice and the guitar, but little else. In his review of the Garden State Arts Center show in Holmdel, New Jersey, Jeff Nisan noted, "The rough and undisciplined play of his band contrasted terribly with the raw, spare brilliance of the legendary singles. The generous space provided the second guitar and the synth—there was a mid-set instrumental that must have been the national anthem of Venus—proved entirely unjustified."

Jeffrey Mayer/Starfile

John with his Kubicki "Louisville Slugger" guitar.

Unfortunately, most fans weren't familiar with about a third of the material John played at the shows on the first leg of the tour—including "Going Back Home" which Nisan described as "the national anthem of Venus"—because *Eye of the Zombie* wasn't set for release until mid-October, but Fogerty insisted on starting the tour in August. Fogerty again blamed Fantasy for the poorly timed tour:

> Going out here before my next album is released wasn't the way I would have planned to do it. I had to start now because of having to take time later for Fantasy's latest lawsuit.
>
> If I'd waited until this trial was over, and then started rehearsal and lighting and sound, I couldn't be touring until January or February. So there they are, screwing me again.

That summer, in fact the day before he left for Memphis, the process of depositions and pretrial hearing began in the case of Fantasy *v.* Fogerty in which Fantasy was suing John for copyright infringment on "The Old Man Down the Road" John was naturally displeased with having to attend to the trial while at the same time maintain his touring schedule: "I was out on the road for about two weeks and I had to do a deposition all day long by conference-call telephone with parties in three different cities across the U.S. This is while I'm on tour now!"

In these early legal wranglings, the judge upped the ante, ruling that if Fantasy won the case, John would have to surrender *both* his publishing and his songwriting royalties from "The Old Man Down the Road" as part of the damages to the copyright that the court might award. Trying to balance this ruling, John's lawyer countersued, claiming that if John won, Fantasy should turn over the songwriter royalties they held in escrow since beginning the action, and relinquish John's long-sought-after publishing rights. However, the judge dismissed the idea of requiring Fantasy to turn over the publishing.

In October, Warner Bros. released *Eye of the Zombie*. Some critics found the new album compelling, and gave it strongly positive reviews. In *Down Beat*, Gene Santoro gave the album five stars, saying "Fogerty—like any intelligent and thoughtful musician—puts the past to his own energetic and idiosyncratic uses, folds it into his own voice rather than simply recycling old riffs. *Eye of the Zombie* demonstrates once more how a master does that, and just happens to be a terrific rock & roll record as well."

"While not a musical grand slam," Scott Isler wrote in *Musician*, "the album has enough line drives—and even impressive fouls—to mark Fogerty as one of the most promising players in the majors. . . . Fogerty's handed us a near-concept album about the breakdown of law and order. . . . John Fogerty has always hewn pop to his needs rather than vice versa, and the result usually coincides with mass taste. Should *Zombie*'s idealism strike a common nerve, that would be as encouraging as Fogerty's return to action."

Awarding the record a B in his "Consumer Guide" column, Robert Christgau noted "Fogerty was an outsider in the '60s. . . . Then, as now he had no interest in fashion, which is why his music retains an undeniable modicum of interest. But like they say, the '60s are over."

Despite these favorable reviews, many other critics in the mainstream rock press were unimpressed by John's political commentary and his reliance on modern studio technology. *Rolling Stone*'s Anthony DeCurtis panned the album, even questioning John's mental health:

> By the time the LP's closing cut, "Sail Away," recommends a spaceship escape as the means of "leavin' all of this pain behind," any rational person would have to worry that the fabled swamp rocker might have water on the brain. . . . Fogerty's great gift with Creedence Clearwater Revival—in songs like "Down on the Corner," "Fortunate Son" or "Who'll Stop the Rain"—was his ability to dramatize sociopolitical realities in unpretentious, flesh-and-blood terms. Of course, his unfailing instinct for irresistible hooks didn't hurt either. Now Fogerty's flesh-and-blood people have become zombies and caricatures, and his hooks don't cut as cleanly as they used to. While we still have to wonder who'll stop the rain, it's evident that, with disheartening albums like *Eye of the Zombie*, it won't be Fogerty.

Creem's Craig Zeller voiced a common view that Fogerty had lost his way amidst all of the new studio technology:

> For Fogerty, it looks like being in the 80s means getting comfortable with microchips, computers, synthesizers and digital samplers in the studio. It also means filtering out plenty of passion, forgetting that brevity is the soul of wit, and letting perspiration take the place of inspiration. The result is . . . a record that's overloaded with excess baggage, belabored social commentary and a batch of unimaginative songs sadly lacking in spirit.

Even one of his staunchest avatars in the press, *Stereo Review*'s Steve Simels, called *Eye of the Zombie* "a snoozer, the sound of a genuine rock original approaching self-parody."

In retrospect, John came to regret the heavy-handed message of the album. "I assume all of that responsibility," John later conceded. "It was a difficult commercial project, but the little boy in me had all this stuff he wanted to get off his chest."

John vacillated between defending the album's political themes, describing the album as

> pretty hard-hitting and even ugly at the time. And maybe totally out of whack with the background and social awareness of the country. And it kind of fell on deaf ears. I mean, a song like "Eye of the Zombie" is right here, right now. And I had to do it. And "Violence Is Golden"—I mean, the song was out and being played for a couple of months, then Iranscam hits, you know, and it was right there in the verses of the song.

and criticizing his own lack of finesse in dealing with them:

> *Eye of the Zombie* was depressing. But I couldn't help it. . . . I was depressed.
> One of the things I glaringly forgot with *Zombie* is if you're trying to reach an audience, if you're trying to give them some insight, you have to make it accessible. And if you go off too far, forgetting the very audience you're trying to reach, then you really can't blame them for not getting it.

The public seemed to feel the same way. After the success of *Centerfield* and "The Old Man Down the Road," the title track from *Zombie* stalled at a very disappointing number 81 scant weeks after its release. The album itself topped out at number 26, also pretty quickly after it came out, not a horrible performance, but pretty dismal considering it was following a chart topper. Nonetheless, the album even managed to go gold.

When John hit the road again for the West Coast leg of the "Rockin' All Over the World" tour, a group called the Fogerty Liberation Front, based about thirty miles South of El Cerrito on the East Bay, started to leaflet shows with their manifesto:

> Excitement is in the air over John Fogerty's concert at the Oakland arena on December 7. But a pall is cast by his stern pronouncement he's "not gonna do the old Creedence songs ever again."
> Fogerty's sound resonates from a place deep inside American popular music. The purging strains of Creedence's best stuff are strikingly relevant today: "Bad Moon Rising," "Who'll Stop the Rain"—these and many others deserve to be played again, live, by the only person who can truly deliver them.
> The FLF is not seeking to turn John Fogerty into an oldies act—with songs as good as those on *Centerfield* and *Eye of the Zombie*, there is no danger of that. But Fogerty's public rationale for not playing the CCR material is not an artistic one, rather, having lost his performance royalties in a legal settlement

with Fantasy records, he now views playing the old songs as nothing more than selling Fantasy's products.

But why take this anger out on the fans? If "Proud Mary" can be performed for the elite at the Rock and Roll Hall of Fame event, why can't it be played for his long time Bay Area fans? Any baseball player knows if he wants the coach to put him in, he's got to give it his *all*.

A CALL TO ACTION

There should be no disturbances during the concert's main set—we have enough respect for John Fogerty to let him make his statement. But *when he returns for the encore, he should be met by a solid wall of sound from us:*
"CREE-DENCE! CREE-DENCE! CREE-DENCE!"
Let him know how you feel!
Our Credo: We love the new songs — We love the old songs.

John, however continued to avoid that part of his musical heritage.

Not having been on the road for a while, and certainly not used to the two-hour shows that the contemporary concert business more or less required, John found himself having problems. While he ran ten miles a day, and had no diffiuclty with stamina, he hadn't used his voice night after night in nearly a decade and a half, and even then, it was for considerably less time onstage. He started missing notes. During some shows, he took to perform-ing the strenuous "Mr. Greed" as an instrumental.

Joe Hannigan, an audio engineer, approached the soundman at the Philly show to ask him about missed cues. "He said it was the opposite," Hannigan reports. "The fader was up, but nothing was coming out. He said they were VERY worried about John's voice (and loss of it during that tour). From where we sat, it looked like [John] was singing but the mic level was down. Depending on who you believe, it was problematic either way."

The tour brought one unexpected benefit to John. After a show in South Bend, Indiana, John first encountered Julie Kramer, a divorcée with a young daughter. "The first time we met, I was on tour and we were in the hotel lounge," John recalled. "We talked and had a nice chat. Her sister was there and it was all quite wholesome. Of course, I tried to ruin it all by asking her back to my hotel room, but she wisely said, 'Uh-uh, ain't going for that.' About the first time I saw her, I recognized that she would be good for me. We both did this very cautiously. We instinctively knew, 'Let's not mess this up.'

"She came and saw me later on the tour," he said. "And again, we just talked at the hotel, down in the restaurant area, for a couple of hours, and she went home with her girlfriend. And as we would meet each other and see each other more often, I began to realize that this was really it. But it hap-pened too soon for me, because I was just getting out of a marriage and she was just getting out of a marriage, too. . . . So we agreed to stay apart for a year. She lived in Indiana and I lived [in Los Angeles]."

Back in Los Angeles after the tour, John became a fixture at after-hours jams. One night after a show by Taj Mahal at the Palomino, he was jamming with Bob Dylan, George Harrison, and Mahal. Dylan called for the song he once referred to as the best song of the year some eighteen years earlier, "Proud Mary." John tried to get him to change the subject, but Dylan insisted.

"He said to me, 'Hey, John, if you don't do these tunes, the world's going to remember "Proud Mary" as Tina Turner's song,'" he recalled in *Rolling Stone.* "I said, 'Yeah! You're right'"

On Independence Day 1987 John had agreed to headline with such notables as Stevie Wonder, Linda Ronstadt, Anita Baker, James Ingram, James Brown, Neil Diamond, and Crosby, Stills & Nash at the long belated "Welcome Home" show for veterans of the Vietnam war to be held in Washington, DC. Despite the relative success of his recent albums, he knew these records held minimal resonance for these vets. The people at this show did not come all this way, some of them from across the country, to hear that music. These former soldiers had listened to him sing "Run Through the Jungle" while they were actually running through the jungle. So many Creedence Clearwater Revival songs had taken on new meaning in that context. The veterans of that conflict wanted to hear him play "Run Through the Jungle" and "Fortunate Son." They especially wanted to hear him play "Who'll Stop the Rain," a tune that had become something of an anthem during the war. As far as the people gathered here were concerned, he'd written the sound track to the most savage part of the war.

Way back in 1970, a lifetime ago, Harvey Siders had asked John whether the band would do a tour, playing for the vets in Vietnam. John had told Siders at the time, "Bring 'em home and we'll play for them."

But now, Fogerty was on the verge of starting a new career, or at least the second act of the one he had started in El Cerrito, California, as a teenager during the waning days of the '50s. He wanted appreciation for the new music he had sweated so hard to create. He certainly didn't want to rely on success that was nearly two decades old. The ascent of *Centerfield* told him that he didn't have to. Some lives did get second acts; some artists could enjoy a second chance.

As he strode up on stage, with a band he'd met in LA called the Boneshakers, it might have been 1970 again. Certainly he had aged well. Musically he was sharper than ever, having just ended his tour. He started with a lick that sounded like "The Old Man Down the Road," but quickly changed into "Born on the Bayou." The audience went nuts. He burned through "Down on the Corner," "Who'll Stop the Rain," "Up Around the Bend," "The Mid-

Elliot Landy/Starfile

John at the Welcome Home concert for Vietnam vets.

night Special," "Bad Moon Rising," and was joined by nearly everyone who had performed that afternoon for an extended "Proud Mary."

Fogerty had to overcome a great deal of bitterness to perform the songs these veterans had come all this way to hear. By playing these songs on a televised concert, the performance royalties definitely made more money for Jondora.

John spoke to the crowd: "I want to tell you something real short and sweet. I'm talkin' to the vets here. I myself have gone through about twenty years of pain. I looked it right in the face and said, 'Well, you got a choice. You can do it for twenty more years or you can just say, "That's what happened." You can't change it, that's just what happened.'

"So I'm telling you guys, that's what happened. You got the shaft. You know it, and we know it. It's reality. So drop it."

Part Four

~

"THE ONLY WAY WE TALK TO JOHN IS THROUGH OUR LAWYERS"

1988–1997

28

"A DIVORCE THAT NEVER HEALS"

John himself was still vying for the title of "King of Pain." He spent a good part of 1987 with his lawyer, Ken Sidle, preparing for the Fantasy v. Fogerty trial scheduled to start in the fall. Despite what he told the vets, the CCR music continued to dredge up new worlds of personal anguish. He hadn't talked to his brother Tom in several years, and his mother, Lucile, was getting on in years. Professionally, he found *Eye of the Zombie* very disappointing. Even he heard the bile in the grooves. "I was a pretty confused and you might say bitter guy," he conceded a decade later.

John's bitterness, at least about having sold his performance royalties, had solid roots. Fantasy had grown into one of the largest independent record companies in America, largely thanks to money it made from CCR. While they didn't have the distribution clout of Warner or Columbia (hence the "independent" tag), they had an enviable catalog.

Despite having been apart nearly five times as long as they recorded, CCR continued to sell beyond anyone's hopes. At the National Association of Recording Merchandiser's Independent Distributors and Manufacturers 1987 fall conference, Creedence shared the top indie Best Seller award with rappers Run-DMC. The East Coast rap group won "best-selling indie 7" and album of the year; CCR laid claim to the top selling indie catalog title.

John continued his new carousing ways, but he discovered that after twenty years of marriage—and marrying young at that—he wasn't very good at being single, dating, and all the rest. "I don't know where I got the high idea that this was fun," he commented, "because I was pretty miserable and pretty much alone a lot. I was not the swinging guy that you see on TV."

Having met Julie during the fall tour, the one-year moratorium that they had set on their relationship was almost over. They started to make plans.

Steven Toepp/Ken Davis

Rocking the heartland:
Duke Tumatoe

During one of his trips to Julie's neck of the woods, he heard an ad on the radio for a band called Duke Tumatoe and the Power Trio. The name intrigued him. He asked around and discovered that ol' Duke had been a regional fixture in the midwest for over a decade. His curiosity piqued, Fogerty went to the show. "These people were having a good time," he said. "They knew the words to the songs, shouted them back and kept the whole thing rolling along. I hadn't experienced that in a long time."

John kept on coming back. The band kept impressing him. He met the group, and accepted an occasional invitation to go on stage and jam with them. And he started thinking that maybe they should make a record. Actually, Duke already had four albums out, two on San Francisco-based, roots/blues indie label Blind Pig, two for Chicago-based blues/roots indie Flying Fish. John had bigger ideas for the band.

"Eventually," he said, "I realized the person to produce the record was me. That was a big leap. I was kind of moving along , and I had to ask myself if I really wanted to do that. It's time-consuming. You're getting involved in the dynamics of a band, which is like getting into someone's household—maybe you don't want to do that.

"Finally I just went backstage one night and said, 'I'd like to produce you guys.' They sort of excitedly went, 'Yeah, yeah, yeah,'" he said.

"John said, 'I'm gonna make you guys famous,'" said Tumatoe. "'I'm gonna make an album for you and get you on Warner Bros. Records, and you guys are gonna be big stars.' It's like, 2:30 in the morning, and how many times have we heard something like that before? Thanks a lot, John, that's wonderful. Take care of yourself, bye.'"

John went back to LA and met with his avatar at Warner Bros., Lenny Waronker. He brought a live tape of Duke and the trio and a portable stereo.

"We all know how controlled rock 'n' roll has become, kind of sedate and middle-aged, I'm ashamed to say, and very manufactured," he recounted the conversation. "We were almost being naughty little boys. Live! It's like 'back to the old days,' almost. He said, 'Go ahead. Go do it.' I went 'Fine, I'll tell the guys in the band.'"

So, in the fall of '87, a friend of John's went to see the band and told them they were going to start making an album that winter, as soon as John got back from hunting. "We had no contract, no budget," Tumatoe mused. "I don't know what the hell's going on, but all of a sudden we're making an album with Warners."

Over the course of a week, toward the end of January 1989, John recorded twenty-four hours worth of tape of Duke Tumatoe and the Power Trio in concert. Then he spent three months mixing and editing them. The album, *I Like My Job*, came out late in the winter 1989 to great fanfare and better sales than Tumatoe's previous albums, though certainly nothing remarkable by Warner Bros. standards.

It gave John a reason to be in South Bend, however, and close to Julie. "When we finally moved in together," he said, "which was just about the end of 1987, just about Christmas time, my life started really changing for the better."

Stu was also feeling pretty satisfied. Southern Pacific was still playing out and recording. They were also pretty successful, though in a different world from any with which Stu had ever dealt.

"We were prepared for a difference between a pop and country hit," he explained, "but it was still a shock. We didn't realize that a number 1 country hit doesn't mean the same thing as a number 1 pop single. You can sell a lot of albums off a pop hit, but that's not necessarily true with a country hit. . . . Guys with hats who sing in baritone voices seem to do best in country. It's harder for a band like us to find acceptance."

By 1988, they had a couple of top-40 country hits and an album that peaked at number 31 on the country album charts. "My personal favorite Southern Pacific record is *Zuma*," Stu said of the album they made in 1988. "Great recorded sound, and several hits as well."

Zuma put the band on the map. While the initial single, "Midnight Highway," topped out at number 14 on the country charts, the following two,

"New Shade of Blue" and "Honey, I Dare You" reached number 2 and number 5, respectively. This success opened some doors, and even earned them some product endorsements—not the sort of thing CCR had been offered (and routinely rejected) or deals like the Rolling Stones enjoyed. The returns from country were more modest. Southern Pacific endorsed Justin Boots. "I've still got a closet full of Justin Boots," Stu laughs. "They didn't pay us in money, just in boots."

Sometime in the spring of 1988, John finished up with the bulk of the work on the Duke Tumatoe album. John and Julie moved housekeeping from South Bend to Los Angeles. John found an element in his life that had been missing for a while: joy.

Tom had endured several operations on his back and neck. In the spring of 1988, he reunited with Randy Oda. Along with his son Jeff and Randy's brother Kevin, they went into Fantasy's recording studio to start work on a new project, Tom's first in nearly a decade. They took a break so that Tom could enjoy some time with his new daughter, Nicole. Then something else cropped up.

"In 1988 I had gone on a backpacking trip up in the Sierra Mountains," Jeff recalls. "I was gone for two and a half weeks. When I came back there was a message on my machine that my dad was sick. Really sick. They said I needed to catch a plane and come down to Arizona. I thought that was really strange, that he would catch pneumonia in the middle of the desert."

The pneumonia was a symptom of something else, however. In the course of the operations on his back over the past decade, his family suspects, Tom was given some tainted blood. Now AIDS had decimated his immune system, leaving him susceptible to pretty much anything the wind blew his way.

"Tom didn't want to have everyone know what his illness was. It was the last thing in his life that he had any kind of control over," says Jeff. "There was a point where Tom and I sat down and talked. We were actually going to have a press conference and discuss it and bring it out in public, but we had the little ones to deal with. Ashley was six. She had no protection for herself. Nikki was just born. She wasn't even one, I don't think."

With a new baby in the house and a new recording project in the works, Tom had a lot to live for. He got himself well again, started working out, and got into good physical shape. "That's when we started working on the second part of Sidekicks," Jeff says. "We actually finished the first side, which became the second side, or the second half of the record. When we came back to do what was going to be side two, there's much more life and energy. My dad was putting everything he had into it. It became stronger than side one, so we made side two side one."

"When Tom returned to the studio," Tom's wife, Trish, wrote in the liner notes to Sidekicks, "his first desire was to finish what now was not just

Jeff and Tom Fogerty rock out.

another recording project, but for Tom, a statement. He truly felt that his illness—and all he had gone through—had happened for a reason, that something positive needed to be the result of it and that he would settle for nothing less than his ideal vision of musical perfection for this album. He and Randy went back into the studio with a totally new sense of direction, inspiration and passion."

Meanwhile, the legal wheels kept grinding for John. In the fall of 1988 a jury started hearing the case of Fantasy *v.* Fogerty. This followed nearly two years of legal shenanigans and depositions involving everyone from Bob Fogerty to a couple of dozen journalists who had interviewed John about *Centerfield.*

"Mal Burnstein conducted the deposition [for Fantasy]," recalls *San Francisco Chronicle* music critic Joel Selvin. "The *Chron* sent a lawyer along with me and I looked at my lawyer for approval before I answered any question, like some mobster at a Senate hearing. I tangled with Burnstein over procedural issues just to warm him up and then sat around for hours while the fucker didn't get his questions answered."

The case covered some generally untrod ground. "When we researched this," John's attorney Ken Sidle related, "we couldn't find a case where a songwriter was accused of plagiarizing his own song. There was a case in which the artist Vargas was accused of painting the same girls in *Playboy* that he used to paint in *Esquire,* and there was a similar case against an artist who painted cardinals for the Franklin Mint and then went out and painted them somewhere else. But this is the only case that ever went to the jury over a songwriter accused of plagiarizing his own song."

Fogerty viewed the case as nothing short of harassment. Fantasy had turned up the volume as early as February 1985. They wrote to John's sheet music publisher, advising them of the impending lawsuit: "We have just learned that Columbia Pictures Publications has published sheet music for the composition 'The Old Man Down the Road,' " Fantasy's lawyer Malcolm Burnstein wrote in a letter to the company. "Enclosed please find a copy of a letter I sent to John C Fogerty on January 29. The letter to Mr. Fogerty therefore applies equally to Columbia Pictures Publications and I must inform you that we are in the process of preparing a suit for infringement of copyright. Columbia Pictures Publications will be named in that lawsuit. . . . Of course you can minimize the damage done to my client by your company and your company's risk by taking such steps as are available to you to recompense Fantasy for it's loss and damage." Fantasy also had the firms that took care of their overseas publishing write similar letters to the companies that handled John's copyrights overseas.

During the deposition process, Fantasy attorney Malcolm Burnstein couldn't get John to deal with "The Old Man Down the Road" and "Run Through the Jungle" in the same sentence. Burnstein questioned John about his playing the finished version of *Centerfield* for the Warner brass:

B: For your music to be vital, it doesn't necessarily have to sound like music that you had previously made that was vital?

F: Not necessarily, no.

B: So in what way was it conveyed to you that there was general agreement at this late September meeting that your ability to make vital music was in some way related to your former ability to create the Creedence music?

F: I don't think it was related that way. I think they were expressing to me that they were happy I was able to make vital music. In other words, I had made a good record.

But what they were telling me was that they were going to put the record out. What I'm getting out of that is "Finally, I'm able to make vital music again." Now when I say that, it's just because what I do comes out like me. It doesn't come out like you.

B: Fortunately, or the record wouldn't have been put out.

But in your mind, at least, that vitality that you were talking about related to the kind of music that you were writing for Creedence, writing and performing?

F: Not necessarily so.

B: What about "Old Man"?

F: What about it?

B: Does it sound like Creedence music?

F: It sounds like swamp music. Basically, it's got a good guitar lick that starts it. It's got a great solo. It's a great rock and roll record . . .

B: Do you recall seeing anywhere yourself quoted as saying "Fantasy sues me for breathing"?

F: I don't recall seeing that . . .

B: You recall thinking it, though, don't you?

F: I think I feel that way right now, yes.

John recalled that the first time he even heard about the action was at a meeting with Warner Bros. Head of Business Affairs Dave Berman:

F: I just recall that we both thought it was ridiculous.

B: Without knowing what song Fantasy was referring to, how did you know it was a ridiculous claim?

F: Because "Old Man Down the Road" is a brand new song. By then, dozens
    of people had listened to the record and nobody ever mentioned or
    brought up the fact that "Old Man" sounded like any other Creedence
    song . . .

B: Did you ever see any article that said ["Old Man Down the Road"]
    sounded like "Run Through the Jungle"?

F: I've seen things in the paper that . . . described "Old Man Down the Road"
    as sounding like either "Run Through the Jungle" or "Green River," and I
    think I even remember some [comparing it to] "Born on the Bayou."

What Burnstein had to prove in court, however, was not that the two songs
sounded alike. He had to prove they were, in fact, essentially the same song.
Through the two weeks of the trial, the six-person jury heard the songs "Run
Through the Jungle" and "The Old Man Down the Road" perhaps half a
dozen times. Fantasy played both songs as programmed from a sequencer:
they played the sequences together, they played the sequences one after the
other, they played them on top of each other. But even the keyboard player
Fantasy hired testified that the sheet music from the two songs was different.

On Halloween, John's team got their "at bats." One radio station called
the it "the concert even Bill Graham couldn't put on: John Fogerty live at the
Federal Building." The gallery was full of fans who had waited by the court-
house as if they were waiting for concert tickets. John entered the courtroom
in a conservative blue suit. His hand was in a plaster cast. John explained the
injury: "I got very angry a couple of months ago [about the case], hit a chair
and broke my right hand."

Despite his injury, John brought a guitar and amp. He ran through a
series of CCR songs. Fantasy's lawyer said that gave John's side an unfair
advantage: "It wasn't testimony," Burnstein was quoted as saying, "It was a
performance." However, "I basically was sitting in a chair and illustrating
how I wrote songs," Fogerty contended.

At one point during the cross-examination, one of Fantasy's lawyers
started asking John musical questions. "Their lawyers did not know anything about music," John recalled. "He asked me, 'Have you ever used a second . . . an interval of that is a progression of a second?'

"So, I'm kinda like helping a tourist from out of town, 'Oh, I think I know
what you mean! You mean, have I ever used an interval that goes up a distance of two semitones, a second!'

"I look at him and I said, 'Yes, I've used that.'"

When the lawyer didn't ask any more questions, John looked at him and,
according to *Billboard*'s Robin Tolleson, snapped, "Yeah, I did use that half
step. What do you want me to do, get an inoculation?"

One musicologist testified that the riffs in both songs showed up repeatedly in John's music. He said John had "made this structure commonplace."

"What's at stake," *Rolling Stone* reported John saying outside the courtroom, "is whether a performer can continue to use his own style as he grows and goes through life. I can feel Lennon, Dylan, Bruce Springsteen and Leiber and Stoller standing behind me going 'Johnny don't blow this.' "

He didn't. After deliberating for only three hours, the jury found that John did not plagiarize himself.

"It would be hard to be a juror," Burnstein opined to *Billboard*, "and hear a day and a half performance by a rock superstar and not be affected, even though it had nothing to do with the issues of the trial. It wasn't related at all to whether or not the songs were substantially similar." However, the jury foreman disagreed, stating: "There may have been similarities, but there were not substantial similarities." Another juror added, "Creative people have got to have rights to create without being harassed by too many business people types."

"It was clearly just harassment," John contended at the time. "Another thing to make me mad and make me spend and lose money and time."

Despite this victory, there were two more suits pending between Fantasy and Fogerty, including the issue of slander. While this trial gave him ample opportunity to publicly air his grievances against Zaentz and Fantasy, at the end of the trial, a more conciliatory Burnstein claimed, "We are discussing settlement of all issues with Mr. Fogerty and his counsel. What we're trying to do is see if we can get everything disposed of at minimal cost to everybody and avoid future lawsuits. That's everyone's hope, on both sides."

Money was on John's mind. Close to three years in the making, his defense had not been cheap. According to *Billboard*'s Bill Holland, John and Warner Bros. had built up in excess of a million dollars in lawyer fees. After winning his victory, John filed suit against Fantasy to recover his legal fees. That suit was turned down, so he pressed his suit to the appeals court.

Money was on the minds of the other three members of CCR as well. Every time a licensing opportunity came up for CCR material, it resulted in a battle. John was adamantly opposed to the use of CCR material in any means, especially since the heating up of his hostilities with Fantasy. Stu and Doug felt this unfairly deprived them of extra income from the group's back catalog. Toward the end of 1988, they decided to do something about it.

"Stu and I provided Fantasy with our written approval for compilations," Doug said. "We stated that our two votes were a majority sufficient to authorize compilations of Revival songs as a trio. Of course, we did not constitute a majority for approval regarding quartet recordings." In exchange for this grant, Fantasy gave Stu and Doug a "substantial royalty increase." Tom almost always voted for these projects, leaving John as the lone voice of dissent.

This assignment infuriated John, who felt he was betrayed by his ex-bandmates:

> I have spent years complaining, to no avail, to Fantasy about its licensing of our CCR songs and recordings for what I believed were inappropriate uses, such as commercials for car wax and beer. A major break in my relationship with Clifford, Cook and Tom occurred when I discovered . . . that they had supposedly "assigned" their individual voting rights on compilation recording requests to Fantasy—the very entity that had caused many of our financial problems. These purported assignments were done without any notice to me and were a slap in the face to me: after I had agreed to defer to their decisions out of compassion for the financial hardship that Fantasy had caused them, they sold out these important artistic rights to Fantasy in exchange for some lump-sum payments from Fantasy.

John made this discovery when he came across a compilation Shell Oil put out in the spring of 1989. Called *Cruisin' Classics*, it was a cassette with songs by the Beach Boys and others, a greatest hits compilation for the car. Fill up, and you got one for a nominal cost. Fantasy licensed "Proud Mary" to them for this compilation.

"John was insistent that this not happen," Jeff says. "Once he found out that it had happened, that it was pressed and already out there on the shelves, he was completely pissed off and threatened to sue everybody. Then he made these little boxes. Inside the box were pictures of dead birds with an empty Shell Oil can in the middle of the box and a nasty letter. He made a box and sent one to every single executive at Fantasy, sent one to Doug, Stu and my dad."

John saw the compilation as a way for the polluting oil companies to polish their image. In his eyes it was a complete violation of the word "Clearwater" in the band's name. "Shame on all of you," he railed. "Don't you guys ever read the paper? Ever heard of Exxon . . . Valdez . . . ALASKA?! . . . Your collective greed in the face of my generosity is repugnant . . . . How about a Charlie Manson benefit tape? Or perhaps 'Live Aid for the Aryan Nation'? Lotta bucks there . . . ."

Whether John had this right, however, was the cause of debate, and eventually a court case, which is still pending judgment.

Three years after *Eye of the Zombie*, Fogerty hadn't even thought of going into the studio to follow it. With his carousing and subsequent relationship with Julie, the Duke Tumatoe album, the court case, and everything else that was going on, little wonder. As Malcolm Burnstein had hinted, John and Fantasy eventually negotiated their various other legal problems, resulting in John issuing a public apology (and a large private check) to Fantasy's principal owner. John further enlisted Bill Graham to help him negotiate the rest of his problems with the company, hiring Graham's company as his first professional manager. John claims that much of 1988–1992 was spent trying to patch up the rift between himself and his former bandmates.

> Around 1989, I spent considerable energy trying to get everything resolved, make everyone happy. Sometimes people just want to retreat into the place where they feel strong and hostile. That's kind of the way things stayed.
>
> My efforts at resolving all the disputes between me and Saul and me and the other members of Creedence Clearwater just didn't work out. But I wasted three years trying to do it—expecting to come to an end where we would all feel better. It just didn't work.
>
> In the end, I decided that I'd never speak to them again because they are liars, treacherous, untrustworthy and above everything else, very much jealous of me."

"I see that in print all the time," Stu mused. "John has never tried to resolve anything with Doug and I. In fact, it's the opposite; Doug and I have made overtures to John throughout the years. It's never been right for him to try and reach out to our extended hand. There's just so many complexities to this whole issue, due to many years of non-communication between John and the rest of his former bandmates."

In court, Stu was blunter still: "Our former high school friend and band member has entirely alienated himself from us. . . . Over the years, John has become increasingly abusive."

"My relationship with them is like a divorce that never heals," John countered, "and the combatants just keep fighting."

29

"DON'T LET HIM GO WITHOUT SAYING GOOD-BYE"

The Fantasy Building underwent a name change to the Saul Zaentz Film Center in 1989, Zaentz expanded the company's capacity, adding on three million dollars worth of film-based utilities. He added a dubbing stage, eight editing rooms, an engineering room, a film vault, an editorial services shop and a forty-eight-seat screening room. In one building, Zaentz had put together a film facility to be reckoned with, and all miles out of the Hollywood sphere of influence.

"Tom and Saul Zaentz came by the Meridian Hotel," Merl Saunders recalls of an evening sometime in 1989, after he hadn't seen either one for a long time. "I was music director for the Meridian Hotel in San Francisco. They walked in, I thought I would have a heart attack. We sat down and just talked and talked. No matter where I played, Saul always popped in."

By early 1990, Tom had taken a turn for the worse. John still had not come to see him, though he had been informed of Tom's condition. His one possible acknowledgment of Tom's illness was playing a May 1989 West Coast AIDS benefit concert at the Oakland Coliseum. John played with Jerry Garcia, Tom's old bandmate in the Group, and other members of the Dead. They did a set of "Born on the Bayou," "Green River," "Down on the Corner," "Rock and Roll Girls," "Centerfield," "Proud Mary," "Suzie Q," and "Long Tall Sally."

In a 1986 conversation with Don Everly, John admitted that he was not talking to Tom. "My poor mom's gotta be . . ." and he made a despairing face. Lucile Fogerty died on December 17, 1988. Her sons never patched up their differences, but there was still the chance when she passed on.

Despite Tom's illness, things had not improved between the brothers. "The extent of John's anger towards us was illustrated by his refusal to visit his dying brother," Doug later stated in court proceedings. "I wrote John a letter asking him to visit Tom before he passed away."

In that letter, he told John about a few days that he and Laurie had spent with Tom and Trish. He warned John that Tom was desperately ill. Although Tom seemed in good spirits and was bearing up well, it was clear how ravaged the disease had left his body. The letter bore Doug's ineffable sadness at the imminent loss of someone who had been a close friend through most of their adult life. "He told me that he had much to live for as we watched his two little girls play in the backyard. It was a sad thing to watch."

He urged John to see his brother, to ignore the issues that had kept them apart all this time, just to visit. He concluded, "Don't let him go without saying goodbye."

Stu was incredulous about actually writing anything sympathetic to John, especially in light of the kind of letters with which John had favored him and the rest of the band over the years. However, for Tom's well-being as well as John's, Stu also wrote to implore John to visit his dying brother. The letter actually expressed a certain amount of empathy for John's situation. He begged John to not only see his brother but to let go of the things in his past that caused John all this pain.

"I hear that you're not going to see him because you'd feel 'uncomfortable' and that would make everyone feel the same way. Please give me a break. You act like you're the person with the problem! . . . This is not your wasteful war with Saul, it's your brother! . . . Be his brother, his friend. He'd love to see you. It would be good for you."

John never responded to Doug or Stu's letters.

Tom tried to spend as much of his remaining time as he could at home. Several times, though, he had to be hospitalized. Jeff came down with mononucleosis and had to stay away from his dad through most of the early summer of 1990 while he recovered. When he returned to Tom's home early in August, Tom was again in the hospital.

"Doug was there and Uncle Bob was there," he recalls. "Stu had just left the day before."

We were kind of rotating shifts at the hospital to always have someone with him. He was pretty sick and out of it at that time. He had a bunch of IVs and he was hooked up to all kinds of machines.

Doug was down there for a week, maybe two. Bob was down there for the first week. He showed me the routine of what to do and was there for support, but he had to get back. So, I sort of took over the night watchman's job. I would go to the hospital at about four or five in the afternoon, stay up all night and go home around ten in the morning. I did that continuously.

John had been down there a couple of days before that. I think he went to see my dad before he died for his own peace of mind, and not for my dad's wishes or spirit.

Tom decided that he'd rather die at home and left the hospital. He spent the last four weeks of his life in his and Trish's house in Scottsdale. He had one last request of his former bandmates.

"My dad said one of the last things he wanted," Jeff says, "he asked Doug and Stu and John if they would get together at my dad's house, in the living room, move the couches aside, set up some gear and just play for themselves. Don't roll tape, don't have anybody there, not play for an audience, just jam again for an hour or two. He said everyone agreed to do it. Then when he got home from the hospital, even though he was really sick, John refused to come, which really sucked. That really broke my dad's spirit."

"During the time Tom was terminally ill," John related, "Bill Graham approached me once again on behalf of Clifford, who wanted the four of us to perform together again. My response was that it was unconscionable to even suggest that my dying brother perform. I later told Tom's wife, Tricia, that I would be happy to play with him again in the privacy of his home, but due to his untimely death, we never had a chance."

"John visited Tom," Doug stated, "but denied Tom his wish to play one more time together, if not in public, at least in Tom's living room."

Tom died on September 6, 1990. "He developed more fluid in his lungs and had respiratory problems," Bob said, "and just didn't get better." Tom was forty-eight years old.

His funeral was a private affair attended by only family and friends, including Doug and several people from Fantasy. Asked to eulogize him, his brother John said Tom was "the eternal optimist, childlike, always positive . . . a hero." He added, "We didn't want to conquer Wall Street or take over nations. We wanted to grow up and be musicians. I guess we achieved half of that, becoming rock and roll stars. We didn't necessarily grow up."

He never did make his peace with his brother, though. "A lot of things were unresolved," he reflected.

When it became sort of imminent, and we both knew he was going to die, I tried to kind of fix stuff up, straighten things out. I really worked hard at resolving, and Tom just sort of stayed, maddeningly, in a sublime, almost unresponsive world. He made up his own frame of reference, his own history about what had occurred before, and where everything was now. A sort of make-believe. It was up to me to either bust him or just be polite. Tom made

Courtesy Graham Niven

Tom Fogerty 1941–90.

me suspend disbelief if I was going to talk to him. But it wasn't the truth, it wasn't reality. So he died leaving me holding that balloon filled with all those things that I had to deal with because he obviously did not. His death was a very sad thing for me. . . . I thought mom would have loved it if we could have resolved this, and that's why I tried so hard. Unfortunately it didn't happen.

As with so much in the long history of Creedence, John managed to view Tom's death primarily as it affected him. "He died," he said, "leaving me with the turmoil."

30

"DOWN TO THE CROSSROADS, TO GET THE SCENT BACK"

Apprently, there was one other legacy that Tom left John. He wanted to bring John back to his roots, and asked his son to help him by making a tape of his favorite music.

"The day before my dad died," Jeff Fogerty recalls,

he said, "I want to have a long conversation with you and tell you what I want you to do in life and stuff." He said, "I want you to go into the music room and get this record and this record and this record.' He knew exactly where the records were. His mind was there, his body was just sick. He knew what cuts he wanted to hear. He wanted me to make a bunch of tapes of this old R&B and blues for John. They had had a long discussion, when John was there, about getting back to their roots when they first started as kids. He told me, "Don't give him the records, but tape every single one and then go down to the store and get this, this and this on CD, because it's out now. And make this big box for him and send it to him, so he can get back into it like when we were little kids again."

So, I wrote all this stuff down. About two weeks after he died, I started compiling this stuff. I probably had twenty CDs and maybe about twenty tapes of this old, rare, stuff that you can't find. I tried to find copies of the records to send them to him. My dad said, "If you can find them, go ahead and send them to him, but you probably won't." So I taped all this stuff, and it was really difficult for me to do. This was the last mission my dad asked me to do. So, I made this huge box and I wrote this little letter. I said, "John, this is the last thing that Tom asked me to do. It's really important that you get this. Please call me or write me or let me know that you got this when you get this so I know that it didn't get lost and I won't have to make you another one." I never got a response, ever.

245

I sent it so John had to sign it himself—his wife couldn't sign it, Bob couldn't sign it, John had to sign it. So I got his signature on the thing. I knew he got it.

"I talked to Bob a while later," Jeff adds about the tapes. "I asked, 'Did John ever get that package I sent you?' Bob said, 'Oh, yeah. He got the package and he listens to it all the time.' I thought, 'What a bastard. He didn't even fucking call me to say thanks or "Yes, I got it," or anything.'"

Although John never acknowledged it, the receipt of this musical message from his brother apparently reignited his desire to find out more about the roots of his music. John had been doing a considerable amount of traveling since finishing the Duke Tumatoe album. In addition to the trip to Arizona to see his dying brother, and a subsequent one for the funeral, he had been making pilgrimages to the South, digging up his blues roots.

"The urge was actually coming to me about a year before I ever went," he said, "but I couldn't explain to myself why I wanted to go so I put off doing it. That's sort of a scary thing when a little voice keeps saying 'Go to Mississippi.'"

"I packed up a suitcase," he says, "took a notebook and a boom box and went on an expedition to Mississippi."

While poking around the overgrown graveyard of the Mount Zion Missionary Baptist Church in Morgan City, Mississippi, John ran into Skip Henderson. Henderson, a used guitar dealer from New Brunswick, New Jersey, had heard a similar voice to the one John heard. Henderson convinced Mount Zion's minister and his parishioners that a monument to blues legend Robert Johnson, supposedly interred there, would help the troubled church raise funds.

This graveyard became Henderson and John Fogerty's particular *Field of Dreams*. Together, they searched for the unmarked grave of Robert Johnson. John gave Henderson some money to continue his work. Henderson got Columbia Records, the company that had recently released a platinum-selling, Grammy-winning boxed set of Johnson's work, to pony up $17,000 to put up a monument for Johnson and pay off the church's mortgage.

Fogerty suggested that Henderson put up a similar monument in the New Jerusalem Missionary Baptist Church cemetery marking the resting place of one of Johnson's mentors, Charley Patton. Fogerty attended the dedication of the Charlie Patton Memorial with Pop Staples. "That big event for Charley Patton, it is an anchor for me," he related, calling it, "one of the really cool things I've done in my life."

At the dedication ceremony, John had dual epiphanies. One had been a long time coming; the second had taken a long time to realize. The one that had simmered for a while in the back of John's head had to do with the performers' legacies, particularly Johnson's. "I thought about how all that was left of Robert Johnson was his music," John said. "Obviously, there was a similarity here and I thought someday, someone will be looking at my [gravestone]. I would much rather that they knew I went out there and sang those songs." And so he decided that the music he wrote for CCR, a good chunk of his musical legacy, was his and he should use it.

The other epiphany had to do specifically with that day. John went dressed in a black suit. He stood next to Pops Staples, who wore the more traditional white summer suit of a southern gentleman. "It's 110," John related. "Guess who's from the city?" That experience became the kernel of a new song, "A Hundred and Ten in the Shade." John added it to a small but growing catalog of songs he had either finished or was close to completing.

It had been close to five years since *Eye of the Zombie*. John's life had been far less hermetic during this time than it had been during the woodshedding period between Shep and *Centerfield*. He became a fixture at the annual Rock and Roll Hall of Fame inductions. He played a handful of benefit shows, like Farm Aid. He did a VH-1 special for the troops in the Persian Gulf. He was visible, if no new music was audible. He had, however, not stopped creating as he had during his earlier stretch of silence. In addition to "A Hundred and Ten in the Shade," he had another tune he was working on called "Hot Rod Heart" and four more besides. He was, however, taking his time.

Meanwhile, Stu's career in country music continued to roll along. Southern Pacific put out *County Line* in 1990. By this time, they were down to a quartet of McFee, Knudsen, keyboard man Kurt Howell, and Stu. Working off of the success of *Zuma*, they reached number 4 on the country charts with their first single, "Any Way the Wind Blows." They had spent the last five years touring intensely, but ran into a similar brick wall to the one Cook had run into half a lifetime earlier.

"Most people in country music don't really know about us, even after five years," Stu commented. "We play 150 dates a year all over the country. When you start going back to some places, you develop a following and they learn about you. We've been fortunate to get on some big shows and that has helped."

Subsequent singles didn't do nearly as well for the group. Despite a guest appearance by Carlene Carter, "Time's Up" failed to crack the top 20, nor did their a cappella cover of "I Go to Pieces." They took it on the road one more time, then called it quits late in 1990. In all, the band had lasted nearly twice as long as CCR (at least under that name).

The time that Southern Pacific had been together, from around 1985 through 1990, were not banner years for Saul Zaentz Company films. After

Jeffrey Mayer/Starfile

John and Julie Fogerty.

his monster hit with *Amadeus,* his subsequent productions—*The Mosquito Coast, The Unbearable Lightness of Being,* and *At Play in the Fields of the Lord*—did marginal box office at best. The latter, a very expensive, location-driven film failed to get a wide release in the United States. For his next film, Zaentz faced the prospect of actually having to scare up financing from outside sources.

In 1991 John and Julie got married. Friends would ask John about her, and he'd tell them, "She is the joy of my life." One of these friends, upon hearing this for the umpteenth time had a suggestion for John.

"The woman finally said, 'John, you need to write a song for Julie, and you should call it "The Joy of My Life."' That was pretty much clear homework," John quipped to journalist Edna Gunderson. It was a piece of homework that took him several years to complete.

"I learned so much about communicating from Julie," he added. "Instead of going around the house stomping, which I of course still do, I have learned to get to the heart of it with her. She is going to be my best friend if I just open the door and let her in. When I'm having a difficult time, she will just talk to me. If we're married, we're supposed to be having a relationship—she says that all the time."

Doug had been on a four-year-long campaign to convince Fantasy to submit the CCR catalog to the Recording Industry Association of America to reevaluate the group's sales record. Until that point, CCR only had the seven gold albums and seven gold singles they earned while they were active. "The way it looks in the record books," he complained, "it doesn't seem we had all that successful a career." It certainly didn't reflect the nearly two million records that they sold annually. It took an additional year of auditing the Fantasy books, but the RIAA eventually awarded the group eight platinum albums, six platinum singles, two gold albums, and five gold singles thanks to Doug's efforts.

John's manager, Bill Graham, died in a tragic helicopter crash on October 25, 1991. In addition to managing John's career for the last three years, Graham had been one of the first major promoters to book CCR. Once again working with the Grateful Dead, Fogerty played four CCR songs at a memorial concert for Graham held in Golden Gate Park.

Unable to "settle things" with Zaentz, John shot a new volley in their decades-long pissing contest. The promoters of the Bay Area Music Awards asked him to present a "Bammy" to Chris Isaak as Bay Area Musician of the Year on May 7, 1992. Instead of extolling Isaak's virtues, however, John threw away his prepared notes and delivered a speech regaling the attendees with "a rock and roll story." As if he really needed to, he reminded the audience that he had once belonged to a Bay Area band called Creedence Clearwater Revival, that he had written most of the songs. These songs, he added, he no longer "owned." "It was a trick, folks," he said.

Fantasy's Al Bendich claimed that Zaentz offered to sell John the publishing. The price Zaentz wanted was too high; the price John countered with was too low. They could not reach an agreement. "There is a written settlement agreement," Bendich said, referring to the pending lawsuits, "and it did not include an agreement to sell the songs."

Bill Graham's associate Nick Clainos countered, "To say that John's agreement to settle the lawsuit was independent of his right to acquire the catalog is not accurate. I was witness to all the fine points and nuances of the negotiations."

While John had started to claim the spiritual ownership of his songs, the publishing rights still belonged to Jondora. John's vendetta against Fantasy's continuing to sell the old Creedence recordings, Doug pointed out, did not really hurt him that much: "Because Fogerty had assigned his record royalties to Fantasy, the boycott has little economic impact on him. In contrast, Stu, Tom, and I had not assigned our interests and therefore, the boycott of Creedence Clearwater Revival's records would directly hurt our royalty income."

Meanwhile, John's creative juices continued to flow. By August, John had a good half a dozen tunes together. He started taking up residence at the Lighthouse recording studio in North Hollywood. According to engineer John Lowson, "John was most concerned about the drums, so we spent the most time on them. The first two or three years, the whole process was trying to get great drum tracks."

"Originally," John says, "I put together a four piece lineup, but after a few weeks of playing together, I began to understand that there were limitations to that, as well. So I went on another search, looking for the best musicians for each song I wanted to record. I realized that while, for instance, one drummer might be great for a certain song, there was someone else who could get what I was after on another track." Fogerty worked diligently on his new record. He recruited musicians and went through nearly forty drummers all told.

In November 1992 Bill Clinton was elected president. Perhaps the first president truly of the rock and roll generation, his nomination was celebrated to Fleetwood Mac's "Don't Stop." In putting together the inaugural festivities for January 20, his office got word out to Doug that they would love for CCR to get together, if just for one night, to play the inaugural.

"Being a liberal kind of guy," John said, "I like Clinton, but I told them, unfortunately, I do not play with those people anymore."

With his newly renewed hostilities toward Fantasy, and his ongoing hostilities toward the rest of the band, John refused.

31

"THE ROCK AND ROLL HALL OF FAME . . . WAS A REALLY UGLY EVENT"

The year 1993 marked the twenty-fifth anniversary of *Creedence Clearwater Revival*, the band's debut. By the bylaws of the Rock and Roll Hall of Fame, that milestone made Creedence eligible for their place in the hall. When that year's inductees were announced, they were among them, along with fellow musicians Van Morrison, Cream, Ruth Brown, Frankie Lyman and the Teen-agers, Sly and the Family Stone, the Doors, and Dinah Washington as an early influence, and Milt Gabler and Dick Clark in the "nonperformers" category.

This award should have been a high point for the band, and offered another opportunitiy for John to reconcile himself with his past. There was reason to believe that John would be honored by this award; he had participated in the induction ceremonies for several years. He had inducted Buddy Holly and participated in the jam sessions that had traditionally followed the actually inductions. However, like so much else in Creedence's tortured story, the event turned out to be a disaster.

When Stu was notified about the honor, his first thought was that he was going to get to play CCR music again. His sons, not even born when the band was together, would have the opportunity to hear what had made their daddy famous lo, those many years ago. "We asked if we were going to be able to play," he related. "They said, 'Yeah, someone will contact you.'" They didn't hear from the Hall again. Without a second thought, he put his bass into a road case for the trip to the induction ceremony.

"If the three of us can be together," Cream bassist Jack Bruce told the *New York Times*'s pop critic Jon Pareles on the day of the induction festivities, "anybody can be back together." This comment was an ironic precursor of the evening's events.

"The Rock and Roll Hall of Fame induction ceremony," Jeff Fogerty recalls, "was a real ugly event."

We had gotten called by the people from the Rock and Roll Hall of Fame about two weeks before saying that we were supposed to be there at two o'clock for sound check, that we got to play three songs. I was going to take my dad's place and play the rhythm guitar parts. So, basically, I sat down and learned every Creedence tune I could. I figured we'd play some of the hits. I talked to Doug on the phone, Stu on the phone, and they were all hyped and ready to go. They said they were really happy that I would be there. They thought it would be cool that I would be representing Tom. I even brought some drumsticks and other stuff down for Doug because I was working at a music store. When I got there at around 12:30, Doug and Stu were already there.

Doug was talking to some guy in the back and he was just totally pissed off. I couldn't figure what was going on. Doug and John were standing about a foot or two apart. Doug was very tense and pissed off. Stu was sitting on an Anvil case. I came walking up, and Stu said, "Can I help you?" in this really, "get-the-fuck-out-of-here'" kind of tone. Then they recognized [me] and he goes, "Jeff, man, how's it going?" And he gets up and gives me a big hug. I said, "Hey, Doug, what's going on?" He gave me a big hug, but I could see he was totally fuming. He said, "There's been a change. We're not going to play. John's going to play with Bruce Springsteen and Robbie Robertson. We don't get to play at all." I said, "What the fuck is that? Who made that decision? The band, Creedence Clearwater Revival is being inducted, not John by himself."

They made a decision because John said that he wasn't going to play with Doug and Stu because he had so many resentments that he couldn't play with them.

Doug was literally ready to beat the crap out of John. I thought for sure he was going to smack him one. Anyway, they're getting into this heated argument, and John's raising his voice, and it's getting louder, and ten feet away is Cream, standing there ready to sound check, and across the room is Bruce [Springsteen] and all these other people, and it's just everybody totally shut up in the room and watched this go on. I was standing there and looking at John.

They were basically discussing why, and John was saying, "Well, you guys basically left me hanging on the flagpole twenty years ago, and you never came to my aid and you wouldn't come to my court trial against Fantasy," and on and on about stuff that happened when I was a little kid.

It was like, "Why can't you just put this shit aside for ten minutes, play these three songs that got you here?" And then he looked at me and started going into shit like, "And his father loved Saul and thought that Saul was great." And I gave him a look like, "You don't even say shit about my dad, because he's not even here. He's dead." That was the last thing that John said about that. He got back into the argument with Doug, and this went on for about twenty minutes. Then John said, "Well, I'm not going to play with you, that's fucking it," and he walked away. And we all just looked at each other.

John's actions astonished Doug:

The extent of John Fogerty's vindictiveness toward Stu and me surprised even us as shown by the events at the ceremony at Creedence Clearwater Revival's induction into the Rock and Roll Hall of Fame. Stu and I were, of course, honored that Creedence Clearwater Revival and its members were to be inducted into the Hall of Fame. As members of Creedence Clearwater Revival, Hall of Fame representatives invited us to play at the ceremony. . . . Both Stu and I were delighted that our children, who had never seen Creedence Clearwater Revival perform live, would finally see us play as a band. I felt it most fitting that the band's likely final performance would be at our induction into the Hall of Fame.

Unbeknownst to us, John Fogerty told the Hall of Fame that he would not perform with Stu and me at the induction and made arrangements to play and represent Creedence Clearwater Revival at the ceremony without us. . . . We had only learned late that afternoon that we would not be playing with Creedence Clearwater Revival at the Hall of Fame ceremony from a stage hand when we came to rehearse. This affront took place in front of our families, friends and the audience.

Without telling Stu or Doug, John had arranged to exclude them from performing. Jeff recalled:

He had scheduled a rehearsal the day before with Bruce and Robbie Robertson and Don Was and Jim Keltner and Benmont Tench and they were going to play instead. Doug and Stu were just livid. Doug was pissed as hell. This was his day. Out of respect for the band that was a pretty fucked up thing to do on the Rock and Roll Hall of Fame people's part. The band as a whole didn't get to perform, didn't get to be there showing what they could do, then part of it shouldn't happen. Especially because the other guys were still there.

If they were a million miles away in Alaska, I could see it, but they were sitting at the table.

Stu adds, "He had arranged to play our music *to our exclusion* with Bruce Springsteen, Robbie Robertson, and the house band. . . . They conspired with John to humiliate us."

"Bad things happened between me, Doug, Stu, and Tom as recently as a few months before that Rock and Roll Hall of Fame," John related (forgetting for the moment that his brother was dead?). "They went and made a separate deal with Saul Zaentz which I didn't find out about until later. It was a bad move, probably illegal. They sold their voting rights in the partnership to him. Which stinks. At the time of the Hall of Fame dinner, we were still fighting about that."

"When Coz and I were having it out with John the afternoon of the Hall of Fame induction," Stu says, "John said the reason we were being boycotted was that we didn't help him get out of his Fantasy contract. We left him 'twisting in the wind' or some such shit."

"Those guys knew damn well what the situation was when the Rock and Roll Hall of Fame asked us perform there," John countered. "I was willing to appear with the guys in a jam, if there were other people on stage with us. That's what I thought was going to happen. I woulda done 'Proud Mary.' Hell, yeah. It should have been a night of celebration. But they've turned it into a martyrdom thing."

"He didn't refuse to let Cook and Clifford up on stage," Bob Fogerty says in John's defense.

The Hall came to him and asked him if he would play on stage with Creedence Clearwater Revival. John told them no. They went away. Then Robbie Robertson came back and said, would you play if we got Bruce Springsteen and I and some other fine musicians to play, would you play. And John said, "Okay, I'll play." He knew the situation and he agreed to play with them. Doug and Stu have a problem with that. I don't know what else to say. They have a problem with that. I'm not going to say they shouldn't have a problem with that, but John never said, in any way, that he would play with them. He agreed to play with Robbie and Bruce. That was how the whole thing was set up to him. How the Rock and Roll Hall of Fame did not approach Doug and Stu, I don't have any clue.

"I was crushed," Stu said. "It was horrible."

Photo Ken Levy/Laurie Clifford Archives

Accepting their rockies. L. ro r.: Doug Clifford, John Fogerty, Jeff Fogerty, Stu Cook, and the man who inducted them, Bruce Springsteen.

They were able to put their hostilities on simmer early in the evening, when they took the stage to accept the statuettes awarded to inductees. It fell to Bruce Springsteen to welcome them into the Hall:

In 1970, suburban New Jersey, still filled with the kind of sixties spirit *Easy Rider* made us all so fond of—I'm referring to the scene where Dennis Hopper gets blown off of his motorcycle by some redneck with a shotgun—a weekend outing at the time was still filled with the drama of possibly getting your ass kicked by a total stranger who disagreed with your fashion sense. Me and my band worked at a club on Route 35, outside of Asbury Park, called the Pandemonium. They'd recently lowered the drinking age with the logic that if you were old enough to die, you were old enough to drink. And so, with five 50-minute sets a night, there was rarely a night without a fight. The crowd was eclectic, rough kids just out of high school who hadn't been snatched up by the draft yet, truck drivers on the way home south in the Jersey pines, who weren't going to make it—not that night at least—and a mixture of college and working girls, women with bouffant hairdos, and a small but steady hippie contingent. A tough crowd to please all at once. We played behind a U-shaped bar that was just three feet—spitting distance—from many of the patrons who came to just drink and stare and hassle the band.

Into New Jersey came the music of John and Tom Fogerty, Doug Clifford, and Stu Cook, Creedence Clearwater Revival. And for the three minutes, seven seconds of "Proud Mary," a very strange brotherhood would actually fill the room. It was simply a great song that everybody liked, and it literally saved our asses on many occasions.

Creedence started out in the long, jamming tradition of other San Francisco bands, realized it wasn't their road, quit cold and went on to great things. 'Green River,' 'Bad Moon Rising,' 'Down on the Corner,' 'Lodi,' 'Who'll Stop the Rain,' 'Fortunate Son,' 'Born on the Bayou,' wasn't only great music, it was great dance music, it was great bar band music. I remember in the late '70s, I'd be out in a club and I'd watch some band struggle through one of my songs, and then just glide effortlessly through a Creedence Clearwater tune. It used to really piss me off.

I stand here tonight, still envious of that music's power and its simplicity. They were hits, hits filled with beauty and poetry and a sense of the darkness of events and of history, of an American tradition shot through with pride, fear, and paranoia. And they rocked hard.

You can't talk about Creedence without talking about John Fogerty. On the fashion front, all of Seattle should bow. John was the father of the flannel shirt. As a songwriter, only few did as much in three minutes. He was an Old Testament, shaggy haired prophet. As Clint Eastwood said, "A man's got to know his limitations," but I never met a man who took them so seriously. He was severe, he was precise, he said what he had to say and got out of there. He was lyrically spare and beautiful, created a world of childhood memories and of men and women with their back to the wall, a landscape of swamps, bayous, endless rivers, gypsy women, back porches, hound dogs chasing ghosts, devils, bad moons rising, straight out of the blues tradition and turned it into a vision all his own. In Doug, Stu, and Tom, he had the band that could back it up. What makes a great rock band is a funny thing. It's not always the obvious thing. You can't ever really know what makes a great band tick. It's not about that the players were exactly like. All I know is that Tom Fogerty's relentless rhythm guitar and Doug and Stu's great rhythm section and John's songwriting and singing, all I know is they played great together.

I bumped into John one day on Mulholland Drive and we laughed about how far he was from the bayou and I was from the New Jersey Turnpike. Creedence made music for all the waylaid Tom Sawyers and Huck Finns, and for the world that would never be able to take them up on their most simple and eloquent invitation, which is "If you get lost, come on home to Green River."

Let me end by saying, in their day, Creedence never got the respect they deserved. Who'd have thought in '69, before the Grateful Dead, Jefferson Airplane, Moby Grape, Strawberry Alarm Clock, or Electric Prunes, Creedence would be inducted into a rock and roll hall of fame if there was going to be one? They committed the sin of being too popular when hipness was all. They played no-frills, American music for the people. In the late '60s and early '70s, they weren't the hippest band in the world, just the best. So let me finish by saying congratulations, men, for a job well done, and call the naysayers, "Ha ha ha, they told you so." Doug Clifford, Stu Cook, Jeff Fogerty accepting for his dad, John Fogerty, I'd like to induct you into the Hall of Fame.

The band shuffled around, trying to figure out what order they would accept the awards. "When we were lining up, Doug and Stu were going to go out there," Jeff remembers. "Then John wanted me to go out there. I said, 'No, no, you should go out there first. It's your band. I'm just here representing Tom. You guys should go out there first and do your thing and I'll just go out there and take the award for Tom.' And he said, 'No. I want to go out there last, because I have some things I want to say.' I didn't want him to go out there and slag everyone like he did at the Bammies the year before. So I insisted, 'No, John, I'm going to go last.' We had a whole argument about it. He finally gave in. So, I didn't get to hear Bruce's speech because I was arguing with John the whole time."

Doug was the first to accept:

Nobody wants to go first, so, guess what? It's me. I can't really begin to describe the feeling that I feel at this moment, so I won't try. What I'd like to do is thank a lot of people, and I'm going to do it chronologically. I was a history major in college for a while. I'd like to start by thanking Tom Fogerty. I miss him. Tom is the one that got the rest of us into a recording studio when we were fifteen years old, backing him up trying to get a record deal. So he was way ahead of his time. Demo tapes are now, guys at the gas station, you drive

in and they have their demo tapes. Nobody had a demo tape in 1959. Tom, I
want to thank you for that. I know you're here. I want to thank John Fogerty
for sharing his immense talent. I want to thank Stu Cook for his solid bass
playing and his friendship for thirty-four years.

I want to thank Fantasy Records for putting our records out when no other
record label was interested in Creedence Clearwater Revival. I want to thank
disc jockeys around the world for playing us then, breaking the band, and
continuing to play the music today. I hear it all the time on the radio. I want to
thank our fans. That's an obvious one. None of this would be happening if
people didn't love us and we love all of you, whoever you are, wherever you
are. I want to thank the Hall of Fame nominating committee for thinking of
us. I want to thank everyone who voted for us, and everyone who didn't vote
for us. What the hell. I can take it.

I have some things I want to say about the future. I want to thank Mr. Cliff
Burnstein for putting the SDQ, formerly the Sir Douglas Quintet, together
with Elektra records Nonesuch label. I want to thank Bob Krasnow for his
support, Nancy Jeffries for her diligent work. Look out around summertime,
there's going to be a great rock and roll band with some young people mixed
in with it. They wanted to call it the best of young and old, but you know
where that put me. I like to call it the best of youth and experience.

And of course, most importantly I want to thank my family, my son Brent,
my son Grady, my daughter Jamie, my wife of twenty-five years, who was with
me when we were the Blue Velvets in High School. She's my high school
sweetheart. We've been together thirty-one years. My wife, Laurie.

John accepted next, also remarking on the awesome and humbling
nature of the occasion. He also took a moment to mention his previous
experiences with the hall, speaking on behalf of the other artists. He
thanked the Hall of Fame, then added: "I'd also like to thank my former
bandmates, Doug and Stu and Tom; we've disagreed a lot over the years,
but there was a time when we made really great music together and I think
that's actually the whole reason, that's the real deal why we're here at all.
Thank you guys."

He then thanked his brother and aide-de-camp Bob for a "lifetime of service." He paid tribute to his new wife, Julie, calling her "the joy of my life."

He concluded by thanking everyone for supporting the music. "I always
enjoy hearing this stuff on the radio and seeing people come up wishing us
well. It's a great feeling. God bless you all and thank you."

Next, Stu came up to the podium:

Wow, this is, as John said, awesome. When we started playing down in the music room of my folk's house, we had no idea that it would end up as something like this, that there would ever be this kind of recognition for the music that we loved so much. As we sat there listening and learning from records of the artists that we loved, copying every note, that was the whole goal then. Then came the goal of, maybe one night we'll earn a hundred bucks each. Then the phone started ringing off the hook, and the rest is more than geography. It's a worldwide thing. The Hall of Fame is more than just the people inducted in it. It's about the fans. If it wasn't for the people that loved the music, there'd be no reason for all of this. So, I really have to thank all of the Creedence fans, the old ones and the new ones who are coming along picking up their folk's CDs, LPs, tapes. I'd like to thank my folks for encouraging me, and my wife, Laura, for putting up with me, thank you babe. There've been some great times. I'd like to thank my bandmates, John, Tom—tonight would have been a big night for Tom and I know he's here with us. I've got to thank my partner, Coz. Outside of Al Jackson and Duck Dunn, I can't think of anyone I'd rather listen to than me and Coz. Really folks. When it comes to rhythm sections, I'm really particular. Jack and Ginger, in this place there are some classic ones, but I know Doug and I are like a hand and glove.

I'd like to thank the Hall of Fame for thinking of the four of us. I know that it means a lot. I'd like to thank the people at Fantasy records for being there when we needed it, in the beginning, buying an amp, paying for the first album. Then the doors opened. A lot of stuff's gone under the bridge since then, but they were there. Thank you all for being here tonight. Have a big ol' time.

Finally, Jeff stepped up to the mike:

I'm very proud and honored to accept this award for my father. I know that he would have really liked to be here tonight and would have gotten a great kick out of being here. I'm sure if he was here, he'd like to thank the guys in the band, Stu and Doug and John, for all the time and music that they made together. This is where they ended up. I'm sure he'd also like to thank the record company for giving him the shot, the opportunity to make the record. It took off on it's own. Dad, wherever you are, Trish, the kids, me, the family, we all love you and we miss you.

The bands did their sets later in the evening. Cream reunited for the event. The Doors played with Eddie Vedder filling in for Jim Morrison. Then

Fogerty came on stage. Instead of Stu, Doug, and Jeff, he was backed by the duo guitars of Bruce Springsteen and Robbie Robertson, Don Was on bass, Jim Keltner on drums, and Benmont Tench on keyboards. When they launched into "Who'll Stop the Rain," Doug and Stu, their wives and families, got up and walked out of the room. The band finished the song to a thin scattering of applause. John looked out at the audience and said, "That's all right. You can clap." No one did.

"Everyone was just blown out by John's behavior," says Jeff. "Afterwards, I ran into Bruce for a minute and he said, 'Hey, man. I'm sorry, man.'"

Stu wanted more than just a say-so apology. He wanted his in writing. He wrote essentially the same letter to both Robertson and Springsteen about their involvement in the ceremony. Stu appreciated the compliments paid the band during the evening, and even praised Springsteen's appraisal of the band's story as very insightful for someone who had not lived it. However, he wrote, "I kept getting the feeling that somehow, in spite of the kind words and the 'Rocky' on my table, I'd been sandbagged. . . . It was a real slap in the face for you to take over the stage . . . on the night of *our* induction into the Hall of Fame (while we were supposed to sit in the audience) and play the songs that Creedence made famous. . . . Now you've let yourself get drawn into Fogerty's sick and petty war against Fantasy Records and his former bandmates."

While Stu acknowledged that John had written most of the songs, the place in the Hall had been set aside for Creedence Clearwater Revival the *band*. The Hall, he pointed out, was just as much to blame. He was mystified as to why the people running the show had not told Doug, Jeff, and him they would not perform that evening. He hoped that when it came time for Springsteen's induction, Bruce would treat his old band better.

"I've had John Fogerty's number for a long time," he wrote. "My consolation is that he's finally shown his mean-spirited and revenge driven nature to his peers, and I'm only sorry it had to happen at the expense of a fine evening for the rest of us in the extended CCR family."

In his letter back to Stu, Bruce agreed that the Hall of Fame had mishandled Creedence's induction. He had known for weeks before the ceremony that he would back John and assumed that the arrangements had been made and cleared with Stu and Doug. Springsteen added that he hoped this might serve as a wake-up call to the Hall as to the delicate nature of defunct bands.

"Personally," he wrote, "I would have loved to have watched Creedence Clearwater Revival play. I realize that what should have been a great night for the whole band ended up being a drag for you, Doug, and your families. . . . Everyone from the band should have had the opportunity to have played that night, or no one at all."

Robertson responded that while he had no idea what went on between the old bandmates in Creedence, he had a job to do as music director for the evening. John told Robertson that it would be impossible for CCR to perform, or at least for CCR to perform with CCR. Since they wanted to have the band's music played at the Hall, he felt it had to be either John's way or no way. Initially, they wanted John to perform solo. Then Robbie inserted himself in on guitar "just to keep it going somewhere." Since Springsteen was handling the actual induction, they decided to let him join them as well.

Robertson claimed no one had told him that Doug and Stu even expected to play until the afternoon of the show. "How could you, if you all don't play together? About 3:30 P.M. the afternoon of the ceremonies it was first mentioned that you and Doug were upset. Bruce and I would've much rather seen you guys play together, but that's between you and John. . . . Complications within the workings of a band is something I understand from my own experience and for the most part it's always a damn shame."

Engaged in a serious writing frenzy, Stu also wrote to the Hall of Fame, leaking the contents of the letter to the *LA Times*'s music correspondent Steve Hochman. Hochman quoted part of the letter in a column: "What the hell were you people thinking when you allowed one member to take the stage and play the songs the band made famous, while the other members were expected to sit in the audience? Did it ever occur to you that by turning what was to be a great evening for all of Creedence into the John Fogerty Show you were hurting the other members and their families?"

"I'm sorry they are hurt," the Hall's executive director, Suzan Evans, replied to Hochman, "but the decision was made to proceed with John Fogerty as he was the singer and songwriter for all their hits. It seemed natural that he should sing those songs. It was never meant to be a snub or cause hurt feelings."

The events at the Rock and Roll Hall of Fame had repercussions within the Hall's organization. While not admitting they did anything malicious, Evans said that the situation would be on the agenda of a future meeting of the board of directors.

Rolling Stone editor and publisher Jann Wenner, the vice chairman of the Hall's board of directors, was not nearly as conciliatory. "It's not our job to reconcile groups," he told Hochman. "Our business is to nominate, elect, and induct members into the Hall of Fame, and we did that according to our rules and procedures.

"If we'd taken a hard line," he added, "you wouldn't have seen John Fogerty up there at all, and I don't think anyone would have been satisfied with two members of the rhythm section doing 'Born on the Bayou.'"

Hall board member Tom Freston, CEO of MTV networks, wasn't so sure. "They've got a gripe," he told Hochman. "It would have been preferable if they had played together. It was a strange, forced, almost surreal situation."

And after the event, as Stu put it, "Practically everyone apologized, except John."

32

"FOGERTY HIJACKED THE WHOLE CREEDENCE THING"

The events at the Hall of Fame induction caused a war of words, airing twenty years of CCR's dirty linens so the curious could examine every stain. Several days after the event, the *LA Times*'s Steve Hochman caught up with Doug and Stu and gave them the venue to vent. "What John did was mean-spirited," Stu told him, "but the Hall of Fame was wrong letting him get away with it."

John retaliated with an open tirade in the *Los Angeles Times* titled "Why We Are Not Friends":

The *Times* recently published an article in which former members of Creedence criticized me for not performing with them at the Rock and Roll Hall of Fame ceremonies. The article also attributed several inaccurate statements to me and I would like to set the record straight.

First of all, I never said to the guys, "I hate you." I felt it was enough to say, "We are not friends." This is why . . .

In 1988, I was forced to endure a very costly and mean-spirited trial, at which Fantasy Records contended that I had plagiarized myself. Of course, I *never* received a word of support from my old bandmates. During the trial, Saul Zaentz, the head of Fantasy, took the stand and testified that he had gotten the whole idea for his lawsuit from Doug Clifford of CCR. He stated, under oath, that Doug had come to his office with a copy of my *Centerfield* album, played a few selections and proclaimed that "John Fogerty is ripping off Creedence." When I expressed my outrage to Doug about this, he told me that "Saul is lying." Now, I have no way of knowing the real truth, given the history of both of these people, but the story does reflect sentiments which all three of the other members of CCR have expressed in the press. Doug was afforded the opportunity to come to the trial and tell the truth about the situation but he refused. This is exactly the kind of wishy-washy morality and unreliability that makes it impossible for us to be friends.

He then went through the group selling their voting rights over the approval of using CCR music on compilations. This opened up the catalog for use in "beer commercials, paint thinner commercials and oil company promotions."

These guys do not care about the music, only the money. Doug and Stu have euphemistically described their relationship with Fantasy Records as "keeping the lines of communication open . . . ." I don't think so. I would call it greedy, devious and cowardly. As you can see, this is not some old grievance from the dim past. It is current. I have asked them to rectify this situation and for more than three years the ball has been in their court. They know where to find me . . .

I believe one of the reasons we were chosen is that our records placed such a high value on musical integrity and moral conviction. *Especially* in that situation, I refused to perform my songs with people who have shown such little regard for me and my music. It just seemed like a fake situation. I hope you all will understand.

"John believes," Stu fumed, "he WAS the band. Somewhere along the line, Fogerty hijacked the whole Creedence thing. It's partly our fault that we didn't speak up sooner."

Life went on. In 1993 it looked like—for a moment—that Stu might be finding a new home with another legendary band. Late in 1992, fifty-six-year-old Bill Wyman, newly married to a teenager, decided that his energy was better spent in that direction than in continuing to work with the Rolling Stones.

"Mick Jagger called me and asked if I'd be interested in auditioning for the gig as bass player in the Rolling Stones," Stu marvels.

They flew me to NYC and we jammed for about two hours:

I was one of the nineteen American bass players they auditioned to replace Bill Wyman. They behaved like almost perfect gentlemen. Keith was the most intense, Ronnie and Charlie the most friendly, and Mick, while aloof, was also cordial. I knew I wasn't the guy they were looking for, but I took full advantage of the situation, calling out tunes even after Mick had signaled the "audition" was over. I was like a kid in a candy store. As a final touch, their crew kept all the patch cords for my bass rig. Oh well, I was still way ahead as far as I was concerned.

John was also having personnel problems. Rock critic Michael Goldberg reported that he was in the studio with an album worth of songs, but "he kept recording them over and over again, he wasn't happy with the results." Jeff reported seeing a master tape at his Uncle Bob's house as early as 1993. Rumors abounded that John was going through drummers faster than guitar strings. He had hired and fired former Toto drummer and all around studio wiz Jeff Porcaro before the drummer's untimely death. He erased Porcaro's tracks and went looking for a another drummer.

"This story is true," Stu claimed. "The way I heard the story is that Porcaro got fed up with Fogerty and told him the LP was going nowhere, and then quit the project. Who knows? Fogerty could certainly fill in the details. Jeff's tracks were wiped after the incident."

"John used so many drummers," long-time studio drummer Kenny Aronoff—who wound up on five songs—postulated, "because his concept was developing as he went along."

"I have to say that I used a lot of drummers to get the finished product," John conceded, adding that he went through "close to thirty drummers—I stopped counting at twenty."

John set a strict recording regime. The sessions started at noon and went on until 6:30 P.M. The band would work on one song, take lunch, then work on a second song. After they learned the second song, they'd record two takes and listen. They'd discuss what changes to make, and do two more takes with those changes. Although John recorded everything, he considered Monday, Tuesday, and Wednesday as rehearsals. The real recording went on Thursday and Friday.

"The first day was real exciting," says Aronoff, "because you were learning the songs. By the second day, you definitely knew the songs, so you weren't looking at the charts any more and you were starting to try a few different things. By the third day, you start to go wacko, because you think they surely must have a usable take by now. But that's when the songs really start to grow. There's something exciting about recording a song you've never played before in two takes, but its also exciting to play a song so much that it evolves into something different than what you had the first day you learned it."

All of the drummers used John's drum set, which John tuned himself. "He also picked the cymbals, and he had 15" hi-hats," Aronoff said. "If you remember, Doug Clifford . . . used huge hi-hats."

During the evenings, John worked on playing the Dobro that had been sitting in storage pretty much since "Lookin' Out My Back Door." He had it in mind for two songs though neither was quite finished yet: one was "A Hundred and Ten in the Shade"; the other was a song he was writing for Julie, "Joy of My Life." "The Dobro was a total mystery to me," he said. "So I got myself some videotapes. I was the perfect candidate for this teaching methodology, because I'm already a musician. I'm already a guitar player and I didn't have to learn how to tune."

In fact, John claims that—similar to the pre-*Centerfield* hiatus—a lot of the time between albums was spent in the woodshed. "Let's just take one song," he said, describing how he forced himself to perfect his instrumental technique in order to perform the songs he was writing:

> "Blue Moon Nights." When I wrote that song, a year or so before we started recording, I had the first part of the song and knew what style it would be. I knew what I wanted. I went and got a thumb pick and got my guitar and started playing. . . . But it became immediately apparent to me: "Uh-oh, you've got some work to do. Because I couldn't play that stuff" . . . Even while I was trying to make the record, trying to get the basic tracks, the bass and drums were very fine, after a fashion. I went out to play the guitar, and it was like, in five minutes I stopped the tape and I told the engineer, "This bass player and this drummer would kick the guitar player out of this band." It was the truth. I just wasn't up to that level, so I had to go to work.

In February 1993, Fogerty was back in court. The Ninth Circuit Court of Appeals finally heard his appeal of the lower court denying him legal fees from the first *Fantasy v. Fogerty* case. It was the Ninth Circuit's practice to award legal fees to plaintiffs only if they won. In a usual case, this practice served to allow plaintiffs—usually the song's creators—to protect their copyrights. Without this provision, a plaintiff might not try to protect a copyright due to the expense of the legal process; even if they won, they might lose. In a sense, this is what happened to Fogerty in this case, even though he was the defendant. He won the case that Fantasy brought against him, but was unable to recoup his costs defending himself. He maintained that, as an artist, he was the wronged party.

Additionally, it was the Ninth Court's practice to award legal fees only if the plaintiff's case was "frivolous." John maintained that not only was Fantasy's case frivolous, it was downright legal harassment. The Ninth didn't buy it, however, and ruled against John. John and his lawyers vowed to pursue the case to the next and last avenue available to them, the U.S. Supreme Court.

Late in 1993 the Supreme Court said they would hear the *Fantasy v. Fogerty* case. On March 1, 1994, the justices overturned the lower court rulings in a 9-0 decision. From a legal standpoint, the *Fantasy v. Fogerty* decisions leveled the playing field for plaintiffs and defendants when it came to the losers reimbursing the winners' legal fees, adding weight to the passage in the 1976 copyright law that allowed judges to "award a reasonable attorney's fee to the prevailing party." Now John Fogerty was not only a major name in American music; his name was also attached to an integral piece of American intellectual property law.

Meanwhile, Doug Clifford had been working with Doug Sahm and his various Sir Douglas bands on and off since CCR split up. As he mentioned at the Hall of Fame inductions, he was busy recording with the band at the time. The Sir Douglas Quintet's *Day Dreaming at Midnight* album was released in 1993. In his liner notes, Sahm set lofty goals for the band:

> We set off on a Rock 'n' Roll journey to make a record for people of all ages— for older rockers who have been left swinging in the wind; for kids who weren't old enough to have been around for the heyday of the sixties, and for people who were looking in vain for the groove of Creedence Clearwater Revival, the jangle of the Byrds, and the raw rock 'n' roll energy of the early Rolling Stones and Beatles records.

Doug cowrote three of the tunes on the album, and coproduced the sessions with Sahm. Stu lent backing vocals to one of the tunes. The album got good critical notices— ". . . the songwriting throughout is smart and funny," wrote Michael Tearson in *Audio*. " . . . *Day Dreaming at Midnight* throbs with fun . . ."—but only sold marginally.

On January 17, 1994, powerful earthquakes hit Los Angeles. The quakes killed sixty-one people and caused countless millions of dollars in damage. One of the property casualties was the John Fogerty home on Mulholland Drive. It took nine months to restore his demolished home.

The Northridge quake had a similar effect on another former member of CCR. With the demise of Southern Pacific, Stu really had nothing to keep him in Los Angeles. Doug was living a more bucolic existence near Lake Tahoe. "Coz invited us up for a week," Stu recalls. "After eight and a half years in LA, the riots, the floods, the Malibu fire — which started about a half mile from my place in Calabasas—and the earthquake, we decided to look for a nicer environment to raise a kid. We left town with an offer on a huge, ignored, log house. It all worked out, and about forty days later the deal was done." So once again the formidable Creedence rhythm section— the Tom and Huck of rock and roll—were living close together.

It took an earthquake to make John miss the ninth annual Rock and Roll Hall of Fame induction ceremonies. For him, like many Los Angelinos, the January 19 festivities were far less important than getting things straightened out at home. This no doubt distressed Fogerty. For years, he had lobbied long and hard to get his guitar idol, Duane Eddy, into the Hall. In 1994 Eddy was finally slated for induction. Because Eddy had been John's hobby-horse, the Hall naturally asked him to induct the rabble-rousing guitarist. Due to the quake, that task fell to someone else.

The summer of '94 marked the twenty-fifth anniversary of Woodstock. In addition to new concerts to commemorate the event, the maker of the original film wanted to update the documentary with footage of CCR, the only act not represented on film or recordings, despite being the first major act to sign on. Once again, John nixed the idea.

"CCR's inclusion in the recut Woodstock film was going to happen," Doug says. "John told them 'no way.' It's so unnecessary. It hurts him as well as everyone else."

"[John] stifled the whole thing with Woodstock, the director's cut," says Jeff.

The director flew from Thailand to LA and said, "I don't care about anything else, I want to put Creedence in the movie. That's the only thing I care about with the director's cut." John was insistent about not letting it happen. They were shooting it back and forth. It went on for weeks and weeks and weeks. Finally, the director said, "The decision has to be made Tuesday at 5 o'clock. If John still doesn't want to do it, then unfortunately we're going to have to cut it from the film." He had it all ready to go and John wouldn't do it. He said if they put it into the film anyway, he was going to block it from being shown. So the director said, "I don't want John's negativity and his bullshit to taint this movie and the wonderful thing that it was, so I'm just going to cut him completely out of it and not let CCR have anything to do with it, unfortunately."

"When the Woodstock twenty-fifth anniversary project came up Doug and I felt it was time to let the world know that CCR was there and played great," Stu said. "John threatened to sue Warner Bros. Pictures if any image of him was included. WB didn't want their big release stained by a lawsuit from a guy they knew to be litigious, so the offer to be included in the director's cut of the film was withdrawn. Doug and I were contacted by Atlantic Records and we agreed to include four tracks in the box set. The performances are classic CCR, and I'm still amazed by the number of people that don't even know we were one of the headliners at Woodstock 69."

"Doug and Stu and my dad would have wanted to be in there. It's part of history," says Jeff. "It would have renewed the public's interest in the band. . . . They were there, they were a big part of it, and nobody knows it except for the people that were there, and half of them don't remember. But it's in John's best interest to have that going. He's working on a new record, that would have revitalized him. Then, I guess Doug and Stu and Trish gave permission to have it on the boxed set CD. There's a couple of Creedence tunes on that, but not in the movie. I thought that was kind of strange."

The quake slowed down work on John's new album, but in September he took enough time off to prepare for a live benefit concert at the House of Blues in LA. His first full-length show since the "Zombie" tour, it consisted of mostly old CCR songs. "Watching Fogerty play guitar and sing with such authority Tuesday," wrote the *LA Times*'s Robert Hilburn, "it was hard to believe that he has been away from the rock arena for even a few weeks. Rock 'n' roll seems to run through the man's veins—100 percent."

The fact was, however, that Jeff was right. John needed something to boost his public image. It had been eight years since *Eye of the Zombie*. Careers in popular music had come and gone in the time John had been away. "One of my friends has put out I think at least three albums during that time," John admitted. "I ran into Clint Black a few weeks ago and he told me that he has been next door [in an adjoining studio] and then he had been next door again. He recorded two albums there. He'd come and gone and come and gone and I'm still there, kind of tied to the rock, you might say."

Where bands from the '60s had developed a steady base of fans so that groups from Steppenwolf to the Stones could still make a living, they were either recording or touring constantly. As far as the public was concerned, John had briefly poked his head out of his cave to go to court or the Hall of Fame, but otherwise they heard nothing from him, and certainly nothing new.

33

"WE'RE NOT DOING THIS TO HURT HIM"

CCR's continued absence from the *Woodstock* film, or from pretty much anything else, didn't keep it from continued popularity on radio. Not a day went by when a classic rock station didn't play one of the sixty-five original CCR tunes. But unless you were lucky enough to catch one of John's charity shows or be at the Rock and Roll Hall of Fame ceremonies, no one had seen anyone from the band play this music live in over two decades.

People were still interested. A record of contemporary bands recording CCR tunes called *John Fogerty: Wrote a Song for Everyone* came out via a Finnish company. One of the artists on the album was former Dream Syndicate guitarist/vocalist Steve Wynn. He wrote in the liner notes:

> So there I was, eight years old and standing at the post office with my $10 money order, a stamped envelope and my application to become a member of the Creedence Clearwater Revival fan club. And when my photo, button, and first newsletter arrived six weeks later (the longest six weeks of my life), I was something more than thrilled. . . . John Fogerty introduced me to a vivid and very foreign world where El Cerrito . . . was just as exotic and elusive as New Orleans and the Mississippi River that they sang about. . . . As I grew older, Creedence made even more sense to me. Through the band, I discovered Bo Diddley, Buck Owens, Hank Williams, Marvin Gaye, Screamin' Jay Hawkins, and especially Sun Records. I pumped some pain in New Orleans, caught a ride on a riverboat queen, always awestruck that I was that much closer to the fantasy world of John Fogerty. As a youth I had many fine teachers, but none of them taught me so much that stuck with me for so long as the lessons I learned from the wondrous music of Creedence Clearwater Revival.

The continued interest in the band, tributes like this from contemporary artists, coupled with the shabby treatment at the Rock and Roll Hall of

Fame, their newfound proximity, their fiftieth birthdays, and a renewed desire to play this music gave Stu and Doug the yen to go back on the road as Creedence Clearwater Revival. Figuring nothing ventured, nothing gained, they once again proposed this to John.

"In June of 1995," John stated,

> I received an inquiry from Cook and Clifford, through our respective attorneys, as to whether I would be interested in a CCR reunion tour. This request came in the wake of announcements of reunions of several other "classic rock" groups that had gone their separate ways, including the Eagles' appropriately-named "Hell Freezes Over" tour. Since my relationship with Cook and Clifford had already been strained for a number of years and I was in the midst of writing songs for a new solo album, my response was that I had no interest in performing with them in a CCR reunion tour.

John had just turned fifty, as well. His wife, Julie, had thrown him a surprise party, and almost got the kind of crowd the group used to have for barbecues on the Fourth of July. Tom's ex-wife was there, with Jeff. All three of John's children from his first marriage came, as did his three surviving brothers. John, of course, wound up sitting in with the band, as did Bruce Springsteen. Eventually Jeff also sat in, finally enjoying the opportunity denied him at the Hall of Fame, to play some CCR with his Uncle John.

John's solo album was crawling to a conclusion. He finally felt he got the Dobro right, and wanted to try out the song he had written for Julie in front of people:

> Our kids' school has a variety show every year, and I usually play at it. . . . I chose that place because she would be in the audience and our friends would be in the audience and the kids would be in the audience. It was our world, you might say. It's the truest world we have.
>
> It's outdoors. It was a great setting. I actually surprised everybody, because we had a rehearsal in the daytime, but I didn't tell anybody what was going to happen. That night, I asked the band to leave the stage, because I didn't want anybody there. Then I basically sang this song directly to my wife. She didn't know I had this prepared. That's how I sprung it on her.
>
> She was sitting there with her family and all the other moms and dads and kids and she was just blown away. She didn't know any of this was coming.

As Fogerty worked away at his project, his old nemesis Saul Zaentz was engaged in a new project of his own. He had acquired the rights to Michael Ondaatje's Booker Prize-winning novel, *The English Patient*. With director

Kelly A. Swift/Retna Limited USA

John Fogerty
(House of Blues, L.A.)

Anthony Minghella shooting, he spent a good chunk of the year traipsing around the desert, recalling his wartime experiences of half a century earlier.

John went into the studio with one of his idols that spring. Carl Perkins is one of the people he credits with putting the fire in his belly to become a musician, but more than that, to become a songwriter. He duetted with Perkins on a track called "All Mama's Children" for Carl's *Go Cat Go* album.

Stu and Doug had made a few overtures to John to join them on the road. Nineteen-ninety-five became the year of the "big reunion tour, "with the Eagles hitting the road. Nearly as much bad blood ran among the members of *that* band. Don Henley had once said that he might consider playing with the band again when hell froze over. Naturally, they called their around the world jaunt the Hell Freezes Over tour. By burying the hatchet, they unburied a treasure chest. The tour, cable special, and live album made a fortune.

John, however, had his album to finish. When that happened, he planned on touring and playing both his new music and his legacy, the CCR songs. While not telling his old band members of his future plans, he simply passed on the opportunity to reunite with them.

After John declined their offer, Stu and Doug regrouped. They decided they still wanted to go out and play this music, and that even without John, there must be a market for it. As Doug put it:

> Stu and I decided that time was running out, that we were not getting any younger, and that we wanted to play our music live. We also feel that fans should be treated to live performances of our music that had not been played publicly by original members of the band in over two decades. Given that John would not be performing with us, we decided to perform as "Creedence Clearwater Revisited," which tells the public that we are part of Creedence Clearwater Revival, but that it is not the same band.

They made a deal with Trish Fogerty, who inherited Tom's share of the CCR partnership. With her cooperation, they had 75 percent of the members allowing them to use the Creedence Clearwater name.

Next they had to put together a band. "A business acquaintance at Atlantic Records in New York introduced me to Elliot Easton," Stu says. "When we needed a guitar player I thought of no other. It was Elliot's playing that made the Cars interesting to me. I became a big fan. It's great to play with him. He's truly one of the best."

"Through word of mouth, we learned about John Tristao," Doug adds. A contemporary of the band, Tristao was the lead vocalist and guitarist in a band called People. Based not all that far from CCR in San Jose, People had one hit in 1968, a tune called "I Love You" that made it to number 14 on the *Billboard* charts just a few months before "Suzie Q" went a few notches higher. "He auditioned for us," Doug continued. "Stu and I liked him and thought he did justice to the vocals. John Tristao brings passion, new energy, and a fuller, richer voice to the music, while keeping the style and integrity of Creedence Clearwater Revival music intact."

On the last day of July 1995, Creedence Clearwater Revisited played their first show. It felt good to get back on the road, playing the music that had made them famous. Easton's stint with the Cars and Tristao's having had a hit predating even Creedence's gave the band an extra fillip. They were not strictly some ghost band trying to capitalize on what once was. They played the old tunes, true, but they brought a new vitality to them.

"The truth is we don't miss him," Stu noted of the absent John. "I must say that John, for his part, hasn't been very friendly toward us or our project."

That didn't stop them from playing. Through the rest of the year, they would only play eight more shows, but two of them marked the beginning of a two-week-long jaunt through the Pacific Rim, where some of the last Creedence shows had taken place. "The response in Japan was enthusiastic," Stu remarked. "People were up dancing at their seats. It was an interesting mix. Older than usual. Asia is more subdued than Europe or the U.S., but I'd say they partied. The Thais were the wildest. Many people had their cell phones on and pointed towards the stage. Beaming us to who knows where."

From then on, they played between seven and fifteen gigs a month, except during June of 1996, when they played nearly every night as they toured through Europe, entertaining in such CCR strongholds as Denmark, Germany, and Sweden. To avoid confusion, they sent the following letter to promoters and media at all of the European stops:

AN OPEN LETTER TO CREEDENCE CLEARWATER REVIVAL FANS
FROM STU COOK AND DOUG "COSMO" CLIFFORD

Dear Creedence Fans:

We, Stu Cook and Doug "Cosmo" Clifford, two of the founding members of Creedence Clearwater Revival, are coming to Europe in May and June to perform with our new band, Creedence Clearwater Revisited. We formed the band last Summer to once again perform live the CCR songs that we recorded and love to play live and which are enjoyed by fans worldwide. As you know, no original CCR member individually or as a group has toured to play these songs since Creedence Clearwater Revival broke up in 1972. John Fogerty declined to join us in reviving our music and touring the world. We elected to go forward without him.

It has now come to our attention that some of our upcoming Creedence Clearwater Revisited shows may have been incorrectly promoted in Europe and some fans may think that Creedence Clearwater Revival has re-formed and is now coming to tour Europe. This is incorrect. The band that is coming to tour Europe is not Creedence Clearwater Revival, but rather our new band, Creedence Clearwater Revisited. Creedence Clearwater Revisited is made up of us, original CCR members Doug "Cosmo" Clifford on drums and Stu Cook on bass, and we are joined by Elliot Easton on lead guitar (formerly of The Cars), Steve Gunner on keyboards, and John Tristao filling big shoes on lead vocals.

We believe that from a live performance standpoint, Creedence Clearwater Revisited is better than any band we have ever played in. However, we certainly do not want anyone to be misled into thinking that the original Creedence Clearwater Revival has re-formed. That is

Courtesy Mason Company

Creedence Clearwater Revisited. L. to r.: Elliot Easton, Stu Cook, Steve Gunner, Doug Clifford, John Tristao.

not the case. If anyone has been misled, we invite you to return your ticket to the promoter that sold it to you for a full refund. Of course, we prefer that you come check out the show and judge for yourself. We are confident that you will agree with the nearly one hundred thousand fans that have seen Creedence Clearwater Revisited concerts here in the United States that our new band is fantastic and it is great to experience the music live again. If not, ask for your money back. Of course, it is not politics and personnel, but good music and good times that wins the day.

People had fun at their concerts. They danced, they sang along. A surprising number of the people at the Revisited shows had not been born when the music was recorded. The group got a mixed, but generally good critical reaction.

"Tristao floored the crowd with his stage presence and left them with no doubts about the true Creedence 'flavor' of the show," wrote Dave Hosik. "Cook and Clifford were comfortable not being the stars of the show and let Easton and Tristao take full reign—which ultimately led to an impressive display of Creedence power and soul. From the opening of 'Born on the Bayou' Creedence fans of every age imaginable jumped to their feet and danced in the aisles."

"All Creedence Clearwater Revisited proved Saturday at the Greek Theater," wrote Steve Hochman in the *Los Angeles Times*, "was the greatness of Fogerty's CCR songs and vision. Sure this presentation was a remarkable simulation. John Tristao . . . has all the vocal grit and force of the real thing, while ex-Cars guitarist Elliot Easton, an unabashed Creedence acolyte, dexterously recreated Fogerty's swamp rock chooglin'."

"This tour," Stu related, "is really a celebration. We don't have to deal with internal problems or record labels. We're not starting out or over. It's just us, the music and the audience."

After the band had been in business a year, John decided he didn't like them using the Creedence Clearwater name. "Creedence no longer exists," he complained. "For a couple of guys to go out and say, 'We are Creedence,' it's wrong. I invented it. I wrote and sang the songs. I taught those people how to play their instruments. Creedence had high ideals. They turned it into a Las Vegas lounge act and smudged my reputation."

This sounded like things John had said nearly a quarter of a century earlier. "Going Vegas" was a pet horror for both Fogerty brothers. As far back as 1970, they were talking about not behaving like Bobby Darin and playing nightclubs. Rather than "Revisited," John saw the group as more like the Creedence Clearwater Revue.

It also resonated of the old riff about John going into the studio and changing everyone's parts. "To read it now," Stu countered, "it's like he dragged us kicking and screaming into the top 10. Right. If we were that crappy, he should have gotten another band."

"Credit should be given where credit is due," Doug said. "When people talk about Creedence, they say, 'it's got a great beat.' Well, Stu and I are 'the beat' of that music. I'm not slighting John Fogerty's brilliant songs—he deserves his due—but that aside, really what's happening is the joy of the people responding to the music we're making now."

John sued the band for violating the band's trademark, copyright infringement, and other charges based on using the Creedence Clearwater part of the name. He got an injunction against them calling themselves Creedence Clearwater ANYTHING until the courts decided.

After a month off, the band started calling themselves Cosmo's Factory. Despite the change, John did not drop the suit—anything but. "When we were playing the Greek Theater in Los Angeles," Stu said, "we were billed as 'Cosmo's Factory—Former Creedence Clearwater Revival Members Stu Cook and Doug Clifford—An Evening of CCR.' John tried to get us held in contempt of court. He claimed that the name violated the injunction, even though the court threw it out. But he still went through it all and it cost him ten grand. I mean, why bother?"

Once again, the former members of CCR entered the labyrinth of depositions and court dates. The irony was, as much as Revisited or Cosmo's Factory was a tribute to Doug and Stu's younger days, it was also a tribute to John. "I am doing this tour because I miss playing the music," Doug related. "I forgot how good the music is and how much fun it is to play."

"For the record," adds Stu, "I try to remember to thank 'Willy, wherever he is tonight' after 'Down on the Corner' at every concert. I might've done it after 'Sky' in one or two instances." Stu continued to offer his "thanks" even after John filed the lawsuit, despite John's claim that: "If [Doug and Stu] are permitted to continue to use the CCR name or a name confusingly similar to it, without my consent and in a manner that is likely to confuse the public as to my involvement in the new group, there will be irreparable harm to my reputation, the reputation of CCR, and to the goodwill associated with CCR's name, music, and reputation that I have helped to generate over the many years."

Stu denied this:

Here's the FACTS concerning the Fogerty/Revisited lawsuit. Several months after CCRv played its first concert Fogerty, through his attorney, demanded: That Doug and I stop using the Creedence Clearwater component of the name; or that we pay him 25% of the gross receipts from the project; or that we agree to his claim that he has a veto over all proposed business uses of Creedence Clearwater Revival product, and/or name; or we get sued by him.

The trademark CREEDENCE CLEARWATER REVIVAL is owned by Stu Cook, Doug Clifford, Tricia Fogerty, and John Fogerty, 25% each. Seventy-five percent of the owners agreed to the use as Creedence Clearwater Revisited. The trademark owners are compensated for the use of the name.

Doug and I believe Fogerty's demand of 25% of the gross proceeds was excessive, and unacceptable. Fogerty also refused to allow Doug and myself to be compensated for our performances in the project. We have never, nor will we ever, agree to give any one of the owners of the trademark a veto.

Fogerty waited sixteen months after he knew about this project before filing his lawsuit. Whatever the lawsuit is about, it's NOT about integrity.

"I hate them," John fumed. "It's just stupid. It's such a bringdown."

"If John doesn't want to play the songs, that's fine," Stu asserted. "He can do whatever he wants. We want to play this music. I haven't spoken with him about this. I imagine he's not very thrilled about it. I hope that he understands we're not doing this to hurt him."

Doug and Stu's reason for wanting to put the band together also has deep roots. As far back as 1971, when they were coming to grips with working as a trio, Stu had said, "Those are the songs that put us where we are. We still like playing them and they keep getting better each night."

"It's great to be playing again," Stu said some twenty-five years later. "There's nothing like the satisfaction of playing."

34

"WHEN ARE YOU GOING TO PLAY SOMETHING WHERE YOU ACTUALLY EARN MONEY?"

In the spring of 1996, word had begun to spread that the world might just see a new John Fogerty record soon. "He's been fine-tuning the album that he hopes to have out and tour behind within the year," Bob Fogerty commented. "The songs are wonderful. They sound like John Fogerty songs. I think everyone will be happy." Bob also let drop that, in the ensuing tour, John "will be singing the songs he wrote, which will certainly include many of these CCR rock standards." It would be the first time he played them live on tour in a quarter of a century.

By the end of January 1997, *Blue Moon Swamp* was done. Warner Bros. put it on their release schedule for the spring of 1997. It had been close to eleven years since *Eye of the Zombie*. While John had maintained a modicum of a public profile, people wondered what kind of record he would make. People wondered whether John Fogerty could be relevant at all after all this time.

John was smart enough to understand the dilemma. "Obviously I'm not twenty-three years old with a shaved head and shorts and trying to catch up with kids that are a lot younger than me," he said. "It'd be silly to pretend to do that. It's better to just be who I am. So, already I may be condemning myself to a certain category rather than another category. But it's the same thing I would tell any kid. Just be yourself. Don't be something you're not.

"While I tried in those days really hard to make hits unashamedly," he added, "and I certainly want to make hits now, unashamedly, I think for me to go and try and catch the latest trend and join in would be silly because I already have a trend. Everybody knows what my trend is. To go off and join some other trend would look like pandering, would look like some old guy trying to pick up a fifteen-year-old at the beach or something. There's something distasteful about it."

In making the album, he had recorded with some fifty musicians. "Hot Rod Heart" featured session ace Bob Glaub on bass and on drums, Kenny Aronoff, who would become the nucleus of his touring band. Among other notables who actually wound up on the album were Duck Dunn, Zappa and Genesis drummer Chester Thompson, vocalists the Waters, awesome gospel singers the Fairfield Four, Red Hot Chili Peppers drummer Chad Smith, and about a dozen other musicians. The budget for the record ran into seven figures, an astonishing amount considering how frugally John had made all of his previous recordings.

"I can believe it," muses CCR engineer Russ Gary. "It took him so much time. He lived at the Lighthouse recording studio, day in and day out for four years. That studio had a nice client there. You've got to hand it to Warner Brothers for sticking with him."

"It must have looked strange from the outside," John said. "Me going to the studio every day for years. I mean, if I saw someone doing that, I'd be the first to ask, 'Are you sure you're okay?'"

"It took longer to complete my album than it took to complete the Chinese wall," he added ironically.

By the time they were ready to mix the sessions, "some of the tape was four and five years old," said John Lowson, the engineer of *Blue Moon Swamp*. "In the end, I had close to 500 analog reels and about twelve of those large digital reels. I had inventory lists that were pretty extensive. There were times when John might say, 'Remember four years ago, when I did that lick? What guitar did I use?' I had it all written down. I had to keep good records."

As per his habit, John erased every tape he didn't use. They'll be no outtake collections of unreleased Fogerty in the future. He wanted his output to speak strictly for itself. That, he claimed, was one of the reasons it took him so long to make the album.

> I save nothing. If it's not good, I'm not going to want to listen to it. I destroy it. It's an old habit of mine. Look what happened to Buddy Holly and Jimi Hendrix: they have released all they could find. Every artist has albums and songs that are not good, and I don't want that to be heard. Imagine if I hadn't destroyed all my material when I was with Creedence. Those guys, you can be sure, would be selling it already. They even did it with material from our beginnings when we were kids.

"We used to have erasing sessions," Russ Gary concurs.

Of course, the question on everyone's mind was the same question everyone asked when he put out *Centerfield*: What took so long?

"I ask you," John posed, tongue in cheek, "who says you have to put out a record more often than every ten years? . . . It was a lot of work trying to make this record. Longer than Creedence's career." John added with self-deprecating humor, "I'm getting better at comebacks than I am at sustaining a solo career."

A couple of months before his record was due for release, John watched Zaentz carry home an armful of Oscars for *The English Patient*. Despite all the things he would say about putting his bitterness behind him, his perception of Zaentz's betrayal was a wound that stayed open and festered. "I like to say 'Yeah, I saw Jabba the Hutt win an award for best actor,'" John said, using his favorite nickname for his nemesis. "I'm not going to say it didn't bother me, but you know what—I haven't seen that movie, but I must say it looked like he won that award in an amazingly weak field this year. It wasn't like he was up against *Gandhi*."

Blue Moon Swamp was being released into a decidedly different musical environment than even *Centerfield*. Over the dozen years since John's first comeback, the music business had grown, changed, mutated, and subdivided. Where in 1985 there were pop, album-oriented rock, and modern rock stations, by 1997 the distinctions between radio formats had grown sharper and more exclusive. Many great albums fell through the cracks in radio, most because the greatness of the music found roots and wings in people's inability to classify and codify them.

In this environment, where did a John Fogerty album fit? Some classic rock stations that played CCR wouldn't play anything new, even by a classic rocker. "Sometimes with an older act," Warner Bros. president Steve Baker commented, "no matter how great the talent, it's not obvious that you're going to reach the maximum audience. If the pop stations or video channels don't play John's music, it doesn't mean he's not brilliant, it just means that another generation has taken over the airwaves."

John and Warners looked to the road to promote the album. It would be John's first tour in eleven years, and he could hardly wait. Even before the record came out, he was rehearsing his road band. They actually had to go out and buy some CCR CDs. For the first time in a quarter century, after arguing over them in court, urging boycotts of them, and telling people he would never play them again, John was going to perform his CCR songs live on tour.

Even back in the *Centerfield* days, when he was busily sniping at the publishers of his CCR catalog, he hinted that he might revive his old songs, "Look, you never say never, right? Ronald Reagan said he'd never cut Social Security. A lot of people really like those songs; there's an attachment in those people's hearts, and that's great. It's just that it's caused me so much pain for so many years, it's hard to contemplate. Maybe there'll come a day when I soften. I don't know."

In retrospect, John regretted not performing his old hits on the Rockin' All Over the World tour. "It was a bad decision, I guess," he told journalist Edna Gunderson before he embarked on his 1997 tour, "but it was where my heart was then. I was a guy that was pretty bitter. One way I put it fairly recently: it's like if you had a guy put in prison for years, unjustly, and then you let him out, which is what happened with *Centerfield*. . . . He's exuberant, he's real happy, joyful, until he thinks about being away in prison, unjustly. Then he gets really pissed off. . . . But the fans want to hear me sing my songs. It's just as simple as that."

While John had played a handful of concerts during his recent withdrawal from public life, most of them had been benefits. Now he would be hitting the road for money. Julie, for one, was proud. "She ribbed me," John noted, "saying, 'When are you going to stop playing benefits? When are you going to play something where you actually earn money?' It's true. I've done a lot of benefits because I believe in them. But they're sort of quirky. It's a little strange when you prepare for a month for just one night. And then you come out and it's all over."

Blue Moon Swamp came out on the twentieth of May; most of the reviews were positive. "Fogerty's wondrous album," wrote *Time*'s Jay Cocks, "follows a decade of anger, frustration, fear and hard-won resolution. But you don't hear the turmoil that went into making these songs. Instead you feel the confidence and ebullience of an artist renewed, covering the ground at the height of his power. . . . "

"John Fogerty's first album in more than a decade turns out to be worth the wait," wrote Steve Simels. "*Blue Moon Swamp* is the work of a still formidable musician, and if there's nothing here that comes up to his best past records, there's nothing here that dishonors them, either."

"It feels like something he might've knocked out over a few weekends," *Entertainment Weekly*'s Chris Willman complimented the record in his A-review. "*Swamp* is much more akin to the unpretentious, poop-kicking '70s solo albums Fogerty issued just after disbanding CCR, and though there's no 'Almost Saturday Night'-style classic around, you'll have a hard time finding a more charming roots-rock record this year."

"For his part, John Fogerty has had more pieces of classic rock than anyone this side of Elvis Presley and Paul McCartney," Grant Alden wrote in his four-star, *Rolling Stone* review. "His newest outing is still a remarkably vibrant batch of songs. . . . 'A Hundred and Ten in the Shade' may be the single best song Fogerty has offered since CCR fell apart."

John, live in 1997.

A day after the record came up, John started playing a short promotional tour beginning at Los Angeles's House of Blues. Steve Mirkin covered the show for *Rolling Stone Random Notes Daily On-line*:

> Fogerty's two-hour, twenty-three-song set leaned heavily on Creedence classics. . . . Fogerty's voice, a wondrous combination of purity and power in Creedence's prime, hasn't aged well. He had trouble reaching some notes, and during "Fortunate Son," his vocals took on the thin, tremulous quality of Neil Young. Still, he sang every song with energy and conviction. . . . To Fogerty's credit, the show never seemed like a cynical greatest hits rehash. . . . When he sang "Centerfield" he came off less as a rookie looking for his big break than a grizzled veteran trying to prove he still has the stuff to stay in the game.

Variety's Phil Gallo was more charitable in his review: "He moved from upbeat vintage hits to stirring renditions—backed by the gospel quintet the Fairfield Four — of the new *Swamp* ballad 'A Hundred and Ten in the Shade' and the traditional 'Midnight Special'; turned to a softer session with the Dobro on 'Workin' on a Building' . . . and 'Joy of My Life' . . . "

John took the show to the Fillmore in San Francisco, then on to Chicago and Toronto, where the crowd sang "Happy Birthday" to him (a couple of days late). By the time he reached New York, the band was broken in. His voice had mellowed from a roar to a growl. Fogerty couldn't reach the high notes in "Heard It Through the Grapevine," but just hearing him sing the songs made the small hairs stand up on the back of your neck. He signed pretty much anything brought up to him on the stage, and looked genuinely happy to be there—almost as happy as the audience was to see him.

"Nearly three decades later, as rock pulls further away from its roots," wrote the *New York Times*'s Jon Pareles in reviewing Fogerty's show, "most rockabilly seems even more antiquated. Yet, for Mr. Fogerty, it hasn't dated at all. . . . while many of Mr. Fogerty's newer songs sound like variations of Creedence songs, in tunes like 'Blueboy' his new riffs have as much rangy spunk as their predecessors. . . . The music wasn't nostalgic, just sure of its shape. As he was in the 1960s, Mr. Fogerty is still unfashionable and still indelible."

"He seemed absolutely at peace and calm in Chicago," reported Eric Schumacher-Rasmussen. "He did a short mini-press conference where he talked easily about the acrimony between him and the other band members and Saul Zaentz. When someone shouted for 'Zanz Can't Danz' at that night's House of Blues show, he said, 'Naaaah, I ain't that pissed off anymore.'"

John's tour created an almost ironic situation. After twenty-five years of no one from the original band playing this music, suddenly all three surviving members of CCR were on the road singing "rolling on the river." The two groups put on very different shows. Revisited/Cosmo's Factory played all sorts of venues, from the Greek Theater to state fairs, private parties, and even casinos. They averaged about 4,000 people a show. John played more traditional, though generally smaller (1,000 seat) venues, clubs like the House of Blues and auditoriums like the Hammerstein. At John's shows, people would sway, but they didn't really dance. At the Cosmo Factory shows, people danced in the aisles, on the seats, anywhere they could.

"There is room for both of us," noted Laurie Clifford. "We rock 'em, he fascinates them."

35

"I GET MORE AMAZED BY THE WEIRDNESS OF IT ALL"

Blue Moon Swamp started slowly in the United States. In Europe, however, particularly Scandinavia, the album jumped to number 1 and stayed in the high reaches of the charts for months. So, soon after the promotional tour and appearances on *Good Morning America*, two nights on *The Late Show with David Letterman*, and filming an episode of *Live at the Hard Rock Cafe* for VH-1, Fogerty, his band, and entourage were off to Europe.

In Germany, John had press conferences, filmed a TV show called "Gottschalk's House Party," and did a show for WEA Europe employees at a small club in Hamburg. He also played the Roskilde Festival in Denmark. He continued to sign things that people brought to the stage, allegedly only rejecting items that had already been signed by Stu and Doug, claiming they were bad luck.

While in Scandinavia, he signed records in department stores as well. An acquaintance in Stockholm reported: "John sat at a raised podium (actually not far from the ladies underwear) signing records with a big smile on his face, despite the no doubt boring work. I had brought my old vinyl *Green River* to have it signed as well, although the store's staff firmly informed me that the rules were that only the CD purchased would be signed. When it was my turn, he shook my hand and when the staff protested loudly (in Swedish) as I slipped my *Green River* on the table, he just said, 'It's cool, it's cool, I understood what she said, don't worry about it,' and then he signed it!"

John's official "World" tour started in Louisville, Kentucky, on July 12. He worked his way up the eastern part of the United States. The show in Philadelphia inspired a Bruce Springsteen fan to write to the Springsteen fanzine *Backstreets*: "I've just come home from seeing John Fogerty at the Tower Theater in Philadelphia. Springsteen should be made a roadie for this tour just so he can watch a man growing old gracefully and rocking the shit out of an audience."

The tour turned out to be the best promotion for *Blue Moon Swamp*. The album hovered around the high 30s and low 40s on the *Billboard* charts. Yet, whenever he played, local sales went up at least 50 to as much as 300 percent. "Everywhere he played," his booking agent commented, "it created a groundswell of much bigger proportions than the normal concert stop. This is one of those instances where the live performance is truly the best marketing tool for the album."

After a couple of weeks in the United States, Fogerty was back off to Europe, playing the Lollipop Festival and various arenas. Another acquaintance in Oslo reported, "There was a singalong with John in Oslo. Just when 'Midnight Special' was over, the audience started to sing 'Cotton Fields'. . . . John was just saying, 'And now I would like to sing another song from *Blue Moon Swamp*' when he suddenly realized what was going on. He stepped forward to listen to what we sang, then urged us to go on, started to pick on the guitar to support and eventually he and the band took up and played the whole song together with us!"

Back in America, John filmed another VH-1 special, this time for the popular *Story Tellers* series in which well-known songwriters comment on the genesis of their songs. He also played on the *Tonight Show*, then started a West Coast swing.

In August Fogerty's legal bete noir, the Ninth Circuit Court of Appeals, announced their reversal of John's injunction preventing Stu and Doug from playing as Creedence Clearwater Revisited:

> "Because we conclude that the District Court clearly erred, we reverse the District Court's grant of a preliminary injunction. The evidence submitted by both parties convincingly demonstrates that the public was unlikely to be, and in fact was not confused about Fogerty's association with Revisited. . . . Here, the record contains virtually no evidence that [Clifford and Cook were] engaged in deceptive or misleading advertising or marketing. It does not support the District Court's finding that Fogerty would probably prevail on the merits. . . . The record contains no evidence that the American public actually was confused or led to believe that Fogerty was associated with Revisited. We therefore assign little weight to the evidence that at least one German and one Thai Fogerty fan was [*sic*]confused as to Fogerty's involvement in the Revisited tour.

"We obviously feel vindicated," Stu said. "From the beginning this project has been only about good music and good fun, not personnel or politics."

Doug added, "Stu and I have great love for CCR music. There is nothing confusing about our show, our band or who's in it. We're glad the Court of Appeals agrees."

The Revisited camp then took the offensive. They sued Fogerty for defamation and breach of fiduciary duty. "Over the years he has done everything he could to devalue [Creedence Clearwater Revival]," Stu explained. "He owes the rest of us a fiduciary duty to protect, enhance and help [the band] grow on a business level. We believe that he has violated that."

Other strange things were happening with John. Nick Clainos of Bill Graham Presents and John severed relations, leaving John's management once more in his own hands, assisted by his wife, Julie, and his brother Bob. A spate of European dates, in England and Germany, suddenly were canceled to the chagrin of many local fans.

Peter Koers, head of the CCR fan club, reported Julie telling him that the cancelations were the result of apparent misunderstandings between John's U.S. management and the European tour agent:

> John NEVER gave his okay for the tour beside the concerts in Scandinavia. Those had been booked by a different organization. The reason the three German tour dates in Berlin, Offenbach, and Munich were canceled later than the others was because John tried to arrange a deal with Warner Bros Germany to meet halfway the costs for the concerts that would have been into largely negative figures. It didn't work out.

Despite the snafu, the German music critics gave *Blue Moon Swamp* the Preis der Deutschne Schallpatternkritik for the summer of 1997 as best "Blues, Pop and Rock" record.

During the summer of 1997, Jeff Fogerty announced his plans to make a benefit CCR tribute record. As the representative for a company making microphones and recording studio equipment, he had talked to a number of artists. He hoped to raise funds for Pediatric AIDS. However, his uncle didn't like the idea. Jeff reported that "Any artist who approaches John or his agent is being told that John is not participating and he is not encouraging their participation." This caused several artists, most with Warner Communication ties, to withdraw their support. Others, like George Clinton, couldn't wait to do it. "They're great songs and it's a good cause," he commented.

When the *Blue Moon Swamp* tour pulled into Julie's home turf of South Bend, the Fogertys announced that they intended to move the family to the area when the tour ended. "Living in Los Angeles, there are so many people," Julie said. "We are going to love having some privacy and some space." Even the videos from *Blue Moon Swamp* were family affairs. Julie showed off her ample charms in the "Walking in a Hurricane" clip. Their son Shane played on a swing in the "Southern Streamline" video. All of the children were in the video for "Blueboy." When John went on tour, he took the entire family with him.

"You can be certain that if Julie and the kids weren't able to come along on the tour then there wouldn't be a tour at all," John's sister-in-law, Lisa Taylor, said. "Julie and John got married to be together. I have a lot of respect for them as a couple and that their marriage is the biggest priority for them. Julie is very active in the day to day operations of the tour. She plays an active role in everything from John's wardrobe to the tour merchandise."

During the fall of 1997 rumors began to circulate. John was unhappy with his high-priced band. Warner Bros. was upset with the sales on *Blue Moon Swamp*. They wanted to produce a live album from the tour featuring the Creedence music. If they didn't pick up his option, it was the last album on John's contract. And despite his legal woes, with pending cases with Fantasy and now with Stu and Doug, John parted company with his longtime attorney, Ken Sidle, who had been with him all the way to the Supreme Court.

In the meantime the National Academy of songwriters presented John a lifetime achievement award on December 3, 1997, along with his Hall of Fame bandmate Robbie Robertson, Quincy Jones, and Ashford and Simpson.

One of the most persistent questions to crop up, though, still had to do with John's next album of new material. Would it take him another ten years to make one? "Can I do it in a year?" he asked rhetorically. "I'll try. But if it takes five years, I'll do that."

"I truly expect this next album by John to be a killer," predicted Russ Gary. "Not so much the live one as the one after. The live one will probably be good if his voice is in shape. I don't know what takes they'll use. Hopefully towards the end of the tour. They've probably got John starting to peak with that voice again. You've got to go out there and work that muscle in your throat to get that growl going. He's not a young fellow anymore. I truly believe that the next studio album will be the one to put him back on the mark again. I think he's quite inspired now. He's out there and he's been received so well. The man doesn't write a bad song."

In November flyers started appearing at the reception counters at Warner Bros. in Burbank announcing free John Fogerty concerts at the Warner Bros. Studio on December 12 and 13. The flyers read "John Fogerty In Concert, performing songs from *Blue Moon Swamp*, songs from *Centerfield* and songs he made famous with Creedence Clearwater Revival like: Grapevine, Proud Mary, Who'll Stop the Rain, Lodi, Travelin' Band, Green River, Centerfield,

Blue Boy, Down on the Corner, Long as I Can See the Light, Old Man Down the Road, Fortunate Son, A Hundred and Ten in the Shade, ETC." It gave a number to call for free tickets.

On December 12 and 13, two audiences of about 800 people got to see the Blue Moon Swamp Tour, along with one new John Fogerty song, "Premonition." Forgerty taped the show for VH-1. Rumors abounded that it might also be the source for the Live album he was supposed to release.

Stu and Doug had plans for a live album as well. They took tapes from a week of Canadian shows to make a live CCRevisited double CD. Setting out to recreate an ideal version of their two-hour show, they spent the better part of December and January picking the songs and performance they wanted to include.

In the mean time, Jeff Fogerty had taken a new gig, touring as minister of promotion for George Clinton and the P-Funk Allstars. He occasionally took the stage with the band, playing guitar during the always chaotic encores.

The first week of January 1998, the National Association of Recording Arts and Sciences announced the nominations for the 1997 Grammy Awards. John got his third and fourth nominations, one for Best Rock Album for *Blue Moon Swamp,* the other for Best Male Rock Vocal Performance for "Blueboy." He had previously been nominated for that award twice before, for "Centerfield" and "Eye of the Zombie" in 1985 and 1986 respectively. Additionally, John Lowson and Bob Clearmountain were given engineering nods for their work on the *Blue Moon Swamp* album.

About a week later, John was at the Rock and Roll Hall of Fame induction ceremonies. Welcoming the late Gene Vincent into the music pantheon, he strode up to the mic and belted out an a cappella verse of Vincent's greatest hit, "Be-Bop-a-Lula," which he called "one of the greatest records ever made."

"Gene Vincent gave me an image perfect for rock 'n' roll," he said. "Loud, self-assured and greasy."

The day before the Grammys, John accepted the 1998 Orville H. Gibson Lifetime Achievement Award at a gala fund-raiser for the Nordoff-Robbins Music Therapy Foundation. In announcing the award, Gibson chairman Henry Juszkiewicz called John "one of America's true guitar heroes." At the Grammys John finally took home a statuette, winning the Best Rock Album award. Then, perhaps to make up for turning down an invitation to play at Clinton's second inaugural, John answered a presidential invitation. He joined several other performers playing the annual presidential gala for the restoration of Ford's Theater in Washington. A condensed version of the show was broadcast on the ABC network.

After eleven years largely out of the public eye, John was making up for lost time. Perhaps, like Stu and Doug, he realized he wasn't getting any younger. As he told Pete Fornatale live on the air at New York City's venerable rock station WNEW-FM before a late summer appearance at Hammerstein Hall, "I can't be fooling around anymore. I don't have that much time left."

Meanwhile, the three ex-bandmates continue to struggle with the legacy—musical, legal, and otherwise—of a group they founded as teenagers. As Doug summed it up, "Thank God the music is in the grooves. The music will never change. That's the legacy, that's what counts. Whether we like each other or not really doesn't matter."

"I think Creedence will be remembered as one of the great bands," Stu said. "That really gives you a sense of accomplishment that [every band member] should have, no matter how things turned out in the end. We really shouldn't be dwelling on how it all came apart.

"Every day, I get more amazed by the weirdness of it all, and it just gets weirder. [But] these lawsuits will be over someday. I don't like them either, but I didn't start them."

Which all just leaves Bob Fogerty shaking his head. He was still in his teens when he started working for his two brothers and two of their friends, taking pictures of one of the most popular bands in the world. Now, once again, he was his brother's chief aide-de-camp. "All three of them," he says of the surviving members of the band, "you can go around and around with those guys. Life isn't easy. They have such animosity towards each other. It's too bad. You get divorces, and everything doesn't always turn out so well. When one side of this starts talking, the other side wants to talk and it just makes matters worse. Dealing with anything to do with Creedence at all. . . . I don't need to cause more hurt feelings than there already are."

DISCOGRAPHY

Compiled by Petri Simala, Paul Garfinkle, and Hank Bordowitz

Tommy Fogerty and the Blue Velvets

Singles

Come on Baby/Oh My Love	(Orchestra 10/61)
Have You Ever Been Lonely/Bonita	(Orchestra 11/61)
Now You're Not Mine/Yes You Did	(Orchestra 6/62)

The Golliwogs

Singles

Don't Tell Me No Lies/	(Fantasy 11/64)
Little Girl (Does Your Mama Know)	
You Came Walking/Where You Been	(Fantasy 4/65)
You Can't Be True/	(Fantasy 7/65)
You Got Nothin' on Me	
Brown-Eyed Girl/	(Scorpio 3/66)
You Better Be Careful	
Fight Fire/Fragile Child	(Scorpio 4/66)
Walking on the Water/	(Scorpio 12/66)
You Better Get It Before It Gets You	

Albums

The Golliwogs (Pre-Creedence)	(Fantasy '75)

Don't Tell Me No Lies - Little Girl (Does Your Mama Know?) - Where You Been - You Came Walking - You Can't Be True - You Got Nothin' on Me - Brown-Eyed Girl - You Better Be Careful - Fight Fire - Fragile Child - Walk

on the Water - You Better Get It Before It Gets You - Porterville (T Spice-
bush Swallowtail*) - Call It Pretending
All songs Rann Wild & Toby Green (Aka Tom Fogerty and John Fogerty)
*Pseudonym for John Fogerty

Creedence Clearwater Revival

Singles

	Porterville/Call It Pretending	(Fantasy 1/68)	
	Suzie Q (Part one)/Suzie Q (Part Two)	(Fantasy 8/68)	#11
	I Put a Spell on You/Walk on the Water	(Fantasy 10/68)	#52
P	Proud Mary/Born on the Bayou	(Fantasy 1/69)	#2
P	Bad Moon Rising/Lodi	(Fantasy 4/69)	#2/52
P	Green River/Commotion	(Fantasy 7/69)	#2/30
P	Down on the Corner/Fortunate Son	(Fantasy 10/69)	#3/14
P	Travelin' Band/Who'll Stop the Rain	(Fantasy 1/70)	#2
G	Up Around the Bend/ Run Through the Jungle	(Fantasy 4/70)	#4
P	Lookin' Out My Back Door/ Long as I Can See the Light	(Fantasy 8/70)	#2
G	Have You Ever Seen the Rain/Hey Tonight	(Fantasy 1/71)	#8
G	Sweet Hitch-Hiker/Door to Door	(Fantasy 7/71)	#6
	Someday Never Comes/ Tearin' Up the Country	(Fantasy 4/72)	#25
	I Heard It Through the Grapevine/ Good Golly Miss Molly	(Fantasy 1/76)	#43

Albums

All songs written by J. C. Fogerty unless otherwise stated

P   Creedence Clearwater Revival   (Fantasy 7/68)   #52 Pop
I Put a Spell on You (J. Hawkins/Slotkin) - The Working Man - Suzie Q
(Hawkins/Lewis) - Ninety-Nine and a Half (Won't Do)(Cropper/Floyd/
Pickett) - Get Down Woman - Porterville - Gloomy - Walk on the Water

2p Bayou Country   (Fantasy 2/69)   #7 Pop
Born on the Bayou - Bootleg - Graveyard Train - Good Golly Miss Molly (R.
Blackwell/J. Marascalco) - Penthouse Pauper - Proud Mary - Keep on Chooglin'

3p Green River   (Fantasy 9/69)   #1 Pop
Green River - Commotion - Tombstone Shadow - Wrote a Song for Every-
one - Bad Moon Rising - Lodi - Cross-Tie Walker - Sinister Purpose -
Night Time Is the Right Time (L. Herman/Cadena)

2p Willy and the Poorboys   (Fantasy 12/69)   #3 Pop
Down on the Corner - It Came Out of the Sky - Cotton Fields (H. Ledbet-
ter) - Poorboy Shuffle - Feelin' Blue - Fortunate Son - Don't Look Now (It
Ain't You or Me) - The Midnight Special (American folk song, arranged by
J. C. Fogerty) - Side o' the Road - Effigy

4p Cosmo's Factory   (Fantasy 7/70)   #1 Pop
Ramble Tamble - Before You Accuse Me (McDaniels) - Travelin' Band -
Ooby Dooby (Moore/Penner) - Lookin' Out My Back Door - Run
Through the Jungle - Up Around the Bend - My Baby Left Me (Arthur
Cruddup) - Who'll Stop the Rain - I Heard It Through the Grapevine
(Whitfield/Strong) - Long as I Can See the Light

P   Pendulum   (Fantasy 12/70)   #5 Pop
Pagan Baby - Sailor's Lament - Chameleon - Have You Ever Seen the Rain? -
(Wish I Could) Hideaway - Born to Move - Hey Tonight - It's Just a
Thought - Molina - Rude Awakening No. 2

G   Mardi Gras   (Fantasy 4/72)   #12 Pop
Lookin' for a Reason - Take It Like a Friend (Cook) - Need Someone to
Hold (Cook/Clifford) - Tearin' Up the Country (Clifford) - Someday
Never Comes - What Are You Gonna Do (Clifford) - Sail Away (Cook) -
Hello Mary Lou (G. Pitney) - Door to Door (Cook) - Sweet Hitch-Hiker

2p Creedence Gold   (Fantasy 12/72)   #15 Pop
Proud Mary - Down on the Corner - Bad Moon Rising - I Heard It
Through the Grapevine - The Midnight Special - Have You Ever Seen the
Rain? - Born on the Bayou - Suzie Q (D. Hawkins/Lewis)

G   More Creedence Gold   (Fantasy 7/73)   #61 Pop
Hey Tonight - Run Through the Jungle - Fortunate Son - Bootleg - Lookin'
Out My Back Door - Molina - Who'll Stop the Rain - Sweet Hitch-Hiker -
Good Golly Miss Molly (R. Blackwell/J. Marascalco) - I Put a Spell on You
(J. Hawkins/Slotkin) - Don't Look Now - Lodi - Porterville - Up Around
the Bend

Live in Europe   (Fantasy 12/73)
Born on the Bayou - Green River/Suzie Q (D Hawkins/Lewis) - It Came
Out of the Sky - Travelin' Band - Fortunate Son - Commotion - Lodi - Bad
Moon Rising - Proud Mary - Up Around the Bend - Hey Tonight - Keep on
Chooglin'

4p Chronicle   (Fantasy 2/76)   #100 Pop
Suzie Q (D. Hawkins/Lewis) - I Put a Spell on You (J. Hawkins/Slotkin) -
Proud Mary - Bad Moon Rising - Lodi - Green River - Commotion -
Down on the Corner - Fortunate Son - Travelin' Band - Who'll Stop the
Rain - Up Around the Bend - Run Through the Jungle - Lookin' Out My
Back Door - Long as I Can See the Light - I Heard It Through the
Grapevine (Whitfield/Strong) - Have You Ever Seen the Rain? - Hey
Tonight - Sweet Hitch-Hiker - Someday Never Comes

P   The Concert   (Fantasy 11/80)   #62 Pop
(Reissue of Royal Albert Hall)
Born on the Bayou - Green River - Tombstone Shadow - Don't Look Now -
Travelin' Band - Who'll Stop the Rain - Bad Moon Rising - Proud Mary -
Fortunate Son - Commotion - The Midnight Special - Night Time Is the
Right Time (L. Herman/Cadena) - Down on the Corner - Keep on
Chooglin'

Creedence Country   (Fantasy 8/81)
Lookin' for a Reason - Don't Look Now - Lodi - My Baby Left Me (Crud-
dup) - Hello Mary Lou (G. Pitney) - Ramble Tamble - Cotton Fields -
Before You Accuse Me (McDaniels) - Wrote a Song for Everyone - Ooby
Dooby (Moore/Penner) - Crosstie Walker - Lookin' Out My Back Door

Chooglin'   (Fantasy '82)
Keep on Chooglin' - Heard It Through the Grapevine (Whitfield/Strong) -
Suzie Q (Hawkins/Lewis) - Pagan Baby - Born on the Bayou

Chronicle 2   (Fantasy '86)
Walk on the Water - Suzie Q (Part 2) - Born on the Bayou - Good Golly
Miss Molly (R. Blackwell/J. Marascalco) - Tombstone Shadow - Wrote a
Song for Everyone - Night Time Is the Right Time - Cotton Fields - It
Came Out of the Sky - Don't Look Now - The Midnight Special - Before
You Accuse Me (McDaniels) - My Baby Left Me (Cruddup) - Pagan Baby -
(Wish I Could) Hideaway - It's Just a Thought - Molina - Born to Move -
Lookin' for a Reason - Hello Mary Lou (Pitney)

John Fogerty

Singles

Blue Ridge Mountain Blues/	(Fantasy 8/72)	
Have Thine Own Way, Lord		
Jambalaya/Workin' on a Building	(Fantasy 10/72)	#16 Pop
Hearts of Stone/Somewhere Listening	(Fantasy 4/73)	#37 Pop
Back in the Hills/You Don't Owe Me	(Fantasy 9/73)	
Comin' Down the Road/Ricochet	(Fantasy 11/73)	
Rockin' All Over the World/The Wall	(Asylum 9/75)	#27 Pop
Almost Saturday Night/Sea Cruise	(Asylum 1/76)	#78 Pop
You Got the Magic/Evil Thing	(Asylum 2/76)	#87 Pop
The Old Man Down the Road/	(Warner 11/84)	#10 Pop
Big Train (From Memphis)		
Rock and Roll Girls/Centerfield	(Warner 5/85)	#20 Pop
Eye of the Zombie/I Confess	(Warner 8/86)	#81 Pop
Change in the Weather/	(Warner 11/86)	
My Toot Toot		
Walkin' in a Hurricane	(Warner 5/97)	

Albums

All songs written by J. C. Fogerty unless otherwise stated.

Blue Ridge Rangers   (Fantasy 4/73)   #47 Pop

Blue Ridge Mountain Blues (Trad.)- Somewhere Listening (for My Name) (Brownlee) - You're the Reason (Edwards/Imes/Terry/Fell) - Jambalaya (Hank Williams) - She Thinks I Still Care (Lipscomb/Duffy) - California Blues (J. Rodgers) - Workin' on a Building (Trad.) - Please Help Me I'm Falling (Robertson/Blair) - Have Thine Own Way, Lord (Stebbins/Pollard) - I Ain't Never (Tillis/Pierce)- Hearts of Stone (Ray/Jackson) - Today I Started Loving You Again (Haggard/Owens)

John Fogerty   (Asylum 10/75)   #78 Pop

Rockin' All Over the World - You Rascal You (Theard) - The Wall - Travelin' High - Lonely Teardrops (Carlo/Gordy Jnr.) - Almost Saturday Night - Where the River Flows - Sea Cruise (Smith) - Dream Song - Flying Away

2p Centerfield   (Warner 1/85)   #1 Pop

The Old Man Down the Road - Rock and Roll Girls - Big Train (From Memphis) - I Saw It on TV - Mr. Greed - Searchlight - Centerfield - I Can't Help Myself - Zanz Kant Danz*

*Original title in the first pressing of the album, later changed to Vanz Kant Danz

G   Eye of the Zombie   (Warner 9/86)   #26 Pop
    Goin' Back Home - Eye of the Zombie - Headlines - Knockin' on Your
    Door - Change in the Weather - Violence Is Golden - Wasn't That a
    Woman - Soda Pop - Sail Away

G   Blue Moon Swamp   (Warner 5/97)   #37 Pop
    Southern Streamline - Hot Rod Heart - Blueboy - A Hundred and Ten in
    the Shade - Rattlesnake Highway - Bring It Down to Jellyroll - Walking in a
    Hurricane - Swamp River Days - Rambunctious Boy - Joy of My Life - Blue
    Moon Nights - Bad Bad Boy

Guest Appearances
Guitar on "Kickin' Asphalt" by Duane Eddy on his self-titled album 1987
"Born on the Bayou" and "Fortunate Son" live on the album featuring Rock
    and Roll Hall of Fame Opening Concert, 1995
"All Mama's Children," duet with Carl Perkins on his *Go, Cat, Go* album 1996

Tom Fogerty

Singles

Good-Bye Media Man, Pt one/	(Fantasy 4/71)
Good-Bye Media Man, Pt Two	
Cast the First Stone/Lady of Fatima	(Fantasy 6/72)
Faces, Places, People/Forty Years	(Fantasy 10/72)
Joyful Resurrection/Heartbeat	(Fantasy 5/73)
Mystic Isle Avalon/Reggie	(Fantasy 11/73)
Money/It's Been a Good Day	(Fantasy 6/74)
Sweet Things to Come	(Fantasy 3/75)
Judy Lee/	(PBR '75)
Baby, What You Want Me to Do	
Life Is But a Dream/	(PBR '76)
Running Back to Me	
Champagne Love/The Secret	(Fantasy 1/82)

Albums
All songs written by Tom Fogerty unless otherwise stated

Tom Fogerty   (Fantasy 5/72)   #78 Pop
The Legend of Alcatraz - Lady of Fatima - Beauty Is Under the Skin - Won-
dering - My Pretty Baby - Train to Nowhere - Everyman - The Me Song -
Cast the First Stone - Here Stands the Clown

Excalibur   (Fantasy 10/72)
Forty Years - Black Jack Jenny - Rocky Road Blues (B. Monroe) - Faces, Places,
People - Get Funky - Sick and Tired (C. Kenner/D. Bartholomew) - Sign of the
Devil - Straight and Narrow - Next in Line - (Hold on) Annie Mae

Zephyr National   (Fantasy 2/74)
It's Been a Good Day - Can You Feel It, Ras? - Mystic Isle Avalon - Reggie -
Money (Root the Root) - Hot Buttered Rum (Tom Fogerty, Russell Gary) -
Joyful Resurrection - Heartbeat - Fate - Goin' Back to Okeefeenokee

Myopia   (Fantasy 11/74)
Give Me Another Trojan Horse - What Did I Know - Theme From 4-D -
Sweet Things to Come - What About Tomorrow - She La La La - And I
Love You - Get Up - There Was a Time - Showdown

Ruby   (PBR '76)
Life Is But a Dream (Oda/Fogerty) - Can You Really Say (Davis) - Bart
(Oda) - Starry Eyed (Cochran) - Baby What You Want Me to Do (Reed) -
Running Back to Me (Oda/Fogerty/Cochran) - Take Me Back to London
(Oda/Fogerty) - It's Taking a Long Time (Oda) - Slippin' and Slidin' (Pen-
niman/Bocage/Collins/Smith) - Big Fat Woman

Rock and Roll Madness   (PBR '78)
Run With Your Love (Oda) - Mistreater (Oda) - Take a Little More Time -
Make Love to You - Evergeen in Mexico - It's Gotta Be You - Take Me
Higher - Singin' the Blues (Mcgreavy)- King Arthur's March - Dance All
Night (Davis)

Deal It Out   (Fantasy 10/81)
Champaign Love (T. Fogerty/Clifford) - Why Me - Real Real Gone (V.
Morrison) - Tricia Suzanne - Mystery Train (Parker/Phillips) - Deal It Out
(Olson) - Open the Window (Park) - You Move Me (Morrison) - The
Secret - Summer Night (Park)

Precious Gems   (Fantasy '84)
Running Back to Me (Oda/T. Forgerty/Cochrane) - Life Is But a Dream
(Oda/Fogerty)- Mistreater (Oda) - Run With Your Love (Oda) - Bart
(Oda)- Take Me Back to London (Oda/Fogerty) - Can You Really Say
(Davis) - Singin' the Blues (Mcgreavy) - Dance All Night (Davis)

Sidekicks   (Fantasy '92)
All songs by Fogerty/Oda except as indicated.
Rainbow Carousel - Money Buys It (on the Funky Side of Town) - Video

Girl - Woman of the Year - Clearwater Rain - Teardrops - We've Been Here
Before - Sometimes - Sloop John B (Wilson) - Unbearable Lightness of
Being (Fogerty) (Recorded '88, Released '92)

Guest Appearances
Guitar on the "Heavy Turbulence" album by Merle Saunders in 1972
Guitar and producer on "Fire Up" by Merle Saunders in 1973

Doug Clifford

Single
Latin Music/Take a Train   (Fantasy 8/72)
Albums
All songs by Doug Clifford except where indicated.

Doug "Cosmo" Clifford   (Fantasy 9/72)
Latin Music - Regret It (for the Rest of Your Life) - Guitars, Drums, & Girls
- I'm a Man (S. Winwood) - She's About a Mover (Doug Sahm) - I Just
Want to Cry - Get Your Raise - Daydream (J. Sebastian) - Take a Train -
Death Machine - Swingin' in a Hammock

Guest Appearances
On Russell Da Shiell's album "Elevator" (Epic 1972)

Stu Cook

Guest Appearances
On Russell Da Shiell's album "Elevator" (Epic 1972)
Bass and producer on Rocky Erickson's album "Evil One" (415 1981)

Don Harrison Band
Featuring Doug Clifford and Stu Cook

Singles
Rock 'n' Roll Records/   (Atlantic '76)
    Ballroom Dancing Girl
Sixteen Tons/Who I Really Am   (Atlantic '76)   #47 Pop

Albums
All songs By Don Harrison unless noted

Don Harrison Band   (Atlantic '76)
Sixteen Tons (M.Travis) - Who I Really Am - Rock 'N' Roll Records - Fame and Fortune - Sometimes Loving You (R. Da Shiell) - Romance - Sweetwater William (R. Da Shiell) - Barroom Dancing Girl - a Bit of Love (R. Da Shiell) - Living Another Day

Red Hot   (Atlantic '76)
Red Hot (Ready to Go) - Jaime - This Ol' Guitar - Rock 'N' Roll Lady - My Heart - In the Rain - Baby Don't Change Your Mind - Love Came Down - Takin' My Time (Da Shiell) - Round and Round

Southern Pacific
Featuring Stu Cook

Singles

A Girl Like Emmy Lou	(Warner '86)	#17 Country
Killbilly Hill	(Warner '86)	#37 Country
Don't Let Go of My Heart	(Warner '87)	#26 Country
Midnight Highway	(Warner '88)	#14 Country
New Shade of Blue	(Warner '88)	#2 Country
Honey, I Dare You	(Warner '88)	#5 Country
Any Way the Wind Blows	(Warner '89)	#4 Country
Times Up (w/Carlene Carter)	(Warner '89)	#26 Country
I Go to Pieces	(Warner '90)	#31 Country
Reckless Heart	(Warner '90)	#32 Country

Albums

Killbilly Hill   (Warner 85)   #31 Country
Road Song (Goodman/Mcfee) - A Girl Like Emmy Lou (Goodman/Mcfee/Knudsen/Cook) - Pink Cadillac (Springsteen) - I Still Look for You (Nobel/Struck) - Pull Your Hat Down Tight (Storey) - Killbilly Hill (Mcfee/Goodman) - Don't Let Go of My Heart (Howell/Maslin) - What's It Gonna Take (Howell/Mcfee/Knudsen/Cook) - Hearts on the Borderline (Rose/Bunch/Kennedy) - Bluegrass Blues (O'Hara/Kane)

Zuma   (Warner '88)   #21 Country
Midnight Highway - Honey I Dare You - New Shade of Blue - Dream on -
The Invisible Man - Wheels on the Line (With Huey Lewis on Harmonica) -
Just Hang on - All Is Lost - Bail Out (With Huey Lewis on Harmonica) -
Trail of Tears

County Line   (Warner '91)
Any Way the Wind Blows - I Can't Complain - Beyond Love - Time's Up
(Duet With Carlene Carter) - Memphis Queen - Side Saddle - One That
Got Away - Reckless Heart - Mary Lou - Help Wanted - G.T.O. (with the
Beach Boys) - I Go to Pieces

Greatest Hits   (Warner '92)
Any Way the Wind Blows - Reno Bound - New Shade of Blue - Thing About
You (with Emmylou Harris) - All Is Lost - A Girl Like Emmy Lou - Honey I
Dare You - Midnight Highway - I Go to Pieces - Perfect Stranger - Time's
Up (with Carlene Carter) - Trail of Tears - Pink Cadillac (live version)

Pink Cadillac Movie Soundtrack
Any Way the Wind Blows - Reno Bound

Where the Pyramid Meets the Eye—a Tribute to Roky Erikson
A Cold Night for Alligators

Sir Douglas Quintet
Featuring Doug Clifford and Stu Cook; all songs by Doug Sahm except
where indicated.

Albums

Groover's Paradise   (Warner '74)
Groover's Paradise - Devil Heart - Houston Chicks - For the Sake of Rock
'N' Roll - Beautiful Texas Sunshine - Just Groove Me - Girls Today Don't
Like to Sleep Alone - La Cacahuta (Peanut) (L. Guerrero) - Her Dream
Man Never Came - Catch Me in the Morning

Day Dreaming at Midnight   (Elektra '94)
Too Little Too Late (D. Sahm/S. Sahm) - Twisted World (D. Sahm/S. Sahm/
Clifford) - Darling Dolores - Day Dreaming at Midnight (D. Sahm/ S.
Sahm) - Into the Night (Clifford/Ortega) - Dylan Come Lately - She
Would If She Could, She Can't So She Won't - You Don't Know How Young
You Are (St. John) - County Line (Ortega) - Romance Is All Screwed Up -
Freedom Is Mine (Clifford/Ortega) - Intoxication

NOTES

Introduction

"John Fogerty is an idol . . .," Siegle, 1997

"Literally everyone . . . ," Gleason, 1970

"It is the saddest . . . ," E-mail, 1997

Chapter 1

"El Cerrito is like the most . . . ," interview, 1997

"I envisioned being exactly . . . ," Hubner, 1986

"I remember as early as 1953 . . . ," Goldberg, 1993.

"Carl Perkins . . . ," Goldberg, 1993/ Hubner, 1986

"We came from a strict . . . ," Hallowell, 1971

"I did use a lot of energy . . . ," Hubner, 1986

"I was always ashamed . . . ," *Time*, 6/27/69

"Most of my struggles were mental . . . ," *In Concert*, 1970

"John used to work relentlessly . . . ," Bryman, 1988

"We had this great series . . . ," Hillburn 1993

"I'll never forget seeing . . . ," Forte 1986

"I remember when I . . . ," Forte 1986

"Tom and I went and," Cole/Gossett, c. 1975

"I convinced my wife . . . ," Lundqvist/ Lindberg/Ekholm, 1994

"For a long time . . . ," Ruby 1969

Info on KWBR and Fogerty's favorite songs from Gleason, 1970

"Doug wasn't the first . . . ," Brewer, 1969

"I was twelve or thirteen . . . ," Brewer, 1969

"Doug and I met in . . . ," Hallowell, 1971

"I was listening to . . . ," Ruby, 1969

"We were all on the same . . . ," Ruby, 1969

"Both my parents worked . . . ," *In Concert*, 1970

"When we started . . . ," Ben Fong-Torres, 1969; Gleason, 1970

"We were really getting down!" Werner, 1997

"We only knew so many songs . . . ," Lundqvist/Lindberg/Ekholm, 1994

"I remember the first time . . . ," interview, 1997

"St. Mary's High—the all-boys school . . . ," Forte, 1986

Chapter 2

"Tom was singing at some . . . ," interview, 1997

"I think it's important to know . . . ," Gleason, 1970

"I was in the ninth grade . . . ," official John Fogerty Web page, 1977

"We somehow landed a contract . . . ," Osborne, 1988

"The Blue Velvets backed . . . ," E-mail correspondence, via River Rising mailing list, 1996–97

"We were high school . . . ," interview, 1997

"I had the money to pay . . . ," Parachini, 1971

" We made, I guess, five . . . ," Gleason, 1970

"We auditioned . . . ," Osborne, 1988

"The Blue Velvets, my back-up . . . ," Osborne, 1988

"Casey Kasem was the program . . . ," Osborne, 1988

"It died . . . ," Settle, 1984

Chapter 3

"There was a time . . . ," Forte, 1986

"Two of us worked . . . ," Delahant, 1969; Dawber, 1969

"We went over there . . . ," Gleason, 1970

"We recorded the kind of jazz . . . ," Saul Zaenta, Fantasy Films biography, c. 1986

"Fantasy is primarily a jazz label . . . ," Tom Fogerty radio interview, 1976

"I mean, I was eighteen years old . . . ," Forte and Soest, 1985

"An eccentric, beatnik type." E-mail correspondence, via River Rising mailing list, 1996–97

"Max and Sol Weiss, they . . . ," interview, 1997

"Max [Weiss] convinced us . . . ," Gleason, 1970

"We made a dumb tape, a . . . ," Gleason, 1970

"The Monkey Inn was . . . ," interview, 1997

"Unfortunately . . . ," Hallowell, 1971

"Our manager, Max Weiss . . . ," E-mail correspondence, via River Rising mailing list, 1996–97

"You know . . . ," Gleason, 1970

"Oh, that was so funny . . . ," Osborne, 1988

"We figured if you . . . ," Gleason, 1970

"With the new name . . . ," Scott Longston, via E-mail, 1988

"The Golliwogs' and funny hats soon . . . ," Settle, 1984

Chapter 4

"We were getting $50 a night . . . ," Creedence Clearwater Revival, Fantasy biography

"I was mainly in it for the beer . . . ," Kris Eric Stevens, WLS (Chicago) audio interview, 1970

"Those frat parties . . . ," Torres, 1969

"Everybody wanted . . . ," Kris Eric Stevens, WLS (Chicago) audio interview, 1970

"I was very self-conscious . . . ," Gleason, 1970

"There was all this beer . . . ," Tiegel, 1969

"I realized John should . . . ," Hallowell, 1971

"I used to get sore throats . . . ," Tiegel, 1969

"One day . . . ," Lundquist/Lindberg/Ekholm/, 1994

"We used the Monkey Inn . . . ," *Fifth Street Flash* 1970

"We never identified with . . . ," Tiegel, 1969

"Back in 1965 . . . ," interview, 1997

"When Doug and I . . . ," E-mail correspondence, via River Rising mailing list, 1996–97

"This is when I started . . . ," interview, 1997

"Very contrived . . . ," Gleason, 1970

"A lot of earnestness about nothing," Lundqvist/Lindberg/Ekholm, 1994

"If 'Brown Eyed Girl' had been a hit . . . ," Gleason, 1970

"The reason it took . . . ," Factory/Fantasy press kit, 1971

"If we had made it then . . . ," Creedence Clearwater Revival, Fantasy Records biography

"I was an auto dealer . . . ," interview, 1997

"I was so downed by . . . ," Kris Eric Stevens, WLS (Chicago) radio interview, 1970

"I was really excited about . . . ," official John Fogerty Web site, 1997

"All through school . . . ," official John Fogerty Web site, 1997

"I developed my style . . . ," Moseley, 1997

"I'd been telling the group . . . ," Gleason, 1970

"Stu's dad ran this high powered . . . ," interview, 1997

"It was a big decision for Stu . . . ," Gleason, 1970

"I think I was nervous . . . ," interview, 1997

"At that time . . . ," Correspondence with journalist Ken Levy, 1975

"The original Factory . . . ," E-mail correspondence, via River Rising mailing list, 1996–97

"I had to work pregnant . . . ," E-mail correspondence

"In 1967 . . . ," letter from Tom to John Fogerty, dated October 11, 1985

"I worked for the electric . . . ," McDonough, 1975

"We said . . . ," Hallowell, 1971

Chapter 5

"There was some disagreement . . . ," interview, 1997

"I used to gamble a lot . . . ," Wloszczyna, 1997

"shuttling troops to the . . . ," Fantasy Films biography, c. 1986

"to see the last two weeks . . . ," Fantasy Films biography, c. 1986

"Norman was an enormous . . . ," Koehler, 1997

"They didn't know anything . . . ," Fantasy Films biography, c. 1986

"We knew Saul mostly . . . ," Gleason, 1970

"In October, we got . . . ," Gleason, 1970

"When Saul bought the company . . . ," Settle, 1985

"You deliver ten . . . ," deposition, Fantasy v. Fogerty, July 8, 1986

"Fogerty, Cook, Clifford and Fogerty . . . ," E-mail correspondence, via River Rising mailing list, 1996–97

"I hated the name . . . ," Saul Zaentz, The South Bank Show, London Weekend TV, 1997

"Many names were thrown," correspondence with Ken Levy, 1985

"Tom brought . . . ," E-mail correspondence, via River Rising mailing list, 1996–97

"We'd been together . . . ," Osborne, 1988

"Finally, John put together . . . ," E-mail correspondence, via River Rising mailing list, 1996–97

"The most important part . . . ," Creedence Clearwater Revival, Fantasy Records biography

"I still have . . . ," Saul Zaentz, *The South Bank Show,* London Weekend TV, 1997

"Blew 'em out at Roger Caulkins' . . . ," Gleason, 1970

"I was afraid of . . . ," Tiegel, 1969

"It was a small narrow . . . ," E-mail correspondence, via River Rising mailing list, 1996–97

"We were finally sure . . . ," Gleason, 1970

"I really didn't like most . . . ," Forte, 1986; Price, 1997; Hillburn, 1985

"I remember when . . . ," Forte, 1986

"We had a lot of fun . . . ," Kris Eric Stevens, WLS (Chicago) audio interview, 1970

"He said . . . ," Gleason, 1970

Chapter 6

"I resolved at that point . . . ," official John Fogerty Web site, 1997

"He was there . . . ," Gleason, 1970

"Early on . . . ," Prodigy chat group with Stu Cook and Doug Clifford, 1997

"John brought . . . ," E-mail correspondence

"I was very careful," Forte, 1986

"We developed the music . . . ," Lundqvist/Lindberg/Ekholm, 1994

"As 1968 became a . . . ," correspondence with Ken Levy, 1985

"Once in the studio . . . ," Gleason, 1970

"We tracked all of the songs . . . ," E-mail correspondence

"We four track . . . ," Brewer, 1969

"I really zip through . . . ," Gleason, 1970

"Everybody listened . . . ," Gleason, 1970

"My son Josh . . . ," Forte, 1986

"A great record . . . ," Zollo, 1997

"I kept telling . . . ," Gleason, 1970

"I was really hot for . . . ," Gleason, 1970

"'Susie Q' was a song . . . ," Bryman, 1988

"I knew I needed to . . . ," Goldberg, 1993

"I could worry about . . . ," Gleason, 1970

"It was my idea . . . ," E-mail correspondence, via River Rising mailing list, 1996–97

"[I] especially [liked] . . . ," Gleason, 1970

"That was kind of . . . ," Bryman, 1988

"You know what we'd . . . ," Siders, 1971

"In the process of arranging . . . ," Goldberg, 1997

"We had supported the strike pretty . . . ," Gleason, 1970

"We joined Local 424 . . . ," E-mail correspondence, via River Rising mailing list, 1996–97

"We were getting ready to . . . ," official John Fogerty Web site, 1997

"We liked the pic . . . ," E-mail correspondence, via River Rising mailing list, 1996–97

"It was a real drag," Gleason, 1970

"We were convinced . . . ," Gleason, 1970

Chapter 7

"Our approach . . . ," Brewer, 1969

"In the beginning . . . ," E-mail correspondence, via River Rising mailing list, 1996–97

"That's my favorite Creedence . . . ," Bryman, 1988

"The riff came before the . . . ," official John Fogerty Web site, 1997

"I can't tell you how . . . ," Bryman, 1988

"People sometimes associate me . . . ," *Rolling Stone*, April 19, 1990

"It is almost the Gordian . . . ," Goldberg 1993

"I was writing many . . . ," Zollo, 1997

"All the really great records . . . ," *Rolling Stone*, April 19, 1990

"I used to listen to the religious . . . ," Clark, 1997

"It is almost . . . ," Goldberg, 1993

"There wasn't a doubt . . . ," official John Fogerty Web site, 1997

"When it came time for . . . ," Hunter, 1991

"At the time . . . ," Goldberg, 1993

"The Army Reserves . . . ," official John Fogerty Web site, 1997

"There's an old Will Rogers . . . ," official John Fogerty Web site, 1997

"A single . . . ," Dubro, 1970

"As a songwriter . . . ," Cole/Gossett, 1975

"We always look ahead . . . ," Siders, 1971

"They made *Bayou Country* . . . ," interview, 1997

"That's John's tribute to . . . ," Bryman, 1988

"I knew I didn't . . . ," official John Fogerty Web site, 1997

"We'd had a big hit with . . . ," Goldberg, 1993

"I told them . . . ," official John Fogerty Web site, 1997

'We're following . . . ," Trakin, 1997; Persson, 1997

Chapter 8

"We went through . . . ," Hallowell, 1971

"Very early on . . . ," deposition, Fantasy *v.* Fogerty, July 8, 1986

"We had learned," Brewer, 1969

"I wouldn't trust anybody . . . ," Gleason, 1970

"After the first album . . . ," Cole and Gossett, 1975

"We decided to begin . . . ," Hilburn, in *Guiness Book of Rock*

"This group . . . ," Hilburn in *Guiness Book of Rock*

"When I heard John sing . . . ," Mattingly, 1997

"I was so impressed . . . ," interview, 1997

"As soon as . . . ," Gleason, 1970

"I loved that lick on . . . ," Steinblatt and Gill, 1997

"I remember one . . . ," Henke, 1987

"The first time I . . . ," official John Fogerty Web site, 1997

"We made a lot of people . . . ," Bryman, 1988

"I went on a fishing trip . . . ," Oakley, 1997

"I wasn't a prude . . . ," Henke, 1987

"We may have looked . . . ," Smith, 1988

"I was personally part . . . ," Prodigy chat group with Stu Clifford

"Good music is just that . . . ," Creedence Clearwater Revival, Fantasy biography

"We were sort of able . . . ," Gleason, 1970

"Nobody would touch . . . ," Levy, 1994

"Creedence was the hottest . . . ," Henke, 1987

"Creedence was not included . . . ," E-mail correspondence, via River Rising mailing list, 1996–97

"After our performance . . . ," deposition, Fantasy *v.* Fogerty July 8, 1986

"The performances are . . . ," E-mail correspondence, via River Rising mailing list, 1996–97

Chapter 9

"Highlanders and flatlanders . . . ," E-mail correspondence with Laurie Clifford, 1997

"I see things through ...," *Time*, 6/27/69

"They got successful ...," interview with Jeff Fogerty, 1997

"The band helps ...," Modderno, 1970

"They would be down ...," interview with Jeff Fogerty, 1997

"Creedence to me is four individuals ...," Creedence Clearwater Revival, Fantasy biography

"I wish marriage could work ...," Dawbarn, 1970

"A jazz record that sold ...," Tiegel, 1969

"There will be no pressure ...," Tiegel, 1969

"They were one of ...," interview with Ross Gary, 1997

"They came in ....," Lundqvist/Lindberg/Ekholm, 1994

"We went in and did ...," Forte, 1986

"John would come in ...," Lundqvist/Lindberg/Ekholm, 1994

"*Green River* was the next ...," Bryman, 1988

"I always considered *Green River* ...," official John Fogerty Web site, 1997

"Green River" was another title ...," official John Fogerty Web site, 1997

"It was exactly like the song ...," Tom Fogerty radio interview

"The day after we recorded ...," official John Fogerty Web site, 1997

"At one point ...," official John Fogerty Web site, 1997

"John was better able ...," Bryman, 1988

"He told John ...," Bryman, 1988

"Most of this is built-in ...," Dubro, 1970

"Our career is just starting ...," Creedence Clearwater Revival , Fantasy biography

Chapter 10

"Every couple of weeks ...," Link, 1969

"We can move faster ...," Hallowell, 1971

"A *contract* ...," Hallowell, 1971

"It took us about a year ...," Price, 1997

"Saul Zaentz or somebody ...," interview,1997

"They wanted to avoid ...," Selvin, 1985

"When I first came to work ...," interview,1997

"It was an atmosphere of unity ...," interview, 1997

"We chartered two ...," interview, 1997

"We used to take all ...," interview, 1997

"Public acceptance is everything to us," Yorke, 1970

"People thought we were a band ...," Bryman, 1988

"When I went to get ...," Gleason, 1970

"At the time ...," interview, 1997

"There were things ...," official John Fogerty Web site, 1997

"That's a song ...," Bryman, 1988

"When Creedence were ...," interview, 1997

"We were Willie ...," Bryman, 1988

"These were songs ...," Bryman, 1988

"John had a vision ...," Bryman, 1988

"The exhausting part ...," Settle, 1985

"'Fortunate Son' ...," Bryman, 1988

"It's a confrontation ...," official John Fogerty Web site, 1997

"It took ...," Fong Torres, 1969

"Nixon ...," Isler, 1985

"The line ...," Bryman, 1988

"I think socially . . . ," Warner Bros. Records, artist biography

"a real heavy political song ...," Bryman, 1988

"Our music ...," Fong Torres, 1969

"The Duck Kee Market . . . ," official John Fogerty Web site, 1997

"The one and only time," Lundqvist/Lindberg/Ekholm, 1994

Chapter 11

"I was a very busy . . . ," *People* Magazine, June 2, 1997

"We were very disciplined . . . ," Lundqvist/Lindberg/Ekholm, 1994

"I was just experimenting . . . ," *Fifth Street Flash*

"I tried to be purposefully symbolic . . . ," *Rolling Stone*, 9/8/88

"Stu and Tom . . . ," interview, 1997

"We're going to try . . . ," *Rolling Stone*, 2/7/70

"I would imagine . . . ," E-mail correspondence, via River Rising mailing list, 1996–97

"Gort Functions . . . ," Gort Functions Partnership Agreement, 1970

"That's where the gift . . . ," official John Fogerty Web site, 1997

"It seems to me . . . ," interview, 1997

"It definitely got adopted . . . ," Werner, 1997

"That'll put a chill . . . ," Bryman, 1998

"Even though it . . . ," Bryman, 1998

"I can write . . . ," Modderno, 1970

"Crazy George would call . . . ," interviews and correspondence with Jake Rohrer, 1997

"It was one of the . . . ," *Rolling Stone*, 7/23/70

"I turned around . . . ," *Rolling Stone*, 7/23/70

"They were supposed . . . ," *Rolling Stone*, 7/23/70

"They had always . . . ," interview, 1997

"They tried to serve . . . ," interview, 1997

"We'd been labeled . . . ," *Rolling Stone*, 7/23/70

"There was a stomping . . . ," interview, 1997

"People may think . . . ," *Rolling Stone*, 7/23/70

"One night at the . . . ," E-mail correspondence, via River Rising mailing list, 1996–97

"We hear some . . . ," Gleason, 1970

"Encores have been . . . ," E-mail correspondence, via River Rising mailing list, 1996–97

"With Creedence Clearwater . . . ," Reece, 1997

"This was good clean living . . . ," Lundqvist/Lindberg/Ekholm, 1994

"We take good care of ourselves . . . ," Creedence Clearwater Revival, Fantasy biography

"Lucy was this sweet . . . ," interview 1997

Chapter 12

"We cut five complete music tracks . . . ," Kris Eric Stevens, WLS (Chicago) radio interview, 1970

"I think we've . . . ," Gleason, 1970

"When I listen to the radio . . . ," Pop Music and Society, 1973

"It was a free jam . . . ," Bryman, 1988

"Our jams were never . . . ," Cole and Gossett, 1975

"That was a tune . . . ," E-mail correspondence, via River Rising mailing list, 1996–97

"That thing in the . . . ," Cole and Goseett, 1975

"It was one of our . . . ," Bryman, 1988

"A real great one . . . ," Bryman, 1988

"John wrote that . . . ," Bryman, 1988

"This one's about . . . ," official John Fogerty Web site, 1997

"During the heyday . . . ," interview, 1997

"*Cosmo's* was the peak in a lot of ways," Forte, 1986

"That was our most . . . ," Bryman, 1988

"John Fogerty was the lead . . . ," Lundqvist/
    Lindberg/Ekholm, 1994
"It may actually be . . . ," Werner, 1997
"When the American . . . ," E-mail corre-
    spondence, via River Rising mailing
    list, 1996–97
"I like my private life," Selvin, 1971

Chapter 13

"In the beginning," Hilburn, 1971
"There must be . . . ," Bryman, 1988
"But he never . . . ," Hilburn, 1971
"We told John . . . ," E-mail correspon-
    dence, via River Rising mailing list,
    1996–97
"He read our . . . ," deposition, *Fantasy v.
    Fogerty*, July 8, 1986
"I told John I wanted . . . ," E-mail corre-
    spondence, via River Rising mailing
    list, 1996–97
"After a couple of years . . . ," deposition,
    Fantasy v. Fogerty, July 8, 1986
"There was a lot of push . . . ," Forte,
    1986
"There's a lot of pressure . . . ," *In Con-
    cert*, 1970
"I could walk away . . . ," Hallowell,
    1971
"This was our first . . . ," Selvin, 1971
"I guess even if the . . . ," Yorke, 1970
"We'd love the . . . ," Siders, 1971
"We are not . . . ," Hallowell, 1971
Disaffected is a good word for it . . . ,"
    interview, 1997
"Things were bad, a struggle . . . ," depo-
    sition, *Fogerty v. Poorboy*, 1996
"I kinda dominated the group . . . ,"
    Cole and Gossett, 1975
"For two years . . . ," Price, 1997
"More keyboard and John's . . . ," E-mail
    correspondence, via River Rising
    mailing list, 1996–97

"We were more involved . . ." Bryman,
    1988
"John said to me while . . . ," interview,
    1997
"We idolized Booker T and the MGs . . . ,"
    Bryman, 1988
"*Pendulum* starts to get into . . . ,"
    Lundqvist/Lindberg/Ekholm, 1994
"We loved them both dearly . . . ," Bry-
    man, 1988
"John was under a lot . . . ," Bryman,
    1988
"I hate that song . . . ," Bryman, 1988
"'Rude Awakening #2' . . . ," E-mail cor-
    respondence, via River Rising mail-
    ing list, 1996–97
"This happens in the Bay Area . . . ,"
    official John Fogerty Web site, 1997
"Two songs . . . ," Carr, 1971
"That was a song . . . ," Bryman, 1988
"People don't know us . . . ," Siders, 1971
"Tom was the energy behind . . . ," E-
    mail correspondence, via River Ris-
    ing mailing list, 1996–97
"He was around . . . ," interview
"At the time. . . ," official John Fogerty
    Web site, 1997

Chapter 14

"This is the first . . . ," Yorke, 1971
"Rogers and Cowan's . . . ," E-mail corre-
    spondence, via River Rising mailing
    list, 1996–97
"After *Pendulum* was recorded . . . ,"
    official John Fogerty Web site, 1997
We had retained this . . . ," interview,
    1997
"I think that the press . . . ," Yorke,
    1971
"Everyone has . . . ," Lombardi, 1971
"Sometimes, reading the reviews . . . ,"
    Selvin, 1970

"Creedence was more . . . ," interview, 1997

"Tom and the other . . . ," interview, 1997

"About a month after . . . ," interview, 1997

Chapter 15

"He decided he'd had enough . . . ," interview, 1997

"I was gone . . . ," KSAN interview, 1976

"I started out . . . ," interview, 1981

"I sang lead . . . , " KSAN interview, 1976

"There was all this dissension . . . ," interview, 1997

"I was always under pressure . . . ," Parachini, 1971

"John was always the most . . . ," Rosenthal, 1971

Somehow, it's an . . . ," Rudis, 1971

"Creedence was together . . . ," interview, 1981/Goldberg, 1982

"That wouldn't work . . . ," interview, 1981

"Tom clashed with . . . ," Doug Clifford deposition, Fogerty *v.* Poor Boy Productions, July 26, 1996

"He only left for . . . ," Gleason, 1973

"The fact is . . . ," E-mail correspondence, via River Rising mailing list, 1996–97

"I almost went stir crazy . . . ," Hillburn, 1971

"After Tom quit . . . ," E-mail correspondence, via River Rising mailing list, 1996–97

"Really, I'd like to . . . ," Dawson, 1970

"I've always had . . . ," Kris Eric Stevens, WLS (Chicago) radio interview, 1970

"I wasn't real open . . . ," official John Fogerty Web site, 1997

Chapter 16

"Ike and Tina Turner . . . ," E-mail correspondence, via River Rising mailing list, 1996–97

"They did it the fast way . . . ," *Rolling Stone,* September 8, 1988

"Fantasy has acquired . . . ," interview, 1997

"The CCR special . . . ," E-mail correspondence, via River Rising mailing list, 1996–97

"We were promised . . . ," *Rolling Stone,* April 29, 1971

"A certain clause . . . ," E-mail correspondence, via River Rising mailing list, 1996–97

"After Tom left . . . ," interview, 1997

"For a band that . . . ," Hilburn, 1971

"It's about rock . . . ," Bryman, 1988

"I was a college student . . . ," Rudis, 1971

"It's the first Creedence . . . ," Rudis, 1971

"I realized there . . . ," Selvin, 1971

"It was either that . . . ," Hilburn, 1971

"We're all compromising . . . ," Rudis, 1971

"We can be friends . . . ," Hilburn, 1971

"It took us two days, . . . ," Aikin, 1972

"It was just like . . . ," Selvin, 1971

"It was necessary . . . ," E-mail correspondence, via River Rising mailing list, 1996–97

"I sang 'Door to Door' . . . ," Aikin, 1972

"On the second European . . . ," interview, 1997

We'd always come . . . ," *Pop Music and Society,* 1973

"We'd have these . . . ," interview, 1997

"CCR was into country music . . . ," E-mail correspondence, via River Rising mailing list, 1996–97

"When I talk about . . . ," Hilburn, *Rolling Stone,* 10/14/71

Chapter 17

"After I quit . . . ," Parachini, 1971

"When I finished . . . ," Fantasy Records biography

"We shot a video . . . ," interview, 1997

"I'm not adverse . . . ," Fantasy Records biography

"Jerry Garcia and . . . ," interview, 1997

"I don't want . . . ," Parachini, 1971

"Probably because the song . . . ," E-mail correspondence, via River Rising mailing list, 1996–97

"He came back . . . ," Cohen, 1979

"John had required . . . ," E-mail correspondence, via River Rising mailing list, 1996–97

"He wouldn't sing . . . ," Lundqvist/Lindberg/Ekholm, 1994; Forte, 1986

"He played leads . . . ," interview, 1997

"John made us . . . ," Cohen, 1979

"The *Mardi Gras* experience . . . ," interview, 1997

"When they were making . . . ," interview, 1981

"I'm not even in . . . ," Selvin, 1971

"I've written a couple . . . ," Aikin, 1972

"Fogerty once told . . . ," E-mail correspondence, via River Rising mailing list, 1996–97

"John was having trouble . . . ," Bryman, 1988

"Ironically, we had the . . . " Traikin, 1997

"My parents divorced when . . . ," Lundqvist/Lindberg/Ekholm, 1994

"That song was for Josh . . . ," interview, 1997

"John had left home . . . ," Bryman, 1988

"I've always felt . . . ," E-mail correspondence, via River Rising mailing list, 1996–97

"Yeah, it's my mother's . . . ," interview, 1997

"The girl in the photo . . . ," E-mail correspondence, via River Rising mailing list, 1996–97

"It's the closest I ever . . . ," *Rolling Stone*, September 8, 1988

"The review in *Rolling Stone* . . . ," Hilburn, 1971

Chapter 18

"The group hadn't officially . . . ," interview, 1997

"He deliberately set . . . ," Cohen, 1979

"Never having written . . . ," E-mail correspondence, via River Rising mailing list, 1996–97

"I didn't want to do . . . ," Persson, 1997

"It was John's . . . ," E-mail correspondence, via River Rising mailing list, 1996–97

"Soon enough . . . ," official John Fogerty Web site, 1997

"Looking back now . . . ," Smith, 1988

"The business pressures . . . ," E-mail correspondence, via River Rising mailing list, 1996–97

"I was not popular . . . ," Goldberg, 1993

"Right after the band . . . ," interview, 1997

"I think we all began . . . ," Gleason, 1973

"The result was . . . ," Hilburn, 1973

"At that point . . . ," Bryman, 1988

"Finally, the bomb exploded," Persson, 1997

"John came to . . . ," E-mail correspondence, via River Rising mailing list, 1996–97

"Ever since Tom split . . . ," *Rolling Stone*, 11/9/72

"They've got to . . . ," *Rolling Stone*, January 9, 1972

"It was the biggest . . . ," Selvin, 1972

"We always had . . . ," Gleason, 1973

"Everything that could . . . ," Cohen, 1979

"The success became a . . . ," Smith, 1988

"After ten years . . . ," deposition, John Fogerty *v.* Poor Boy Productions, Inc., July 26, 1996

Chapter 19

"Fantasy's big mistake . . . ," E-mail correspondence, via River Rising mailing list, 1996–97

"We were always . . . ," interview with KSAN, 1975

"Tom's real . . . ," Tolces, 1973

"In our shit kicker sessions . . . ," *Popular Music & Society*, 1973

"I prefer now doing . . . ," Tolces, 1973

"I was doing . . . ," Settle, 1984

"John came up . . . ," interview, 1997

"That's the first . . . ," *Popular Music & Society*, 1973

"My conviction . . . ," Gleason, 1973; Hilburn, 1973

"We don't intend . . . ," Yorke, 1970

"The *Blue Ridge Ranger* . . . ," Cole and Gossett, 1975

"We played a lot . . . ," interview, 1997

"We've always had . . . ," Delahant, 1969

"When we toured . . . ," Gleason, 1973

"I was walking . . . ," Gleason, 1973; Cole and Gossett, 1975

"There were a multitude . . . ," Gleason, 1973

"We played baseball . . . ," Rosen, 1991

"The contract was so . . . ," Price, 1997

"I had meetings . . . ," deposition, Fantasy *v.* Fogerty, July 8, 1986

"We had a good relationship . . . ," Crowe, 1976

"I think John's . . . ," interview, 1997

Chapter 20

"I owed so much product . . . ," Selvin, 1985

"He's hell . . . ," Goldstein, 1997

"He can spot . . . ," Goldstein, 1997

"He's the most . . . ," Guthmann, 1996

"an unhappy John . . . ," deposition, Fantasy *v.* Fogerty, July 8, 1986; Forte, 1985; Gunderson, 1997

"Here they had . . . ," Hubner, 1986; Hillburn, 1975

"He made himself . . . ," interview, 1997

"It was the very . . . ," Crowe, 1976

"They had a . . . ," interview, 1997

"I built a real nice echo . . . ," interview, 1997

"It should never . . . ," Hillburn, 1975; Crowe, 1976

"They discovered. . . ," Hubner, 1986

"I had a solemn . . . ," Crowe 1976; Hillburn, 1975

"I was strictly . . . ," interview, KSAN, 1975

"The Golliwogs LP . . . ," E-mail correspondence, via River Rising mailing list, 1996–97

"because of the . . . ," Crowe, 1976

"I have four . . . ," interview, KSAN, 1975

"This is Tom's . . . ," McDonough, 1975

"I was twenty-two years . . . ," Inteview, KSAN, 1975

"His records . . . ," interview, 1997

"I'm talking . . . ," McDonough, 1975

"They tried to hang . . . ," Forte, 1985

"Geffen says . . . ," Crowe, 1975

"John went with Geffen . . . ," interview, 1997

"Asylum purchased . . . ," interview, 1997

"I went, 'Wow . . . ,'" Forte, 1985

"When I'm hot . . . ," Cole and Gossett, 1975

"because my dog . . . ," Moseley, 1997

"Everything inside me is . . . ," Cole and Gossett, 1975

Chapter 21

"Something was wrong . . . ," Zimmerman, 1985; Forte, 1985

"By the time I entered . . . ," Smith, 1988

"My grandfather . . . ," interview, 1997

"When he died . . . ," Hubner, 1986

"who were kind of . . . ," Fantasy Records biography

"We felt we had a lot . . . ," Fantasy Records biography

"I think I'm getting . . . .," *Billboard*, November 8, 1975

"I realize I need . . . ," *Billboard*, November 8, 1975

"It didn't take me . . . ," Fantasy Records biography

"I had done lots of . . . ," interview, 1997

"Don was signed as . . . ," E-mail correspondence, via River Rising mailing list, 1996–97

"I rehearsed a . . . ," interview, 1997

"When I did '16 Tons' . . . ," interview, 1997

"The first DHB album . . . ," E-mail correspondence, via River Rising mailing list, 1996–97

"'You Got the Magic' . . . .," Isler, 1985; Hillburn, 1985

"I remember when . . . ," interview, 1997

"[Joe] said, 'John . . . ,'" Forte, 1985; Zimmerman, 1985; Sutherland, 1985

"That was a crusher . . . ," interview, 1997

"I started working . . . ," Forte, 1985

"Barrie Engel . . . ," interview, 1997

"Practically all . . . ," Forte, 1985; Selvin, 1985

"They stole our . . . ," interview, 1997

"Rumors are that . . . ," interview, 1981

"The day I found . . . ," Isler, 1985

"That whole fiasco . . . ," interview, 1997

"Some of it had . . . ,' interview, 1997

"I guess a nice . . . , interview, 1997

"My mom wanted . . . ," interview, 1997

"He had quit . . . ," interview, 1997

Chapter 22

"He's been working . . . ," interview, 1997

"He runs my office . . . ," deposition, Fantasy *v.* Fogerty, 1986

"It didn't get much . . . ," Fantasy Records biography

"He got on the . . . ," interview, 1997

"For a six month . . . ," interview, 1981

"I moved there . . . ," interview, 1997

"We knew from . . . ," *New York Times*, December 8, 1978

"When Fogerty's name . . . ," Hilburn, 1985

"It's hard to decide," Marsh, 1981

"We had been informed . . . ," deposition in Fogerty *v.* Poorboy Productions, July 26, 1996

"I felt it was time . . . ," letter from Tom Fogerty to Malcolm Bernstein, Sept. 24, 1979

"Tom wanted to earn . . . ," Fogerty v. Poorboy Productions, July 12, 1996

"In light of Tom's . . . ," letter from John Fogerty to Tom Fogerty, Stu Cook, and Doug Clifford, October 1, 1979

"worn down by Tom's . . . ," deposition, Fogerty *v.* Poor Boy, July 12, 1996

"John was really against . . . ," interview, 1997

"The inner conflict . . . ," Isler, 1985; Forte, 1985; Selvin, 1985

"I was hung up . . . ," interview, 1981

"With Doug and Stu, . . . ," interview, 1981

"I wanted to concentrate . . . ," interview, 1981

"Their own music . . . ," interview, 1981

"We all did . . . ," anonymous source, close to the band

"He still wants . . . ," interview, 1981

"He's become like Brian . . . ," Cohen, 1979

Chapter 23

"It was a real job . . . ," Forte, 1985; Cocks and Worrell, 1985

"Where my family . . . ," Cocks and Worrell, 1985

"When things aren't right . . . ," Oakley, 1997

"I went to the studio . . . ," Hubner, 1986

"I had no confidence . . . ," Miller, 1985; Hillburn, 1985

"I tried to hit all . . . ," John Fogerty Warner Bros. Records biography, c. 1984

"I took my kids . . . " Goldberg, 1982

"I bought socks . . . ," Hubner, 1986

"They came back . . . ," Settle, 1985

"BMI won't pay . . . ," Isler, 1985

"I told Joe Smith . . . ," Zimmerman, 1985; Hilburn, 1985

"A few years ago . . . ," Hillburn, 1985

"Dad was always mad," Cocks/Worrell, 1985

"I came home . . . ," Isler, 1985

"I was hoping there . . . ," Goldberg, 1982

"Obviously, John doesn't . . . ," Matsumoto, 1985

"I don't think . . . ," letter from John Fogerty to Doug Clifford, 1980

"Since you assume . . . ," letter from John Fogerty to Doug Clifford, c. 1980

"During the course of . . . ," deposition, Fantasy v. Fogerty, 1986

"The Concert CD . . . ," E-mail correspondence via River Rising mailing list, 1996–97

"They put 'em in . . . ," *Musician*, July, 1986

"Their records . . . ," Golberg, 1982

"We felt that since reissue product . . . ," McDonough, 1982

"It's like, how can you rape . . . ," Settle, 1985

"I was informed that . . . ," deposition, Fantasy v. Fogerty, 1986

"Lenny Waronker said . . . ," Forte, 1985

"They just let Castle . . . ," *Variety*, May 11, 1983

"I think I felt. . . ," deposition, Fantasy v. Fogerty, 1986

"It still goes on . . . ," Isler, 1985

"I feel more relieved. . . ," *Rolling Stone*, July 7, 1983

Chapter 24

"I went to the San Pablo . . . ," official John Fogerty Web Page, 1997

"Then the first line came . . . ," official John Fogerty Web page, 1997; Hubner, 1986; Smith, 1988

"Doug and I didn't . . . ," Matsumoto, 1985

"I was shocked that . . . ," Settle, 1985

"It was very . . . ," Settle, 1985; Forte, 1985

"We played a mixture . . . ," Matsumoto, 1985

"An hour and ten . . . ," Settle, 1985

"We dropped . . . ," Matsumoto, 1985

"I tried a little . . . ," Isler, 1985

"'Rock and Roll Girls . . . ," Selvin, 1985

"I do most of my . . . ," Forte 1985; Isler, 1985

"[It's] just those three . . . ," Warner Bros. biography

"A title will help me . . . ," Zimmerman, 1985
"I was never good . . . ," Isler, 1985
"You can get . . . ," Settle, 1985
"I came down . . . ," Isler, 1985; *Time*, January 28, 1985

Chapter 25

"They flew in . . . ," deposition, Fantasy *v.* Fogerty July 8, 1986
"I am not impressed . . . ," Matsumto, 1985
"I'm a pretty good bar band." Cocks and Worrell, 1985
"My problems were . . . ," Isler, 1985
"This is more than . . . ," Isler, 1985; Settle, 1985
"I'm not gonna do the . . . ," Isler, 1985
"When I hear . . . ," deposition, Fantasy *v.* Fogerty, July 8, 1986
"I think the reason . . . ," Hubner, 1986
"John didn't *have* . . . ," E-mail via River Rising mailing list, 1996–97
"The best example in the . . . ," letter from Tom Fogerty to John Fogerty, dated October 11, 1985
"I thought . . . ," Fantasy Records biography
"The video consists . . . ," Fantasy Records biography
"The recording by . . . ," trade advertisment for *Precious Gems*
"Lenny Waronker called . . . ," deposition, Fantasy *v.* Fogerty July 8, 1986
"Saul was hurt, injured . . . ," Goldberg, 1985
"It's defamatory . . . ," Goldberg, 1985
"to the max." Gans, 1985
"a mediocre . . . ," Gans, 1985
"And you should know . . . ," Bond, 1997
"This is a total load of crap . . . ," E-mail via River Rising mailing list, 1996–97
"It would have been . . . ," Novak, 1985

"I was up in Oregon . . . ," Henke, 1987

Chapter 26

"Stu—What a load of . . . ," letter from John Fogerty to Stu Cook, January 28, 1986
"The same contract . . . ," E-mail via River Rising mailing list, 1996–97
"I was living . . . ," Gunderson, 1997; Price, 1997
"I stopped him . . . ," E-mail via River Rising mailing list, 1996–97
"Creedence was pretty . . . ," Forte, 1986
"I find it interesting . . . ," Forte, 1986
"We drove rental . . . ," E-mail via River Rising mailing list, 1996–97
"Jim Ed Norman is quite . . . ," E-mail via River Rising mailing list, 1996–97
"It's totally democratic . . . ," Forte, 1986
"In Southern Pacific . . . ," E-mail via River Rising mailing list, 1996–97
"I had to let go of the . . . ," Warner Bros. biography
"While it was nice that . . . ," Edelstein, 1986
"I decided I needed . . . ," Warner Bros. biography
"'Eye of the Zombie' . . . ," Edelstein, 1986; Isler, 1989
"I'm truly, deeply honored . . . ," Osborne, 1988

Chapter 27

"That's the energy that's . . . ," Hubner, 1986
"I wanted to start here . . . ," Palmer, 1986
"I forgot totally . . . ," Hubner, 1986
"I know they're doing . . . ," Brogan, 1997; Palmer, 1986

"Going out here . . . ," Palmer, 1986; Brogan, 1997

"I was out on . . . ," official John Fogerty Web site

"I assume all of that responsibility . . . ," Scoppa, 1990

"Pretty hard hitting . . . ," Henke, 1987

"*Eye of the Zombie* . . . ," Willman, 1997; Scoppa, 1990

"Excitement is in the air . . . ," Osborne, 1988

"He said it was the . . . ," E-mail via River Rising mailing list, 1996–97

"The first time we met . . . ," Selvin, 1997

"She came and saw me later . . . ," Gunderson, 1997

"He said to me . . . ," *Rolling Stone*, September 8, 1988

"Bring 'em home and we'll play for them," Siders, 1971

"I want to tell you something . . . ," HBO telecast of the "Welcome Home" concert, 1987

Chapter 28

"I was a pretty confused . . . " Gunderson, 1997

"I don't know where . . . ," Gunderson, 1997

"These people were having . . . ," Warner Bros. biography

"Eventually . . . ," Popson, 1989

"We all know . . . ," Warner Bros. biography

"We had no contract, no budget . . . ," Popson, 1989

"When we finally moved in together . . . ," Gunderson, Music Central, 1997

"We were prepared . . . ," Marymount, 1990

"My personal favorite . . . ," E-mail via River Rising mailing list, 1996–97

"I've still got a closet full . . . ," E-mail via River Rising mailing list, 1996–97

"In 1988, I had gone on . . . ," interview, 1997

"Tom didn't want to have . . . ," interview, 1997

"That's when we started . . . ," interview, 1997

"Mal Burnstein conducted . . . ," E-Mail correspondence with Joel Selvin, 1997

"When we researched this . . . ," McDougal, 1988

"We have just learned . . . ," letter from Malcom Bernstein to Columbia Pictures, February 28, 1985

"*B:* For your music to be vital . . . ," deposition, Fantasy *v.* Fogerty July 8, 1986

"the concert even . . . ," Isler, 1989

"I got very angry . . . ," Isler, 1989

"It wasn't testimony . . . ," Isler, 1989

"I basically was . . . ," Isler, 1989

"Their lawyers . . . ," Isler, 1989

"Yeah, I did use . . . ," Tolleson, 11/12/88

"What's at stake . . . ," Goldberg, 1989

"It would be hard to be a juror . . . ," Tolleson, 11/19/88

"There may have . . . ," Tolleson, 11/19/88

"Creative people . . . ," Tolleson, 11/19/88

"It was clearly just harassment . . . ," Isler, 1989

"We are discussing settlement . . . ," Isler, 1989

"Stu and I provided Fantasy . . . ," deposition, Fogerty *v.* Poor Boy Productions, July 26, 1996

"I have spent years complaining . . . ," deposition, Fogerty *v.* Poor Boy Productions, July 12, 1996

"John was insistent that this not happen . . . ," interview, 1997

"Shame on you . . . . ," letter From John Fogerty, August 17, 1989

"Around 1989 . . . ," Oakley, 1997; Stein-
    blatt, 1997; Gausch, 1997
"I see that in print all the time . . . ,"
    Graff, 1997
"Our former high school . . . ," deposi-
    tion, Fogerty v. Poor Boy Produc-
    tions, July 26, 1996
"My relationship with them . . . ,"
    Strauss, 1997

Chapter 29

"Tom and Saul Zaentz . . . ," interview,
    1997
"My poor mom's gotta be . . . ," *Musi-
    cian*, July 1986
"The extent of . . . ," deposition, Fogerty
    v. Poor Boy Productions, July 26,
    1996
"Doug was there . . . ," interview, 1997
"My dad said one . . . ," interview, 1997
"During the time . . . ," deposition,
    Fogerty v. Poor Boy Productions,
    August 1, 1996
"John visited Tom . . . ," deposition,
    Fogerty v. Poor Boy Productions, July
    26, 1996
"He developed more . . . ," Goldberg,
    1993
"The eternal optimist . . . ," Goldberg,
    1990
"A lot of things were . . . ," Gunderson,
    Music Central, 1997
"He died . . . ," Price, 1997

Chapter 30

"The day before my dad . . . ," interview,
    1997
"The urge was actually . . . ," Stevenson,
    1997
"That big event . . . ," Yellin, 1997

"I thought about . . . ," McJunkin, 1997
"It's 110 . . . ," Steinblatt and Gill, 1997
"Most people in country . . . ," Mary-
    mount, 1990
"The woman finally . . . ," Gunderson,
    1997
"The way it looks in . . . ," Selvin, 1992
"Howdy! Well it is my job . . . ," speech
    given at the Bammy Awards, May 7,
    1992
"There is a written . . . ," Selvin, 1992
"To say that . . . ," Selvin, 1992
"Because Fogerty . . . ," deposition,
    Fogerty v. Poor Boy Productions, July
    26 1996
"John was most concerned . . . ," *Mix*,
    September 1997
"Originally, I put together . . . ," Warner
    Bros. biography
"Being a liberal kind of . . . ," Steinnblatt
    and Gill, 1997

Chapter 31

"We asked if . . . ," Graff, 1996
"If the three of us can be together . . . ,"
    Pareles, 1993
"The Rock and Roll Hall . . . ," interview,
    1997
"The extent of John Fogerty's . . . ,"
    deposition, Fogerty v. Poor Boy Pro-
    ductions, July 26 1996
"He had scheduled a . . . ," interview,
    1997
"He had arranged . . . ," E-Mail via River
    Rising mail group, 1996–97; Traikin,
    1997
"Bad things happened . . . ," Traikin,
    1997
"When Coz and I . . . ," E-Mail via River
    Rising mail group, 1996–97
"Those guys knew damn well . . . ,"
    Traikin, 1997

"He didn't refuse to let . . . ," interview, 1997

"I was crushed . . . ," E-Mail via River Rising mail group, 1996–97

"In 1970, suburban New Jersey . . . ," VH1 coverage of the 1993 Rock and Roll Hall of Fame induction

"When we were lining up . . . ," interview, 1997

"Nobody wants to go first . . . ," VH1 coverage of the 1993 Rock and Roll Hall of Fame induction

"The first thing I want to . . . ," VH1 coverage of the 1993 Rock and Roll Hall of Fame induction

"Wow, this is, as . . . ," VH1 coverage of the 1993 Rock and Roll Hall of Fame induction

"That's all right . . . ," VH1 coverage of the 1993 Rock and Roll Hall of Fame induction

"Everyone was just blown . . . ," interview, 1997

"I'm writing you in regards . . . ," letter

"I agree that the events . . . ," letter

"What the hell were you . . . ," Hochman, 1993

"I'm sorry they are hurt . . . ," Hochman, 1993

"It's not our job to . . . ," Hochman, 1993

"They've got a gripe . . . ," Hochman, 1993

"Practically everyone apologized . . . ," E-Mail via River Rising mail group, 1996–97

Chapter 32

"What John did was . . . ," Hochman, 1993

"John believes . . . ," Graff, 1996

"Mick Jagger called . . . ," E-Mail via River Rising mailing list, 1996–97

"This story is true . . . ," E-Mail via River Rising mailing list, 1996–97

"John used so many drummers . . . ," Mattingly, 1997

"I have to say. . . ," Clark, 1997; Levine, 1997

"The first day was real exciting . . . ," Mattingly, 1997

"The dobro was a total . . . ," Stout, 1997

"Let's just take one song . . . ," Gunderson, 1997

"Coz invited us up for a week . . . ," E-Mail via River Rising mailing list, 1996–97

"CCR's inclusion in the . . . ," Levy, 1994

"[John] stifled the whole thing . . . ," interview, 1997

"When the Woodstock twenty-fifth anniversary . . . ," Levy, 1994

"Doug and Stu and my dad . . . ," interview, 1997

"One of my friends has . . . ," Goldberg, 1997

Chapter 33

"In June of 1995," deposition, Fogerty *v.* Poor Boy Productions, July 12, 1996

"Our kids' school has a variety . . . ," Gunderson, Music Central, 1997; McJunkin, 1997

"Stu and I decided . . . ," Fogerty *v.* Poor Boy Productions July 12, 1996

"A business acquaintance . . . ," E-Mail via River Rising mailing list, 1996–97

"Through word of mouth . . . ," Fogerty *v.* Poor Boy Productions, July 12, 1996

"He auditioned for us . . . ," Levy, 1997

"The response in Japan . . . ," E-Mail via River Rising mailing list, 1996–97

"AN OPEN LETTER . . . ," press release, 1997

"This tour . . . ," Gilbert, 1996

"Creedence no longer exists . . . ," Gunderson, *USA Today*, 1997

"To read it now . . . ," Saidman, 1997
"Credit should be given where . . . ," Levy, 1997
"When we were playing . . . " Saidman, 1997
"I am doing this tour . . . ," Willis, 1997
"For the record . . . ," E-mail via River Rising mail list, 1996–97
"If [Doug and Stu] are permitted . . . , " deposition, Fogerty v. Poor Boy Productions, July 12, 1996
"Here's the FACTS concerning . . . ," E-mail via River Rising mail list, 1996–97
"I hate them . . . ," Stout, 1997
"If John doesn't want . . . ," Brown, 1996
"Those are the songs . . . ," Rudis, 1971
"It's great to be playing again . . . ," Spera, 1996

Chapter 34

"He's been fine-tuning . . . ," Brown, 1996
"Obviously I'm not . . . ," Goldberg, 1997
"I can believe it . . . ," interview, 1997
"It must have looked . . . ," Hilburn, 1997
"It took longer . . . ," Musikexpress, June 1997
"some of the tape was . . . ," Lowson, Mix, September 1997
"I save nothing . . . ," Gausch, 1997
"We used to have . . . , " interview, 1997
"I ask you . . . ," Steinblatt and Gill, 1997; Levine, 1997
"I'm getting better . . . ," Band, 6/3/97
"I like to say . . . ," Stevenson, 1997
"Sometimes with an older act . . . ," Reece, 1997

"Look, you never say never . . . ," Forte and Soest, 1985
"It was a bad decision, I guess . . . ," Gudnerson, 1997
"She ribbed me . . . ," Werner, 1997
"He seemed absolutely at . . . ," E-mail, 1997
"There is room for both of us . . . ," E-mail, 1997

Chapter 35

"Everywhere he played . . . ," Reece, 1997
"We obviously feel vindicated . . . ," CCRevisited press release
"Stu and I have great . . . ," CCRevisited press release
"Over the years he has . . . ," Saidman, 1997
"The whole blame . . . ," E-mail via the River Rising mail list, 1997
"Any artist who approaches . . . ," Saidman, 1997
"They're great songs and it's a good cause," Saidman, 1997
"Living in Los Angeles . . . ," Hughes, Sept. 17, 1997
"Can I do it in a year? . . . ," Cocks, 1997
"I truly expect this next album . . . ," interview, 1997
"I can't be fooling around . . . ," Fornatale, 1997
"Thank God the music . . . ," Lundqvist/ Lindberg/ Ekholm, 1994
"I think Creedence will . . . ," Matsumoto, 1985
"Every day . . . ," Saidman, 1997
"All three of them . . . ," interview, 1997

BIBLIOGRAPHY

"A Special Special for Creedence." *Rolling Stone*, February 7, 1970
"Bad Blood and Clear Water." *The Bergen Record*, May 29, 1996
"*Blue Ridge Ranger* review," *Pop Music in Society*, 1973
"CCR Break Up." *Melody Maker*, October 28, 1972
"CCR Break Up." *Melody Maker*, September 11, 1972
"CCR Breakthrough." *Disc and Music Echo*, June 21, 1969
"Concert Review." *Variety*, April 22, 1970
"Concert Review." *Variety*, June 4, 1969
"Concert Review." *Variety*, May 27, 1970
"Court Clears Way for Creedence." Associated Press, August 16, 1997
"Creedence & Run-DMC Top NARM Best Sellers at Independent Confab." *Variety*, November 4, 1987
"Creedence Calls It Quits." *San Francisco Chronicle*, October 18, 1972
"Creedence Clearwater Feud Still Going Strong Years Later." *Las Vegas Review Journal*, May 19, 1966
"Creedence Clearwater Gets $8-Mil Judgment Against Accounting Firm." *Variety*, May 11, 1983
"Creedence Clearwater Revisited." *Bergen Record*, May 29, 1996
"Creedence Defunct as Trio Dissolves." *Variety*, October 25, 1972
"Creedence Enters Hall of Fame." *The Bergen Record*, January 12, 1993
"Creedence Escapes Europe Intact." *Rolling Stone*, July 23, 1970
"Creedence Gets Its Own Revival." *Las Vegas Review-Journal*, August 16, 1887
"Creedence Revival Sales Pace Otherwise Dull February Awards." *Variety*, March 5, 1986
"Creedence Splits. No More Chooglin'." *Rolling Stone*, November 9, 1972
"Creedence Sued in Living Color." *Rolling Stone*, April 29, 1971
"Creedence Three to Go It Alone." *San Francisco Herald Examiner*, October 18, 1972
"Deaths: Tom Fogerty." *New York Times*, September 15, 1990

"Don (Everly) and John (Fogerty) Brother to Brother." *Musician*, July 1986

"Farewell to Tom Fogerty." *Rolling Stone*, December 13, 1990

"Fogerty to Revive Career." *Rolling Stone*, July 7, 1983

"Fogerty Wins Self-Plagerism Case." *Melody Maker*, December 3, 1988

"Frisco Jury Clears John Fogerty of Charge He Copied CCR Song." *Variety*, November 16, 1988

"Here to Stay." *The Bergen Record*, January 14, 1993

"John Fogerty Interview." *Pop Music and Society*, 1973

"Lean Clean and Bluesy." *Time*, June 27, 1969

"Live Review." *Variety*, October 15, 1986

"Lord of the Rings." *New York Times*, December 8, 1978

"Modern Rockers Pick Their Top Ten Hits of the Fifties." *Rolling Stone*, April 19, 1990

"Pro's Reply: John Fogerty." *Guitar Player*, January 1971

"Proud Mary." *Rolling Stone*, September 8, 1988

"Randy Oda." *The Complete Marquis Who's Who in Entertainment*, Reed Elsevier, Inc, 1988

"Reflections on Fame." *The Bergen Record*, January 12, 1993

"Rock and Roll Is Here to Stay." *Publisher's Weekly*, January 25, 1971

"Saul Zaentz." *Celebrity Bios*, Baseline II, 1997

"Saul Zaentz Files Suit. Charges Fogerty Tunes, Interviews Libeled Him." *Variety*, July 31, 1985

"Springsteen Installs CCR." *Bergen Record*, January 14, 1993

"Supreme Court Rules." *Billboard*, March 12, 1995

"The Top 100 Singles of All Time: #8 'Fortunate Son.'" *Rolling Stone*, September 8, 1988

"Tom Fogerty Forms Label In Berkeley." *Billboard*, November 8, 1975

"Tom Fogerty interview." KSAN 1975

"Tom Fogerty Obituary." *Variety*, September 24, 1990

"Tour Gossip." *Pollstar*, November 25, 1996

"Underground Groove." *Tiger Beat*, May 1969

"Zaentz expanding studios." *Variety*, May 29, 1989

"John Fogerty Item." *Musikexpress*, June 1997

Abel, Bob, Pierre Adidge, and Tom Donahue. "In Concert." *National General Television*, 1971

Aikin, Jim. "Stu Cook Creedence." *Guitar Player*, February 1972

Alden, Grant. "*Blue Moon Swamp* Review." *Rolling Stone*, June 12, 1997

Anderson, Susan Heller. "Chronicle." *New York Times*, January 28, 1991

Arendt, Lawrence. "Southern Pacific Plays Pure Country." *Lansing Economist Pointer*, December 29, 1985

Aronowitz, Al. "Creedence Clearwater Survival." *Melody Maker*, January 2, 1971

Associated Press. "Fillmore West Rolls into Rock Age Past." *New York Times*, July 6, 1971

Bail. "Concert Review." *Variety*, April 23, 1970

Band, Ira. "Fogerty Rekindles the Old Fire." *Toronto Star*, June 3, 1997

————— . "New Moon Rising." *Toronto Star*, June 1 1997

Barnes, Ken. "*Pre-Creedence the Golliwogs* Review." *Rolling Stone*, April 24, 1975

Barry Lazell. *Rock Movers and Shakers*, Billboard Books, 1989

Bessman, Jim. "Blue Moon Swamp." *Billboard*, April 19, 1997

Blake, Joseph. "Creedence More Than Revisited." *Victoria Times-Columnist*, May 9, 1996

Brennan, Carol. *Contemporary Musicians, Volume 16*. Detroit: Gale Research

Brewer, James. "Bayou Country." *Guitar Player*, August, 1969

Brogan, Daniel. "Getting Past John Fogerty." *Creem*, January 1997

Bronson, Fred. *The Billboard Book of Number One Hits*. New York: Billboard Publications, 1985

Brown, G. "Creedence Clearwater Duo Keeps the Music Flowing." *Denver Post*, November 8, 1996

Brown, Mark. "New Album Due (Finally) from Former CCR Leader John Fogerty." *Addicted to Noise*, May 16, 1996

Bryman, Wayne. "A Revival Interview With Fortunate Son Doug Clifford." *DISCoveries*, November, 1988

Buday, Don. "Fogerty's 1 Man Quartet on the Tube." *Los Angeles Free Press*, May 28, 1971

Campbell, Mary. "Rock Legends Inducted into Hall." The Associated Press, January 13, 1998

Carpenter, Dick. "Creedence Wins $8.6 Millon." *The Boston Globe*, May 1, 1983

Carr, Roy. "Cosmorama of Creedence." *New Musical Express*, January 30, 1971

Chapple, Steve, and Reebee Garofalo. *Rock 'n' Roll Is Here to Pay*. Chicago: Nelson-Hall, 1977.

Christgau, Robert. "Christgau's Consumer Guide." *Creem*, February, 1987

Christgau, Robert. "Where Do You Go from the Top?" *The Village Voice*, March 4, 1971

Christgau, Robert. *Any Old Way You Choose It*. Baltimore: Penguin Books, 1973

Christgau, Robert. *Christgau's Record Guide: Rock Albums of the '70s*. New York: Ticknor & Fields, 1981.

Clark, Rick. "The Mix Interview." *Mix*, September, 1997

Cocks, Jay and Denise Worrell. "High Tide on the Green River." *Time*, January 28, 1985

Cocks, Jay. "Songs of Survival." *Time*, June 2, 1997

Cohen, Debra Rae."Creedence Clearwater Revival's Rock & Roll: It's a Gift." *Rolling Stone*, June 11, 1981

Cohen, Elliot. "Rock History from A to Z: Creedence Clearwater Revival." *Grooves*, September 1979

Cole, Bobby, and Richard Gosett. John Fogerty KSAN radio interview, 1975

Considine, J. D. "Centerfield Review." Musician, March, 1985

Cook, Richard. "The Lizard King Is Dead." *Punch*, April 30, 1991

Coppage, Neil. "*Blue Ridge Rangers* Review." *Stereo Review*, October 1973

Coughlin, Janice. "*Cosmo's Factory* Review." *Jazz & Pop*, November 1970

Crockett, Lane. "Creedence Got Big Welcome from Students." *Shreveport Times*, April 18, 1972

Cromelin, Richard. "*Inside Creedence* Review." *Coast FM & Arts*, April 1971

———. "Rock Stars Find Making Up Is Hard to Do." *Los Angeles Times*, January 14, 1993

Crowe, Cameron. "John's Clearwater Credo." *Rolling Stone*, May 6, 1976

Dawbarn, Bob. "A Day With Creedence, The Traveling Band." *Melody Maker*, April 10, 1970

Dawbarn, Bob. "Would You Believe Creedence Clearwater?" *Melody Maker*, May 10, 1969

DeCurtis, Anthony. "Fogerty Eyes the Apocalypse." *Rolling Stone*, January 31, 1985

———. "Fogerty Plays Creedence Songs at Vets Benefit." *Rolling Stone*, August 13, 1987

Delahant, Jim, and John Fogerty. "John Fogerty: Lead Guitarist, Creedence Clearwater Revival." *Hit Parader*, July 1969

Denselow, Robin. "Rock and Roll." *The Guardian*, September 28, 1971

Dubro, Alec. "Records." *Rolling Stone*, January 21 1970

Dunn, Kate. "From 'Cuckoo's Nest' and 'Amadeus' to an Italian Hillside." *New York Times*, December 3, 1995

Edelstein, Albert. "John Fogerty: Mr. October." *Rockbill*, October, 1986

Editors of *Rolling Stone*. *Rolling Stone Rock Almanac*. Rolling Stone Press, 1983

Elwood, Phillip. "Creedence Playing Better Than Ever." *San Francisco Examiner*, March 14, 1969

Fogerty, John. "John Fogerty on His Bandmates: Why 'We Are Not Friends.' " *Los Angeles Times*, February 7, 1993

Fogerty, John. Speech to the Bammy Awards. May 7, 1992

Fogerty, Lucile Lytle. "Remembering the Early Years." Unpublished oral history.

Fogerty, Trish. Liner notes to *Sidekicks*, 1992

Fong-Torres, Ben. "Creedence Clearwater Revival at the Hop." *Rolling Stone*, April 5, 1969

Forte, Dan. "Return of the Swamp Thing." *Record*, May 1985

———. "Stu Cook, Southern Pacific." *Guitar Player*, November, 1986

———, and Steve Soest. "John Fogerty Returns." *Guitar Player*, April 1985

Forte, Dan. "Woodsheds." *Guitar Player*, April, 1985

Freedland, Nat. "Talent in Action." *Billboard*, November 13, 1971

Gallo, Phil. "Live Review." *Variety*, May 22, 1997

Gans, David. "Paper Bullets." *Record*, May 1985

Gausch, Alberto, "Life After Creedence." *El Dominical de El Periodico de Calalunya*, September 24, 1997

Gilbert, Melanie. "CC Gets a New R — For 'Revisited Tour.' " *The Detroit News*, August 22, 1996

Gitler, Ira. Liner notes to *Charles Mingus, the Complete Debut Recordings*. Fantasy Records, 1990

Gleason, Ralph. "The *Rolling Stone* Interview With John Fogerty." *Rolling Stone*, February 21, 1970

————. "A Fantastic Tale." *Downbeat*, July 11, 1956

————. "Inside the *Blue Ridge Rangers*." *Rolling Stone*, July 5, 1973

————. "Let It Evolve." *BMI Music World*, February, 1970

Goldberg, Michael. "Fogerty Wins Unusual Self-Plagiarism Suit." *Rolling Stone*, January 12, 1989

————. "Fortunate Son." *Rolling Stone*, February 4, 1993

————. "John Fogerty Alters Album: 'Zanz' becomes 'Van.'" *Rolling Stone*, March 28, 1985

————. "On the Road Again." *Rolling Stone*, October 8, 1986

————. "The Triumphant Return of John Fogerty." *Addicted To Noise*, May 2, 1997

————. "Tom Fogerty Dies." *Rolling Stone*, November, 1990

————. "Will Creedence Clearwater Ever Be Revived?" *Rolling Stone*, September 2, 1982

Goldman, Albert. "Purity, Not Parody in a Real Rock Revival." *Life*, May 9, 1969

Goldstein, Patrick "The Producer and his Fine Madness." *Los Angeles Times*, March 23 1997

Goldstein, Richard "Creedence Clearwater Revival Energy." *Vogue*, May 1970

Goodman, Fred, and Parke Putterbaugh, eds. *The 100 Greatest Albums of the 80's.* New York: St. Martin's, 1990

Goodman, Fred. "Creedence Delights at Forest Hills." *Billboard*

Graff, Gary. "Creedence Clearwater Revisited." *Oakland Press*, August 19 1996

————. "Creedence's Legacy: Fortunate Sons or Bad Moon Rising?" *Jam TV*, July 1997

Graham, Jefferson. "West Coast Rockers to stage AIDS Benefit." *USA Today*, May 27, 1989

Greenhouse, Linda. "High Court Eases Rule on Paying Lawyers' Fees in Copyright Suits." *New York Times*, March 2, 1994

Grissim, John. "*Cosmo's Factory* Review." *Rolling Stone*, September 3, 1970

Gunderson, Edna. "Swamp Thing: John Fogerty's Blue Moon Dance." *Microsoft Musiccentral*, August 29, 1997

————. "With *Blue Moon Swamp*, a John Fogerty Revival." *USA Today*, May 19, 1997

Guzman, Pablo. "Creedence Rollin' On." *The Village Voice*, June 17, 1981

Guthmann, Edward. "A Patient Producer from the Old School." *San Francisco Chronicle*, November 17, 1996

Hallowell, John. *Inside Creedence.* New York: Bantam, 1971

Harmetz, Aljean. "Theroux Tale to Be Filmed This Year." *New York Times*, April 25, 1985

Harada, Wayne. "Talent in Action." *Billboard*, September 14 1968

Showtime Productions. "John Fogerty's All-Stars." Showtime Network, 1985

Heckman, Don. "*Green River* Review." *Stereo Review*, March 1970

Heineman, A. "*Cosmo's Factory* Review." *Down Beat*, March 1971

Henke, James "John Fogerty." *Rolling Stone*, November 5, 1987

Hilburn, Robert. "Chooglin' Again." *Melody Maker*, October 18, 1975

————. "7th Creedence Album Also a 1st." *Los Angeles Times*, April 9, 1972

———. "Creedence in a Return to Recording Wars." *LA Times Calendar,* June 20, 1971

———. "Creedence Knocks 'Em Out in Europe." *Rolling Stone,* October 14, 1971

———. "Fogerty Rocks Again as Lone Ranger." *Los Angeles Times,* April 8, 1973

———. "Fogerty Shows His Creedence Credentials." *Los Angeles Times,* September 22, 1994

———. "The Force Behind Creedence." *Los Angeles Times,* January 12, 1993

———. "The Long Nightmare Is Over." *Los Angeles Times Calendar,* January 6, 1985

———. "Way Beyond Centerfield." *Los Angeles Times,* May 6, 1997

Hirschberg, Lynn. "Pure Profit." *New York Times Magazine,* January 1, 1997

Hiltbrand, David. "Picks & Pans." *People,* March 4, 1985

Hochman, Steve. "Pop Eye." *Los Angeles Times,* January 31, 1993

———. "These Guys' Bad Moon Rose a Loooong Time Ago." *Los Angeles Times,* January 31, 1993

———. "'Proud Mary' Fans Would Be Proud." *Los Angeles Times,* May 30, 1997

———. "*Blue Moon Swamp* Review." *Los Angeles Times,* May 30, 1997

———. "Creedence Revisits Classics but Lacks Fogerty's Vision." *Los Angeles Times.,* May 13, 1996

Holland, Bill. "Lawyer's Fees at Issue After Decision in Fogerty Case." *Billboard* December 16, 1993

Hollingsworth, Roy. "Creedence — too fast, too precise." *Melody Maker,* September 11, 1971

———. "Creedence Invite You to Dinner." *Melody Maker,* September 25, 1971

———. "Creedence." *Melody Maker,* October 26, 1970

Hosik, Dave. "Cosmos Factory Fine Creedence." *Daily Journal,* November 25, 1996

Hounsome, Terry. *Rock Record.* New York: Facts on File, 1987

Hubner, John. "The Demon Fighter of Rock 'n' Roll." *West,* December 7, 1986

Hughes, Andrew S. . "Tour Delays Michiana Move." *South Bend Tribune,* September 17, 1997

Hunter, James. "Years of Bad Road: John Fogerty Meets Duane Eddy." *Musician,* November, 1991

Isler, Scott. "John Fogerty's Creedence Revival." *Musician,* October 1987

———. "John Fogerty's Triumph Over Evil." *Musician,* March 1985

———. "Fogerty vs. Fogerty." *Musician,* February 1989

———. "The Hoodoo Man Puts On the Anti-War Paint." December, 1986

Jaeger, Barbara, "Winwood Strikes Gold with 5 Grammy Nominations." *The Bergen Record,* January 9, 1987

———. "HBO Encore For Fogerty." *The Bergen Record,* July 19, 1987

———. "The Welcome Home Concert." *The Bergen Record,* July 19, 1987

Jahn, Mike. "Bo Diddley Returns on Guitar at Forest Hills Rock Concert." *New York Times,* July 19, 1971

———. "Californians Play Refreshing Rock at Fillmore East." *New York Times,* March 24, 1969

Johnson, Rick. "Concert Review." *Jazz & Pop,* December 1970

Jones, Allan. "Centre Points." *Melody Maker,* February 2, 1985

Jones, Ben. "A Handful of Lawsuits Later, Creedence Clearwater Revival Is Finally Back on Tour." *USA Today*, September 17, 1997

Kamstra, Rex. Southern Pacific Web Page, 1997

Keough, Peter. "Producer Saul Zaentz Affirms 'Lightness' of Being." *Chicago Sun Times*, February 7, 1988

Kernfeld, Barry, ed. *The New Grove Dictionary of Jazz*. New York: Grove Press, 1988

Kirby, Fred. "Beach Boys Tripped Up by Past. Turtles Take Past in Fine Stride." *Billboard*, October 26, 1968

———. "Creedence Clearwater, Aum Big Fillmore East Successes." *Billboard*, August 2, 1969

Koehler, Robert. "Producer Zaentz Rises to Lit Challenge." *Variety* January 13, 1997

Lammers, Tjerk. "John Fogerty: The Monkey Is Off His Back." *Rock*, October 1985

Landau, Jon. "*Blue Ridge Rangers* Review." *Rolling Stone*, July 5, 1973

———. "*Mardi Gras* Review." *Rolling Stone*, May 25, 1972

———. "*Pendulum* Review." *Rolling Stone*, February 4, 1971

Larkin, Colin, ed. *The Guinness Encyclopedia of Popular Music*. Middlesex: Guinness Press, 1975

Lawson, John. "Sweating the Details." *Mix* , September 1997

Levine, Robert. "Creedence Clearwater Revisited." *Rolling Stone On-line*, June 12, 1997

Levitin, Daniel. "Blue Moon Rising." *Audio*, January 1998

Levy, Arthur. "*Mardi Gras* Review." *Zoo World*, May 4, 1972

Levy, Ken. "John Fogerty on a Tear." *Relix*, October 1997

———. "Stricken From the Record." *San Francisco Examiner*, August 9, 1994

Lewis, Alan. "Caught in the Act." *Melody Maker*, April 25, 1970

Lichtman, Irv. "*Billboard* Bulletin." *Billboard*, July 17, 1993

Link, Geoffrey. "Creedence — Fantasy Fancies." *Billboard*, November 8, 1969

Loder, Kurt. "Fogerty Still Hits With Power." *Rolling Stone*, January 31, 1985

Lombardi, John. "Creedence Clearwater Throws Serious Party." *Rolling Stone*, January 21, 1971

Lundqvist, Lena (writer), Clara Lindberg (dir.), and Kjell Ekholm (prod.). *Rockens Roll*. Fiktionen/FST 1994

Marcus, Greil. "*Mardi Gras* Review." *Creem*, June 1972

———. Liner notes to *Chronicle*, 1976

Marsh, Dave. "Where Has John Fogerty Gone." *Musician*, April, 1981

Martin, Nina. "How Vicious Rock Became." *The Examiner*, January 28, 1986

Marymont, Mark. "Southern Pacific Seeks Recognition." *Arkansas Democrat-Gazette*, May 25, 1990

Matsumoto, Jon., "Where Did the Rest of Creedence Go?" *Los Angeles Times*, January 6, 1985

Mattingly, Rick. "Kenny Aronoff: Mr. 'Less Is More' Is Everywhere." *Modern Drummer*, November 1997

McCullaugh, Jim. "Claymation Creator Molds Fogerty Clip." *Billboard*, July 13, 1985

McDonough, Jack. "A Fogerty Calling Card: His New *Myopia* Album." *Billboard*, February 22, 1975

———. "New Creedence Anthology Aims at Audiophile Buyers." *Billboard*, November 13, 1982

McDougal, Dennis. "The Trials of John Fogerty." *Los Angeles Times*, November 15, 1988

McJunkin, Jennifer. "John Fogerty." *House of Blues On-line*, September, 1997

McManus, Linda. "Ripe Tumatoe." *South Bend Tribune*, January 31, 1988

Miles, Milo. "*The Royal Albert Hall Concert* Review." *Boston Phoenix*, January 20, 1981

Milkowski, Bill. "Centerfield Review." *Down Beat*, April 1985

Miller, Jim. "Another Clearwater Revival." *Newsweek*, February 18, 1985

Mirkin, Steve. "Live Review." *Rolling Stone Random Notes Daily On-line*, May 23, 1997

Miroff, Bruce. "*Green River* Review." *Rolling Stone*, October 18, 1969

Modderno, Craig. "East Bay Rock Group May Claim the Beatles' Crown." *Oakland Tribune*, August 9, 1970

Morris, Chris. "Live WB Tumatoe & Power Trio Album Gets Fuel From Fogerty." *Billboard*, April 8, 1989

Morthland, John. "The 'Toot-Toot' Wars." *The Village Voice*, August 6, 1985

Moseley, Willie G.. "Ol' Flannel Shirt Is Back." *Vintage Guitar*, August 1997

Muirhead, Bert. *The Record Producer's File*. Dorset: Blandford Press, 1984

Natale, Richard. "Hard Work Ahead for 'At Play' Producer." *Variety*, February 3, 1992

Newman, Melinda. "Inductees Gather in NY for 9th Hall of Fame Dinner." *Billboard*, January 29, 1994

Nisan, Jeff. "Pop Flies." *Creem*, February, 1987

Novak, Ralph. "Picks & Pans." *People*, April 15, 1985

O'Connor, John J. "Creedence Clearwater Special Tomorrow." *New York Times*, June 19, 1971

Oakley, John. John Fogerty interviewed on *Live on Life*, The Life Network (Canadian Cable), June, 1997

Oberman, Mike. "Music Makers." *Washington Evening Star*, September 25, 1971

Ochs, Ed. "Creedence Live at the Filmore East." *Billboard*, April 4, 1969

Oldfield, Michael. "Fogerty: Sweet Rock 'n' Roller: *John Fogerty* Review." *Melody Maker*, November 1 1975

———. "*Mardi Gras* Review." *Melody Maker*, May 20, 1972

———. "The Circle Is Broken." *Melody Maker*, February 28, 1981

Osbourne, Jerry. "Creedence Clearwater Revival." *DISCoveries*, November, 1988

Palmer, Robert. "Show by Fogerty in Memphis." *New York Times*, August 30, 1986

Parachini, Alan. "Tom Fogerty: Free of Creedence." *Los Angeles Herald Examiner*, August 22, 1971

Pareles, Jon. "Playing in Reunion, Cream Is Finale of Rock Ceremony." *New York Times*, January 14, 1993

Pareles, Jon. "To the Good Times, With a Twang." *New York Times*, June 4, 1997

Paul, Alan. "The Old Man Down the Road: Fogerty Comes Back Without a Vengence." *People*, June 2, 1997

Persson, Lennart. "John Fogerty." *Pop* (Sweden), June, 1997

Pirone, Rich. "Letter." *Backstreets*, September 1997

Popson, Tom. "Discovering Tumatoe." *Chicago Tribune*, March 31, 1989

Price, Bill. "Rock Now, Pay Later." *Q*, July 1997

Radcliffe Joe, "Talent in Action." *Billboard*, May 23, 1970

Reece, Doug. "Fogerty Roadwork Driving Sales of Artist's WB Set." *Billboard*, October 18, 1997

Reilly, Peter. "Pendulum Review." *Stereo Review*, May, 1971

———. "Bayou Country Review." *Stereo Review*, June, 1969

Rohrer, Jake. Liner notes to *Chronicle*. Fantasy Records, 1976

Romanowski, Patricia, and Holly George-Warren, eds. *The New Rolling Stone Encyclopedia of Rock & Roll*. New York: Fireside Books, 1995

Rosen, Steve. Foreword. *Guitar Anthology Series: Creedence Clearwater Revival*. Miami: Warner Bros. Publications, 1991

Rosenthal, Marshal. "Tom Fogerty Leaves Creedence." *Rolling Stone*, March 3, 1971

Ruby, Jay. "Creedence Clearwater Revival." *International Musician*, June ,1969

———. "Creedence Clearwater Revival." *Jazz & Pop*, April/May 1969

Rudis, Al. "Keep On Chooglin.'" *Melody Maker*, July 24 1971

———. "Smash Revival by Creedence." *Melody Maker*, July 1971

———. "Why Tom Quit Creedence." *Melody Maker*, March 20 1971

Saidman, Sorelle. "Creedence Courtroom Revival." *Rolling Stone On-line*, August 22, 1997

Sanjeck, Russell, and David Sanjeck. *Pennies From Heaven*. New York: Da Capo, 1996

Santoro, Gene. "*Eye of the Zombie* Review." *Down Beat*, January, 1987

Schruers, Fred. "Top Records of 1985." *Rolling Stone*, January 2, 1986

Scoppa, Bud. "Here Comes Functional Fogerty, One Man Supergroup: *John Fogerty* Review." *Rolling Stone*, October 23, 1975

———. "John Fogerty Gets the Zombie Off His Back." *Cashbox*, 1991

Sculatti, Gene. "*John Fogerty* Review." *Creem*, December 1985

Seigal, Buddy. "Thorogood Puts Creedence into His Music." *Los Angeles Times*, March 19, 1997

———. "The Fortunate Son Returns." *San Francisco Chronicle*, May 12, 1997

Selvin, Joel. "A Revival for Creedence." *San Francisco Chronicle*, July 5, 1971

———. "Angry Fogerty Urges Fantasy Records Boycott." *San Francisco Chronicle*, May 12, 1992

———. "Big Wheels Stop Turning — End of Line for Creedence." *San Francisco Examiner & Chronicle*, November 5, 1972

———. "CCR Rock the Filmore West." *San Francisco Chronicle*, December 20, 1972

———. "Creedence Got a Kinda New Bag." *Rolling Stone*, December 24 1970

———. "John Fogerty on Threshold of Big Comeback." *San Francisco Chronicle*, January 6, 1985

———. "Many Musicians Are Messing With 'Toot Toot.'" *San Francisco Chronicle*, March 12, 1988-

———. "The Remarkable Recordings of Creedence Clearwater." *San Francisco Chronicle*, November 26, 1978

———. "The Strength of Creedence Is Creedence." *Hit Parader*, April 1971

Settle, Ken "John Fogerty Returns." *Creem*, June 1985

———. "Bayous and Backstreets." *Goldmine*, June 8 1984

Shaw, Arnold. "John Fogerty." *BMI Music World*, April, 1971

Shaw, Greg. "The John Fogerty Years." *Phonograph Record*, September 1973

Siders, Harvey. "Lending Creedence to Rock." *Down Beat*, January 7, 1971

Simels, Steve ."*Blue Moon Swamp* Review." *TV Guide Entertainment On-line*, May 27, 1997

———. "*Eye of the Zombie* Review." *Stereo Review*, January, 1987

———. "The Return of John Fogerty: *John Fogerty* Review." *Stereo Review*, November, 1975

Simila, Petri. "Set Lists of Major John Fogerty Concerts." Finland: CCR Web Page

Sippel, John. "Creedence Awarded $8.6 Million." *Billboard*, May 14, 1983

———. "Zaentz Sues John Fogerty." *Billboard* August 10, 1985

Smith, Joe. *Off the Record*. New York: Warner Books, 1988

Spera, Keith. "Band Puts a Lot of Creedence into Playing the Hits." *The New Orleans Times Picayune*, October 8, 1996

Spitz, Robert Stephen. *Barefoot in Babylon*. New York: Viking, 1979

Stambler, Irwin. *Encyclopedia of Pop Rock & Soul*. New York: St. Martins, 1989

Steinblatt, Harold, and Chris Gill. "New Moon Rising." *Guitar World*, July 1997

Stevens, Kris. Interview on WLS, 1969

Stevenson, Jane. "Fogerty Stages 'Revival' of CCR." *Toronto Sun*, May 31, 1997

Stout, Gene. "It's a Revival, John Fogerty-style." *Seattle Post-Intelligencer*, August 22, 1997

Strauss, Neil. "A Lurking Album Is Freed." *New York Times*, May 21, 1997

Strong, M. C. *Great Rock Discography, 3rd Edition*. Music Sales, 1996

Sugarman, Robert, and Joseph Salvo. "Commentary." *Billboard*, March 19, 1994

Sutherland, Sam. "Rock Recluse Fogerty Returns." *Billboard*, February 2, 1985

Swenson, John. "Centerfield Review." *Saturday Review*, March/April 1985

Tearson, Michael. "*Daydreaming at Midnight* review." *Audio*, July 1994

Thomas, Elizabeth. *Contemporary Musicians*, vol. 2. Detroit: Gale Research, 1990

Tiegel, Elliot. "Creedence Supports Old Rock Sounds." *Billboard*, November 29, 1969

———. "Fantasy's Future Spelled Expansion." *Billboard*, August 12, 1989

Toches, Todd. "Home on the Range." *Melody Maker* September 8, 1973

Tolleson, Robin. "Fogerty, Fantasy Face Off in Frisco Court." *Billboard*, November 12, 1988

———. "John Fogerty Wins Lawsuit." *Billboard*, November 19, 1988

Trakin, Roy (Moderator). *Rant and Rave* on-line Chat, Prodigy, 1997

———. "Back to the Swamp." *Hits*, June 30, 1997

Twitty, Georgia. "John Fogerty Picks Country." *Music City News*, July, 1973

UPI. "Creedence Wins Bank Appeal." March 29, 1986

Wasserman, John L. "Lively Arts." *San Francisco Chronicle*, March 19,1972

Watkins, Roger. "Zaentz High on Back-End Deals as 'Amadeus' B.O Tops $90-Mil." *Variety*, November 20, 1985

Werner, Craig. "John Fogerty." *Goldmine* July 18, 1997

Whitburn, Joel. *Billboard Book of Top 40 Albums*. New York: Billboard Books, 1987

———. *Billboard Book of Top 40 Hits*. New York: Billboard Books, 1989

Wilde, David. "John Fogerty Q&A." *Rolling Stone*, December 25, 1997

Willis, Ellen. "Centerfield Review." *Village Voice*, January 29, 1985

———. "Musical Events." *The New Yorker*, September 2, 1972

———. *Rolling Stone Illustrated History of Rock*. New York: Random House/Rolling Stone Press, 1980

Willis, Tim. "Creedence Clearwater Lives Again." *The Bonanza*, July 2, 1996

Willman, Chris. "Fogerty Comes Back With a Vengeance." *Entertainment Weekly*, May 30, 1997

———. "Vet Sounds." *Entertainment Weekly*, May 30, 1997

Wilson, Tony. "Creedence — Keeping the Music in Shape." *Melody Maker*, September 20, 1969

Wloszczyna, Susan. "Oscar Salutes Producer Saul Zaentz." *USA Today*, March 24, 1997

Wynn, Steve. "Liner Notes." *John Fogerty Wrote a Song for Everyone*. Rubber Rabbit Rock 'n' Roll Records (Finland), 1996

Yellin, Emily. "Homage at Last for Blues Makers." *New York Times*, September 30, 1997

York, William. *Who's Who in Rock Music*. New York: Scribners, 1982

Yorke, Ritchie. "Public Acceptance Is Everything to Us." *Toronto Telegram Syndicate*, January 11, 1971

———. "The Rock Scene." *Toronto Telegram Syndicate*, January 11, 1971

Zeller, Craig. "*Eye of the Zombie* Review." *Creem*, February, 1987

Zimmerman, Kent and Keith. "New Moon on the Rise." *Gavin Report*, January 18, 1985

Zollo, Paul. "John Fogerty Takes His Time." *Musician*, November 1997

Primary Sources

E-mail correspondence with Eric Schumacher-Rasmussen, 1997

E-mail correspondence with Joe Hannigan, October 9, 1996

E-mail correspondence with Joel Selvin, 1997

E-mail correspondence with Lars Petersson, via the River Rising mail list, 1997

E-mail correspondence with Laurie Clifford, 1997

E-mail correspondence with Lisa Taylor, via the River Rising mail list, 1996–7

E-mail correspondence with Michael Bernander, via the River Rising mail list, 1997

E-mail correspondence with Peter Koers, via the River Rising mail list, 1996–7
E-mail correspondence with Petri Silmala, August 14, 1996
E-mail correspondence with Stu Cook, via River Rising mail list, 1996–7
E-mail correspondence with Trish Fogerty, 1997
Interview and correspondence, Al Bendich, 1997
Interview and correspondence, Bob Fogerty, 1997
Interview and E-mail correspondence, Jeff Fogerty, 1996–7
Interview, Gail Fogerty, 1997
Interview, Merl Saunders, 1997
Interview, Russ Gary, 1997
Interview, Tom Fogerty, 1981
Interviews and correspondence, Jake Rohrer, 1997

Secondary Correspondence

Letter from Bob Fogerty to Doug Clifford, Stu Cook, and Tom Fogerty, June 18, 1986
Letter from Bob Fogerty to Paul Zaentz, November 27, 1984
Letter from Bob Fogerty to Tom Fogerty, June 29, 1985
Letter from Bruce Springsteen to Stu Cook, March 8, 1993
Letter from David Dover to Lowell C. Brown, Esq., May 28, 1985
Letter from Jim Bickhart, Warner Special Products, to Paul Zaentz, Esq., May 7, 1979
Letter from John Fogerty to Doug Clifford, c. 1980
Letter from John Fogerty to Stu Cook, January 28, 1986
Letter from John Fogerty to Stu Cook, Tom Fogerty, and Doug Clifford, October 1, 1979
Letter from John Fogerty, August 17, 1989
Letter from Malcolm Burnstein, Esq., to Seymour Bricker, Esq, August 21, 1979
Letter from Malcolm Burnstein, Esq., to Seymour Bricker, Esq. and Barry Engel, Esq, May 18, 1979
Letter from Michael R. Blaha (Columbia Pictures) to Allan Shapiro, Esq. (John's attorney), April 1, 1985
Letter From Robbie Robertson to Stu Cook, February 19, 1993
Letter from Seymour Bricker, Esq., to Harris Zimmerman, Esq., August 8, 1985
Letter from Seymour Bricker, Esq., to Kenneth Sidle, Esq., October 24, 1989
Letter from Seymour Bricker, Esq., to Kenneth Sidle, Esq., September 25, 1989
Letter from Seymour Bricker, Esq., to Malcolm Burnstein, Esq, June 8, 1979
Letter from Seymour Bricker, Esq., to Malcolm Burnstein, Esq, October 24, 1978
Letter from Stu Cook to Bruce Springsteen, January 14, 1993
Letter from Stu Cook to John Fogerty, November 9, 1990
Letter from Stu Cook to Robbie Robertson, January 14, 1993
Letter from Tom Fogerty to John Fogerty, Dated October 11, 1985

Letter from Tom Fogerty to Ken Levy, 1985.
Letter from Tom Fogerty to Malcolm Burnstein, September 24, 1979
Open Letter from CCR, February 1, 1971

Legal Sources

American Federation of Musicians Contract, Creedence Clearwater Revival at the Sacremento Civic Auditorium, March 5, 1969
Application for Service Mark Registration for Creedence Clearwater Revival, April 4, 1981
Assignment of Trademark, 1992
Deposition, Doug Clifford, John Fogerty *v.* Poor Boy Productions, Inc. July 26, 1996
Deposition, John Fogerty, Fantasy *v.* Fogerty, July 8 1986
Deposition, John Fogerty, Fogerty *v.* Poor Boy Productions, August 1, 1996
Deposition, John Fogerty, Fogerty *v.* Poor Boy Productions, July 12, 1996
Deposition, Stu Cook, Fogerty *v.* Poor Boy Productions, July 26 1996
Gort Functions Partnership Agreement, March 29, 1970
The King David contract, June 5, 1969
U.S. Ninth Circuit Court of Appeals opinion, Fantasy *v.* Fogerty, 1996
U.S. Ninth Circuit Court of Appeals opinion, Fogerty *v.* Poor Boy Productions, 1997
U.S. Patent and Trademark Office Service Mark Principal Register, January 4, 1983

Web-Based Sources

BMI Repertoire Song Title Database
CCR Web Page, Finland
Fantasy Record Web Site
Official John Fogerty Web Site
RIAA Gold and Platinum Database
Southern Pacific Web Page
River Rising Web Page, John Fogerty concert dates
Woodstock Web Page
Yahoo! Print Map

Publicity Sources

Creedence Clearwater Revisited itinerary
Creedence Clearwater Revisited press release, August 18, 1997
Creedence Clearwater Revisited press release, May 24, 1996
Creedence Clearwater Revival Fantasy Records biography, c. *Bayou Country*
Creedence Clearwater Revival Fantasy Records biography, c. *Cosmo's Factory*

Creedence Clearwater Revival Fantasy Records biography, c. *Creedence Clearwater Revival*

Creedence Clearwater Revival Fantasy Records biography, c. *Green River*

Creedence Clearwater Revival Fantasy Records biography, c. *Mardi Gras*

Creedence Clearwater Revival Fantasy Records biography, c. *Pendulum*

Creedence Clearwater Revival Fantasy Records biography, c. *Willie and the Poorboys*

Factory press release re: Tom leaving CCR, February 1, 1971

Fantasy Records press release, "New Creedence Album Launches Spring Tour," March 24, 1972

Fifth Street Flash, April, June , September, and December 1970

Fogerty, John. Warner Bros. Records biography, c. *Blue Moon Swamp*

Fogerty, John. Warner Bros. Records biography, c. *Centerfield*

Fogerty, John. Warner Bros. Records biography, c. *Eye of the Zombie*

Fogerty, Tom. Fantasy Records biography, c. *Tom Fogerty*

Fogerty, Tom. Fantasy Records biography c. *Deal It Out*

Fogerty, Tom. Fantasy Records biography c. *Precious Gems*

Fogerty, Tom. Fantasy Records biography, c. *Myopia*

Gibson Guitar press release, "John Fogerty to Receive 1998 Orville H. Gibson Lifetime Achievement Award." January 12, 1998

Minnesota Vikings. "Rock the Dome" press release, August 13, 1997

Tumatoe, Duke. Warner Bros. Records biography, c. *I Love My Job*

Warner Bros. press release, "Blue Moon Over Scandinavia." June, 16, 1997

Warner Bros. Records press release, June 16, 1997

Zaentz, Saul. Fantasy Films biography, c. *Amadeus*

Zaentz, Saul. Saul Zaentz Film Co. biography, c. *The Unbearable Lightness of Being*

INDEX